# FOUNDATIONS
# OF CODING

# FOUNDATIONS OF CODING

## Theory and Applications of Error-Correcting Codes with an Introduction to Cryptography and Information Theory

**Jiří Adámek**
*Czech Technical University in Prague*

A Wiley-Interscience Publication
JOHN WILEY & SONS, INC.
Chichester • New York • Brisbane • Toronto • Singapore

In recognition of the importance of preserving what has been
written, it is a policy of John Wiley & Sons, Inc., to have books
of enduring value published in the United States printed on
acid-free paper, and we exert our best efforts to that end.

*Library of Congress Cataloging in Publication Data:*

Adámek, Jiří, ing.
   Foundations of coding: theory and applications of error-
   correcting codes, with an introduction to cryptography and
   information theory / Jiří Adámek.

      p.   cm.

   "A Wiley-Interscience publication."
   Includes bibliographical references and index.

   ISBN 0-471-62187-0
   1. Coding theory.    I. Title.

QA268.A36 1991
003'.54 — dc20
                                    90-20905
                                    CIP
                                    Rev.

10   9   8   7   6   5   4

*To Honza, Kuba, Jirka, and Ondřej*

# Preface

Coding theory is a fascinating field combining elegant mathematical theories with constructions of a major practical impact.

This book is devoted to constructions of

(1) error-correcting codes,

(2) secrecy codes, and

(3) codes used in data compression.

The stress is on the first direction: we introduce a number of important classes of error-detecting and error-correcting codes, and we present their decoding methods. Some of these constructions require a deep background in modern algebra, and we carefully provide such background. Secret codes are treated only briefly; we mainly explain the role of error-correcting codes in modern cryptography. Data compression and other topics related to information theory are briefly discussed in the first part of the book.

The material is presented in a way making it possible to appreciate both the beauty of the theory and the scope of practical applications. We use the definition-theorem-proof style usual in mathematical texts (since the reader can thus skip a proof to keep continuity of the text and return to it later), but formalism is avoided as much as possible.

The book evolved from a series of lectures I held at the Czech Technical University in Prague in 1985–1990. They were based primarily on the following excellent textbooks which the reader may use for further reading: *Information Theory and Coding*, Abramson (1963),* *Theory and Practise of Error Control Codes*, Blahut (1983), *The Theory of Error-Correcting Codes*, MacWilliams and Sloane (1981), and *An Introduction to Cryptology*, van Tilborg (1988).

Jiří Adámek

---

*A name followed by a year in parentheses refers to the list of references at the end of the book.

# Contents

# FOUNDATIONS OF CODING

# Introduction

Data transmision and data storage suffer from errors created by noise. Techniques for combatting noise have been used for a long time. They range from simple ones, e.g., adding a parity check symbol to every byte, to modern complex error-correcting techniques described in this book. The basic idea of error correction by a block code (i.e., a code in which all code words have the same length) is simple: code words must be "wide apart" from each other. That is, two distinct code words have a large Hamming distance, which means the number of symbols in which the words differ. Then the code corrects errors as follows: the word received is corrected to the nearest code word (in the sense of the Hamming distance). If the number of errors created by noise is smaller than one-half of the minimum Hamming distance of code words, then the correction is well done. Thus, the theory of error-correcting block codes is concerned with a construction of "good" codes with large Hamming distances. "Good" means that (1) the number of code words is as high as possible (to keep the redundancy low) and (2) an efficient technique for error correction is known (to make the search for the nearest code word fast).

Besides block codes, there is another class of error-correcting codes, called convolutional codes, in which memory plays a role: the message is again divided into blocks, but each block sent depends on a certain number of preceding blocks. The theory of convolutional codes is less rich than that of block codes: whereas good convolutional codes have been found by computer search, good block codes result from the algebraic theory presented in this book. However, the importance of convolutional codes in practical applications is ever increasing.

The theory of error-correcting codes is closely related to the theory of information, and the first part of this book is devoted to the foundations of information theory. Both of these theories were initiated by the pioneering paper of Claude Shannon (1948) in which he introduced entropy as a measure of information contained in an average symbol of a message. Shannon proved, *inter alia*, that entropy gives a precise estimate of how

1

much can be achieved by data compression. Combined with the famous Huffmann construction of the shortest code, this result of Shannon leads to a simple technique of data compression, presented in Chapters 2 and 3. (However, data compression is restricted to the case of information sources without memory.) The fourth chapter discusses the Fundamental Theorem of Shannon, which states that for every channel there exist error-correcting codes which remove noise while keeping the redundancy within the channel capacity. This result is purely theoretical: no algorithm for finding such codes has ever been found. The theory of error-correcting codes today has a lesser goal, viz., constructing codes with a reasonable redundancy and a fast decoder.

Constructions of efficient error-correcting and error-detecting codes with fast decoders are presented in the second part of the book. Some of the constructions require a deeper background in modern algebra and geometry, and we provide a thorough presentation of the relevant topics. The most important classes of error-correcting codes are the following:

Hamming codes (Chapter 5), perfect codes for single errors;

Reed-Muller codes (Chapter 9), multiple-error-correcting codes with a particularly efficient and easily implemented decoder;

Golay code (Chapter 10), the unique perfect code for triple errors;

BCH codes (Chapters 12 and 13), strong multiple-error-correcting codes with a fast decoder;

Convolutional codes (Chapter 14), multiple-error-correcting codes with memory.

The last part of the book is a short introduction to modern cryptography, stressing the role which error-correcting codes play here. Some of the well-known secret codes used in cryptography are based on constructions of error-correcting codes (e.g. the cryptosystem of McEliece, see 15.3). However, the main relation between cryptography and error-correcting codes is that, since noise is fatal for decryption, secret codes are usually combined with error-correcting codes. Furthermore, since encryption is costly, secret codes are usually combined with data compression.

The book is organized in chapters numbered consecutively throughout the three parts. Each chapter is divided into sections, and cross-references are always related to the number of section. For example, Theorem 3.2 means (the only) theorem in Section 3.2 of Chapter 3.

# Part I

# Coding and Information Theory

# Chapter 1

# Coding and Decoding

We are often faced with the task of converting a message, i.e., a sequence of symbols from a finite set (called a *source alphabet*), into a binary message, i.e., a sequence of 0's and 1's. The most common method is to translate each source symbol into a binary word. [*Word* means precisely a finite sequence; we often write $a_1 a_2 \ldots a_n$ instead of the more precise $(a_1, a_2, \ldots, a_n)$. Thus, 00101 is an example of a binary word.] Then the message is encoded symbol by symbol: we simply concatenate the words corresponding to the first, second, etc., symbol of the source message. The question of *how* to encode the source symbols is very important. There are two major criteria: we want to compress data, i.e., we want the resulting binary message to be as concise as possible, and we want to protect information against noise. These two requirements are rather contradictory, since by compressing data in the presence of noise, we are apt to increase, rather than decrease, the loss of information. In the present part, we therefore disregard noise: assuming that no errors occur, we try to find a concise code.

In the present chapter we introduce the important class of instantaneous codes, i.e., codes which can be decoded letter by letter, and we show how to construct such codes. The construction of the shortest code will be presented in Chapter 2.

## 1.1  Coding

**Definition.** *Given finite sets A* (source alphabet) *and B* (code alphabet), *a* coding *is a rule assigning to each source symbol exactly one word in the code alphabet, i.e., a function from A to the set of all words in B. We speak about* binary coding *if the code alphabet B has two symbols.*

5

| Source Symbol | Code Word |
|:---:|:---:|
| 1 | 11000 |
| 2 | 10100 |
| 3 | 01100 |
| 4 | 10010 |
| 5 | 01010 |
| 6 | 00110 |
| 7 | 10001 |
| 8 | 01001 |
| 9 | 00101 |
| 0 | 00011 |

| Decoding | 01247 |
|:---:|:---:|

**Figure 1:** 2-out-of-5 code

**Example of Binary Coding.**   Observe that among binary words of length 5, the number of those having two 1's is $\binom{5}{2} = 10$. This can be used to the *2-out-of-5 code* of decimal digits, see Figure 1.

The message "173" has the following code: 110001000101100. Observe that no space is left between the code words since "space" is a code symbol too. Thus, for example, the famous Morse code has code alphabet $B = \{ \cdot , -- , \text{space} \}$.

How do we decode the 2-out-of-5 code? Of course, the first five binary digits correspond to the first decimal one, and after decoding them, we proceed to the second group of five binary digits, etc. A helpful mnemonic rule: use 01247 as a "weight" of the five columns, and add the weights of all 1's in your words. Examples: $11000 \longmapsto 0+1 = 1$ and $01100 \longmapsto 1+2 = 3$. Unfortunately, 0 is an exception.

**Remark.**   Given a coding (i.e., a function $K$ from $A = \{a_1, \ldots, a_n\}$ to the set of all words in $B$), the words $K(a_1), \ldots, K(a_n)$ are called *code words*, and the set of all code words is called a *code*. When the concrete symbol in $A$ is not important, "code" and "coding" are usually identified.

## 1.2   Unique Decoding

**Definition.** *For each coding $K$ (of source symbols), we define the* coding *of source messages as the rule $K^*$, which to each word $x_1 x_2 \ldots x_m$ in the* source alphabet assigns the word $K^*(x_1 x_2 \ldots x_m) = K(x_1)K(x_2)\ldots K(x_m)$ obtained by concatenation of the code words $K(x_i)$, $i = 1, \ldots, m$.

The coding $K$ is said to be uniquely decodable *provided that arbitrary two distinct source messages have distinct codes. In other words, provided that $K^*$ is one-to-one.*

For example, the 2-out-of-5 code is uniquely decodable. The assignment of a binary word to "173" is a sample of coding source messages.

In contrast, the following coding

$$a \longmapsto 00 \quad b \longmapsto 10 \quad c \longmapsto 101 \quad d \longmapsto 110 \quad e \longmapsto 1001$$

is not uniquely decodable: try to decode 10110.

We now introduce two important types of uniquely decodable codes.

## 1.3  Block Codes and Instantaneous Codes

We now introduce two important types of codes: instantaneous codes, which are codes of variable word lengths decodable symbol per symbol, and block codes, which are the special case of instantaneous codes with constant word length:

**Definition.** (1) *A coding using only pairwise distinct code words of a certain length $n$ is called a* block coding *of length $n$.*

(2) *A coding is called* instantaneous *provided that no code word is a prefix of another code word; i.e., if a source symbol has a code $b_1 b_2 \ldots b_n$ then no other source symbol has a code $b_1 b_2 \ldots b_n b_{n+1} \ldots b_m$.*

**Remark.** Block codes (e.g., the 2-out-of-5 code above) are very convenient for decoding since we know in advance which code symbols correspond to the first (second, third, etc.) source symbol. And they are certainly efficient whenever all source symbols appear with equal frequency. However, if the frequencies of various source symbols differ substantially, then block codes become clumsy, and it is preferable to use instantaneous codes of variable lengths of words.

**Examples**

(1) The famous *Morse code* is exhibited in Figure 2. This is an instantaneous code with the code alphabet $\{ \cdot, -, \text{space} \}$. Since "space" is only used at the end of each code word, the decoding procedure is simple: we always look for the first "space". There is an obvious reason for not using a block code: the frequency of, say, "E" in the English language is much higher than that of "F".

| A | .— | N | —. |
| B | —... | O | ——— |
| C | —.—. | P | .——. |
| D | —.. | Q | ——.— |
| E | . | R | .—. |
| F | ..—. | S | ... |
| G | ——. | T | — |
| H | .... | U | ..— |
| I | .. | V | ...— |
| J | .——— | W | .—— |
| K | —.— | X | —..— |
| L | .—.. | Y | —.—— |
| M | —— | Z | ——.. |

**Figure 2:** Morse code

(2) An important example of a block code is the *octal code*:

| 0 | 000 | 4 | 100 |
| 1 | 001 | 5 | 101 |
| 2 | 010 | 6 | 110 |
| 3 | 011 | 7 | 111 |

(3) Suppose that we are to find a binary coding for the alphabet $\{0, 1, 2, 3\}$, and we observe that 0 appears much more often in source messages than any other symbols. Then the following coding seems reasonable:

$$0 \longmapsto 0 \quad 1 \longmapsto 01 \quad 2 \longmapsto 011 \quad 3 \longmapsto 111.$$

We can decode quite easily: count the number of 1's among the last three symbols of the encoded message. If the number is $i$, then the last source symbol is $i$. However, the above coding is not instantaneous. Indeed, when receiving a long message

$$011111111111\ldots,$$

we will not know whether the first source symbol is 0, 1, or 2 until the message stops.

# 1.4 Some Important Block Codes

Long binary codes are difficult to handle. It is thus often suitable to group the binary symbols: we get shorter codes in more complex alphabets. For example, by forming groups of three symbols, we obtain the octal code, see 1.3. Representation by the octal code is usually indicated by the subscript 8. Example:

$$(01)_8 = 000001.$$

By forming groups of four binary symbols, we obtain the *hexadecimal code* in Figure 3.

| Binary | Hexadecimal | Binary | Hexadecimal |
|--------|-------------|--------|-------------|
| 0000 | 0 | 1000 | 8 |
| 0001 | 1 | 1001 | 9 |
| 0010 | 2 | 1010 | A |
| 0011 | 3 | 1011 | B |
| 0100 | 4 | 1100 | C |
| 0101 | 5 | 1101 | D |
| 0110 | 6 | 1110 | E |
| 0111 | 7 | 1111 | F |

**Figure 3:** Hexadecimal code

A very important code used for a standard binary representation of alphabetic and numeric symbols is the ASCII code* (Figure 4). It has $2^7 = 128$ source symbols encoded into binary words of length 8: the first seven symbols carry the information, and the eighth one is set in such a way that the *parity* is even (i.e., each code word contains an even number of 1's). The role of this eighth symbol is to enable detection of single errors—we explain this in detail in Chapter 5. For example, the letter A has code

$$A \longleftrightarrow \underbrace{1000001}_{\substack{\text{inform.} \\ \text{symbols}}}\underbrace{0}_{\substack{\text{check} \\ \text{symbol}}},$$

which in Figure 4 is represented by its seven information bits: $1(01)_8 = 1\,000\,001$.

---

*American Standard Code for Information Interchange

| Source Symbol | Code | Source Symbol | Code | Source Symbol | Code | Source Symbol | Code |
|---|---|---|---|---|---|---|---|
| @ | $1(00)_8$ | ` | $1(40)_8$ | NUL | $0(00)_8$ | SP | $0(40)_8$ |
| A | $1(01)_8$ | a | $1(41)_8$ | SOH | $0(01)_8$ | ! | $0(41)_8$ |
| B | $1(02)_8$ | b | $1(42)_8$ | STX | $0(02)_8$ | " | $0(42)_8$ |
| C | $1(03)_8$ | c | $1(43)_8$ | ETX | $0(03)_8$ | # | $0(43)_8$ |
| D | $1(04)_8$ | d | $1(44)_8$ | EOT | $0(04)_8$ | $ | $0(44)_8$ |
| E | $1(05)_8$ | e | $1(45)_8$ | ENQ | $0(05)_8$ | % | $0(45)_8$ |
| F | $1(06)_8$ | f | $1(46)_8$ | ACK | $0(06)_8$ | & | $0(46)_8$ |
| G | $1(07)_8$ | g | $1(47)_8$ | BEL | $0(07)_8$ | ' | $0(47)_8$ |
| H | $1(10)_8$ | h | $1(50)_8$ | BS | $0(10)_8$ | ( | $0(50)_8$ |
| I | $1(11)_8$ | i | $1(51)_8$ | HT | $0(11)_8$ | ) | $0(51)_8$ |
| J | $1(12)_8$ | j | $1(52)_8$ | LF | $0(12)_8$ | * | $0(52)_8$ |
| K | $1(13)_8$ | k | $1(53)_8$ | VT | $0(13)_8$ | + | $0(53)_8$ |
| L | $1(14)_8$ | l | $1(54)_8$ | FF | $0(14)_8$ | , | $0(54)_8$ |
| M | $1(15)_8$ | m | $1(55)_8$ | CR | $0(15)_8$ | − | $0(55)_8$ |
| N | $1(16)_8$ | n | $1(56)_8$ | SO | $0(16)_8$ | . | $0(56)_8$ |
| O | $1(17)_8$ | o | $1(57)_8$ | SI | $0(17)_8$ | / | $0(57)_8$ |
| P | $1(20)_8$ | p | $1(60)_8$ | DLE | $0(20)_8$ | 0 | $0(60)_8$ |
| Q | $1(21)_8$ | q | $1(61)_8$ | DC1 | $0(21)_8$ | 1 | $0(61)_8$ |
| R | $1(22)_8$ | r | $1(62)_8$ | DC2 | $0(22)_8$ | 2 | $0(62)_8$ |
| S | $1(23)_8$ | s | $1(63)_8$ | DC3 | $0(23)_8$ | 3 | $0(63)_8$ |
| T | $1(24)_8$ | t | $1(64)_8$ | DC4 | $0(24)_8$ | 4 | $0(64)_8$ |
| U | $1(25)_8$ | u | $1(65)_8$ | NAK | $0(25)_8$ | 5 | $0(65)_8$ |
| V | $1(26)_8$ | v | $1(66)_8$ | SYN | $0(26)_8$ | 6 | $0(66)_8$ |
| W | $1(27)_8$ | w | $1(67)_8$ | ETB | $0(27)_8$ | 7 | $0(67)_8$ |
| X | $1(30)_8$ | x | $1(70)_8$ | CAN | $0(30)_8$ | 8 | $0(70)_8$ |
| Y | $1(31)_8$ | y | $1(71)_8$ | EM | $0(31)_8$ | 9 | $0(71)_8$ |
| Z | $1(32)_8$ | z | $1(72)_8$ | SUB | $0(32)_8$ | : | $0(72)_8$ |
| [ | $1(33)_8$ | { | $1(73)_8$ | ESC | $0(33)_8$ | ; | $0(73)_8$ |
| \ | $1(34)_8$ | \| | $1(74)_8$ | FS | $0(34)_8$ | < | $0(74)_8$ |
| ] | $1(35)_8$ | } | $1(75)_8$ | GS | $0(35)_8$ | = | $0(75)_8$ |
| ^ | $1(36)_8$ | ~ | $1(76)_8$ | RS | $0(36)_8$ | > | $0(76)_8$ |
| _ | $1(37)_8$ | DEL | $1(77)_8$ | US | $0(37)_8$ | ? | $0(77)_8$ |

**Figure 4:** ASCII code (7 information bits)

Let us finally mention an "everyday" code we meet in most textbooks. It is called the *international standard book number*, ISBN, and it is a block code of length 10. (Various hyphens are often inserted between the symbols, but we can ignore them here since they are used just for optical orientation.) The code alphabet has 11 symbols: 0, 1, ..., 9 and X (read: ten). For example, the book of Lin and Costello (1983) has

$$\text{ISBN } 0\text{-}13\text{-}283796\text{-}X.$$

The first number 0 denotes the country (USA), 13 denotes the publisher (Prentice-Hall), and the next six digits are assigned by the publisher as an identification number of the book. The last symbol is a check symbol (analogously as in the ASCII code above). It is set in such a way that for each ISBN code word $a_1 a_2 a_3 \ldots a_9 a_{10}$, the sum

$$\sum_{i=1}^{10} i a_{11-i} = 10a_1 + 9a_2 + 8a_3 + \cdots + 2a_9 + a_{10}$$

be divisible by 11. For example, in the ISBN above:

$$10 \times 0 + 9 \times 1 + 8 \times 3 + 7 \times 2 + 6 \times 8 +$$
$$5 \times 3 + 4 \times 7 + 3 \times 9 + 2 \times 6 + 1 \times 10 \;=\; 132 \;=\; 11 \times 12.$$

Some publishers have a three-digit identification (e.g., Wiley-Interscience has 471) and then they assign a five-digit number to each publication.

## 1.5  Construction of Instantaneous Codes

Suppose you want to construct a binary instantaneous code of the source alphabet $\{a_1, \ldots, a_n\}$. It is sufficient to specify the lengths $d_1, \ldots, d_n$ of the expected code words. In fact, we can certainly assume that $d_1 \leq d_2 \leq \cdots \leq d_n$. Then we choose an arbitrary binary word $K(a_1)$ of length $d_1$. Next we choose a binary word $K(a_2)$ of length $d_2$, but we avoid all those which have the prefix $K(a_1)$. This is possible: the number of all binary words of length $d_2$ is $2^{d_2}$. The number of those having the prefix $K(a_1)$ is $2^{d_2 - d_1}$ (because you can choose the $d_2 - d_1$ digits remaining after the prefix $K(a_1)$ arbitrarily). Since $2^{d_2} \geq 2^{d_2 - d_1} + 1$, we have at least one choice of $K(a_2)$.

Next, we want to choose a word of length $d_3$ which has neither prefix $K(a_1)$ nor $K(a_2)$. Thus, from the $2^{d_3}$ possible words, we must avoid all the $2^{d_3 - d_1}$ words with the prefix $K(a_1)$ and all the $2^{d_3 - d_2}$ words with the prefix $K(a_2)$. This is possible if (and only if)

$$2^{d_3} \geq 2^{d_3 - d_1} + 2^{d_3 - d_2} + 1.$$

Dividing the last inequality by $2^{d_3}$, we obtain

$$1 \geq 2^{-d_1} + 2^{-d_2} + 2^{-d_3}.$$

Analogously, we can see that the following inequality

$$1 \geq 2^{-d_1} + 2^{-d_2} + \cdots + 2^{-d_n}$$

makes it possible to fulfil our task. It turns out that this inequality is both necessary and sufficient for a construction of instantaneous codes.

**Example.** We want to find an instantaneous code with the same lengths of code words as that in Example 1.3(3) above. This is possible since

$$1 \geq 2^{-1} + 2^{-2} + 2^{-3} + 2^{-3}.$$

Here is such a code:

$$0 \longmapsto 0 \quad 1 \longmapsto 10 \quad 2 \longmapsto 110 \quad 3 \longmapsto 111.$$

## 1.6   Kraft's Inequality

**Theorem.** *Given a source alphabet of n symbols and a code alphabet of k symbols, then an instantaneous code with given lengths $d_1, d_2, \ldots, d_n$ of code words exists, whenever the following Kraft's inequality*

$$k^{-d_1} + k^{-d_2} + \cdots + k^{-d_n} \leq 1$$

*is fulfilled.*

**Proof.** We can assume that the source alphabet $\{a_1, a_2, \ldots, a_n\}$ is presented in the order imposed by the lengths of the expected code words; i.e., $d_1 \leq d_2 \leq \cdots \leq d_n$. We define instantaneous coding $K$ by the following induction:

(1) Choose an arbitrary word $K(a_1)$ of length $d_1$.

(2) Suppose $K(a_1)$, $K(a_2)$, ..., $K(a_{s-1})$ have been chosen. Then choose an arbitrary word $K(a_s)$ of length $d_s$ with no prefix among $K(a_1)$, ..., $K(a_{s-1})$. This is possible: the number of words with the prefix $K(a_i)$ is $k^{d_s - d_i}$, and thus we have a choice of

$$k^{d_s} - \sum_{i=1}^{s-1} k^{d_s - d_i}$$

words. From Kraft's inequality, we get

$$1 - \sum_{i=1}^{s-1} k^{-d_i} \geq k^{-d_s}$$

and multiplying by $k^{d_i}$, we conclude

$$k^{d_s} - \sum_{i=1}^{s-1} k^{d_s - d_i} \geq 1.$$

$\square$

## 1.7  McMillan's Theorem

**McMillan's Theorem.** *Every uniquely decodable coding satisfies Kraft's inequality.*

**Remark.** We see that Kraft's inequality is not only sufficient, but also necessary for the construction of an instantaneous code. However, McMillan's Theorem says much more: instantaneous codes are just as efficient as uniquely decodable codes. More precisely, for every uniquely decodable code there exists an instantaneous code with the same lengths of code words.

**PROOF.** Let $K$ be a uniquely decodable coding. Denote by $d_i$ the length of the code word $K(a_i)$, $i = 1, 2, \ldots, n$. Observe that for each number $j = 1, 2, 3, \ldots$, we can form exactly $k^j$ words of length $j$ in the ($k$-symbol) code alphabet. By unique decodability, the number of source messages $a_{i_1} a_{i_2} \ldots a_{i_r}$ whose code has length $j$ cannot exceed $k^j$. The length of the code is $d_{i_1} + d_{i_2} + \cdots + d_{i_r}$. Thus, we observe that the number of all sums of the form

$$d_{i_1} + d_{i_2} + \cdots + d_{i_r} = j \tag{1.7.1}$$

is smaller or equal to $k^j$.

It is our task to prove that the number

$$c = \sum_{i=1}^{n} k^{-d_i}$$

is smaller or equal to 1. For this, we will verify that the numbers $\frac{c^r}{r}$ are bounded for all $r = 1, 2, 3, \ldots$. In fact, each number $c > 1$ clearly fulfils

$\lim_{r \to \infty} \frac{c^r}{r} = \infty$, and, therefore, the theorem will then be proved. Let us compute the powers of $c$:

$$c^2 = \left( \sum_{i=1}^{n} k^{-d_i} \right) \left( \sum_{j=1}^{n} k^{-d_j} \right) = \sum_{i,j=1}^{n} k^{-(d_i + d_j)}$$

and, in general,

$$c^r = \sum_{i_1, \ldots, i_r = 1}^{n} k^{-(d_{i_1} + d_{i_2} + \cdots + d_{i_r})}. \tag{1.7.2}$$

We can reorder the last sum by collecting all the summands $k^{-j}$, where $j$ satisfies (1.7.1). The largest possible $j$ is $j = d + d + \cdots + d = rd$, where $d = \max(d_1, \ldots, d_n)$. As observed above, the number of all summands $k^{-j}$ in sum (1.7.2) is smaller or equal to $k^j$. Thus,

$$c^r \leq \sum_{j=1}^{rd} k^j \cdot k^{-j} = \sum_{j=1}^{rd} 1 = rd.$$

Consequently, $\frac{c^r}{r} \leq d$, which proves that $c \leq 1$.    □

# Exercises

**1A**  What is the smallest length of a block code with the same source alphabet $\{A, B, \ldots, Z\}$ and the same code alphabet $\{ \cdot , - , \text{space} \}$ as the Morse code?

| 1 | ... | 01   |
| 2 | ... | 011  |
| 3 | ... | 10   |
| 4 | ... | 1000 |
| 5 | ... | 1100 |
| 6 | ... | 0111 |

| A | ... | 1010 |
| B | ... | 001  |
| C | ... | 101  |
| D | ... | 0001 |
| E | ... | 1101 |
| F | ... | 1011 |

**Figure 5**                    **Figure 6**

**1B**    Is the code in Figure 5 uniquely decodable? Is it instantaneous? Can you find an instantaneous code with the same lengths of code words?

**1C**    Is the code in Figure 6 uniquely decodable? If not, exhibit two source messages with the same code.

**1D**    Is the code in Figure 7 uniquely decodable?

| | | |
|---|---|---|
| 0 | ... | AA |
| 1 | ... | AABAB |
| 2 | ... | ABBBBB |
| 3 | ... | ABABA |
| 4 | ... | ABBAA |
| 5 | ... | BABBA |
| 6 | ... | BBBAB |
| 7 | ... | AAAABB |
| 8 | ... | AAAABA |
| 9 | ... | AAAAAB |

| | | | | | |
|---|---|---|---|---|---|
| A | ... | 001 | A | ... | 00 |
| B | ... | 1001 | B | ... | 10 |
| C | ... | 0010 | C | ... | 011 |
| D | ... | 1110 | D | ... | 101 |
| E | ... | 1010 | E | ... | 111 |
| F | ... | 01110 | F | ... | 110 |
| G | ... | 0101 | G | ... | 010 |

**Figure 7**                                        **Figure 8**

**1E**    Can you decide unique decodability of the two codes in Figure 8 by using Kraft's inequality?

**1F**    Construct a binary instantaneous code for the following source alphabet with the prescribed lengths of code words:

| Symbol | A | B | C | D | E | F | G | H | I | J | K | L |
|---|---|---|---|---|---|---|---|---|---|---|---|---|
| Length | 2 | 4 | 7 | 7 | 3 | 4 | 7 | 7 | 3 | 4 | 7 | 7 |

**1G**    Construct a ternary (three code symbols) instantaneous code for the following source alphabet with the prescribed lengths of code words:

| Symbol | 1 | 2 | 3 | 4 | 5 | 6 | 7 | 8 | 9 | 0 |
|---|---|---|---|---|---|---|---|---|---|---|
| Length | 1 | 3 | 3 | 3 | 3 | 2 | 2 | 2 | 2 | 2 |

**1H**   How many code symbols are needed if the following source alphabet is to be encoded into an instantaneous code with the prescribed lengths of code words:

| A | B | C | D | E | F | G | H | I | J | K | L | M | N | O | P |
|---|---|---|---|---|---|---|---|---|---|---|---|---|---|---|---|
| 1 | 2 | 2 | 2 | 1 | 2 | 2 | 2 | 1 | 2 | 2 | 2 | 2 | 2 | 1 | 2 |

**1I**   Prove that for each instantaneous code for which Kraft's inequality is not an equality, it is possible to add a new source symbol and extend the given code to an instantaneous code (with the same code alphabet). Demonstrate this on the code found in Exercise 1.6.

## Notes

Coding theory and information theory have their origin in the fundamental work of Claude E. Shannon (1948), reprinted in Slepian (1974), although many of the ideas were understood and used before. The small interesting book of Richard N. Hamming (1980), one of the founders of coding theory, provides further historical remarks.

    Kraft's inequality was formulated by Kraft (1949). The source of McMillan's Theorem is McMillan (1956), the present proof is from Karush (1961).

# Chapter 2

# Huffman Codes

We have mentioned that if the frequencies of source symbols vary, then instantaneous codes can be preferable to block codes: the most frequent symbols will be encoded into the shortest code words. We now make these considerations more precise. If the frequencies of source symbols are known exactly (i.e., if the probability distribution of source symbols in messages has been determined), we want to find the most efficient coding.

## 2.1 Information Source

**Definition.** *An* information source *is a source alphabet together with a probability distribution; i.e., a set* $\{a_1, \ldots, a_n\}$ *together with numbers* $P(a_1), \ldots, P(a_n)$ *satisfying* $\sum_{i=1}^{n} P(a_i) = 1$ *and* $0 \leq P(a_i) \leq 1$.

More precisely, we should speak about a discrete, zero-memory information source: discrete because we have discrete source symbols, and zero-memory because we assume that the source symbols appear independently. In other words, the probabilities $P(a_i)$ fully describe the statistics of the source messages, and the probability of a message $a_{i_1} a_{i_2} \ldots a_{i_r}$ can be computed from the probabilities of the individual symbols:

$$P(a_{i_1} a_{i_2} \ldots a_{i_r}) = P(a_{i_1}) P(a_{i_2}) \ldots P(a_{i_r}).$$

## 2.2 Huffman Codes

Let $K$ be a coding of an information source. That is, for each source symbol $a_i$, we have a code word $K(a_i)$ and we know the probability $P(a_i)$

of $a_i$. Denoting by $d_i$ the length of the word $K(a_i)$, we can compute the *average length* $L$ of code words:

$$L = \sum_{i=1}^{n} d_i P(a_i).$$

The most efficient coding is the one which has the smallest average length (because this means that the resulting code messages are as compressed as possible in the long run). By McMillan's Theorem 1.7 no harm is done if we confine ourselves to instantaneous codes.

**Definition.** *Given an information source $S$ and a code alphabet, by a* Huffman code *is meant an instantaneous code with the minimum average length of code words; the minimum average length is denoted by $L_{\min}(S)$.*

**Example.** Find a binary Huffman code for the source alphabet $A$, $B$, $C$, $D$, $E$, $F$ if $A$ appears twice as often as $E$ and $E$ twice as often as any consonant.

Thus, we have the following information source:

| Symbol | $A$ | $E$ | $B$ | $C$ | $D$ | $F$ |
|---|---|---|---|---|---|---|
| Probability | 0.4 | 0.2 | 0.1 | 0.1 | 0.1 | 0.1 |

We can assign a word of length 1 to $A$ and a word of length 2 to $E$. Then the remaining lengths are 4 by Kraft's inequality: $\frac{1}{2} + \frac{1}{2^2} + \frac{4}{2^4} = 1$. Here is a such code:

| $A$ | $E$ | $B$ | $C$ | $D$ | $F$ |
|---|---|---|---|---|---|
| 0 | 10 | 1100 | 1101 | 1110 | 1111 |

Its average length is

$$L = 0.4 + 2\,(0.2) + 4.4\,(0.1) = 2.4.$$

Is this $L_{\min}(S)$? Or would it be better to assign a word of length 3 to $E$ in order to escape the length 4? The following algorithm answers such questions.

## 2.3   Construction of Binary Huffman Codes

A source of two symbols has an obvious Huffman code with the code words 0 and 1 [and $L_{\min}(S) = 1$]. A source with three symbols, $a_1$, $a_2$, $a_3$, of which $a_1$ is the most probable, can be reduced to the case of two symbols,

$a_1$ and $a_{2,3}$, where $P(a_{2,3}) = P(a_2) + P(a_3)$. We find a Huffman code for the reduced source

| $a_1$ | $a_{2,3}$ |
|-------|-----------|
| 0     | 1         |

and then we "split" the code word 1 into two words, 10 and 11, thus obtaining a Huffman code for the original source:

| $a_1$ | $a_2$ | $a_3$ |
|-------|-------|-------|
| 0     | 10    | 11    |

In general, let $S$ be an information source with symbols $a_1, a_2, \ldots, a_n$ *ordered by probability*, i.e.,

$$P(a_1) \geq P(a_2) \geq \cdots \geq P(a_n).$$

The *reduced source* $S^*$ has symbols $a_1, a_2, \ldots, a_{n-2}$ and a new symbol $a_{n-1,n}$, and its probabilities are $P(a_1), \ldots, P(a_{n-2})$ (as before), whereas $P(a_{n-1,n}) = P(a_{n-1}) + P(a_n)$. Suppose that we are able to find a Huffman code $K^*$ for the reduced source $S^*$. Then the following code

| $a_1$ | $a_2$ | $\cdots$ | $a_{n-2}$ | $a_{n-1}$ | $a_n$ | |
|-------|-------|----------|-----------|-----------|-------|---|
| $K^*(a_1)$ | $K^*(a_2)$ | $\cdots$ | $K^*(a_{n-2})$ | $K^*(a_{n-1,n})0$ | $K^*(a_{n-1,n})1$ | (2.3.1) |

[obtained by "splitting" the last code word $K^*(a_{n-1,n})$ into two words] is a Huffman code for $S$. This will be proved below.

If we cannot find a Huffman code for $S^*$, we continue in the same way, finding a reduction of $S^*$ and a reduction of this reduction, etc. Eventually, we end up with two source symbols.

*Caution!* Before further reducing the reduced source $S^*$, we must move the new symbol $a_{n-1,n}$ in order to maintain the ordering by probability.

**Remark.** Observe that the average length $L(K)$ of the code in (2.3.1) is related to the average length $L(K^*)$ of the original code by

$$L(K) = L(K^*) + P(a_{n-1}) + P(a_n). \qquad (2.3.2)$$

In fact, if the lengths of code words of $K^*$ are $d_1, d_2, \ldots, d_{n-2}, d^*$, then the lengths of code words of $K$ are $d_1, d_2, \ldots, d_{n-2}, d^* + 1, d^* + 1$. Thus,

$$
\begin{aligned}
L(K) &= \sum_{i=1}^{n-2} d_i P(a_i) + (d^* + 1)P(a_{n-1}) + (d^* + 1)P(a_n) \\
&= \sum_{i=1}^{n-2} d_i P(a_i) + d^*[P(a_{n-1}) + P(a_n)] + P(a_{n-1}) + P(a_n) \\
&= L(K^*) + P(a_{n-1}) + P(a_n).
\end{aligned}
$$

**Theorem.** *Suppose that $K^*$ is a Huffman code for the reduced information source $S^*$, then the code (2.3.1) is a Huffman code for the original information source $S$.*

PROOF. Let $a_1, \ldots, a_n$ be all source symbols ordered by probability. We assume $P(a_n) > 0$ since the theorem is obvious if $P(a_n) = 0$.

I. $S$ has a Huffman code $K_0$ with nondecreasing word lengths, i.e.,

$$d_1 \leq d_2 \leq \cdots \leq d_n,$$

where $d_i$ denotes the length of the word $K_0(a_i)$.

To prove this, we start with an arbitrary Huffman code $K$ for $S$. If there exists a symbol $a_i$ such that $d_i > d_{i+1}$, denote by $K'$ the code obtained from $K$ by switching the code words for $a_i$ and $a_{i+1}$. Then $K'$ is certainly an instantaneous code, and the difference of the average lengths $L = L_{\min}$ (of $K$) and $L'$ (of $K'$) is

$$
\begin{aligned}
L_{\min} - L' &= \left[ d_i P(a_i) + d_{i+1} P(a_{i+1}) \right] - \left[ d_{i+1} P(a_i) + d_i P(a_{i+1}) \right] \\
&= (d_i - d_{i+1}) \left[ P(a_i) - P(a_{i+1}) \right].
\end{aligned}
$$

The last number is a product of a positive and a nonnegative number—thus, $L_{\min} \geq L'$, and from the minimality we conclude that $L_{\min} = L'$. In other words, $K'$ is another Huffman code. We continue the process of switching "unsuitable" pairs of neighbor code words until we obtain a Huffman code $K_0$ as above.

II. $S$ has a Huffman code $K_1$ such that the last code words $K_1(a_{n-1})$ and $K_1(a_n)$ differ only in the last symbol.

In fact, let $K_0$ be a Huffman code with nondecreasing word lengths (as in I) and let $\tilde{K}_0$ be the code obtained from $K_0$ by deleting the last symbol of the last code word $K_0(a_n)$. The average length of $\tilde{K}_0$ is clearly smaller than that of $K_0$ [since $P(a_n) > 0$] and, therefore, $\tilde{K}_0$ cannot be instantaneous. The word $\tilde{K}(a_i) = K(a_i)$ ($i \leq n-1$) is not a prefix of any code word; thus, $\tilde{K}(a_n)$ must be a prefix of some $K(a_i)$, $i \leq n-1$. This is not possible if $d_i < d_n$; therefore, $d_i = d_n$ (since $K_0$ has nondecreasing word lengths). The fact that $\tilde{K}(a_n)$ is a prefix of $K(a_i)$ implies that $K(a_i)$ differs from $K(a_n)$ in the last symbol only. If $i = n-1$, we put $K_1 = K_0$. If $i < n-1$, observe that $d_i = d_n$ implies $d_i = d_{i+1} = d_{i+2} = \cdots = d_n$. Therefore, we can switch the code words of $K_0$ for $a_i$ and $a_{n-1}$. This gives us a code $K_1$ of the same average length as $K_0$; thus, a Huffman code.

III. We are ready to prove the theorem. Suppose that a Huffman code $K^*$ of the reduced source $S^*$ is given, and define a code $K$ for $S$ by (2.3.1). The average lengths $L(K)$ and $L(K^*)$ of those codes are related by (2.3.2).

Let us now use the Huffman code $K_1$ of II above. Since the last two code words differ only in the last symbol, $K_1$ can be obtained from an (obvious) code $K_1^*$ of $S^*$ by "splitting" the last code word. Moreover, $K_1^*$ is clearly instantaneous. The same computation as in the remark above shows that

$$L(K_1) - L(K_1^*) = P(a_{n-1}) + P(a_n).$$

Thus, the two differences are equal, and we conclude that

$$L(K) = L(K_1) - L(K_1^*) + L(K^*).$$

Now $L(K^*) = L_{\min}(S^*)$ and, hence, $-L(K_1^*) + L(K^*) \leq 0$. This proves that $L(K) \leq L(K_1) = L_{\min}(S)$. Thus, $K$ is a Huffman code. $\quad\square$

## 2.4  Example

Let us compute a Huffman code for the source of Example 2.2. We start by reducing the symbols $D$ and $F$ to one symbol of probability 0.2. We must put the new symbol between $A$ and $E$ or betweeen $E$ and $B$. Let us choose, for example, the former, and continue with the reduction process (see Figure 1). We finally obtain two symbols (of probabilities 0.6 and 0.4),

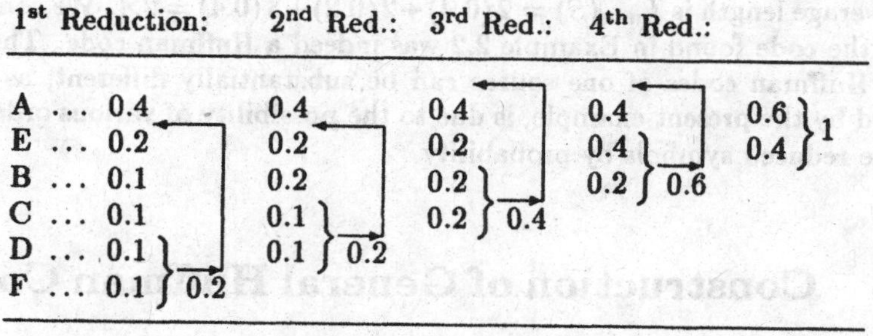

**Figure 1:** Iterated reduction

which are encoded by 0 and 1. We now proceed backwards by "splitting" each code word $w$ assigned to a sum of two probabilities to two words, $w0$ and $w1$ (see Figure 2).

The resulting Huffman code is the following:

| $A$ | $E$ | $B$ | $C$ | $D$ | $F$ |
|-----|-----|-----|-----|-----|-----|
| 00 | 11 | 010 | 011 | 100 | 101 |

1st Splitting:          2nd Splitting:

| | | |
|---|---|---|
| 0.6 ... 0 | 0.4 ... 1 | 0.4 ... 00 |
| 0.4 ... 1 | 0.4 ... 00 | 0.2 ... 01 |
|  | 0.2 ... 01 | 0.2 ... 10 |
|  |  | 0.2 ... 11 |

2nd Splitting:          3rd Splitting:          4th Splitting:

| | | |
|---|---|---|
| 0.4 ... 00 | 0.4 ... 00 | 0.4 ... 00 |
| 0.2 ... 01 | 0.2 ... 10 | 0.2 ... 11 |
| 0.2 ... 10 | 0.2 ... 11 | 0.1 ... 010 |
| 0.2 ... 11 | 0.1 ... 010 | 0.1 ... 011 |
|  | 0.1 ... 011 | 0.1 ... 100 |
|  |  | 0.1 ... 101 |

**Figure 2:** Iterated splitting

Its average length is $L_{\min}(S) = 2(0.4) + 2(0.2) + 3(0.4) = 2.4$. We conclude that the code found in Example 2.2 was indeed a Huffman code. The fact that Huffman codes of one source can be substantially different, as illustrated by the present example, is due to the possibility of various orderings of the reduced symbols by probability.

# 2.5   Construction of General Huffman Codes

The idea of constructing a Huffman code in, say, the code alphabet 0, 1, 2 is quite analogous to the binary case: reduce the three least important symbols to one, and, in the opposite direction, "split" the code word of the reduced symbol by concatenating 0, 1, 2 at the end. There is just one exception: the first (least important) reduction is performed on either three or just two symbols. For example, the source alphabet $a_1$, $a_2$, $a_3$, $a_4$ requires a reduction of two symbols, whereas $a_1$, $a_2$, $a_3$, $a_4$, $a_5$ requires a reduction of three. The rule is as follows:

(1) order the $n$ source symbols by probability,

(2) reduce the three least important symbols ($n$ odd), or the two least important symbols ($n$ even), and re-order by probability,

(3) in the next reductions, always reduce the three least important symbols and re-order by probability.

Observe that after each reduction, the resulting number of symbols is odd (since by reducing the three least important symbols to one symbol, the number of source symbols is decreased by two). Thus, we eventually end up with one symbol of probability 1. Then we start the splitting process.

In general, given a code alphabet of $k$ symbols, we construct a Huffman code by repeated reductions of the $k$ least important symbols. The only exception is the first reduction, when we reduce $k_0 = 2, 3, \ldots, k$ symbols in such a way that $k - 1$ is a divisor of the number $n - k_0$ (of nonreduced symbols).

**Example.** A ternary Huffman code for the information source in Example 2.2 is constructed as shown in Figures 3 and 4.

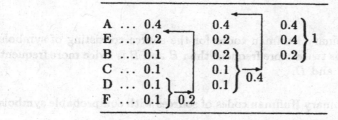

**Figure 3:** Iterated reduction

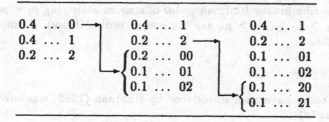

**Figure 4:** Iterated splitting

# Exercises

**2A**  Find binary Huffman codes for the sources shown in Figure 5.

| Symbol | A | B | C | D | E | F | G | H |
|---|---|---|---|---|---|---|---|---|
| Prob. (1st source) | $\frac{1}{8}$ | $\frac{1}{8}$ | $\frac{1}{8}$ | $\frac{1}{8}$ | $\frac{1}{8}$ | $\frac{1}{8}$ | $\frac{1}{8}$ | $\frac{1}{8}$ |
| Prob. (2nd source) | 0.1 | 0.2 | 0.1 | 0.3 | 0.05 | 0.1 | 0.05 | 0.1 |
| Prob. (3rd source) | 0.15 | 0.15 | 0.15 | 0.15 | 0.1 | 0.1 | 0.1 | 0.1 |

**Figure 5**

**2B**  Find ternary and quaternary (three and four code symbols) Huffman codes for the sources shown in Figure 5.

**2C**  Find the smallest number of code symbols necessary to construct an instantaneous code of average length $L \leq 1.5$ for each of the three sources of Figure 5.

**2D**  Find all binary Huffman codes for the source consisting of symbols $A, B, C, D$ if $A$ is twice more frequent than $B$ and $B$ is twice more frequent than either of $C$ and $D$.

**2E**  Describe binary Huffman codes of sources with equiprobable symbols

(1) if the number of source symbols is a power of 2,

(2) if it is not a power of 2.

**2F**  Describe binary Huffman codes of sources satisfying $p_1 < p_{n-1} + p_n$ (where $p_1 \geq p_2 \geq \cdots \geq p_n$ are the source probabilities).  Compare with Exercise 2E.

# Notes

Huffman codes have been introduced by Huffman (1952) reprinted in Berlekamp (1974).

# Chapter 3

# Data Compression and Entropy

Huffman codes can be used for data compression, in particular, when combined with extensions of the information source (i.e., with dividing messages into bytes). We first show an example of how this compression is performed, and then we discuss its effectiveness. The discusion uses the concept of entropy, or amount of information in the message, introduced by Claude Shannon. We prove the famous Shannon's Noiseless Coding Theorem, which states that Huffman codes of extensions represent the most effective data compression possible. (The reader should be aware of our standing assumption that we work with zero memory sources, see 2.1. Data compression for sources with memory is much more subtle.)

## 3.1   An Example of Data Compression

Suppose we obtain a very large binary message, and we observe that it contains almost no 1's. Say, there are nine times more 0's than 1's. This means, of course, that the information contained in the message is somewhat "thin". There are many methods of "compressing" the information. One is to divide the source message into bytes and encode the individual bytes.

For example, let us use bytes per two symbols. Thus, the message is now presented in the following symbols: 00, 01, 10, 11. Since 0 has probability 0.9 and 1 has probability 0.1, we can compute the new probabilities (using our assumption of zero memory, see 2.1):

| Symbol | 00 | 01 | 10 | 11 |
|---|---|---|---|---|
| Probability | 0.81 | 0.09 | 0.09 | 0.01 |

The Huffman code for this new information source is obvious:

| Symbol | 00 | 01 | 10 | 11 |
|---|---|---|---|---|
| Code | 0 | 10 | 110 | 111 |

Its average length is

$$L_{\min} = 0.81 + 2\,(0.09) + 3\,(0.1) = 1.29.$$

Thus, we need 1.29 bits to express a pair of source symbols; in other words, we need

$$\frac{1.29}{2} = 0.645 \text{ bits/symbol.}$$

This is a dramatic improvement to the 1 bit/symbol used without any coding.

This whets our appetite to try larger bytes. For example, in byte length 3, we get the following Huffman code (which can be guessed, or constructed as in the previous chapter):

| Symbol | 000 | 100 | 010 | 001 | 110 | 101 | 110 | 111 |
|---|---|---|---|---|---|---|---|---|
| Probab. | 0.729 | 0.081 | 0.081 | 0.081 | 0.009 | 0.009 | 0.009 | 0.001 |
| Code | 0 | 100 | 101 | 110 | 11100 | 11101 | 11110 | 11111 |

Here $L_{\min} = 0.729 + 3\,(0.243) + 5\,(0.028) = 1.598$, which is the average number of bits per three symbols, and thus we need approximately

$$\frac{1.598}{3} = 0.533 \text{ bits/symbol.}$$

Using this simple technique, we compress data to slightly more than one-half of their original size!

How much further can we compress? Can we really achieve one-half? Or even one-quarter? We now try to give clear answers to such questions.

## 3.2   The Idea of Entropy

In the late 1940s, Claude E. Shannon introduced the concept of the "amount of information" contained in a message. We must be very careful when trying to understand the idea well: "information" has a semantic meaning (what does the message say? what does it imply?) and a syntactic one (how does the message look?). We are absolutely disinterested in the semantics here because it is far beyond our aim of transmitting messages. Thus, our concept of "information" is purely syntactical. One can say that we regard messages in the same way a computer would: as sequences of symbols. In order to avoid misunderstanding, Shannon used the name entropy rather than information.

Thus, for each information source $S$, we want to introduce a number $H(S)$, called the entropy of the source $S$, which would express the intuitive idea of the "average amount of information" contained in one source symbol (or, from the opposite direction, the average uncertainty, i.e., the amount of information needed to specify one symbol of the source message). The main observation about the entropy $H(S)$ is that it depends only on the statistics of the source $S$, not on the names of source symbols. Since we assume that $S$ is a zero-memory source (2.1), we can consider $H(S)$ as a function of the probabilities $p_1, \ldots, p_n$ of the individual source symbols. Thus, $H(p_1, \ldots, p_n)$ is a function assigning to each probability distribution $(p_1, \ldots, p_n)$ (i.e., each $n$-tuple of nonnegative numbers summing up to 1) a number $H(p_1, \ldots, p_n)$ — the entropy of any source of information with the given probability distribution of source symbols.

Now, the entropy function $H(p_1, \ldots, p_n)$ can be expected to have the following properties:

(1) *Positivity*. $H(p_1, \ldots, p_n)$ is greater or equal to zero, and for some sources, it is positive.

(2) *Continuity*. A small change in the probabilities causes only a small change in the entropy; i.e., the function $H(p_1, \ldots, p_n)$ is continuous.

(3) *Symmetry*. A change in the ordering of the source symbols does not change the entropy, i.e.,

$$H(p_1, \ldots, p_n) = H(p_{t(1)}, \ldots, p_{t(n)})$$

for each permutation $t$ of the numbers $1, \ldots, n$.

(4) *Coherence*. The entropy of a source of $n$ symbols $a_1, \ldots, a_n$ can be computed from entropies of smaller sources for the following reason. Suppose we read the message twice: the first time we fail to distinguish between the symbols $a_1$ and $a_2$. This means that we work with a source of $n - 1$ symbols of probabilities $p, p_3, \ldots, p_n$, where $p = p_1 + p_2$. On the second reading, we can ignore the symbols $a_3, \ldots, a_n$ because we only want to distinguish $a_1$ from $a_2$. Thus, we read a $p$-times smaller message consisting of $a_1$'s (with probability $\frac{p_1}{p}$)

and $a_2$'s (with probability $\frac{p_2}{p} = 1 - \frac{p_1}{p}$). The first reading gives us the entropy $H(p, p_3, p_4, \ldots, p_n)$ and the second one, when a $p$-times smaller message is read, the entropy $pH\left(\frac{p_1}{p}, \frac{p_2}{p}\right)$. The two readings, then, give us the entropy of the original source:

$$
\begin{aligned}
H(p_1, p_2, p_3, \ldots, p_n) &= H(p_1 + p_2, p_3, \ldots, p_n) \\
&\quad + (p_1 + p_2)H\left(\frac{p_1}{p_1 + p_2}, \frac{p_2}{p_1 + p_2}\right).
\end{aligned}
$$

**Remark.** We have listed four "obvious" properties of entropy. Nobody is forced to accept them. But everyone who believes, as we do, that entropy must satisfy the properties above, obtains a unique formula for entropy:

**Theorem.** *There exists, up to a multiplicative constant $k > 0$, precisely one positive, continuous, symmetric, and coherent function, viz.,*[*]

$$
H(p_1, \ldots, p_n) = k \sum p_i \log \frac{1}{p_i},
$$

*where we add over all $p_i \neq 0$.*

We refrain from presenting the (very technical) proof due to Fadeiev (1956) improving an analogous result of Shannon (1948).

## 3.3   The Definition of Entropy

Theorem 3.2 is a clue to the following definition of entropy. The multiplicative constant $k$ is, obviously, just the choice of a unit of entropy. Let us express $k$ in the form

$$
k = \frac{1}{\log r} \qquad \text{(for } r = e^{-\frac{1}{k}}\text{)}.
$$

Then, by virtue of the formula

$$
\log_r x = \frac{\log x}{\log r}
$$

for logarithm of radix $r$, we get

$$
H(p_1, \ldots, p_n) = \sum p_i \log_r \frac{1}{p_i}
$$

---

[*]The natural logarithm is denoted by log, and the logarithm of radix $r$ by $\log_r$.

or, equivalently,

$$H(p_1, \ldots, p_n) = -\sum p_i \log_r p_i \, .$$

The most common choice of radix is $r = 2$. The corresponding unit is called a *bit*. Observe that if $S$ has two equiprobable symbols, then

$$H(S) = \frac{1}{2} \log_2 2 + \frac{1}{2} \log_2 2 = 1 \text{ bit}.$$

Thus, *one bit is the entropy of flipping an ideal coin once.*

The (unpleasant) condition of adding over all nonzero probabilities only is overcome by a (pleasant but imprecise) convention:

$$0 \log \frac{1}{0} = 0 \log 0 = 0.$$

Summarizing, we get the following:

**Definition.** *By the* entropy *of an information source $S$ with symbol probabilities $p_1, \ldots, p_n$ is meant the number*

$$H(S) = \sum_{i=1}^{n} p_i \log_2 \frac{1}{p_i} = -\sum_{i=1}^{n} p_i \log_2 p_i \qquad \text{(bits)}.$$

# 3.4 An Example

The entropy of the information source $S$ in Example 3.1 is

$$H(S) = -0.1 \log_2 0.1 - 0.9 \log_2 0.9 \approx 0.469 \text{ bits}.$$

Thus, by reading one source symbol, we obtain, in the average, less than half a bit of information. In 3.1, we have seen a concrete coding requiring, in the average, 0.533 bits per source symbol. It can be expected that no coding can compress data to below the 0.496 bits/symbol expressed by the entropy. We show below that this is indeed the case.

More generally, for an arbitrary information source with two symbols, we have a probability distribution $p$, $1 - p$, where $p \in [0, 1]$, and the corresponding entropy is

$$H(p, 1 - p) = p \log_2 \frac{1}{p} + (1 - p) \log_2 \frac{1}{1 - p} \quad \text{(bits)}.$$

Its graph is shown in Figure 1; observe how the positivity, symmetry, and continuity of entropy are demonstrated by the graph.

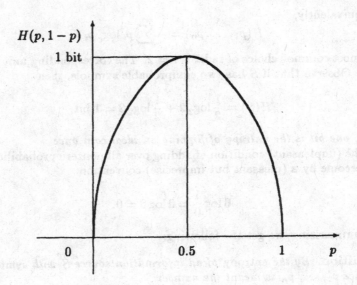

Figure 1: The entropy function $H(p, 1 - p)$

## 3.5   Maximum and Minimum Entropy

**Theorem.** (1) *The minimum entropy is $H(S) = 0$, and it is reached by precisely those sources $S$ which have a symbol of probability 1.*

(2) *The maximum entropy on an $n$-symbol source $S$ is $H(S) = \log_2 n$ bits, and it is reached by precisely those sources $S$ in which all symbols are equiprobable, $p_i = \frac{1}{n}$.*

**PROOF.** (1) We have $H(S) = \sum p_i \log_2 \frac{1}{p_i}$ and both $p_i$ and $\log_2 \frac{1}{p_i}$ are nonnegative (since $\frac{1}{p_i} > 1$). Thus, $H(S) \geq 0$, and if $H(S) = 0$, then for each $i$, either $\log_2 \frac{1}{p_i} = 0$ (which happens exactly if $p_i = 1$) or $p_i = 0$. We conclude that $H(S) = 0$ takes place precisely when all probabilities are 0 or 1; the latter must then happen exactly once.

(2) If all symbols are equiprobable, i.e., $p_i = \frac{1}{n}$, then

$$H(S) = \sum_{i=1}^{n} \frac{1}{n} \log_2 n = \log_2 n \quad \text{(bits)}.$$

In order to prove that this is the maximum value, we use the following (easily established) fact from calculus: the natural logarithm $\log x$ lies entirely below its tangent line in $x = 1$ (which is the line $y = x - 1$), see Fig. 2.

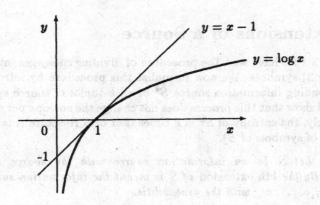

**Figure 2**

Thus,

$$\log x \leq x - 1 \quad \text{with equality only for} \quad x = 1. \quad (3.5.1)$$

We now compute the difference between the entropy of any source $S$ and the value $\log_2 n = \sum_{i=1}^{n} p_i \log_2 n$:

$$
\begin{aligned}
H(S) - \log_2 n &= \sum_{i=1}^{n} p_i \log_2 \frac{1}{p_i} - \sum_{i=1}^{n} p_i \log_2 n \\
&= \frac{1}{\log 2} \sum_{i=1}^{n} p_i \left( \log \frac{1}{p_i} - \log n \right) \\
&= \frac{1}{\log 2} \sum_{i=1}^{n} p_i \log \frac{1}{p_i n} \\
&\leq \frac{1}{\log 2} \sum_{i=1}^{n} p_i \left( \frac{1}{p_i n} - 1 \right) \\
&= \frac{1}{\log 2} \left( \sum_{i=1}^{n} \frac{1}{n} - \sum_{i=1}^{n} p_i \right) \\
&= \frac{1}{\log 2} (1 - 1) = 0.
\end{aligned}
$$

Thus, $H(S) \leq \log_2 n$, and the equality takes place only if $\frac{1}{p_i n} = 1$, i.e., $p_i = \frac{1}{n}$, for all $i$.                                    $\square$

## 3.6   Extensions of a Source

In Example 3.1 we have seen the procedure of dividing messages into bytes of $k$ (= 2 or 3) symbols. We now formalize this procedure by introducing the corresponding information source $S^k$ of all $k$-tuples of source symbols. Then we will show that this process does not change the entropy per symbol. More precisely, the entropy of $S^k$ is $k$ times that of $S$ (because it is related to a $k$-tuple of symbols of $S$).

**Definition.** *Let $S$ be an information source with the source symbols $a_1, \ldots, a_n$. By the $k$th extension of $S$ is meant the information source $S^k$ of symbols $a_{i_1} a_{i_2} \ldots a_{i_k}$ with the probabilities*

$$P(a_{i_1} a_{i_2} \ldots a_{i_k}) = P(a_{i_1}) \, P(a_{i_2}) \ldots P(a_{i_k})$$

*(for $i_1$, $i_2$, $\ldots$, $i_k$ taking arbitrary values 1, 2, $\ldots$, $n$).*

For example, in 3.1, we have seen $S^2$ and $S^3$ for the binary source $S$ with probabilities 0.9 and 0.1.

**Theorem.** *For each information source $S$,*

$$H(S^k) = kH(S).$$

**PROOF.** We prove just that $H(S^2) = 2H(S)$ and leave it to the reader to perform the (completely analogous) computation for $k = 3, 4, \ldots$. The source $S^2$ has symbols $a_i a_j$ with probabilities $p_i p_j$, where $p_i$ denotes the $i$th probability in $S$ ($i = 1, \ldots, n$). Thus,

$$
\begin{aligned}
H(S^2) &= -\sum_{i=1}^{n} \sum_{j=1}^{n} p_i p_j \log_2(p_i p_j) \\
&= -\sum_{i=1}^{n} \sum_{j=1}^{n} p_i p_j (\log_2 p_i + \log_2 p_j) \\
&= -\sum_{i=1}^{n} p_i \log_2 p_i \sum_{j=1}^{n} p_j - \sum_{i=1}^{n} p_i \sum_{j=1}^{n} p_j \log_2 p_j \\
&= H(S) + \sum_{i=1}^{n} p_i H(S) = 2H(S).
\end{aligned}
$$

$\square$

## 3.7 Entropy and Average Length

We now compare the average length $L$ of a binary instantaneous code $K$ with the entropy $H(S)$. The number $L$ tells us how many bits are required per symbol by the code $K$. The entropy $H(S)$ expresses the average number of bits "contained" in a symbol. Whatever the construction of the code $K$ may be, we expect that the actual number $L$ of bits per symbol will not be smaller than $H(S)$. This is what we prove now.

**Theorem.** *Every binary instantaneous code of a source $S$ has the average length larger or equal to the entropy of $S$ (in bits), i.e.,*

$$L \geq H(S).$$

PROOF. Denote by $d_i$ the length of the $i$th code word. Then

$$L = \sum_{i=1}^{n} p_i d_i = \sum_{i=1}^{n} p_i \log_2 2^{d_i}$$

and we compute the difference

$$
\begin{aligned}
H(S) - L &= \sum_{i=1}^{n} p_i \log_2 \frac{1}{p_i} - \sum_{i=1}^{n} p_i \log_2 2^{d_i} \\
&= \sum_{i=1}^{n} p_i \log_2 \frac{1}{p_i 2^{d_i}} \\
&= \frac{1}{\log 2} \sum_{i=1}^{n} p_i \log \frac{1}{p_i 2^{d_i}}.
\end{aligned}
$$

We now use the inequality (3.5.1):

$$
\begin{aligned}
H(S) - L &\leq \frac{1}{\log 2} \sum_{i=1}^{n} p_i \left( \frac{1}{p_i 2^{d_i}} - 1 \right) \\
&= \frac{1}{\log 2} \left( \sum_{i=1}^{n} \frac{1}{2^{d_i}} - \sum_{i=1}^{n} p_i \right) \\
&= \frac{1}{\log 2} \left( \sum_{i=1}^{n} 2^{-d_i} - 1 \right).
\end{aligned}
$$

By Kraft's inequality (1.6), we conclude that $H(S) - L \leq 0$. $\qquad \square$

# 3.8   Shannon's Noiseless Coding Theorem

Let us once again return to Example 3.1. The source $S$ has entropy $H(S) = 0.469$ bit (per symbol), see 3.4. By coding the second extension $S^2$, we have obtained a code of average length 1.29 (bits per two symbols), thus getting $L_{min}(S^2)/2 = 0.645$ bits per symbol. A better result is obtained by coding the third extension, which yields $L_{min}(S^3)/3 = 0.533$ bits per symbol. (See 3.1.) This process will never compress data to below the entropy of the source. In fact, by applying Theorem 3.7 to the extended source $S^k$, we get

$$L_{min}(S^k) \geq H(S^k) = k \cdot H(S)$$

and, thus,

$$\frac{L_{min}(S^k)}{k} \geq H(S).$$

One of the crucial results of information theory is that the compression can be arbitrarily close to the entropy $H(S)$:

**Shannon's Noiseless Coding Theorem.** *For each information source, the average length $L_{min}(S)$ of a binary Huffman code is related to the entropy $H(S)$ by*

$$H(S) \leq L_{min}(S) \leq H(S) + 1$$

*and, thus, the $k$th extensions $S^k$ of the source fulfil*

$$\frac{L_{min}(S^k)}{k} \longrightarrow H(S) \quad for \ k \to \infty.$$

**Remark.** Two mistakes live on in the literature on information theory [ever since Shannon's paper (1948)]. One is minor: it is usually claimed that $L_{min}(S) < H(S) + 1$; however, if $S$ is a source of two symbols of probabilities 1 and 0, then $L_{min}(S) = 1 = H(S) + 1$. The other one is presenting the simpler proof without assuming nonzero probabilities.

**PROOF.** The latter statement follows from the former one by applying it to the source $S^k$ [of entropy $kH(S)$, see 3.6]:

$$kH(S) \leq L_{min}(S^k) \leq kH(S) + 1,$$

In fact, divide the inequalities through $k$:

$$H(S) \leq \frac{L_{min}(S^K)}{k} \leq H(S) + \frac{1}{k}$$

and use the sandwich theorem for limits to conclude that $\frac{L_{min}(S^k)}{k} \to H(S)$.

In view of Theorem 3.7, it remains to prove that

$$L_{\min}(S) \leq H(S) + 1. \tag{3.8.1}$$

Let $a_1, a_2, \ldots, a_n$ be the source symbols of $S$ and denote by

$$P(a_i) = p_i \qquad \text{for } i = 1, 2, \ldots, n$$

their probabilities.

(1) Suppose that $p_i \neq 0$ for $i = 1, 2, \ldots, n$. For each $i$, there exists a (unique) natural number $d_i$ such that

$$\log_2 \frac{1}{p_i} \leq d_i < 1 + \log_2 \frac{1}{p_i}. \tag{3.8.2}$$

We can construct an instantaneous code with code word lengths $d_1, d_2, \ldots, d_n$. In fact, Kraft's inequality is satisfied:

$$\sum_{i=1}^{n} \frac{1}{2^{d_i}} \leq \sum_{i=1}^{n} \frac{1}{2^{\log_2 \frac{1}{p_i}}} = \sum_{i=1}^{n} \frac{1}{\frac{1}{p_i}} = \sum_{i=1}^{n} p_i = 1.$$

That instantaneous code has the following average length:

$$L = \sum_{i=1}^{n} p_i d_i < \sum_{i=1}^{n} p_i + \sum_{i=1}^{n} p_i \log_2 \frac{1}{p_i} = 1 + H(S).$$

This proves (3.8.1).

(2) The case of an arbitrary source $S$ (with $p_i = 0$ for some $i$) can be derived from the above case as follows: choose a sequence $S^k$ of sources on the same source symbols as $S$ and with positive probabilities $p_1^k, p_2^k, \ldots, p_n^k$, which tend to the probabilities of $S$:

$$\lim_{k \to \infty} p_i^k = p_i \qquad \text{and} \qquad p_i^k > 0 \quad \text{for all } i = 1, 2, \ldots, n.$$

[Such sources exist: if, say, $p_1 > 0$, then put $p_i^k = p_i + \frac{1}{k}$ $(i = 2, \ldots, n)$ and $p_1^k = p_1 - \frac{n-1}{k}$ for all $k \geq \frac{n-1}{p_1}$.] By (1) we know that for each $k$,

$$L_{\min}(S^k) \leq 1 + H(S^k).$$

Thus, to prove (3.8.1), it is sufficient to verify that

$$L_{\min}(S^k) \to L_{\min}(S) \qquad \text{and} \qquad H(S^k) \to H(S) \quad \text{for } k \to \infty.$$

The first limit is clear: the Huffman codes of sources $S^k$ will not change infinitely many times. More precisely, there exists $k_0$ such that a Huffman code for $S^{k_0}$ will also be a Huffman code for all $S^k$ with $k \geq k_0$ (and, thus, for $S$ too). The latter limit follows from the continuity of entropy. □

## 3.9    Concluding Remarks

1. For each source $S$, we have introduced the entropy $H(S)$, which is, roughly speaking, the average number of bits contained in a source symbol. No data compression can represent $S$ by a smaller amount of bits symbol (see Theorem 3.6).

2. An optimum data compression can be achieved by using Huffman codes of the extension $S^k$ of the source $S$.

3. We have, so far, restricted ourselves to binary codes. However, the same results hold for coding by $r$ code symbols for any $r > 2$, except that logarithms of radix $r$ must be used. That is, for the radix-$r$ entropy,

$$H_r(S) = \sum p_i \log_r p_i,$$

one has, as in 3.8,

$$H_r(S) \le L_{\min}(S) \le H_r(S) + 1,$$

and hence

$$\frac{L_{\min}(S^k)}{k} \longrightarrow H_r(S) \qquad \text{for } k \to \infty.$$

Here $L_{\min}(S^k)$ is the minimum average length of an $r$-symbol code for the $k$th extension of $S$.

The proof is quite analogous to that of 3.8, and we leave it to the reader.

## Exercises

**3A**    A message is written in source symbols $A$, $B$, $C$, $D$, and $A$ appears seven times more often than any of the other symbols. Find a binary coding which does not require more than 1.4 bits per symbol in the average. (Use extensions.)

**3B**    Find the entropy of the following information source:

| Symbol | 1 | 2 | 3 | 4 | 5 | 6 |
|---|---|---|---|---|---|---|
| Probability | 0.1 | 0.1 | 0.45 | 0.05 | 0.2 | 0.1 |

**3C**    A shooter who hits the target with probability $\frac{1}{2}$ shoots twice. Another shooter has the probability $\frac{1}{3}$ of hitting the target, and he shoots three times. Whose target carries "more information" (i.e., has a larger entropy)?

**3D**  Given information sources $S_1$ and $S_2$, denote by $S_1 \times S_2$ the information source of all pairs of symbols $(s_1, s_2)$ with $s_i$ a symbol of $S_i$ ($i = 1, 2$). Prove that

$$H(S_1 \times S_2) \leq H(S_1) + H(S_2)$$

and the equality takes place iff $S_1$ and $S_2$ are independent [i.e., the probability of $(s_1, s_2)$ is the product of the probability of $s_1$ (in $S_1$) and $s_2$ (in $S_2$)].

**3E**  A channel transmits equiprobable symbols 0 and 1. What is the probability of receiving the message 01101? What is the entropy of five-symbol messages?

**3F**  An information source consists of 128 equiprobable symbols. What is the length of a message of entropy 42 bits?

**3G**  What is the entropy of a message consisting of three words of length 8 each, if the source alphabet has symbols $A$, $B$, $C$ which

  (1) are equiprobable?

  (2) have probabilities 0.58, 0.33, and 0.09?

**3H**  The *effectivity* of an information source is defined as the ratio between the entropy (in bits) and the average length of a binary Huffman code. Prove that the effectivity lies between 0 and 1, and discuss the two extremal values. Find the effectivity of the three sources of Figure 5 in Chapter 2.

**3I**  Find the effectivity of

  (1) the source $A$, $B$, $C$, $D$ in which $A$ has double the frequency of the other three symbols,

  (2) the second extension of that source.

**3J**  What is the effectivity of a binary source $S$ in which 0 has probability 0.89? Find an extension of $S$ with effectivity at least 90%.

**3K**  Find binary instantaneous codes for the sources in Figure 4 and compute their effectivity.

| Symbol | A | B | C | D | E | F | G | H |
|---|---|---|---|---|---|---|---|---|
| Prob. (1st source) | 6% | 15% | 15% | 7% | 5% | 30% | 18% | 4% |
| Prob. (2nd source) | $\frac{1}{4}$ | $\frac{1}{4}$ | $\frac{1}{8}$ | $\frac{1}{8}$ | $\frac{1}{16}$ | $\frac{1}{16}$ | $\frac{1}{16}$ | $\frac{1}{16}$ |
| Prob. (3rd source) | 0.2 | 0.18 | 0.16 | 0.14 | 0.1 | 0.1 | 0.6 | 0.4 |

**Figure 4**

**3L**  Suppose a huge binary message contains twice more 0's than 1's. Find a coding which uses

(1)  at most 0.94 bits per symbol

(2)  at most 0.9 bits per symbol.

## Notes

Entropy in information theory has been introduced by Shannon (1948), who was inspired by entropy in physics (where logarithms of the probabilities of states had been used by Boltzmann already in 1896). Foundations of information theory are presented, e.g., in the excellent textbook of Abramson (1963), where some generalizations of Shannon's Noiseless Coding Theorem can also be found.

# Chapter 4
# Reliable Communication Through Unreliable Channels

So far we have not taken into consideration the role of noise in communication. In practice, communication channels and storage media add a certain level of noise to messages. We can use coding to restore the original information. Codes designed for this task are called error-correcting (or error-detecting) codes. They are typically block codes.

The construction of good error-correcting codes goes, in a sense, in the opposite direction to the data compression studied in the preceding chapters: there we tried to minimize the redundancy, whereas here we create it. Observe that all natural languages contain a certain redundancy which is used for correction of errors. That is, our words contain more letters than what would be absolutely necessary for communication, and we are thus usually able to correctly read a sentence even if one or two letters are corrupted. In artificial languages (i.e., codes), designed without redundancy, this error-correcting capability is missing. (When we receive a binary word, there is no telling whether this word has actually been sent.) We thus extend code words by redundant symbols, making it possible to detect or even correct errors. These new symbols, called check symbols, make the coding less effective, and the fundamental task of the theory of error-correcting codes is to find good codes which would correct sufficiently many errors while remaining sufficiently effective.

In the present chapter, we introduce the basic parameters of error-correcting codes, and we introduce the surprising result of Claude Shannon, stating that each unreliable channel can be encoded with a specified level of effectivity in such a way that communication becomes reliable, i.e., practically error-free. Concrete constructions of good error-correcting codes are presented in subsequent chapters.

## 4.1   Binary Symmetric Channels

We now turn to communication through channels which add a certain level of noise. This means that when we send a symbol through the channel, we can receive a different symbol. (We disregard the possibility of synchronization errors, i.e., of receiving a symbol when none was sent, or not receiving any symbol although some was sent. In most of the usual applications, synchronization errors are less probable than corruptions of symbols.)

For simplicity, we confine ourselves to *binary symmetric channels*, which means that

(1) our communication is binary, i.e., the inputs and outputs of the channel are the symbols 0 and 1,

(2) the probability $p$ that when sending 1 we will receive 0 is equal to the probability that when sending 0 we will receive 1,

(3) the channel has no memory, i.e., when sending a symbol, the probability of receiving 0 (or 1) does not depend on the preceding symbols sent.

Although all results of the present chapter hold for a much wider variety of channnels, binary symmetric channels form the most frequently met model of communication (in data transmission, storage, etc.), and the idea of reliable communication is much easier to understand in such a simple model.

The probability $p$ of (2) above is called the *error probability* of the binary symmetric channel. The opposite probability of a correct transmission of a symbol is denoted by

$$q = 1 - p.$$

We can assume that

$$0 \leq p \leq 0.5$$

because if $p > 0.5$, then it is sufficient to switch the roles of 0 and 1 at the receiving end.

As a concrete example, consider a binary symmetric channel which corrupts one symbol in a thousand (on the average), i.e., $p = 0.001$ and $q = 0.999$. In many applications, this is not a sufficient reliability. Let us assume that we cannot afford more than two corrupted symbols per ten thousand. The first of idea of how to increase the reliability is to repeat each symbol several times. This is called a *repetition code*. For example, when we repeat three times, we use the following code $K_3$:

$$0 \quad 000$$
$$1 \quad 111$$

Repetition code $K_3$

Thus, to each information symbol we, add two check symbols. Let us compute the increase in reliability. When $a_1 a_2 a_3$ is received, we determine the word sent by a majority vote: if at least two of the symbols $a_i$ are 0, then 000 was sent; if at least two are 1, then 111 was sent. This decision is incorrect only if the noise has either corrupted three bits in a row (probability $p^3$) or two in one word (probability $3pq^2$, see 4A). Thus, the probability of error when $K_3$ is applied is

$$P_{\text{err}}(K_3) = p^3 + 3pq^2 = (0.001)^3 + 3(0.001)(0.999)^2 \approx 0.003.$$

This is not yet enough, so we can try five repetitions. (Observe that four repetitions clearly would not help.)

$$0 \quad 00000$$
$$1 \quad 11111$$

Repetition code $K_5$

Again, we decode by majority vote. This is incorrect only if noise has corrupted five bits (probability $p^5$) or four bits (probability $5p^4q$) or three bits [probability $\binom{5}{3}p^3q^2$]. Thus, the code $K_5$ has the following error probability:

$$
\begin{aligned}
P_{\text{err}}(K_5) &= p^5 + 5p^4q + \binom{5}{3}p^3q^2 \\
&= (0.001)^5 + 5(0.001)^4 0.999 + 10(0.001)^3(0.999)^2 \\
&\approx 10^{-8}.
\end{aligned}
$$

This certainly is a major improvement.

It is obvious that repetition codes can make communication *arbitrarily reliable*. That is, the repetition codes $K_n$ of length $n$ have the property that $P_{\text{err}}(K_n)$ tends to zero with increasing $n$. This simple technique is, however, too costly (from the point of view of time, space, or equipment). Therefore, we will try to find better codes. Before continuing, observe that an application of error-correcting codes makes the scheme of communications more complex (see Figure 1). We first turn the source message to

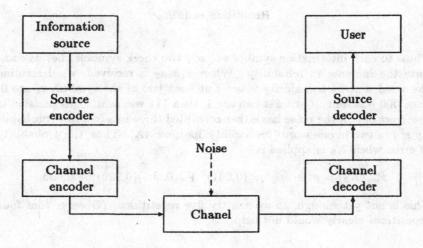

**Figure 1:** Block diagram of a communication system

the binary form (source encoder) and add the check bits (channel encoder). Then we send the message through the channel, where noise is added. In the opposite direction, we use the redundancy to estimate what code word has been sent (channel decoder), then we delete the redundant symbols (source decoder) and, finally, we translate to the form required by the user.

Beware: when speaking of decoding in the realm of error-correcting codes, what is usually meant is the channel decoder (estimating the code word sent).

## 4.2   Information Rate

In the case of the repetition code, we send a word of length $n$, but only one bit carries information, and the other $n-1$ bits just repeat it—thus, they are redundant. In a more efficient code designed for noise protection, we often have the $n$ bits of each code word divided into $k$ *information bits* which carry information (i.e., which can be chosen arbitrarily), and $n - k$ *check bits* which are redundant (i.e., are completely determined by the information bits). The arbitrary choice of $k$ bits then implies that the number of code words is $2^k$. Conversely, whenever a binary block code $K$ of length $n$ has $2^k$ code words, we can say that each word "contains" $k$ information bits and $n - k$ check bits. More precisely, since the number of all binary words of length $k$ is $2^k$, we have a bijection between those $2^k$ words and all code words. Any such bijection provides an encoder which turns a $k$-bit information word (a binary word of $k$ symbols) into a code word (of length $n$).

The ratio

$$R(K) = \frac{k}{n}$$

of the number of information bits to the number of all bits sent is called the *information rate* of the code $K$. This important concept actually need not be restricted only to the binary case. Recall that a *block code* of length $n$ in a given alphabet $B$ is a nonempty set $K$ of words of length $n$ in $B$. We call $K$ *trivial* if it has one code word only; all other codes are called *nontrivial*.

**Definition.** *A block code $K$ of length $n$ in a code alphabet of $r$ symbols is said to have the* information rate

$$R(K) = \frac{k}{n}$$

*provided that the number of all code words is $r^k$.*

**Remark.** The information rate lies between 0 and 1. The two extreme values correspond to the trivial codes $[k = 0, R(K) = 0]$, which carry no information, and to the codes in which every word is a code word $[k = n, R(K) = 1]$, which provide no noise protection. In general, information rates near to 0 are typical for codes which are not very efficient from the point of view of time and/or space they require, but which often provide good noise protection. A code with information rate near to 1 is a very efficient code, but it often provides weaker noise protection.

**Examples**

(1) The repetition code has an information rate $1/n$.

(2) One of the most frequently used codes for error control is the *even-parity code* which has $n - 1$ information bits and one parity check bit such that every code word has even parity (i.e., an even number of 1's).

| Information Bits | Code Word | Information Bits | Code Word |
|:---:|:---:|:---:|:---:|
| 000 | 0000 | 110 | 1100 |
| 100 | 1001 | 101 | 1010 |
| 010 | 0101 | 011 | 0110 |
| 001 | 0011 | 111 | 1111 |

**Figure 2:** The even-parity code of length 4

The information rate is $(n-1)/n = 1-1/n$, and the code detects single errors. The encoding in the case $n = 3$ is shown in Figure 2.

## 4.3   An Example of Increased Reliability

Let us return to the situation of a binary symmetric channel with the error probability $p = 0.001$, and to our requirement of at most two errors per ten thousand of symbols. Suppose our channel can transmit two bits per second, and the source message is a continuous flow of information of one bit per second. This means that we can add redundant bits, but the amount of the information bits must be at least one-half of the transmitted bits. In other words, we can only use codes $K$ of information rates $R(K) \geq 1/2$.

In this situation, repetition codes are no good, of course. In order to achieve the required increase in reliability, we use the same trick as for data compression in Chapter 2: we organize the source message into bytes. For example, if we use bytes of length $k = 2$, we can send words of length $n = 4$. A simple idea is to repeat the second bit three times; i.e., to use the code $K_4^*$ in Figure 3. We decode as follows: we assume that the first bit is

| Information Bits | Code Word |
|:---:|:---:|
| 00 | 0000 |
| 01 | 0111 |
| 10 | 1000 |
| 11 | 1111 |

**Figure 3:** Code $K_4^*$

correct, and for the second bit we have a majority vote (like in the case of the repetition code $K_3$ in 4.1). Thus, our decoding will be correct whenever all four bits are correct (probability $q^4$) or the first bit is correct and there is at most one corrupted bit in the word (probability $3pq^3$, see 4A). The average error probability $P_{\text{err}}(K_4^*)$ of our decoding then fulfils

$$1 - P_{\text{err}}(K_4^*) = q^4 + 3pq^3 = (0.999)^4 + 3(0.001)(0.999)^3 \approx 0.9997,$$

i.e.,

$$P_{\text{err}}(K_4^*) \approx 0.0003.$$

This is not sufficient.

To find a better code, we choose $k = 3$ and $n = 6$. We can use the code $K_6^*$ in Figure 4, which has the property that any two distinct code words differ in three bits or more. It follows that this code can correct any

| Information Bits | Code Word |
|:---:|:---:|
| 000 | 000000 |
| 100 | 100011 |
| 010 | 010101 |
| 001 | 001110 |
| 011 | 011011 |
| 101 | 101101 |
| 110 | 110110 |
| 111 | 111000 |

**Figure 4:** Code $K_6^*$

single error: the received word differs in one bit from exactly one of the code words, the code word sent. Thus, we know which symbol to correct. In other words, we decode by finding the most similar code word. This decoding is correct whenever no error has occurred (probability $q^6$) or just one bit has been corrupted (probability $6pq^5$, see 4A). Thus,

$$1 - P_{\text{err}}(K_6^*) \geq q^6 + 6pq^5 \approx 0.99985,$$

i.e.,

$$P_{\text{err}}(K_6^*) \leq 0.00015.$$

We see that the percentage of computed bytes is better than required: 1.5 per ten thousand. (The percentage of corrupted bits is, then, even slightly smaller, since a corrupted byte can have some correct bits.)

We can ask whether an *arbitrary* reliability can be achieved this way. That is: do there exist codes $K_n^*$ of information rate $\frac{1}{2}$ such that the decoding error probabilities $P_{err}(K_n^*)$ tend to zero with increasing $n$? We will see from Shannon's Fundamental Theorem that the answer is affirmative.

This might whet our appetite to ask for more: can an arbitrary reliability be achieved with the information rate 0.9? (yes, by Shannon's Fundamental Theorem), or even 0.99? (no, by the Converse of Shannon's Fundamental Theorem).

## 4.4   Hamming Distance

The main idea of error correction is that we want to have code words sufficiently "wide apart" in order to recognize the corrupted positions of the received word. For that reason, the following concept of distance of two words (not necessarily binary, but necessarily of the same length) plays a fundamental role:*

**Definition.** *Given two words* $\mathbf{a} = a_1 a_2 \ldots a_n$ *and* $\mathbf{b} = b_1 b_2 \ldots b_n$, *their* Hamming distance *is defined as the number of positions in which* $\mathbf{a}$ *and* $\mathbf{b}$ *differ. We denote it by* $d(\mathbf{a}, \mathbf{b})$:

$$d(\mathbf{a}, \mathbf{b}) = number\ of\ indices\ i = 1, 2, \ldots, n\ with\ a_i \neq b_i.$$

For example, the repetition code has the property that the two distinct code words have Hamming distance $n$. In 4.3, we introduced the code $K_6^*$ in which arbitrary two code words have distance at least 3. We deduced that the code is capable of correcting single errors. We will see below that this is no coincidence.

**Proposition.** *For each alphabet and each number* $n$, *the Hamming distance is a metric on the set of all words of length* $n$. *That is:*

(1)  $d(\mathbf{a}, \mathbf{a}) = 0$ *and* $d(\mathbf{a}, \mathbf{b}) > 0$ *whenever* $\mathbf{a} \neq \mathbf{b}$,

(2)  $d(\mathbf{a}, \mathbf{b}) = d(\mathbf{b}, \mathbf{a})$,

(3)  $d(\mathbf{a}, \mathbf{b}) + d(\mathbf{b}, \mathbf{c}) \geq d(\mathbf{a}, \mathbf{c})$      (triangle inequality)

*for arbitrary words* $\mathbf{a}$, $\mathbf{b}$, $\mathbf{c}$ *of length* $n$.

---

*This is the distance function suitable for the white noise, i.e., for the random distribution of corrupted symbols (as opposed, say, to burst errors).

PROOF. (1) and (2) follow immediately from the definition of the Hamming distance. To verify (3), put $d(\mathbf{a}, \mathbf{b}) = v$ and $d(\mathbf{b}, \mathbf{c}) = w$. Thus, we have indices $i_1, \ldots, i_v$ in which $\mathbf{a}$ differs from $\mathbf{b}$, and indices $j_1, \ldots, j_w$ in which $\mathbf{b}$ differs from $\mathbf{c}$. Moreover, $a_i = b_i$ whenever $i \neq i_1, \ldots, i_v$, and $b_i = c_i$ whenever $i \neq j_1, \ldots, j_w$. Consequently, $a_i = c_i$ whenever $i \neq i_1, \ldots, i_v, j_1, \ldots, j_w$. Therefore, the number of indices in which $\mathbf{a}$ differs from $\mathbf{c}$ is at most $v + w$. This proves that $d(\mathbf{a}, \mathbf{c}) \leq v + w = d(\mathbf{a}, \mathbf{b}) + d(\mathbf{b}, \mathbf{c})$.      □

**Example.** Let us illustrate the role of the Hamming distance in the case of binary codes of length 3. There are altogether 8 binary words of length 3, and we can depict them as vertices of the corresponding cube (see Figure 5). The Hamming distance is just the number of sides of the cube on the path

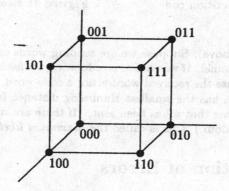

**Figure 5:** Binary words of length 3

from one word to another. If all eight words are code words, then no noise protection is obtained, and the information rate is $R = 1$. The repetition code has code words 000 and 111 of Hamming distance 3 (see Figure 6). This code has information rate $\frac{1}{3}$, and it corrects single errors. Further, we have the even-parity code (see Figure 7). Arbitrary two code words have Hamming distance 2. Therefore, the code detects a single error, but cannot correct it. Its information rate is $\frac{2}{3}$.

**Remark.** Now we can make precise the decoding rule used throughout the book* for error-correcting codes (which has already been illustrated in

---

*The only exceptions are codes for burst-error protection, see 10.7.

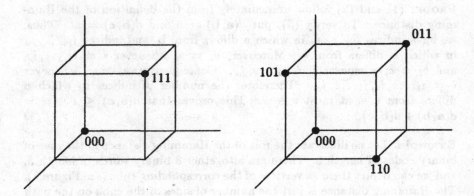

**Figure 6:** Repetition code          **Figure 7:** Even-parity code

several examples above). Suppose we are sending words of a block code $K$ through a noisy channel. If we receive a code word, we assume that no error has occurred. In case the received word is not a code word, we find the code word **a** in $K$ which has the smallest Hamming distance from the received word, and we assume that **a** has been sent. (If there are more choices of **a**, we pick one at random.) This is called the *maximum likelihood decoding*.

## 4.5   Detection of Errors

The idea of error detection is clear: if we receive a word which is no code word, then we know that an error has been made. Recall that a block code of length $n$ in the code alphabet $B$ is a nonempty set of words of length $n$ in that alphabet. A block code $K$ is said to *detect $t$ errors* provided that for each code word **a** and each word **a'** obtained from **a** by corrupting 1, 2, ..., $t$ symbols, **a'** is not a code word. In other words, no two code words have Hamming distance 1, 2, ..., $t$. This is an important property of codes used in situations where communication can be repeated whenever errors are detected.

**Definition.** *The* minimum distance $d(K)$ *of a nontrivial block code $K$ is the smallest Hamming distance of two distinct code words, i.e.,*

$$d(K) = \min\{\, d(\mathbf{a}, \mathbf{b}) \mid \mathbf{a}, \mathbf{b} \text{ are words in } K \text{ and } \mathbf{a} \neq \mathbf{b} \,\}.$$

**Examples.** The repetition code of length $n$ has $d = n$. The even-parity code has $d = 2$. The code $K_6^*$ of 4.3 has $d = 3$.

**Proposition.** *A code detects t errors if and only if its minimum distance is greater than t.*

PROOF. If $d(K) > t$, then $K$ detects $t$ errors. In fact, suppose a is a code word and a' is a word which satisfies $1 \leq d(\mathbf{a}, \mathbf{a}') \leq t$. Then a' cannot be a code word, since else $d(K) \leq d(\mathbf{a}, \mathbf{a}') \leq t$.

Conversely, if $d(K) \leq t$, then $K$ does not detect $t$ errors. In fact, let a, a' be code words with $d(\mathbf{a}, \mathbf{a}') = d(K)$. Then $d(\mathbf{a}, \mathbf{a}') \leq t$ and the error which changes the originally sent code word a to the received word a' escapes undetected. □

## 4.6 Correction of Errors

The concept of error correction is somewhat more subtle. A block code $K$ is said to *correct t errors* provided that for each code word a and each word a' obtained from a by corrupting $1, 2, \ldots, t$ symbols, the maximum likelihood decoding (4.4) leads uniquely to a. In other words, the Hamming distance $d(\mathbf{a}, \mathbf{a}')$ is strictly smaller than the Hamming distance from a' to any other code word. In symbols: for each code word a in $K$ and each word a' such that $1 \leq d(\mathbf{a}, \mathbf{a}') \leq t$, it follows that $d(\mathbf{a}, \mathbf{a}') < d(\mathbf{b}, \mathbf{a}')$ for all words b in $K$, $\mathbf{b} \neq \mathbf{a}$.

**Proposition.** *A code corrects t errors if and only if its minimum distance is greater than 2t.*

PROOF. Let $d(K) \leq 2t$. Then we will show that $K$ cannot correct $t$ arbitrarily distributed errors. In other words, we will find a code word a and a word a' which has Hamming distance $t$ or less from a and yet its Hamming distance from a different code word is even smaller. To this end, let a, b be two code words with $d(\mathbf{a}, \mathbf{b}) = d(K)$. Let $i_1, i_2, \ldots, i_r$ be all the indices in which a differs from b. Then $r \leq 2t$. Suppose that we send a and the noise changes all the symbols $a_i$ with $i = i_2, i_4, i_6, \ldots$ (i.e., all the even indices in which a and b differ) to the values in b. That is, we receive the word a', where

$$a_i' = \begin{cases} a_i = b_i & \text{if } i \neq i_1, i_2, \ldots, i_r, \\ a_i & \text{if } i = i_1, i_3, \ldots, \\ b_i & \text{if } i = i_2, i_4, \ldots. \end{cases}$$

Then, obviously, $d(\mathbf{a}, \mathbf{a}') \leq \frac{r}{2} \leq t$ and yet $d(\mathbf{a}', \mathbf{b}) \leq d(\mathbf{a}', \mathbf{a})$. This can lead to decoding a' incorrectly as b.

Conversely, let $d(K) > 2t$. Then $K$ corrects $t$ errors. In fact, suppose that we send a word a and we receive a word a' of Hamming distance

$d(\mathbf{a}, \mathbf{a}') \leq t$. We have the following situation with any code word $\mathbf{b} \neq \mathbf{a}$ : $d(\mathbf{a}, \mathbf{b}) \geq d(K) > 2t$ and, by the triangle inequality (4.4),

$$d(\mathbf{a}, \mathbf{a}') + d(\mathbf{a}', \mathbf{b}) \geq d(\mathbf{a}, \mathbf{b}) > 2t.$$

Thus,

$$d(\mathbf{a}', \mathbf{b}) > 2t - d(\mathbf{a}, \mathbf{a}') \geq 2t - t = t \geq d(\mathbf{a}, \mathbf{a}').$$

We conclude that the maximum likelihood decoding will (correctly) lead to $\mathbf{a}$. □

**Remark.** We see that error correction is more demanding than error detection. For example, a code with the minimum distance $d = 4$ corrects single errors only, but it detects triple errors. However, in situations when no re-transmission is possible (e.g., in information storage), error-correcting codes have to be applied. In 8.6, we study the combination of detection and correction of errors.

## 4.7   Channel Capacity

In this section, we introduce an important parameter of the binary symmetric channel: its capacity. We first take a broader view and discuss discrete channels with an arbitrary number of inputs. Suppose a channel has inputs $x_1, x_2, \ldots, x_n$ and outputs $y_1, y_2, \ldots, y_m$. As in the case of binary symmetric channels (4.1), we assume that the channel has no memory, i.e., the present output $y_i$ only depends on the present input $x_i$ and not on the previous inputs. Then the full function of the channel is known when we test what happens if $x_j$ is put to the input for all $j = 1, 2, \ldots, n$. The result of such tests is the conditional probability distribution $P(y_1 \mid x_j)$, $P(y_2 \mid x_j)$, $\ldots, P(y_m \mid x_j)$ of the output under the condition that the input is $x_j$. This leads to the following mathematical model of a discrete channel:

**Definition.** *A discrete memoryless information channel consists of a finite set $\{ x_1, x_2, \ldots, x_n \}$ (of input symbols), a finite set $\{ y_1, y_2, \ldots, y_m \}$ (of output symbols), and, for each $j = 1, 2, \ldots, n$, a probability distribution $P(y_i \mid x_j)$ on the set of output symbols. That is, $P(y_i \mid x_j)$ are numbers between 0 and 1 ($i = 1, 2, \ldots, m$ and $j = 1, 2, \ldots, n$) such that for each $j$, we have $\sum_{i=1}^{m} P(y_i \mid x_j) = 1$.*

**Examples**

(1) The case $n = m = 2$ and $P(y_2 \mid x_1) = P(y_1 \mid x_2) = p$ is the binary symmetric channel of Section 4.1.

(2) Suppose a channel with inputs 0, 1 has outputs 0, 1, E. Statistical testing shows that 1% of the inputs results in the output E and 99% are transmitted correctly. Then the channel is described by the two probability distributions in Figure 8.

| $y_i$ | 0 | 1 | E |
|---|---|---|---|
| $P(y_i \mid 0)$ | 0.99 | 0 | 0.01 |
| $P(y_i \mid 1)$ | 0 | 0.99 | 0.01 |

**Figure 8:** The description of a channel

**Remark.** (1) Suppose we know the probability $P(x_i)$ of the input $x_i$ of an information channel. More succinctly, we know what information source:

| input | $x_1$ | $x_2$ | ... | $x_n$ |
|---|---|---|---|---|
| probability | $P(x_1)$ | $P(x_2)$ | ... | $P(x_n)$ |

is being fed into the channel (Figure 9). Then we can compute the prob-

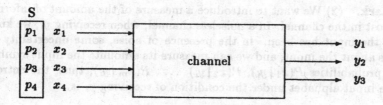

**Figure 9:** An information channel with an information source

ability $P(x_j, y_i)$ of the input/output pair of symbols by the well-known formula

$$P(x_j, y_i) = P(x_j)P(y_i \mid x_j). \qquad (4.7.1)$$

The (marginal) probability distribution of the outputs is then given by

$$P(y_i) = \sum_{j=1}^{n} P(x_j, y_i). \qquad (4.7.2)$$

We can use the formula (4.7.1) also in the reverse order: $P(x_j, y_i) = P(y_i, x_j) = P(y_i)P(x_j \mid y_i)$. Thus, we obtain the following expression for the probability $P(x_j \mid y_i)$ that, when receiving $y_i$, the input is $x_i$:

$$P(x_j \mid y_i) = \frac{P(x_j, y_i)}{P(y_i)} = \frac{P(x_j)P(y_i \mid x_j)}{\sum_{k=1}^{n} P(x_k)P(y_i \mid x_k)}. \qquad (4.7.3)$$

**Example.** (2) (continued) An information source at the input consists of the probabilities $p_0 = P(0)$ and $p_1 = P(1) = 1 - p_0$. The probabilities $P(x_j, y_i)$ and $P(x_j \mid y_i)$ are listed in Figure 10. Observe that $P(x_j \mid y_i)$ has

| $y_i$ | 0 | 1 | E |
|---|---|---|---|
| $P(0, y_i)$ | $0.99p_0$ | 0 | $0.01p_0$ |
| $P(1, y_i)$ | 0 | $0.99p_1$ | $0.01p_1$ |
| $P(y_i)$ | $0.99p_0$ | $0.99p_1$ | $0.01$ |

| $y_i$ | 0 | 1 | E |
|---|---|---|---|
| $P(0 \mid y_i)$ | 1 | 0 | $p_0$ |
| $P(1 \mid y_i)$ | 0 | 1 | $p_1$ |

**Figure 10:** Probabilities $P(x_j, y_i)$ and $P(x_j \mid y_i)$

the obvious interpretation: when receiving 0, the input must be 0; when receiving 1, the input must be 1; and when receiving E, the probabilities of 0 and 1 have their original values, $p_0$, $p_1$.

**Remark.** (2) We want to introduce a measure of the amount of information lost in the channel. In a noiseless channel, when receiving $y_i$, we know what the input has been. In the presence of noise, some uncertainty remains about the input, and we can measure its amount: the input symbols have probabilities $P(x_1 \mid y_i)$, $P(x_2 \mid y_i)$, $\ldots$, $P(x_m \mid y_i)$, thus, the entropy of the input alphabet under the condition of receiving $y_i$ is

$$H(X \mid y_i) = -\sum_{j=1}^{n} P(x_j \mid y_i) \log_2 P(x_j \mid y_i) \quad \text{(bits)}.$$

Taking the mean value over all output symbols $y_i$, we obtain the expected uncertainty about the input after reading the output. This mean value is denoted by $H(X \mid Y)$. Let us compute it:

$$H(X \mid Y) = -\sum_{i=1}^{n} H(X \mid y_i)P(y_i)$$

$$= \sum_{i=1}^{m} \sum_{j=1}^{n} P(y_i)P(x_j \mid y_i) \log_2 P(x_j \mid y_i)$$

$$= \sum_{i=1}^{n} \sum_{j=1}^{m} P(x_j, y_i) \log_2 P(x_j \mid y_i).$$

**Definition.** *Given an information channel and an information source S at its input, the number*

$$H(X \mid Y) = -\sum_{i=1}^{m} \sum_{j=1}^{n} P(x_j, y_i) \log_2 P(x_j \mid y_i) \quad \text{(bits)}$$

*is called the* **conditional input-output entropy.** *The number*

$$I(X, Y) = H(S) - H(X \mid Y)$$

*is called the* **mutual information.**

**Example.** (2) (continued) From the tables in Figure 10, we see that the conditional input-output entropy is

$$
\begin{aligned}
H(X \mid Y) &= 0.99 p_0 \log_2 1 + 0 + 0.01 p_0 \log_2 p_0 \\
&\quad + 0 + 0.99 p_1 \log_2 1 + 0.01 p_1 \log_2 p_1 \\
&= 0.01 (p_0 \log_2 p_0 + p_1 \log_2 p_1) \\
&= 0.01 H(S).
\end{aligned}
$$

We can say that 1% of information is lost in the channel. The mutual information is

$$I(X, Y) = H(S) - 0.01 H(S) = 0.99 H(S).$$

**Remarks**

(3) The mutual information is the difference of the uncertainties about the input before and after reading the output. It depends on the information channel and on the type of messages that are put into the channel, i.e., on the information source $S$.

(4) A more compact formula for the mutual information is

$$I(X, Y) = \sum_{i=1}^{m} \sum_{j=1}^{n} P(x_j, y_i) \log_2 \frac{P(x_j, y_i)}{P(x_j) P(y_i)}.$$

(Observe the symmetry of the inputs and outputs in the formula, which explains the term "mutual".) In fact,

$$I(X, Y) = -\sum_{j=1}^{n} P(x_j) \log_2 P(x_j) + \sum_{i=1}^{m} \sum_{j=1}^{n} P(x_j, y_i) \log_2 P(x_j \mid y_i)$$

$$= -\sum_{i=1}^{m}\sum_{j=1}^{n} P(x_j, y_i) \log_2 P(x_j)$$

$$+ \sum_{i=1}^{m}\sum_{j=1}^{n} P(x_j, y_i) \log_2 \frac{P(x_j, y_i)}{P(y_i)}$$

$$= \sum_{i=1}^{m}\sum_{j=1}^{n} P(x_j, y_i) \log_2 \frac{P(x_j, y_i)}{P(x_j)P(y_i)}.$$

(5) The maximum mutual information obtained by taking the most convenient source $S$ for the given channel is called capacity:

**Definition.** *By the* capacity $C$ *of an information channel is meant the maximum value of the mutual information (over all information sources at the input).*

**Theorem.** *The capacity of a binary symmetric channel of error probability $p$ is*

$$C = 1 - H(p, 1-p) = 1 + p \log_2 p + (1-p) \log_2(1-p) \quad \text{(bits)}.$$

**Proof.** Let $S$ be an arbitrary information source of the input, given by the probabilities $p_0 = P(0)$ and $p_1 = P(1)$. Using (4.7.1) and (4.7.2), we can compute the output probabilities $\overline{p}_0$ and $\overline{p}_1$ of 0 and 1, respectively (see Figure 11), and we obtain an output information source $\overline{S}$ given by $\overline{p}_0 = P(0)$ and $\overline{p}_1 = P(1)$.

From the symmetrical formula for $I(X, Y)$ in Remark (4), we conclude that

$$I(X, Y) = H(S) - H(X \mid Y) = H(\overline{S}) - H(Y \mid X),$$

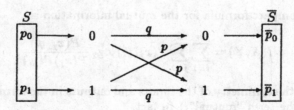

**Figure 11:** A binary symmetric channel with an input source $S$ and an output source $\overline{S}$

where $H(Y \mid X)$ is the output-input conditional entropy:

$$H(Y \mid X) = -\sum_{i=1}^{m} \sum_{j=1}^{n} P(y_i, x_j) \log_2 P(y_i \mid x_j).$$

The probabilities $P(y_i \mid x_j)$ and $P(y_i, x_j) = P(x_j, y_i)$ for the binary symmetric channel are shown in Figure 12. (Recall that $q = 1 - p$.)

| $y_i$ | 0 | 1 |  | $y_i$ | 0 | 1 |
|---|---|---|---|---|---|---|
| $P(y_i \mid 0)$ | $q$ | $p$ |  | $P(0, y_i)$ | $p_0 q$ | $p_0 p$ |
| $P(y_i \mid 1)$ | $p$ | $q$ |  | $P(1, y_i)$ | $p_1 p$ | $p_1 q$ |

**Figure 12:** Binary symmetric channel

Thus,

$$
\begin{aligned}
H(Y \mid X) &= -p_0 q \log_2 q - p_0 p \log_2 p - p_1 p \log_2 p - p_1 q \log_2 q \\
&= -(p_0 + p_1) q \log_2 q - (p_0 + p_1) p \log_2 p \\
&= -q \log_2 q - p \log_2 p \\
&= H(p, 1 - p).
\end{aligned}
$$

We conclude that $H(X \mid Y)$ is independent of the source $S$, thus,

$$C = \big(\max H(\overline{S})\big) - H(p, 1 - p).$$

The value of $H(\overline{S})$ cannot exceed 1 bit. On the other hand, the value of 1 bit can be achieved by choosing $p_0 = p_1 = 0.5$. In fact, using (7.4.1) and (7.4.2), we obtain $\overline{p}_0 = \overline{p}_1 = 0.5$, thus, $\max H(\overline{S}) = 1$ bit. Consequently,

$$C = 1 - H(p, 1 - p) \qquad \text{(bit)}.$$

□

**Examples**

(3) The binary symmetric channel with error probability $p = 0.001$ has capacity

$$C = 1 + 0.001 \log_2 0.001 + 0.999 \log_2 0.999 \approx 0.989 \text{ bits.}$$

(4) The binary symmetric channel with error probability $p = 0.5$ has capacity

$$C = 1 - H(0.5, 0.5) = 0 \text{ bits.}$$

This is a channel which mixes up 0's and 1's completely, thus, it loses all the information.

(5) The channel of Example (2) fulfils

$$I(X, Y) = 0.99 H(S).$$

The maximum value of $H(S)$ is 1 bit; thus, the channel has capacity

$$C = 0.99 \text{ bits.}$$

## 4.8   Shannon's Fundamental Theorem

We have observed in 4.1 that repetition codes $K_n$ make communication in a binary symmetric channel reliable in the sense that their error probabilities $P_{\text{err}}(K_n)$ tend to zero with increasing $n$. However, the information rates also tend to zero. We now present a surprising result of Claude Shannon concerning the probability of reliable communication with quite large information rates. Given a binary block code $K$ of length $n$, we denote by $P_{\text{err}}(K)$ the *average error probability* of the maximum likelihood decoding introduced in 4.4. In more detail, suppose we send a certain code word a in $K$. We can receive, in general, any binary word of length $n$. Some of the received words will be correctly decoded as a. The remaining words (e.g., all the other code words) will be decoded incorrectly, and the sum of the probabilities of receiving those words when a was sent is called the error probability related to a. Then $P_{\text{err}}(K)$ is the mean value of the error probability related to all code words a of $K$. (See Exercise 4B for a useful estimate.)

**Shannon's Fundamental Theorem.**   *Every binary symmetric channel of capacity $C > 0$ can be encoded with an arbitrary reliability and with information rate arbitrarily close to $C$. That is, there exist codes $K_1$, $K_2$, $K_3$, ... such that $P_{\text{err}}(K_n)$ tends to zero and $R(K_n)$ tends to $C$ with increasing $n$. In symbols:*

$$\lim_{n \to \infty} P_{\text{err}}(K_n) = 0 \quad \text{and} \quad \lim_{n \to \infty} R(K_n) = C.$$

SKETCH OF PROOF. It is our task to show that for an arbitrarily small number $\varepsilon_1 > 0$, there is a code $K_n$ of length $n$ with the information rate

$R(K_n) = C - \varepsilon_1$ and with an arbitrarily small value of $P_{\mathrm{err}}(K_n)$. The first requirement is met whenever we choose, out of the $2^n$ possible binary words, $M$ code words for $K_n$, where

$$M = 2^{n(C - \varepsilon_1)}.$$

In fact, by the definition of the information rate (4.2), we then have

$$R(K_n) = \frac{n(C - \varepsilon_1)}{n} = C - \varepsilon_1.$$

(We must be careful to choose our $n$ in such a way that $n(C - \varepsilon_1)$ is an integer. No problem: we can easily guarantee that $C - \varepsilon_1$ is a rational number, say, $C - \varepsilon_1 = u/v$, and then we choose $n$ to be a multiple of $v$.) From now on, $\varepsilon_1$ is a constant, and we choose $n$ and $M$ binary words of length $n$. Whether or not the chosen words will form codes satisfying the second condition that the error probability tends to 0 depends on the choice, of course.

The surprising and ingenious move in Shannon's proof is that, instead of trying to invent a clever way of choosing the $M$ code words, he has shown that a *random* choice works. More precisely, given any number $n$, we can pick $M$ out of the $2^n$ binary words in a random way, and we obtain a random code $K_n$. Each of these random codes satisfies $R(K_n) = C - \varepsilon_1$, as observed above, but the value of $P_{\mathrm{err}}(K_n)$ is now a random variable. Denote by $\widetilde{P}_{\mathrm{err}}$ the mean value of this random variable (for a fixed value of $n$, but a completely random choice of $M$ code words). The technically difficult part of the proof is to estimate the value of $\widetilde{P}_{\mathrm{err}}$ in order to verify that

$$\widetilde{P}_{\mathrm{err}} \longrightarrow 0 \quad \text{as} \quad n \longrightarrow \infty.$$

We omit the details [which the interested reader can find, e.g., in Hamming (1980), where a very careful exposition is presented]. Now the proof is finished: given arbitrarily small numbers $\varepsilon_1 > 0$ and $\varepsilon_2 > 0$, we can find $n$ such that $\widetilde{P}_{\mathrm{err}} < \varepsilon_2$. Since the mean value is smaller than $\varepsilon_2$, then at least one realization $P_{\mathrm{err}}(K_n)$ is also smaller than $\varepsilon_2$. Thus, $K_n$ is a code with

$$R(K_n) = C - \varepsilon_1 \quad \text{and} \quad P_{\mathrm{err}}(K_n) < \varepsilon_2.$$

$\square$

**Remarks**

(1) Observe that the proof of Shannon's Theorem says more than the statement, and this "more" is highly surprising: in every symmetric binary

channel of capacity $C$, by choosing a *random* code of length $n$ and information rate $C - \varepsilon_1$, we can be sure that reliability increases arbitrarily with increasing $n$.

However, this feature of the proof makes it absolutely nonconstructive: nobody would seriously advise a code designer to choose a good code at random.

(2) No practical coding scheme realizing the parameters promised by Shannon's Theorem has ever been presented. Thus, coding theory (and practice) concentrates today on a smaller but practically very important goal: finding good codes which are capable of the correction of a lot of errors. Here "good" means that the information rate is as high as possible (but not related to any concrete channel), and that there is an efficient decoding method. This is the subject of the subsequent chapters.

(3) The *Converse of Shannon's Fundamental Theorem* is the following statement (which further explains the role of capacity): In every binary symmetric channel of capacity $C$, whenever codes $K_n$ of lengths $n$ have information rates at least $C + \varepsilon$ (where $\varepsilon > 0$ is an arbitrarily small number), then the codes tend to be totally unreliable, i.e., their error probability tends to 1 with increasing $n$. In symbols:

$$R(K_n) \geq C + \varepsilon \implies \lim_{n \to \infty} P_{\text{err}}(K_n) = 1.$$

This has been proved by Wolfowitz (1959).

**Example.** The binary symmetric channel with error probability $p = 0.001$ has a capacity $C \approx 0.989$. It follows that there exist arbitrarily reliable codes with information rate $R = 0.9$. From the above Converse of Shannon's Fundamental Theorem, it further follows that codes with information rate $R = 0.99$ cannot be arbitrarily reliable (in fact, with increasing length, the reliability always decreases to zero).

## Exercises

**4A**    Suppose that a memoryless binary information source (2.1) has probabilities $p$ (for 0) and $q = 1 - p$ (for 1). Let $n$ symbols be emitted.

(1) Prove that the probability that the binary word of length $n$ has 1 on positions $i_1, i_2, \ldots, i_k$ and 0 on the remaining ones is $p^k q^{n-k}$.

(2) Conclude that the probability that the word has 1 on exactly $k$ positions is $\binom{n}{k} p^k q^{n-k}$.

**4B**   Verify the following error estimates for codes in a binary symmetric channel of error probability $p$:

(1) Prove that the probability that in a word of length $n$, precisely $i$ bits are corrupted is $\binom{n}{i} p^i q^{n-i}$.

(2) Let $K$ be a binary block code of length $n$ and minimum distance $2t$ or $2t + 1$. Prove that

$$P_{\text{err}}(K) \leq \sum_{i=t+1}^{n} \binom{n}{i} p^i q^{n-i}.$$

[Hint: if $t$ or less bits are corrupted, the maximum likelihood decoding is correct; this gives a lower bound on $1 - P_{\text{err}}(K)$.]

(3) Verify that the estimate in (2) holds with equality for the repetition codes.

**4C**   In a binary symmetric channel of error probability $p = 0.1$:

(1) find the length of a repetition code $K$ with $P_{\text{err}}(K) < 10^{-4}$;

(2) find $P_{\text{err}}(K_6^*)$ for the code $K_6^*$ of 4.3.

**4D**   Prove that the mutual information $I(X,Y)$ has the following properties:

(1) $I(X,Y) \geq 0$, with equality holding only if the inputs and outputs are stochastically independent.

(2) $I(X,Y) \leq H(S)$, with equality holding only if the outputs completely determine the inputs.

**4E**   Let $S$ be an information source at the input of an information channel, and $\overline{S}$ the information source at the output, given by (4.7.2). Prove that

$$I(X,Y) = H(S) + H(\overline{S}) - H(S,\overline{S}),$$

where $H(S,\overline{S})$ is the entropy of the input-output pairs [with probabilities given in (4.7.1)].

# Notes

The first known error-correcting code was the $(7, 4)$-Hamming code invented by Richard Hamming, and mentioned already in the fundamental work of Shannon (1948). The progress which the theory of error-correcting codes has made in the 40 years of its existence is enormous. A thorough treatise devoted to various aspects of the theory is the monograph of MacWilliams and Sloane (1981).

Shannon's Fundamental Theorem was proved by Claude E. Shannon in 1948. In our sketch of the proof, we have followed the detailed presentation in Hamming (1980).

# Part II

# Error-Correcting Codes

# Chapter 5

# Binary Linear Codes

For construction of effective error-correcting codes, and for good encoding and decoding techniques of such codes, it is desirable to add more "structure" to the code alphabet. In this chapter, we discuss an algebraic structure of the binary alphabet. In subsequent chapters, we will take a broader view by structuring other code alphabets, and we will show how coding is related to linear algebra.

We first show how binary codes can be described by equations, and then we use this description to introduce the important class of Hamming codes for single-error correction.

## 5.1   Binary Addition and Multiplication

We define the following operations $+$ (addition modulo 2) and $\cdot$ (multiplication modulo 2) on the binary symbols 0, 1:

| $+$ | 0 | 1 |     | $\cdot$ | 0 | 1 |
|-----|---|---|-----|---------|---|---|
| 0   | 0 | 1 |     | 0       | 0 | 0 |
| 1   | 1 | 0 |     | 1       | 0 | 1 |

Observe that multiplication is defined as if 0 and 1 were ordinary numbers, whereas the only "interesting" entry in the table of addition is

$$1 + 1 = 0.$$

This can be inerpreted as

$$1 = -1,$$

i.e., in binary computations, subtraction coincides with addition.

In the subsequent chapter, we will see that the operations $+$ and $\cdot$ turn the binary alphabet into a field $\mathbf{Z}_2$ (and we will also explain why they have been chosen this way).

## 5.2　Codes Described by Equations

Important binary codes can be described by systems of linear equations with binary coefficients (which practically means without coefficients: a variable is either present, if the coefficient is 1, or absent, if the coefficient is 0). For example, the repetition code (4.1) is described by the following equations

$$x_1 = x_2,$$
$$x_1 = x_3,$$
$$\vdots$$
$$x_1 = x_n,$$

or, which is the same, by the following homogenous system:

$$x_1 + x_2 = 0,$$
$$x_1 + x_3 = 0,$$
$$\vdots$$
$$x_1 + x_n = 0.$$

In fact, the system has just two solutions, $000\ldots0$ and $111\ldots1$, and those are precisely all code words.

Another example: the even-parity code (4.2) is described by a single equation, viz.,

$$x_1 + x_2 + \cdots + x_n = 0.$$

In fact, every solution of that equation has an even number of 1's (recall that $1 + 1 = 0$!) and, conversely, every word with an even number of 1's is a solution.

Let us mention another useful binary code: the *rectangular code*. This is a binary code of length $n = rs$, whose words are written (or, at least, considered) as $r \times s$ matrices. Each row has $r - 1$ information bits and one parity check bit—thus, all rows have even parity. Analogously, each column has $s - 1$ information bits and one parity check bit. A typical code word for $r = 4$ and $s = 3$ is shown in Figure 1. This code corrects single errors: the error corrupts the parity of a single row (say, the $i$th one) and a single column (the $j$th one), and then we correct the entry $a_{ij}$. However, the theory of error-correcting codes provides us with better codes than the rectangular code. For example, the $8 \times 4$ rectangular code has length 32 (21 information bits and 11 check bits). In comparison, the extended Hamming code of length 32, which also corrects single errors, has 26 information bits (see 8.6), and the extended BCH code of length 32 has 21 information

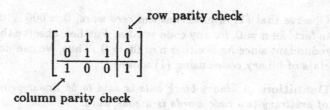

**Figure 1:** A code word of the 4 × 3 rectangular code

bits and corrects double errors (see 12.2). Rectangular codes are suitable, e.g., for error correction of punch cards.

Rectangular codes can also be described by equations. For example, the 4 × 3 code is described by the system of equations in Figure 2 (where the last equation is actually redundant: if all parities of rows and all but one parities of columns are even, then the last column parity must also be even).

$$a_{11} + a_{12} + a_{13} + a_{14} = 0$$
$$a_{21} + a_{22} + a_{23} + a_{24} = 0$$
$$a_{31} + a_{32} + a_{33} + a_{34} = 0$$
$$a_{11} + a_{21} + a_{31} = 0$$
$$a_{12} + a_{22} + a_{32} = 0$$
$$a_{13} + a_{23} + a_{33} = 0$$
$$a_{14} + a_{24} + a_{34} = 0$$

**Figure 2:** Equations describing the 4 × 3 rectangular code

## 5.3  Binary Linear Codes

Whenever a binary code $K$ can be described by a system of homogenous linear equations, then its code words form a *linear space*, i.e.,

(1) a sum $\mathbf{a} + \mathbf{b}$ of code words $\mathbf{a}$ and $\mathbf{b}$ (i.e., the word whose $i$th symbol is $a_i + b_i$) is a code word,

(2) a scalar multiple $\lambda\mathbf{a}$ of a code word (whose $i$th symbol is $\lambda a_i$) is a code word, for $\lambda = 0, 1$.

Observe that (1) implies that the *zero word*, $0 = 000\ldots00$, is a code word: in fact, $a+a = 0$, for any code word $a$. Further, observe that condition (2) is redundant since $\lambda a$ is either $a$ or $0a = 0$. Thus, we can define an important class of binary codes using (1) alone:

**Definition.** *A binary block code is said to be* linear *provided that the sum of arbitrary two code words is a code word.*

**Examples.** The repetition code, the even-parity code, and the rectangular code are examples of linear codes. In contrast, the 2-out-of-5 code (1.1) is not linear.

**Remarks**

(1) As observed above, every homogenous system of linear equations defines a linear code (consisting of all the solutions). Conversely, as we will prove in 7.7, every linear code can be described by a homogenous system of linear equations. The importance of such descriptions for decoding will be seen in many instances of codes studied below.

(2) If we send a code word $v$ and receive a word $w$, then by the *error pattern*, we mean the word $e$ which has 1 in precisely those positions in which $v$ and $w$ disagree:

$$e_i = \begin{cases} 1 & \text{if } v_i \neq w_i, \\ 0 & \text{if } v_i = w_i. \end{cases}$$

It then follows that

$$w = v + e$$

(i.e., we receive the sum of the code word which was sent and the error pattern).

(3) We saw in 4.5 the importance of the minimum distance of a block code. We now prove that this concept can be simplified in the case of linear codes:

**Definition.** *By a* Hamming weight *of a (not necessarily binary) word is meant the number of symbols distinct from 0. For each nontrivial block code $K$, the smallest Hamming weight of a code word distinct from $0 = 000\ldots00$ is called the* minimum weight *of $K$.*

**Example.** The word 11000 has Hamming weight 2. It is a code word of the even-parity code of length 5. Every code word of that code, except 00000, has Hamming weight either 2 or 4. Thus, the minimum weight of the even-parity code is 2.

**Proposition.** *For each nontrivial binary linear code the minimum distance is equal to the minimum weight.*

PROOF. Denote by $d(K)$ the minimum distance and by $w(K)$ the minimum weight. Let $\mathbf{a}$ be a code word of $K$ of Hamming weight $w(K)$. Then the Hamming distance of the code words $\mathbf{a}$ and $\mathbf{0}$ is, clearly, equal to the Hamming weight of $\mathbf{a}$, thus,

$$w(K) = d(\mathbf{a}, \mathbf{0}) \geq d(K).$$

To prove the opposite inequality, we choose code words $\mathbf{a}$ and $\mathbf{b}$ of Hamming distance $d(K)$. Then $\mathbf{a} + \mathbf{b}$ is also a code word (since $K$ is linear) and it has 0's precisely on those positions on which $\mathbf{a}$ and $\mathbf{b}$ agree. Thus, the Hamming distance of $\mathbf{a}$ and $\mathbf{b}$ is equal to the Hamming weight of $\mathbf{a} + \mathbf{b}$:

$$d(K) = d(\mathbf{a}, \mathbf{b}) \geq w(K).$$

Consequently, $d(K) = w(K)$. ◻

**Corollary.** *A linear code corrects (or detects) $t$ errors if and only if its minimum weight is larger than $2t$ (or larger than $t$, respectively).*

This follows from 4.6 and 4.5. ◻

**Example.** The rectangular code (5.2) has the minimum distance 4. In fact, if a code word $(a_{ij})$ has some nonzero entry, say, $a_{i_0 j_0} = 1$, then the $i_0$th row must contain at least two 1's, and the same is true about the $j_0$th column. Thus, the code word of the smallest weight has the following form:

$$
i_0 \rightarrow
\begin{pmatrix}
\vdots & & \vdots & & & \vdots & & & \vdots \\
0 & \cdots & 0 & 1 & 0 & \cdots & 0 & 1 & 0 & \cdots & 0 \\
\vdots & & \vdots & & & \vdots & & & \vdots \\
0 & \cdots & 0 & 1 & 0 & \cdots & 0 & 1 & 0 & \cdots & 0 \\
\vdots & & \vdots & & & \vdots & & & \vdots
\end{pmatrix}
\overset{\displaystyle j_0}{\downarrow}
$$

Consequently, the rectangular code detects triple errors.

## 5.4 Parity Check Matrix

Given a linear code $K$ described by a system of homogenous equations, we denote by $H$ the matrix of coefficients of that system. That is, the $i$th row of $H$ expresses the $i$th equation (in the sense that the $j$th entry is 1 if the $j$th variable is included, and 0 otherwise). As we will see in 7.5 below, the matrix notation of the system of equations is the following

$$H \begin{bmatrix} x_1 \\ x_2 \\ \vdots \\ x_n \end{bmatrix} = \begin{bmatrix} 0 \\ 0 \\ \vdots \\ 0 \end{bmatrix}.$$

For example, the equations in 5.2 describing the repetition code take the following form:

$$\begin{bmatrix} 1 & 1 & 0 & 0 & 0 & \cdots & 0 & 0 \\ 1 & 0 & 1 & 0 & 0 & \cdots & 0 & 0 \\ 1 & 0 & 0 & 1 & 0 & \cdots & 0 & 0 \\ \multicolumn{8}{c}{\dotfill} \\ 1 & 0 & 0 & 0 & 0 & \cdots & 1 & 0 \\ 1 & 0 & 0 & 0 & 0 & \cdots & 0 & 1 \end{bmatrix} \begin{bmatrix} x_1 \\ x_2 \\ x_3 \\ \vdots \\ x_{n-1} \\ x_n \end{bmatrix} = \begin{bmatrix} 0 \\ 0 \\ 0 \\ \vdots \\ 0 \\ 0 \end{bmatrix}$$

**Definition.** *A binary matrix $H$ is called a* parity check matrix *of a linear binary code $K$ of length $n$ provided that the code words of $K$ are precisely those binary words $x_1 x_2 \ldots x_n$ which fulfil*

$$H \begin{bmatrix} x_1 \\ x_2 \\ \vdots \\ x_n \end{bmatrix} = \begin{bmatrix} 0 \\ 0 \\ \vdots \\ 0 \end{bmatrix}.$$

**Example.** The even-parity code has a one-row parity check matrix:

$$H = [1111\ldots1].$$

The $4 \times 3$ rectangular code (see Figure 2 in 5.2) has the following parity check matrix (provided that the code words are now written as words of length 12 by concatenating the three rows):

$$H = \begin{bmatrix} 1 & 1 & 1 & 1 & 0 & 0 & 0 & 0 & 0 & 0 & 0 & 0 \\ 0 & 0 & 0 & 0 & 1 & 1 & 1 & 1 & 0 & 0 & 0 & 0 \\ 0 & 0 & 0 & 0 & 0 & 0 & 0 & 0 & 1 & 1 & 1 & 1 \\ 1 & 0 & 0 & 0 & 1 & 0 & 0 & 0 & 1 & 0 & 0 & 0 \\ 0 & 1 & 0 & 0 & 0 & 1 & 0 & 0 & 0 & 1 & 0 & 0 \\ 0 & 0 & 1 & 0 & 0 & 0 & 1 & 0 & 0 & 0 & 1 & 0 \\ 0 & 0 & 0 & 1 & 0 & 0 & 0 & 1 & 0 & 0 & 0 & 1 \end{bmatrix} \begin{array}{l} \left.\begin{array}{l} \\ \\ \end{array}\right\} \text{row parity} \\ \text{checks} \\ \left.\begin{array}{l} \\ \\ \\ \end{array}\right\} \text{column parity} \\ \text{checks} \end{array}$$

Since the last equation in Figure 2 is redundant, another parity check matrix of the same code is obtained by deleting the seventh row of $H$.

**Remark.** Let $K$ be a linear code described by a system of linear homogenous equations, none of which is redundant. Then each of the equations determines one bit of a code word. Thus, the number of equations (or rows of $H$) is the number of check bits, see 4.2. This will be made precise in Chapter 7, where we will also see that, conversely, each linear code with $k$ information symbols and $n - k$ check symbols can be described by $n - k$ equations. Thus, $H$ is an $n$ by $n - k$ matrix.

# 5.5 Hamming Codes—Perfect Codes for Single Errors

We are now going to introduce an important class of binary linear codes, the Hamming codes, whose basic properties are listed in Figure 3. In Sec-

| | |
|---|---|
| Length: | $n = 2^m - 1$ |
| Information symbols: | $k = 2^m - m - 1$ |
| Minimum distance: | $d = 3$ |
| Error control capability: | Perfect codes for correcting single errors |

Figure 3: Properties of Hamming codes

tion 8.6, we shall investigate the closely related class of extended Hamming codes with properties listed in Figure 4.

| | |
|---|---|
| Length: | $n = 2^m$ |
| Information symbols: | $k = 2^m - m - 1$ |
| Minimum distance: | $d = 4$ |
| Error control capability: | Corrects single errors and detects double errors (8.6) |

Figure 4: Properties of extended Hamming codes

**Proposition.** *A binary linear code $K$ corrects single errors if and only if every parity check matrix of $K$ has nonzero and pairwise distinct columns.*

PROOF. Denote by $d_i$ the binary word with all zeros except a 1 in the $i$th position, and by $d_{ij}$ the binary word with exactly two 1's in the $i$th and $j$th positions. (All nonzero binary words except $d_i$ and $d_{ij}$ have Hamming weight at least 3.)

I.　Let $K$ correct single errors, i.e., have minimum weight at least 3 (see 5.3). Let $H$ be a parity check matrix for $K$. If the $i$th column of $H$ is an all-zero column, then the product of $H$ and $d_i$ (written as a column) is 0:

$$
H
\begin{bmatrix}
0 \\
0 \\
\vdots \\
0 \\
1 \\
0 \\
\vdots \\
0
\end{bmatrix}
i
=
\begin{bmatrix}
0 \\
0 \\
\vdots \\
\vdots \\
\vdots \\
\vdots \\
0
\end{bmatrix}.
$$

This implies that the word $d_i$ is a code word of $K$, in contradiction to the minimum weight at least 3. Similarly, if the $i$th column of $H$ is the same as the $j$th column, $j \neq i$, then the word $d_{ij}$ is a code word—a contradiction again.

II.　Let $H$ be a parity check matrix for a code $K$, and let $H$ have nonzero and pairwise distinct columns. Then none of the words $d_i$ can be a code word: if it were, we would have

$$
H d_i^{\mathrm{tr}} = H
\begin{bmatrix}
0 \\
0 \\
\vdots \\
0 \\
1 \\
0 \\
\vdots \\
0
\end{bmatrix}
=
\begin{bmatrix}
0 \\
0 \\
\vdots \\
\vdots \\
\vdots \\
\vdots \\
0
\end{bmatrix}.
$$

However, the left-hand side is clearly equal to the $i$th row of $H$, which is nonzero by assumption. Also none of the words $d_{ij}$ can be a code word (because by multiplying $H$ with the transpose of $d_{ij}$, we clearly obtain the sum of the $i$th and $j$th columns of $H$, which is nonzero by assumption).

Consequently, every nonzero code word has Hamming weight at least 3. This implies that $d(K) \geq 3$ by 5.3. Thus, $K$ corrects single errors. □

**Remark.** The above proposition suggests a procedure for constructing efficient codes correcting single errors: design the parity check matrix as a matrix with the largest number of nonzero pairwise distinct columns. In this way, we obtain single-error-correcting codes of the largest number of information symbols (see Remark 5.4), and, thus, with the best information rate.

Observe that if the parity check matrix has $m$ rows (i.e., its columns are binary words of length $m$), then the number of columns is smaller or equal to $2^m - 1$. In fact, of the $2^m$ possible binary words, we consider all but one, the all-zero word. This leads us to the following:

**Definition.** *A binary linear code is called a* Hamming code *provided that it has, for some number $m$, a parity check matrix $H$ of $m$ rows and $2^m - 1$ columns such that each nonzero binary word of length $m$ is a column of $H$.*

**Example.** (1) For $m = 3$, the parity check matrix has 3 rows and 7 columns. It is not uniquely determined by the above definition: we can choose any ordering of the columns. A convenient approach is to use as columns the binary expansions of the numbers $1, 2, \ldots, 7$:

$$H = \begin{bmatrix} 0 & 0 & 0 & 1 & 1 & 1 & 1 \\ 0 & 1 & 1 & 0 & 0 & 1 & 1 \\ 1 & 0 & 1 & 0 & 1 & 0 & 1 \end{bmatrix}.$$

This means that the code is determined by the following equations

$$\begin{aligned} x_4 + x_5 + x_6 + x_7 &= 0, \\ x_2 + x_3 + \quad\quad x_6 + x_7 &= 0, \\ x_1 + \quad x_3 + \quad x_5 + \quad x_7 &= 0. \end{aligned} \tag{5.5.1}$$

It is easy to see that (5.5.1) is equivalent to the following:

$$\begin{aligned} x_5 &= x_2 + x_3 + x_4, \\ x_6 &= x_1 + x_3 + x_4, \\ x_7 &= x_1 + x_2 + x_4. \end{aligned} \tag{5.5.2}$$

We conclude that the symbols $x_1, \ldots, x_4$ can be chosen arbitrarily (i.e., these are the information symbols), and the last three symbols are the check symbols. Thus, this Hamming code has the information rate $R = 4/7$.

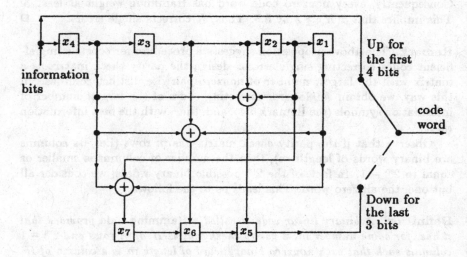

**Figure 5:** An encoder for the Hamming code of length 7

*Encoding.* Given a binary word of length 4, we encode it to a code word by concatenating the three symbols $x_5$, $x_6$, and $x_7$ computed as in (5.5.2).

A shift-register encoder is shown in Figure 5, where $\oplus$ denotes a binary adder (i.e., an exclusive-or gate) and $\rightarrow \square \rightarrow$ a shift register stage (i.e., a flip-flop). All code words of the Hamming code are listed in Figure 6.

| Information Symbol | Code word | Information Symbol | Code word |
|---|---|---|---|
| 0000 | 0000000 | 0110 | 0110011 |
| 1000 | 1000011 | 0101 | 0101010 |
| 0100 | 0100101 | 0011 | 0011001 |
| 0010 | 0010110 | 1110 | 1110000 |
| 0001 | 0001111 | 1101 | 1101001 |
| 1100 | 1100110 | 1011 | 1011010 |
| 1010 | 1010101 | 0111 | 0111100 |
| 1001 | 1001100 | 1111 | 1111111 |

**Figure 6:** Code words of the Hamming code of length 7

*Decoding.* The method of correcting single errors when a Hamming code is used is very simple. When receiving a word $\mathbf{w} = w_1 w_2 \ldots w_7$, compute the left-hand sides of the equations (5.5.1) above (binary addition). The results are denoted $s_1$, $s_2$, and $s_3$, respectively, and the binary word $s_1 s_2 s_3$ is called a *syndrome* of the received word.

(a) If the syndrome is 000, then the received word is a code word (and there is nothing to correct).

(b) If the syndrome is different from 000, then it is a binary expansion of some number $i = 1, 2, \ldots, 7$. Then correct the $i$th bit $w_i$ of the received word $\mathbf{w}$.

For example, we send 1111111 and receive 1110111. The syndrome is

$$
\begin{aligned}
s_1 &= w_4 + w_5 + w_6 + w_7 = 1, \\
s_2 &= w_2 + w_3 + w_6 + w_7 = 0, \\
s_3 &= w_1 + w_3 + w_5 + w_7 = 0.
\end{aligned}
$$

Since $s_1 s_2 s_3 = 100$ is the binary expansion of 4, we correct $w_4$, and we conclude that 1111111 has been sent.

In order to explain why this decoding technique works, observe that in the matrix notation, we have

$$
\begin{bmatrix} s_1 \\ s_2 \\ s_3 \end{bmatrix} = \mathbf{H} \begin{bmatrix} w_1 \\ w_2 \\ \vdots \\ w_7 \end{bmatrix}.
$$

Suppose we send a code word $\mathbf{v}$ and one bit is corrupted. Then we receive the word $\mathbf{w} = \mathbf{v} + \mathbf{d}_i$, where $\mathbf{d}_i$ is the word with all zeros except one 1 in the $i$th position. Since $\mathbf{v}$ is a code word, its product with the matrix $\mathbf{H}$ is the all-zero word, and, thus,

$$
\begin{bmatrix} s_1 \\ s_2 \\ s_3 \end{bmatrix} = \mathbf{H} \left( \begin{bmatrix} v_1 \\ v_2 \\ v_3 \\ \vdots \\ v_6 \\ v_7 \end{bmatrix} + \begin{bmatrix} 0 \\ 0 \\ \vdots \\ 1 \\ \vdots \\ 0 \end{bmatrix}_i \right) = \mathbf{H} \begin{bmatrix} 0 \\ \vdots \\ 1 \\ \vdots \\ 0 \end{bmatrix}_i = i\text{th column of } \mathbf{H}.
$$

Finally, the $i$th column of $\mathbf{H}$ is just the binary expansion of $i$; thus, we correct the corrupted bit.

**Examples**

(2) For $m = 4$, we have the following parity check matrix based on the binary expansions of $1, 2, \ldots, 15$:

$$\mathbf{H} = \begin{bmatrix} 0 & 0 & 0 & 0 & 0 & 0 & 0 & 1 & 1 & 1 & 1 & 1 & 1 & 1 & 1 \\ 0 & 0 & 0 & 1 & 1 & 1 & 1 & 0 & 0 & 0 & 0 & 1 & 1 & 1 & 1 \\ 0 & 1 & 1 & 0 & 0 & 1 & 1 & 0 & 0 & 1 & 1 & 0 & 0 & 1 & 1 \\ 1 & 0 & 1 & 0 & 1 & 0 & 1 & 0 & 1 & 0 & 1 & 0 & 1 & 0 & 1 \end{bmatrix}.$$

This Hamming code has length $n = 15$ and the number of check symbols is 4. Thus, there are 11 information symbols and the information rate is $R = 11/15 \approx 0.73$.

The error correction is performed quite analogously to the case when $m = 3$: by multiplying the matrix $\mathbf{H}$ with the received word (as a column), we obtain a 4-symbol syndrome $s_1 s_2 s_3 s_4$. If the syndrome is nonzero, then it is a binary expansion of a number $i = 1, 2, \ldots, 15$, and we correct the $i$th bit.

(3) For $n = 5$, the Hamming code has length 31, with 5 check symbols and 26 information symbols. Here $R \approx 0.81$.

**Concluding Remarks**

(1) For every $m = 2, 3, 4, \ldots$, we have a Hamming code of $m$ check symbols. It has

length $n = 2^m - 1$ (= the number of all nonzero binary words
　　　　　　　of length $m$, i.e., columns of the matrix $\mathbf{H}$),
number of information bits $k = 2^m - 1 - m$,
minimum distance $d = 3$.

The last can be seen as follows: choose the parity check matrix whose columns are the binary expansions of the numbers $1, 2, \ldots, 2^m - 1$. Then the word $11100\ldots00$ is clearly a code word; thus, $d \leq 3$, see Proposition 5.3. We have seen a simple decoding technique correcting single errors above; thus, $d \geq 3$, see Corollary 5.3.

(2) Hamming codes are *perfect* for single-error correction because they have the following property: every binary word of length $n$ is either a code word or it has a Hamming distance 1 from (precisely one) code word. In fact, this property can be readily deduced from the above decoding technique. And this implies that Hamming codes use the absolutely smallest possible redundancy for correction of single errors. We will

explain the idea of perfect codes in more detail in 10.6, but let us remark here that there is a shocking lack of perfect binary codes: besides Hamming codes and some trivial cases, only one perfect code exists (a triple-error correcting-code of length 23).

(3) The information rates of Hamming codes

$$R = 1 - \frac{m}{2^m - 1}$$

tend rapidly to 1 with increasing $m$. On the other hand, the larger $m$ we choose, the smaller error protection we obtain, of course.

## 5.6 The Probability of Undetected Errors

Let us return to the binary symmetric channel (4.1). When a binary linear code $K$ of length $n$ is used, what is the probability that an error escapes undetected? In other words, what is the probability that a code word $\mathbf{v}$ is sent and a different code word $\mathbf{w}$ is received?

To answer this question, denote by

$$\mathbf{e} = \mathbf{w} - \mathbf{v}$$

the error-pattern word (5.3). Then an undetected error occurs if and only if $\mathbf{e}$ is a nonzero code word. (In fact, if $\mathbf{e} \neq \mathbf{0}$ is a code word, then $\mathbf{w} = \mathbf{v} + \mathbf{e}$ is a code word, and $\mathbf{w} \neq \mathbf{v}$. Conversely, if $\mathbf{w}$ is a code word, then so is $\mathbf{e} = \mathbf{w} - \mathbf{v} = \mathbf{w} + \mathbf{v}$, and $\mathbf{w} \neq \mathbf{v}$ implies $\mathbf{e} \neq \mathbf{0}$.) Now, suppose that the Hamming weight of $\mathbf{e}$ is $i$, i.e., $i$ bits have been corrupted. The probability of this error pattern is $p^i q^{n-i}$, where $p$ is the error probability of the binary symmetric channel, and $q = 1 - p$ (see Exercise 4A). Thus, if we put

$A_i =$ the number of code words of Hamming weight $i$,

then the probability $P_{\text{und}}$ of an undetected error is the sum of the probabilities $p^i q^{n-i}$, where each of these summands appears $A_i$ times for $i = 1, 2, \ldots, n$. That is,

$$P_{\text{und}} = \sum_{i=1}^{n} A_i p^i q^{n-i}. \tag{5.6.1}$$

Observe that $A_1 = A_2 = \cdots = A_{d-1} = 0$, where $d$ is the minimum weight of the code—thus, $P_{\text{und}} = \sum_{i=d}^{n} A_i p^i q^{n-i}$.

**Example.** The Hamming (7,4)-code in Figure 6 (see 5.5) has one code word of Hamming weight 0 (viz. **0**), seven code words of each of Hamming weights 3 and 4, and one code word of Hamming weight 7. Thus,

$$P_{und} = 7p^3q^4 + 7p^4q^3 + p^7.$$

Suppose we use this code in a binary symmetric channel of error probability $p = 0.01$. Then

$$P_{und} = 7(0.01)^3(0.99)^4 + 7(0.01)^4(0.99)^3 + (0.01)^7 \approx 7 \times 10^{-6},$$

which means that seven words in a milion are incorrectly taken to be error-free (on the average).

**Definition.** *If $K$ is a block code with exactly $A_i$ code words of Hamming weight $i$ $(i = 0, 1, \ldots, n)$, then the polynomial*

$$A(x) = \sum_{i=0}^{n} A_i x^i$$

*is called the* weight enumerator *of the code $K$.*

**Proposition.** *Let $K$ be a binary linear code of length $n$ with a weight enumerator $A(x)$. The probability of an undetected error when using the code $K$ in a binary symmetric channel is*

$$P_{und} = q^n \left[ A\left(\frac{p}{q}\right) - 1 \right],$$

*where $p$ is the error probability of the channel, and $q = 1 - p$.*

PROOF. The above expression (5.6.1) for $P_{und}$ can be multiplied and divided by $q^n$ to obtain

$$P_{und} = q^n \sum_{i=1}^{n} A_i p^i q^{-i} = q^n \sum_{i=1}^{n} A_i \left(\frac{p}{q}\right)^i.$$

Since $A_0 = 1$ (the only code word of Hamming weight 0 is **0**), we can rewrite the last sum as follows

$$P_{und} = q^n \left[ \sum_{i=0}^{n} A_i \left(\frac{p}{q}\right)^i - 1 \right] = q^n \left[ A\left(\frac{p}{q}\right) - 1 \right]. \qquad \square$$

**Example** (continued). The Hamming (7,4)-code has the weight enumerator

$$A(x) = 1 + 7x^3 + 7x^4 + x^7.$$

Thus,

$$
\begin{aligned}
P_{\text{und}} &= q^7\left[1 + 7\left(\frac{p}{q}\right)^3 + 7\left(\frac{p}{q}\right)^4 + \left(\frac{p}{q}\right)^7 - 1\right] \\
&= 7p^3q^4 + 7p^4q^3 + p^7.
\end{aligned}
$$

# Exercises

**5A**  Is the binary code of all palindromes (i.e., words which are the same when read backward or forward) linear? Describe it by equations, and determine the number of errors it detects.

**5B**  Describe an algorithm for detection of triple errors when the rectangular code (5.2) is used.

**5C**  Let $K$ be the binary code of all words of length 7 such that (a) the third bit is a parity check for the first two bits, (b) the sixth bit is a parity check for the fourth and fifth bits, and (c) the last bit is an overall parity check. Describe $K$ by equations and determine the number of errors it can correct or detect.

**5D**  The rectangular code (5.2) can also be called a two-dimensional even-parity code. Define, more generally, $m$-dimensional even-parity codes. For which $m$ is such a code capable of correcting double errors? And triple errors?

**5E**  Hamming codes:

(1)  Compute the error probability $P_{\text{err}}(K)$ (4.8) of the Hamming code $K$ of length 7 used in a binary symmetric channel corrupting 1 bit per hundred on the average. (Hint: use the error estimate in 4A.)

(2)  More in general, express the error probability of the Hamming code of length $2^m - 1$ as a function of $m$.

(3)  What is the probability $P_{\text{und}}(K)$ of an undetected errror of the Hamming code of length $2^m - 1$?

**5F**    Prove that every single-error-correcting code of length $2^m - 1$ has at least $m$ check symbols.

**5G**    Prove that the decoding of Hamming codes is always incorrect if two bits are corrupted in a code word.

**5H**    A binary linear code of length 8 is described by the following equations:

$$
\begin{aligned}
x_5 &= x_2 + x_3 + x_4, \\
x_6 &= x_1 + x_2 + x_3, \\
x_7 &= x_1 + x_2 + x_4, \\
x_8 &= x_1 + x_3 + x_4.
\end{aligned}
$$

Find its parity check matrix and verify that the minimum distance is 4.

**5I**    Find the weight enumerator (5.6) of the code in 5H.

**5J**    Draw a scheme of a shift-register encoder of the Hamming code of length 15.

**5K**    Draw a scheme of a shift-register encoder of the code in 5H.

## Notes

The theory of binary linear codes was initiated by the discovery of Hamming codes by Golay (1949) and Hamming (1950). The formalism of linear algebra was introduced by Slepian (1956, 1960). Further historical notes can be found in Berlekamp (1974).

# Chapter 6

# Groups and Standard Arrays

The algebraic structure of commutative groups is used extensively in the theory of error-correcting codes. In this chapter, we introduce groups and cosets, and we show how algebraic ideas can be used for a very thorough (but, unfortunately, very slow) decoding of binary linear codes by so-called standard arrays.

## 6.1   Commutative Groups

**Definition.** *A commutative group $(G, +)$ is a set $G$ together with a binary operation $+$ (i.e., a rule assigning to every pair $x$, $y$ of elements of $G$ a new element $x + y$ of $G$) satisfying the following axioms:*

(1) *associative law: $x + (y + z) = (x + y) + z$ for all $x$, $y$, $z$ in $G$,*

(2) *commutative law: $x + y = y + x$ for all $x$, $y$ in $G$,*

(3) *existence of a neutral element: there exists an element $0$ of $G$ such that $x + 0 = x$ for all $x$ in $G$,*

(4) *existence of opposite elements: for every element $x$ in $G$, there exists an element $-x$ in $G$ such that $x + (-x) = 0$.*

**Remark.** The binary operation is often denoted by juxtaposition ($xy$ instead of $x + y$) and then the neutral element is denoted by 1 and the opposite element by $x^{-1}$ (and it is called the *inverse* element of $x$).

79

**Examples**

(1) The set **Z** of all integers is a commutative group under the usual addition.

(2) The set **R** of all real numbers is a commutative group under the usual addition. But not under the usual multiplication. The multiplication of real numbers satisfies (1), (2), (3), and "almost" satisfies (4): 0 is the only element which fails to have an inverse. A group can be obtained by discarding 0. Since a product of two nonzero numbers is always different from zero, the multiplication defines a binary operation on the set $\mathbf{R} - \{0\}$ of all nonzero real numbers. It is easy to check that $(\mathbf{R} - \{0\}, \times)$ is a commutative group.

(3) Denote by $\{0, 1\}^n$ the set of all binary words of length $n$. With the addition considered in 5.3, this is a commutative group: the associative and commutative laws are obvious, $\mathbf{0} = 000\ldots00$ is the neutral element, and each word a is its own opposite, since $\mathbf{a} + \mathbf{a} = \mathbf{0}$.

(4) For each natural number $p$, put

$$\mathbf{Z}_p = \{0, 1, \ldots, p - 1\},$$

and define the following addition on the set $\mathbf{Z}_p$:

$$x \oplus y = \begin{cases} x + y & \text{if } x + y < p, \\ x + y - p & \text{if } x + y \geq p. \end{cases}$$

Then $(\mathbf{Z}_p, \oplus)$ is a commutative group: the associative and commutative laws are obvious, 0 is the neutral element, and the opposite element to $x$ is $p - x$ (for all $x$ in $\mathbf{Z}_p$ except $x = 0$), and $-0 = 0$.

In particular, in $\mathbf{Z}_2 = \{0, 1\}$, the addition $\oplus$ agrees with that in 5.1: $1 \oplus 1 = 1 + 1 - 2 = 0$. When no misunderstanding is possible, the addition in $\mathbf{Z}_p$ is denoted by $+$. For example, the addition in $\mathbf{Z}_3$ is shown in Figure 1.

| + | 0 | 1 | 2 |
|---|---|---|---|
| 0 | 0 | 1 | 2 |
| 1 | 1 | 2 | 0 |
| 2 | 2 | 0 | 1 |

**Figure 1:** Addition in $\mathbf{Z}_3$

**Remark.** In every group, we have, besides addition, the operation of *subtraction*: $x - y = x + (-y)$. In the multiplicative notation, we call this operation division: $x : y = xy^{-1}$.

Observe that the associative law means that we do not have to use parentheses for the group operation: the meaning of $x + y + z$ is unambiguous.

# 6.2 Subgroups and Cosets

**Definition.** *Let G be a commutative group.*

(1) *By a* subgroup *of G is meant a subset K closed under the group operations, i.e., satisfying the following conditions:*

    (a) *if x and y lie in K, then $x + y$ lies in K,*

    (b) *0 lies in K,*

    (c) *if x lies in K, then $-x$ lies in K.*

(2) *By the* coset *of an element x of G modulo the subgroup K is meant the set $x + K$ of all sums $x + k$, where k are elements of K. In symbols:*

$$x + K = \{\, x + k \mid k \in K \,\}.$$

**Examples**

(1) In the group $(\mathbf{Z}, +)$ of integers, the set $\mathbf{Z}_e$ of all even integers is a subgroup. The coset of the number 1 is the set $\mathbf{Z}_o$ of all odd numbers:

$$1 + \mathbf{Z}_e = \{\, 1 + k \mid k \text{ even} \,\} = \mathbf{Z}_o.$$

The same is true about any odd number:

$$\mathbf{Z}_o = 1 + \mathbf{Z}_e = 3 + \mathbf{Z}_e = -1 + \mathbf{Z}_e \ldots.$$

The coset of the number 0 is $\mathbf{Z}_e$ itself:

$$0 + \mathbf{Z}_e = \mathbf{Z}_e,$$

and the same is true about any even number:

$$\mathbf{Z}_e = 2 + \mathbf{Z}_e = 4 + \mathbf{Z}_e = -2 + \mathbf{Z}_e \ldots.$$

Thus, there are precisely two cosets of integers modulo $\mathbf{Z}_e$, viz., $\mathbf{Z}_e$ and $\mathbf{Z}_o$.

(2) Every binary linear code $K$ of length $n$ is a subgroup of the group $\{0,1\}^n$ [see Example (3) of 6.1]. In fact, (a) if $\mathbf{x}$ and $\mathbf{y}$ are code words, then $\mathbf{x} + \mathbf{y}$ is a code word, by definition of linearity, (b) $\mathbf{0} = \mathbf{x} + \mathbf{x}$ is always a code word, and (c) every code word is opposite to itself. Cosets modulo a linear code form a basis of an important decoding method, which we study in the next section.

We will now show that the structure of all cosets is pleasantly regular: no two cosets overlap, they cover the given group, and they have the same size.

**Proposition.** *Cosets in a group $G$ modulo an arbitrary subgroup $K$ have the following properties:*

(1) *every element of $G$ lies in some coset,*

(2) *no two distinct cosets have a common element,*

(3) *two elements $x$ and $y$ lie in the same coset if and only if their difference $x - y$ is an element of $K$,*

(4) *if the subgroup $K$ has $r$ elements, then each coset has $r$ elements.*

**PROOF.** (1) Each element $x$ of $G$ lies in the coset $x + K$: in fact, $K$ contains 0, and $x = x + 0$.

(2) If the cosets $x + K$ and $y + K$ have a common element, say, $z$, then we can express $z$ in two ways:

$$z = x + k' = y + k'', \qquad \text{for } k', k'' \text{ in } K.$$

Now we will prove that every element $t$ of the coset $x + K$ lies in $y + K$; by symmetry, we then conclude that $x + K = y + K$. Express $t$ as $t = x + k$ for some $k$ in $K$. Then

$$t = x + k = (y + k'' - k') + k = y + (k'' - k' + k).$$

The subgroup $K$ contains $k'' - k' + k$, thus, $t$ lies in $y + K$.

(3) If $x$ and $y$ belong to the same coset, say, to $z + K$, then $x = z + k$ for some $k$ in $K$ and $y = z + k'$ for some $k'$ in $K$. Then $K$ contains $k - k'$, and we have

$$x - y = z + k - (z + k') = k - k' \in K.$$

Conversely, if $x - y$ lies in $K$, then put $k = x - y$, in other words $x = y + k$. We conclude that $x$ and $y$ lie in the same coset $y + K$.

(4) Let $K = \{ k_1, k_2, \ldots, k_r \}$ with $k_i \neq k_j$ for $i \neq j$. Every coset has the form

$$x + K = \{ x + k_1, x + k_2, \ldots, x + k_r \},$$

and $x + k_i \neq x + k_j$ for $i \neq j$. (In fact, if $x + k_i = x + k_j$, then we can subtract $x$ and obtain $k_i = k_j$.) Thus, $x + K$ has $r$ elements.  □

**Remarks**

(1) The above proposition tells us that cosets form a very nice decomposition of the original group $G$: the group decomposes into disjoint cosets of the same size. Thus, if $G$ is a finite group of $s$ elements and $K$ is a subgroup of $r$ elements, then the number of cosets is $s/r$.

(2) An interesting construction of a new group (from a given group $G$ and its subgroup $K$) can be performed as follows. Let us choose in each coset an element, called the *coset leader*. The set of all coset leaders is denoted by $G/K$, and the following operation can be defined on $G/K$:

$$x + y \text{ is the coset leader of the coset } x + y + K.$$

Then $G/K$ becomes a commutative group:

(a) the associative law is clear since $(x + y) + z$ is the coset leader of the coset $(x + y) + z + K$, and $x + (y + z)$ is the coset leader of (the same) coset $x + (y + z) + K$,

(b) the commutative law is clear since $x + y + K = y + x + K$,

(c) the neutral element is the coset leader of $0 + K = K$,

(d) the opposite element of $x$ is the coset leader of $-x + K$.

The concrete form of the group $G/K$ depends, of course, on the choice of coset leaders. However, all the resulting groups are essentially the same (see Exercise 6F).

**Example.** (3) For each natural number $p$, let $p\mathbf{Z}$ denote the set of all multiples of $p$ (i.e., all integers divisible by $p$). This is a subgroup of $(\mathbf{Z}, +)$. There are precisely $p$ cosets modulo $p\mathbf{Z}$: the coset of 0 is $0 + p\mathbf{Z}' = p\mathbf{Z}$, the coset of 1 is the set $1 + p\mathbf{Z}$ of all integers which, divided by $p$, have remainder 1, etc. For each $i = 0, 1, 2, \ldots, p - 1$, the coset $i + p\mathbf{Z}$ consists of all integers of the form $i + pn$ ($n \in \mathbf{Z}$), in other words, all integers whose (integer) division by $p$ has the remainder $i$. For $i = p$, we get the first coset: $p + p\mathbf{Z} = p\mathbf{Z}$, for $i = p + 1$; the second one: $p + 1 + p\mathbf{Z} = 1 + p\mathbf{Z}$, etc. Also $-1 + p\mathbf{Z} = (p - 1) + p\mathbf{Z}$, etc. We usually choose the numbers $0, 1, \ldots, p - 1$ as coset leaders. In that case,

$$\mathbf{Z}/p\mathbf{Z} = \mathbf{Z}_p$$

is the group of Example (4) in 6.1. In fact, $x + y$ in $\mathbf{Z}_p$ is just the usual addition if the result is smaller then $p$ (i.e., it is one of the coset leaders), and otherwise we just subtract $p$. However, an important example of everyday life uses somewhat different coset leaders (see Figure 2). If someone comes

**Figure 2: $\mathbf{Z}_{12}$**

three hours late to a meeting scheduled for eleven, then the person arrives at

$$11 + 3 = 2.$$

Here we compute in $\mathbf{Z}/12\mathbf{Z}$, but the coset leaders are $1, 2, \ldots, 12$ (instead of $0, 1, \ldots, 11$). Nevertheless, if time is measured modulo $24\mathbf{Z}$ (e.g., as in airline schedules), the usual choice of coset leaders is $0, 1, \ldots, 23$.

**Definition.** *We say that two integers $x$ and $y$ are* congruent modulo $p$, *in notation*

$$x \equiv y \pmod p$$

*provided that they lie in the same coset modulo $p\mathbf{Z}$; in other words, provided that the difference $x - y$ is divisible by $p$.*

**Example.** (4) Two integers are congruent modulo 2 if and only if they have the same parity.

Congruence modulo 12 is well known from (old-fashioned) watches: 14 is congruent to 2 and to 26 and to $-10$, etc.

## 6.3   Decoding by Standard Arrays

Let $K$ be a binary linear code of length $n$. As observed in 6.2, $K$ is a subgroup of the group $\{0,1\}^n$ of all binary words of length $n$. It follows that $\{0,1\}^n$ decomposes into cosets modulo $K$. In each coset, we choose a coset leader of the smallest Hamming weight (5.3); thus, e.g., the coset leader of $0 + K = K$ is $0$. The *standard array* is a rectangular array containing all binary words of length $n$ arranged so that

(1) each row is one coset modulo $K$; the first one is $K$ itself,

(2) the first column is formed by the chosen coset leaders,

(3) the word in the $i$th row and the $j$th column is the sum of the $i$th coset leader and the $j$th code word.

The first row, then, is the code $K$, arranged arbitrarily except that the first code word is $0$. Every other row is obtained from the first one by adding the coset leader.

**Example.** (1) The even-parity code of length 4 is a subgroup $K$ of $\{0,1\}^4$. One coset is $K$ with the coset leader 0000. The word 1000 does not lie in the coset $K$, and it has the smallest Hamming weight. Thus, we can choose it as a coset leader of $1000 + K$. This leads to the rectangle in Figure 3.

| | Coset Leader | | | | | | | |
|---|---|---|---|---|---|---|---|---|
| Code $K$ | 0000 | 1100 | 1010 | 1001 | 0101 | 0110 | 0011 | 1111 |
| | 1000 | 0100 | 0010 | 0001 | 1101 | 1110 | 1011 | 0111 |

**Figure 3:** Standard array of the even-parity code

**Remark.** If a linear code $K$ has $k$ information symbols, and thus $2^k$ code words, then the number of cosets modulo $K$ is $2^{n-k}$ (see Remark 6.2). Thus, we know that we have to choose $2^{n-k}$ coset leaders. The choice is simple: choose any word of length $n$ which is not contained in any of the preceding cosets, and take care to keep the Hamming weight to the minimum.

**Example.** (2) Let $K_5$ be the linear code of length 5 in which the fourth bit checks the parity of the first two bits, and the last bit is an overall parity check. Thus, $K_5$ is given by the following equations:

$$x_4 = x_1 + x_2,$$
$$x_5 = x_1 + x_2 + x_3 + x_4.$$

In the standard array, we start with the code $K_5$. Since $K_5$ has 3 information bits, it has $2^3 = 8$ code words. Therefore, we have $2^{5-3} = 4$ cosets. Next, we choose as a coset leader some word of Hamming weight 1, for example, 10000. This is not a code word, thus, we can choose it as a coset leader of $10000 + K_5$. See Figure 4. We now want to choose another coset

| Coset Leader | | | | | | | |
|---|---|---|---|---|---|---|---|
| 00000 | 10010 | 01010 | 00101 | 11000 | 10111 | 01111 | 11101 |
| 10000 | 00010 | 11010 | 10101 | 01000 | 00111 | 11111 | 01101 |

**Figure 4:** Code $K_5$ and one of the cosets

leader of Hamming weight 1. But beware: 01000 cannot be chosen since it lies in the coset of 10000:

$$10000 + K_5 = 01000 + K_5 \qquad \text{(verify!)}.$$

The only word of weight 1 not contained in Figure 4 is 00001. Thus, we choose it as a coset leader. The last coset leader already has Hamming weight 2; we can choose, for example, 10001. See Figure 5.

| Coset Leader | | | | | | | |
|---|---|---|---|---|---|---|---|
| 00000 | 10010 | 01010 | 00101 | 11000 | 10111 | 01111 | 11101 |
| 10000 | 00010 | 11010 | 10101 | 01000 | 00111 | 11111 | 01101 |
| 00001 | 10011 | 01011 | 00100 | 11001 | 10110 | 01110 | 11100 |
| 10001 | 00011 | 11011 | 10100 | 01001 | 00110 | 11110 | 01100 |

**Figure 5:** A standard array of the code $K_5$

*Decoding by a standard array.* When receiving a word, we assume that the word sent is that code word in whose column the received word lies. In symbols, we receive a word $\mathbf{y}$ and we find its position in the standard array:

$$\mathbf{y} = \mathbf{x} + \mathbf{e},$$

where $\mathbf{e}$ is the coset leader of the row of $\mathbf{y}$, and $\mathbf{x}$ is the code word of the column of $\mathbf{y}$. Then we assume that $\mathbf{x}$ has been sent.

When is this decoding correct? Whenever the error pattern (5.3) is one of the coset leaders. In fact, if we send a code word **x** and the error pattern is **e**, then we receive **y** = **x** + **e**. If **e** is a coset leader, we correctly decode **x**. However, if the error pattern is not a coset leader, then we (always!) decode incorrectly.

**Example.** (3) Suppose that when using the above code $K_5$, we received 11111. We use the standard array in Figure 5: 11111 lies below 01111; thus, we decode 01111. This decoding is correct if (and only if) the error pattern is one of the coset leaders. That is, the first or the fifth bit can be corrupted, or both. But when some of the middle bits is corrupted, the decoding is wrong. For example, if we send 01111 and receive 00111, we decode 10111.

**Remark.** Decoding by standard arrays is very thorough, since it corrects the largest possible collection of error patterns. (Observe, for example, that the code $K_5$ has minimum weight 2 and, thus, it cannot correct single errors. Yet, with the standard array above, we correct any errors occurring on the first and last bits only.) However, this decoding is very slow. A substantial simplification will be presented in 8.3; yet, even then, the decoding is quite slow, and we will present more powerful decoding techniques for concrete classes of codes later. We have seen one such example in 5.5 already: for the Hamming code of length 7, we presented a fast decoding. In comparison, decoding by the standard array would require checking the array of $2^7 = 128$ words per each received word.

# Exercises

**6A**    Verify that every subgroup of the group $(\mathbf{Z}, +)$ has the form $p\mathbf{Z}$ for some $p = 0, 1, 2, \dots$.

**6B**    Describe all finite subgroups of the groups $(\mathbf{R}, +)$ and $(\mathbf{R} - \{0\}, \times)$. Verify that the set of all rational numbers is a subgroup of both the groups.

**6C**    Find all subgroups of the group $(\mathbf{Z}_{12}, +)$.

**6D**    Verify that each commutative group $G$ has precisely one neutral element, and each element of $G$ has precisely one inverse element.

**6E**   Let $M$ be a finite set. Denote by $\exp M$ the collection of all subsets of $M$ (including $M$ and the empty set). The operation of *symmetric difference* on subsets of $M$ is defined by

$$A \triangle B = \{\, m \mid m \text{ lies in } A \text{ or } B, \text{ but not in both of them}\,\}.$$

Verify that $(\exp M, \triangle)$ is a commutative group. If $A \cup B$ denotes the usual operation of union, is $(\exp M, \cup)$ a commutative group?

**6F**   Two commutative groups $G$ and $G'$ are said to be *isomorphic* provided that there exists a bijective correspondence between their elements, $f: G \to G'$, which preserves the group operations [i.e., $f(x + y) = f(x) + f(y)$, $f(0) = 0$, and $f(-x) = -f(x)$]. Such groups can be considered as "essentially the same": the name of an element $x$ of $G$ is just changed to $f(x)$.

(1) Prove that there exists essentially just one commutative group of 1 element (i.e., any two one-element groups are isomorphic).

(2) Prove that there exists essentially just one commutative group of 2 elements [i.e., any two-element group is isomorphic to $(\mathbf{Z}_2, +)$].

(3) Let $K$ be a subgroup of a commutative group $G$. Prove that there is essentially just one group $G/K$ of coset leaders (i.e., various choices of coset leaders lead to isomorphic groups).
   Describe the group $\mathbf{Z}_4/K$, where $K = \{\, 0, 2 \,\}$.

(4) Prove that the group $(\exp M, \triangle)$ of 6E is isomorphic to $(\mathbf{Z}_2^n, +)$.

**6G**   Describe the standard array for the repetition codes.

**6H**   Find a standard array of the code for Exercise 5E.

**6I**   Find a standard array for the Hamming code of length 7.

**6J**   Prove that the binary code of length 5 described by the following equations

$$
\begin{aligned}
x_3 &= x_1 + x_2, \\
x_4 &= x_1, \\
x_5 &= x_1 + x_2,
\end{aligned}
$$

corrects single errors. Find a standard array and observe that the corresponding decoding corrects more than single errors.

**6K**  Let $K$ be the linear code obtained by all possible sums of the following words: 101011, 011101, 011010.

(1)  Find a parity check matrix.

(2)  Find a standard array, and decode 111011.

## Notes

More on classical algebraic topics like groups and cosets can be found, e.g., in Birkhoff and MacLane (1953).  Standard arrays were introduced by Slepian (1956, 1960).

# Chapter 7

# Linear Algebra

The reader has probably already encountered the concepts of a linear (or vector) space, matrix, and solutions of a system of linear equations. However, these topics are often restricted to the field of real numbers, whereas in coding theory they are used over finite fields. We therefore present linear algebra over a finite field, and prove all the results needed later. In the sections devoted to basis, matrices, and linear equations, the exposition is somewhat quicker than in other chapters since all the material is actually quite analogous to the case of real vector spaces, and we only present it for sake of easy reference.

## 7.1   Fields and Rings

Finite fields represent one of the most basic concepts of the algebraic theory of error-correcting codes. We introduce here the simple $p$-element fields $\mathbf{Z}_p$, and later (in Chapter 11) the more complex Galois fields.

The aim of the abstract concept of a field is to express all the basic properties of real numbers, the "prototype" field. Thus, in a field, we have addition, subtraction, multiplication, and division, and we require enough axioms to be sure that the computation techniques we are used to with real numbers can be applied in any field. Recall that the addition of real numbers forms a commutative group, and the multiplication forms a commutative group on the set $R - \{0\}$ of all nonzero real numbers.

**Definition.** *A* field *is a set $F$ together with binary operations $+$ and $\cdot$ such that*

(1) *$(F, +)$ is a commutative group with the neutral element 0,*

(2) $(F - \{0\}, \cdot)$ *is a commutative group,*

(3) *distributive law:* $x(y + z) = xy + xz$ *holds for all* $x$, $y$, $z$ *in* $F$.

**Remarks**

(1) In every field, we have *subtraction:* $a - b = a + (-b)$, and, if $b \neq 0$, *division:* $a : b = ab^{-1}$.

(2) A product of two nonzero elements is a nonzero element (because multiplication is a group operation on the set $F - \{0\}$ of all nonzero elements). In other words:

$$xy = 0 \quad \text{implies} \quad x = 0 \text{ or } y = 0.$$

(3) Since the axiom (2) in the above definition deals only with products of nonzero elements, we must specify the multiplication by 0: Every field fulfils

$$x \cdot 0 = 0 \qquad \text{for all } x.$$

In fact, since $x = x + 0$, by the distributive law, we obtain $x \cdot x = x(x + 0) = x \cdot x + x \cdot 0$ and subtracting $x \cdot x$, we get $0 = x \cdot 0$.

(4) In every field, we can cancel by any nonzero element:

$$ax = ay \quad \text{implies} \quad x = y \qquad \text{(whenever } a \neq 0\text{)}.$$

In fact, $a(x - y) = 0$ implies either $a = 0$ or $x - y = 0$, by (2).

(5) Although the definition of a field is quite concise, it represents a large number of axioms:

    (a) associative law for both addition and multiplication,

    (b) commutative law for both addition and multiplication,

    (c) distributive law,

    (d) the existence of the neutral elements 0 and 1,

    (e) each element has an opposite,

    (f) each nonzero element $x$ has an inverse.

The last axiom is the most subtle one: there are lots of natural algebraic structures which satisfy all the axioms but the last one. An algebraic structure satisfying the axioms (a)–(e) is called a *ring* (in more detail: a commutative unitary ring). Thus, a field can be defined as a ring in which all nonzero elements have inverses.

**Examples**

(1) Real numbers form a field. Also rational numbers and complex numbers are fields.

(2) The set $\{0,1\}$ with the operations introduced in 5.1 is a field. It is easy to check the axioms (a)–(f) mechanically, but a more elegant proof is given below.

(3) Integers do not form a field; they fail badly with respect to (f): 1 and $-1$ are the only integers with an inverse. However, integers form a ring.

## 7.2   The Fields $Z_p$

Let $p$ be a nonzero element of a ring $F$. We can create a new ring (in fact, often a field) by requiring that the equation

$$p = 0 \tag{7.2.1}$$

become true. This obscure statement will be made precise below. However, observe first that the above equation implies $pk = 0k = 0$ for each element $k$ of $F$, and, thus,

$$x = x + pk, \qquad \text{for each } x \text{ and } k \text{ in } F. \tag{7.2.2}$$

Now denote [as in Example (3) of 6.2] by $pF$ the set of all multiples of $p$:

$$pF = \{\, pk \mid k \in F \,\}.$$

This is a subgroup of $(F, +)$, and (7.2.2) tells us that each coset modulo the subgroup $pF$ (see 6.2) shrinks to a single element—the coset leader. Cosets modulo the subgroup $pF$ are shortly called *cosets modulo p*. By Proposition 6.1, two elements $x$, $y$ of $F$ are *congruent modulo p* (i.e., lie in the same coset modulo $p$) if and only if $x - y$ is a multiple of $p$. Shortly: if $x - y$ is divisible by $p$. The vague idea of forcing the equation $p = 0$ can be formalized as follows:

**Definition.** *If $p$ is a nonzero element of a ring $F$, denote by*

$$F/\mathrm{mod}\, p$$

*the ring whose elements are (arbitrarily chosen) coset leaders modulo p, and the operations are as follows:*

$$\begin{aligned} x + y &\quad \text{is the coset leader of } x + y + pF, \\ xy &\quad \text{is the coset leader of } xy + pF \end{aligned}$$

*(for arbitrary coset leaders $x$ and $y$).*

**Example.** If $\mathbf{Z}$ is the ring of integers, we can choose, for each $p > 0$, the coset leaders $0, 1, \ldots, p - 1$. The operation $+$ has been described in 6.2. We now also have the operation of multiplication:

$xy$ is the remainder of the usual product $xy$ divided by $p$.

We use the shorter notation

$$\mathbf{Z}_p = \mathbf{Z}/\mathrm{mod}\, p.$$

For example, $\mathbf{Z}_2$ is the set $\{0, 1\}$ together with the operations introduced in 5.1. The operations of $\mathbf{Z}_3$ are given in Figure 1. We see that $\mathbf{Z}_3$ is a

| + | 0 | 1 | 2 |
|---|---|---|---|
| 0 | 0 | 1 | 2 |
| 1 | 1 | 2 | 0 |
| 2 | 2 | 0 | 1 |

| · | 0 | 1 | 2 |
|---|---|---|---|
| 0 | 0 | 0 | 0 |
| 1 | 0 | 1 | 2 |
| 2 | 0 | 2 | 1 |

**Figure 1: Operations of $\mathbf{Z}_3$**

field. In contrast, $\mathbf{Z}_{12}$ is not a field because $3 \cdot 4 = 0$ (whereas in a field, the product of nonzero elements cannot be zero, see Remark 7.1). In general, $\mathbf{Z}_p$ is not a field for any composite number.

**Remark.** To show that the above definition is correct, we must verify that $F/\mathrm{mod}\, p$ satifies all the axioms (a)–(e) of 7.1. In Remark 6.2, we verified that the operation $+$ defines a commutative group. The verification of the associative and comutative laws for the multiplication are equally easy: $(xy)z$ is the coset leader of $(xy)z + pF$, and $x(yz)$ is the coset leader of (the same) coset $x(yz) + pF$; analogously with $xy$ and $yx$. Also the distributive law is clear. The neutral element for the multiplication is the coset leader of $1 + pF$.

**Theorem.** *For every prime $p$, $\mathbf{Z}_p$ is a field.*

**PROOF.** Since $\mathbf{Z}_p$ is a ring (see Remark above), we only have to prove that every element $i = 1, 2, \ldots, p - 1$ has an inverse. We proceed by induction, denoting multiplication in $\mathbf{Z}_p$ by $\otimes$.

(1) $i = 1$ has an inverse element: $1^{-1} = 1$.

(2) Suppose $i > 1$ and all the inverse elements $1^{-1}, 2^{-1}, \ldots, (i-1)^{-1}$ exist. Perform the integer division $p : i$, denoting the quotient by $q$ and the remainder by $r$. Then

$$p - r = iq,$$

which clearly implies that

$$-r = i \otimes q \quad \text{in } \mathbf{Z}_p.$$

Moreover, $r$ is smaller then $i$ (being the remainder of $p : i$) and is nonzero: $p$ is a prime and $i$ lies between 2 and $p - 1$, thus $p \neq iq$. By the induction hypothesis, $r^{-1}$ exists. It follows that the inverse to $i$ is the element $-q \otimes r^{-1}$:

$$i \otimes (-q \otimes r^{-1}) = -(i \otimes q) \otimes r^{-1} = -(-r) \otimes r^{-1} = 1.$$

$\square$

**Concluding Remark.** We are now equipped with a number of finite fields: $\mathbf{Z}_2, \mathbf{Z}_3, \mathbf{Z}_5, \mathbf{Z}_7, \ldots$. Later we will construct fields of $p^k$ elements for any prime $p$, for example, a four-element field (see also Exercise 7F). However, no six-element field exists: every finite field has a number of elements which is a power of a prime (this will be proved in 11.8).

# 7.3 Linear Spaces

The reader has certainly encountered the three-dimensional Euclidean space and has used vectors in that space. A vector is described by a triple of real numbers or a word of length 3 over the alphabet $\mathbf{R}$. The basic operations on vectors are addition (which turns $\mathbf{R}^3$ into a commutative group) and scalar multiplication. The concept of a linear space is a generalization which admits an arbitrary word length and substitutes $\mathbf{R}$ by an arbitrary alphabet with field operations defined on it.

**Definition.** *Let $F$ be a field (the elements of which are called* scalars*). By a* linear space, *or* vector space, *is meant a set $L$ (the elements of which are called* vectors*) together with operations $+$, called* addition, *and $\cdot$, called* scalar multiplication, *satisfying the following axioms:*

(1) $(L, +)$ *is a commutative group,*

(2) $\cdot$ *assigns to each scalar $t$ and each vector* **a** *a unique vector $t\,\mathbf{a}$,*

(3) *associative law:* $(st)\mathbf{a} = s(t\,\mathbf{a})$ *for all scalars $s$, $t$ and all vectors* **a**,

(4) *distributive laws* $t\,(\mathbf{a} + \mathbf{b}) = t\,\mathbf{a} + t\,\mathbf{b}$ *and* $(s + t)\mathbf{a} = s\,\mathbf{a} + t\,\mathbf{a}$ *for all scalars $s$, $t$ and all vectors* **a, b**,

(5) $1\mathbf{a} = \mathbf{a}$ *for all vectors* **a** *(where 1 is the unit of $F$).*

**Remark.** Some further properties of linear spaces can be derived from the above ones, e.g.,

(6) $0\mathbf{a} = \mathbf{0}$ for each vector $\mathbf{a}$,

(7) $(-1)\mathbf{a} = -\mathbf{a}$ for each vector $\mathbf{a}$,

(8) $t\,\mathbf{0} = \mathbf{0}$ for each scalar $t$.

In fact, (6) follows from (3), (4), and $1 = 1 + 0$ (in $F$):

$$\mathbf{a} = (1 + 0)\mathbf{a} = \mathbf{a} + 0\mathbf{a};$$

now subtract $\mathbf{a}$ from both sides. (7) follows from (3), (4), and the definition of the opposite vector $-\mathbf{a}$:

$$\mathbf{a} + (-1)\mathbf{a} = (1 - 1)\mathbf{a} = 0\mathbf{a} = \mathbf{0}.$$

Finally, from (7), we obtain $(-t)\mathbf{a} = -(t\,\mathbf{a})$, and then (8) follows:

$$t\,\mathbf{0} = t\,(\mathbf{0} - \mathbf{0}) = t\,\mathbf{0} - (t\,\mathbf{0}) = \mathbf{0}.$$

**Examples**

(1) The set $F^n$ of all words of length $n$ in the alphabet $F$ is a linear space with coordinatewise addition:

$$a_1 a_2 \ldots a_n + b_1 b_2 \ldots b_n = c_1 c_2 \ldots c_n, \quad \text{where} \quad c_i = a_i + b_i,$$

and coordinatewise scalar multiplication:

$$t\,(a_1 a_2 \ldots a_n) = c_1 c_2 \ldots c_n, \quad \text{where} \quad c_i = ta_i,$$

In particular,

$$\mathbf{Z}_2^n$$

is the linear space of all binary words of length $n$ (the fundamental linear space of coding theory).

(2) The usual (real) plane $\mathbf{R}^2$ is a linear space over the field $\mathbf{R}$ of real numbers. Since points in the plane are described by their coordinates (which are words of length 2 over $\mathbf{R}$), this linear space is a special case of the space $F^n$ above.

Analogously, the usual (real) three-dimensional space $\mathbf{R}^3$ is a linear space over the field $\mathbf{R}$.

**Definition.** *Let $L$ be a linear space. A nonempty subset $K$ of $L$ is called a* linear subspace *provided that it is closed under addition and scalar multiplication, i.e.,*

(1) *if two vectors* **a**, **b** *lie in $K$, then* **a** + **b** *also lies in $K$, and*

(2) *if a vector* **a** *lies in $K$, then each scalar multiple* **ta** *lies in $K$.*

**Remark.** (1) Every subspace contains the zero vector because, given a vector **a** in $K$, then $0 = 0\mathbf{a}$ lies in $K$. Thus, the smallest subspace of any linear space is $\{\,0\,\}$—this subspace is called *trivial*.

**Examples**

(3) Binary linear codes of length $n$ are precisely the linear subspaces of the space $\mathbf{Z}_2^n$.

(4) Linear subspaces of the real plane $\mathbf{R}^2$ are, beside the trivial subspace and $\mathbf{R}^2$ itself, precisely all the lines passing through the origin.

Linear subspaces of the three-dimensional space $\mathbf{R}^3$ are, beside $\{\,0\,\}$ and $\mathbf{R}^3$, precisely all the lines and all the planes passing through the origin.

**Definition.** *By a* linear combination *of vectors* $\mathbf{a}_1, \ldots, \mathbf{a}_m$ *is meant any vector of the form* $t_1\mathbf{a}_1 + t_2\mathbf{a}_2 + \cdots + t_m\mathbf{a}_m$, *where* $t_1, \ldots, t_m$ *are scalars.*

**Proposition.** *Let* $\mathbf{a}_1, \ldots, \mathbf{a}_m$ *be vectors of a linear space $L$. Then all linear combinations of those vectors form a subspace of $L$, which is the smallest subspace containing the given vectors.*

PROOF. We must first prove that the collection $K$ of all linear combinations $\sum_{i=1}^{m} t_i\mathbf{a}_i$ of the given vectors is a linear subspace of $L$. In fact, $K$ is closed under addition:

$$\sum_{i=1}^{m} s_i\mathbf{a}_i + \sum_{i=1}^{m} t_i\mathbf{a}_i = \sum_{i=1}^{m} (s_i + t_i)\mathbf{a}_i,$$

and scalar multiplication:

$$s\sum_{i=1}^{m} t_i\mathbf{a}_i = \sum_{i=1}^{m} (st_i)\mathbf{a}_i.$$

Further, if $K'$ is a linear space containing each $\mathbf{a}_i$ $(i = 1, \ldots, m)$, then $K'$ contains each linear combination: $t_i\mathbf{a}_i$ lies in $K'$ for each $i$ and each scalar $t_i$, hence, $\sum_{i=1}^{m} t_i\mathbf{a}_i$ also lies in $K'$. Thus, $K$ is a subspace of $K'$. □

**Remark.** (2) Vectors $a_1, \ldots, a_n$ of a linear space $L$ are said to *span* the space $L$ provided that every vector in $L$ can be expressed as a linear combination of $a_1, \ldots, a_n$. The above proposition says that every $m$-tuple of vectors of $L$ spans a subspace of $L$.

**Examples**

(5)

(6) The vector $(1, 0, -1)$ in the three-dimensional space $\mathbf{R}^3$ spans the line $K \equiv t(1, 0, -1)$ consisting of all vectors $(t, 0, -t)$, $t \in \mathbf{R}$.

   The vectors $(1, 0, -1)$ and $(0, 1, 1)$ span the plane $K \equiv t(1, 0, -1) + s(0, 1, 1)$.

(7) The even-parity code of length 4 is spanned by the vectors 1100, 1010, and 1001. In fact, all the remaining code words are linear combinations of those three words:

$$
\begin{aligned}
0000 &= 1100 + 1100, \\
0110 &= 1100 + 1010, \\
0101 &= 1100 + 1001, \\
0011 &\doteq 1010 + 1001, \\
1111 &= 1100 + 1010 + 1001.
\end{aligned}
$$

Observe that in the binary field $\mathbf{Z}_2$, the only scalars are $t = 0, 1$ and they just determine whether a given vector is present ($t = 1$) or absent ($t = 0$) in a linear combination.

## 7.4   Finite-Dimensional Spaces

**Definition.** *Let $L$ be a linear space.*

(1) *Nonzero vectors $a_1, \ldots, a_m$ are said to be* linearly independent *provided that none of them is a linear combination of the others.*

(2) *By a* basis *of $L$ is meant a linearly independent collection of vectors which span $L$ [see Remark (2) of 7.3]. If $L$ has a finite basis, then it is said to be* finite-dimensional; *more specifically, $L$ is $k$-dimensional provided that it has a basis of $k$ vectors.*

**Examples**

(1) The real plane $\mathbf{R}^2$ is two-dimensional: the vectors $(1, 0)$ and $(0, 1)$ form a basis. The three-dimensional space $\mathbf{R}^3$ deserves its name: $(1, 0, 0)$, $(0, 1, 0)$, and $(0, 0, 1)$ form a basis.

(2) The linear space $F^n$ of all words of length $n$ is $n$-dimensional. It is easy to see that the $n$ words of Hamming weight 1 form a basis of $F^n$.

(3) The even-parity code of length 4 is three-dimensional: the three vectors of Example (6) in 7.3 clearly form a basis.

(4) As an example of a linear space which is not finite-dimensional, consider the set of all sequences $\mathbf{a} = a_1 a_2 a_3 \ldots$ of 0's and 1's. This is a linear space over $\mathbf{Z}_2$ with coordinatewise addition and scalar multiplication.

**Remarks**

(1) Vectors $\mathbf{a}_1, \ldots, \mathbf{a}_m$ are linearly independent if and only if none of their linear combinations except the trivial one (with all-zero scalars) is equal to the zero vector. In symbols:

$$\sum_{i=1}^{m} t_i \mathbf{a}_i = 0 \qquad \text{implies} \qquad t_i = 0 \text{ for all } i = 1, \ldots, m.$$

In fact, whenever $\sum t_i \mathbf{a}_i = 0$ and $t_{i_0} \neq 0$, then $\mathbf{a}_{i_0}$ is a linear combination of the other vectors, viz.,

$$\mathbf{a}_{i_0} = \sum_{\substack{i=1 \\ i \neq i_0}}^{m} (-t_i t_{i_0}^{-1}) \mathbf{a}_i.$$

Conversely, whenever $\mathbf{a}_{i_0} = \displaystyle\sum_{\substack{i=1 \\ i \neq i_0}}^{m} s_i \mathbf{a}_i$, then we have the following non-trivial linear combination:

$$s_1 \mathbf{a}_1 + \cdots + s_{i_0-1} \mathbf{a}_{i_0-1} - \mathbf{a}_{i_0} + s_{i_0+1} \mathbf{a}_{i_0+1} + \cdots + s_m \mathbf{a}_m = 0.$$

(2) For finite fields $F$, the following holds: a linear space over $F$ is finite-dimensional if and only if it has a finite number of vectors.

More concretely, let $F$ have $r$ elements. Then each $k$-dimensional linear space has $r^k$ elements. This follows from the next result:

**Proposition.** *Let $\mathbf{e}_1, \ldots, \mathbf{e}_m$ be a basis of a linear space $L$. Then for each vector $\mathbf{a}$ of $L$, there exists a unique word $t_1 \ldots t_m$ of scalars (i.e., an element of $F^m$) with $\mathbf{a} = \sum_{i=1}^{m} t_i \mathbf{e}_i$.*

**PROOF.** Since the basis spans $L$, the existence of such a word is clear. To prove the uniqueness, let $s_1 \ldots s_m$ be another word with $\mathbf{a} = \sum_{i=1}^{m} s_i \mathbf{e}_i$. Then $\sum_{i=1}^{m} (s_i - t_i) \mathbf{e}_i = \mathbf{a} - \mathbf{b} = 0$ is a linear combination which, by Remark (1) above, is trivial. Thus, $s_i = t_i$ for each $i$. $\qquad \square$

**Remark.** (3) By choosing a basis $e_1, \ldots, e_m$ in a finite-dimensional space $L$, we obtain a bijective correspondence between vectors in the linear space $F^m$ and vectors in $L$:

$$t_1 \ldots t_m \longleftrightarrow \sum_{i=1}^{m} t_i e_i.$$

This correspondence preserves the operations of linear space: it assigns to a sum $t + t'$ in the space $F^m$ the sum $\sum t_i e_i + \sum t'_i e_i = \sum(t_i + t'_i)e_i$ in the space $L$, and to a scalar product $rt$ in the space $F^m$ the scalar product $r \sum t_i e_i = \sum(rt_i)e_i$ in $L$.

Thus, the linear spaces $F^m$ and $L$ are essentially the same.

**Theorem.** *Any linearly independent vectors* $a_1, \ldots, a_m$ *in a* $k$-*dimensional linear space form a part of some basis* $a_1, \ldots, a_m, b_{m+1}, \ldots, b_k$ *of that space.*

PROOF. We proceed by induction on the number $m$.

(1) $m = 1$. Given a vector $a$ which is linearly independent (i.e., nonzero) in a $k$-dimensional space $L$, we first choose an arbitrary basis of $k$ vectors in $L$: $b_1, \ldots, b_k$. We can express $a$ as a linear combination $a = \sum_{i=1}^{m} t_i b_i$. Some of the coefficients $t_i$ is nonzero (since $a \neq 0$). Suppose, for example, that $t_1 \neq 0$. Then we will show that $a, b_2, \ldots, b_k$ form a basis of $L$. In fact:

(a) The vectors $a, b_2, \ldots, b_k$ span the space $L$ because each of the vectors $b_i$ (which span $L$) is a linear combination of those vectors. This is obvious for $i = 2, \ldots, k$, and for $i = 1$, we have

$$b_1 = t_1^{-1} a - \sum_{i=2}^{m}(t_1^{-1} t_i)b_i.$$

(b) To prove linear independence, we use Remark (1) above. Consider any linear combination

$$s_1 a + s_2 b_2 + \cdots + s_k b_k = 0.$$

Since $a = \sum_{i=1}^{k} t_i b_i$, we have

$$s_1 t_1 b_1 + (s_2 + s_1 t_2)b_2 + \cdots + (s_k + s_1 t_k)b_k = 0.$$

From the linear independence of $b_1, \ldots, b_k$, we conclude that $s_1 t_1 = 0$ (thus, $s_1 = 0$ because $t_1 \neq 0$ by assumption) and $s_i + s_1 t_i = 0$, which implies $s_i = 0$ ($i = 2, \ldots, k$). Therefore, the above linear combination is trivial, which was to be proved.

(2) Induction step: Let the theorem hold for $a_1, \ldots, a_{m-1}$, i.e., let there be a basis $a_1, \ldots, a_{m-1}, b_m, \ldots, b_k$. We are to prove that the theorem holds for $a_1, \ldots, a_m$. We can express $a_m$ as a linear combination

$$a_m = t_1 a_1 + \cdots + t_{m-1} a_{m-1} + s_m b_m + \cdots + s_k b_k.$$

Some of the coefficients $s_i$ is nonzero (since $a_m$ is not a linear combination of $a_1, \ldots, a_{m-1}$). Suppose, for example, that $s_m \neq 0$. Then $a_1, \ldots, a_{m-1}, a_m, b_{m+1}, \ldots, b_k$ is a basis of $L$. This follows, analogously to the above step $m = 1$, from the fact that $b_m$ is a linear combination of those vectors:

$$b_m = \sum_{i=1}^{m-1} (-s_m^{-1} t_i) a_i + s_m^{-1} a_m + \sum_{i=m+1}^{k} (-s_m^{-1} s_i) b_i.$$

□

**Corollary.** *Every $k$-dimensional space $L$ has the following properties:*

(1) *Each basis of $L$ has $k$ vectors.*

(2) *Each $k$-tuple of linearly independent vectors forms a basis.*

(3) *$k$ is the largest number of linearly independent vectors in $L$.*

(4) *Every linear subspace of $L$, except $L$ itself, has dimension smaller than $k$.*

In fact, (1) follows from the above Proposition and the obvious fact that no basis contains a smaller basis; (2) and (3) follow directly from the Proposition. For (4), let $K$ be a linear subspace of $L$ and let $m$ be the largest number of linearly independent vectors in $K$. By (3), we know that $m \leq k$. Any linearly independent collection $a_1, \ldots, a_m$ of vectors in $K$ is a basis of $K$. (In fact, for each vector $a \neq 0$, the collection $a, a_1, \ldots, a_m$ is linearly dependent, thus, there is a nontrivial linear combination $t a + \sum t_i a_i = 0$. The linear independence of $a_1, \ldots, a_m$ implies that $t \neq 0$, and then $a = \sum (-t^{-1} t_i) a_i$. Therefore, $a_1, \ldots, a_m$ span $K$.) If $m = k$, then, by (2), $a_1, \ldots, a_m$ form a basis of $L$, and thus, $L = K$. In other words, if $K \neq L$, then $m < k$.

□

# 7.5 Matrices

We are now going to show that solutions of a system of linear homogenous equations can be found over any field $F$ analogously to the well-known

$$
\begin{array}{rcl}
a_{11}x_1 + a_{12}x_2 + \cdots + a_{1n}x_n & = & 0 \\
a_{21}x_1 + a_{22}x_2 + \cdots + a_{2n}x_n & = & 0 \\
\cdots\cdots\cdots\cdots\cdots\cdots\cdots\cdots\cdots\cdots\cdots\cdots & & \\
a_{m1}x_1 + a_{m2}x_2 + \cdots + a_{mn}x_n & = & 0
\end{array}
$$

**Figure 2:** A system of linear homogenous equations

case of real numbers. A *system of linear homogenous equations* over $F$ is a system as in Figure 2, where the coefficients $a_{ij}$ are elements of $F$. It is obvious that the all-zero vector solves the system, but we want to describe *all* solutions. We first rewrite the system more succinctly, using matrices. An $m \times n$ *matrix* over $F$ is an $(m\,n)$-tuple of elements of $F$ arranged in a rectangular array of $m$ rows and $n$ columns. For example, the coefficients of the system in Figure 2 form the following matrix

$$
\mathbf{A} = \begin{bmatrix}
a_{11} & a_{12} & a_{13} & \cdots & a_{1n} \\
a_{21} & a_{22} & a_{23} & \cdots & a_{2n} \\
\cdots\cdots\cdots\cdots\cdots\cdots\cdots\cdots\cdots\cdots & & & & \\
a_{m1} & a_{m2} & a_{m3} & \cdots & a_{mn}
\end{bmatrix}.
$$

Every vector $\mathbf{a}$ of the linear space $F^n$ is considered as a one-row matrix:

$$
\mathbf{a} = \begin{bmatrix} a_1 & a_2 & a_3 & \cdots & a_n \end{bmatrix}.
$$

Conversely, every row of an $m \times n$ matrix is a vector of $F^n$. The linear subspace of $F^n$ spanned by all rows of the matrix $\mathbf{A}$ is called the *row space* of $\mathbf{A}$. The dimension of the row space is called the *rank* of the matrix $\mathbf{A}$. It is obvious that the solutions of the system of equations in Figure 2 depend on the row space of $\mathbf{A}$ only, and not on the concrete form of the matrix. In order to find all solutions of the system of equations in Figure 2, we perform so-called *elementary row operations* on the matrix $\mathbf{A}$. These are the following three types of operations, which change the matrix $\mathbf{A}$, but do not change the row space of $\mathbf{A}$:

(1) An interchange of two rows.

(2) A scalar multiplication of a row by a nonzero scalar.

(3) A replacement of a row by the sum of itself and a scalar multiple of another row.

By a successive application of elementary row operations, every matrix can be put into *row-echelon form*, which means that

(a) each row with nonzero terms has the leading term (i.e., the first nonzero term) equal to 1;

(b) the leading term of each nonzero row lies to the right of the leading terms of all higher rows;

(c) each all-zero row lies below all nonzero rows.

Observe that (a), (b), and (c) imply that all entries below a leading term are zeros.

**Example.** Let us solve the following system of equations over the field $Z_3$:

$$
\begin{aligned}
x_4 + 2x_5 &= 0, \\
2x_2 + x_4 + 2x_5 &= 0, \\
2x_2 + 2x_4 + x_5 &= 0, \\
2x_2 + x_4 &= 0.
\end{aligned}
$$

We first write down the matrix of coefficients:

$$
A = \begin{bmatrix}
0 & 0 & 0 & 1 & 2 \\
0 & 2 & 0 & 1 & 2 \\
0 & 2 & 0 & 2 & 1 \\
0 & 2 & 0 & 1 & 0
\end{bmatrix}.
$$

Next, we interchange the first and fourth rows and divide the new first row by 2. (In the field $Z_3$, division by 2 is the same as multiplication by 2, since $2 \times 2 = 1$.)

$$
A \longrightarrow \begin{bmatrix}
0 & 2 & 0 & 1 & 0 \\
0 & 2 & 0 & 1 & 2 \\
0 & 2 & 0 & 2 & 1 \\
0 & 0 & 0 & 1 & 2
\end{bmatrix}
\longrightarrow
\begin{bmatrix}
0 & 1 & 0 & 2 & 1 \\
0 & 2 & 0 & 1 & 2 \\
0 & 2 & 0 & 2 & 1 \\
0 & 0 & 0 & 1 & 2
\end{bmatrix}.
$$

We now add the first row to the third and fourth rows:

$$
\longrightarrow \begin{bmatrix}
0 & 1 & 0 & 2 & 1 \\
0 & 0 & 0 & 0 & 0 \\
0 & 0 & 0 & 1 & 2 \\
0 & 0 & 0 & 1 & 2
\end{bmatrix}.
$$

Finally, we add the third row to the fourth one, and interchange the second and third rows:

$$\longrightarrow \begin{bmatrix} 0 & 1 & 0 & 2 & 1 \\ 0 & 0 & 0 & 1 & 2 \\ 0 & 0 & 0 & 0 & 0 \\ 0 & 0 & 0 & 0 & 0 \end{bmatrix}.$$

Thus, we obtain a new system of equations in the row-echelon form:

$$x_2 + 2x_4 + \quad x_5 \;=\; 0,$$
$$x_4 + 2x_5 \;=\; 0.$$

Its solutions are precisely all vectors $(p, q, r, 2q, 2q)$, where $p$, $q$, $r$ are scalars from $\mathbf{Z}_3$.

*Putting a matrix into row-echelon form.* Let $\mathbf{A}$ be a matrix. If the entries are all zeros, then $\mathbf{A}$ is in row-echelon form. Otherwise perform the following steps:

(1) Interchange the first row with the row having the leftmost leading term of all rows. After the interchange, the leading coefficient $a_{1j}$ has the property that either $j = 1$ or every row has the first $j - 1$ terms equal to zero.

(2) Multiply the first row by $a_{1j}^{-1}$. The leading coefficient of the first row becomes 1.

(3) For all $i > 1$, add the scalar multiple of the first row by the scalar $-a_{ij}$ to the $i$th row. All entries of the $j$th column become zero except for $a_{1j} = 1$.

If $m = 1$, we are finished, and if $m > 1$, we now delete the first row of $\mathbf{A}$, and perform the same steps on the smaller matrix. After the smaller matrix is put (recursively) into row-echelon form, we return the first row.

### Remarks

(1) The row-echelon form has the property that the nonzero rows are linearly independent. In fact, let $a_1, \ldots, a_k$ be all the nonzero rows, and let $\sum_{i=1}^{k} t_i a_i = 0$ be a linear combination. Then $\sum_{i=1}^{k} t_i a_{ij} = 0$, where $j$ denotes the column in which the first row has its leading coefficient. Since $a_{1j} = 1$ and $a_{2j} = \cdots = a_{kj} = 0$, we get $t_1 = 0$. Analogously, from $\sum_{i=2}^{k} t_i a_i = 0$, we conclude that $t_2 = 0$, etc. This proves the linear independence by Remark (1) of 7.4.

Therefore, the row rank of a matrix $\mathbf{A}$ is equal to the number of nonzero rows of the row-echelon form of $\mathbf{A}$.

, (2) The row-echelon form always enables an easy characterization of all solutions of the corresponding homogenous system as illustrated by the above example.

**Theorem.** *Every matrix of rank $k$ has $k$ linearly independent columns.*

PROOF. If a matrix $\mathbf{A}$ is in row-echelon form, then it has $k$ nonzero rows, and we can pick the $k$ columns in which the leading coefficients of the rows lie. Those columns are linearly independent because if we write them as rows (from the top downward), we clearly get a matrix of $k$ nonzero rows in row-echelon form.

Since every matrix can be put into row-echelon form by a succession of elementary row operations, it is sufficient to show that none of the row operations changes the linear independence of columns. We present the proof for the case of the interchange of two rows (the other two cases of elementary row operations are analogous). Consider $k$ columns of the matrix $\mathbf{A}$; the columns number $j_1, j_2, \ldots, j_k$. If we write them as rows, we get $k$ vectors $\mathbf{b}_{j_1}, \ldots, \mathbf{b}_{j_k}$. Now we interchange the $i$th and $i'$th rows of the matrix $\mathbf{A}$. The corresponding columns $\overline{\mathbf{b}}_{j_1}, \ldots, \overline{\mathbf{b}}_{j_k}$ of the new matrix are obtained from the original vectors $\mathbf{b}_{j_1}, \ldots, \mathbf{b}_{j_k}$ by interchanging the $i$th and $i'$th positions. It is our task to show that the vectors $\mathbf{b}_{j_1}, \ldots, \mathbf{b}_{j_k}$ are linearly independent if and only if so are the new vectors $\overline{\mathbf{b}}_{j_1}, \ldots, \overline{\mathbf{b}}_{j_k}$. This follows from Remark (1) of 7.4 since, given scalars $t_1, \ldots, t_k$, we clearly have

$$t_1 \mathbf{b}_{j_1} + \cdots + t_k \mathbf{b}_{j_k} = 0 \quad \text{if and only if} \quad t_1 \overline{\mathbf{b}}_{j_1} + \cdots + t_k \overline{\mathbf{b}}_{j_k} = 0.$$

$\square$

# 7.6 Operations on Matrices

Recall the following operations on matrices.

*Sum* $\mathbf{A} + \mathbf{B}$ is defined for two $m \times n$ matrices componentwise:

$$\mathbf{A} + \mathbf{B} = [a_{ij} + b_{ij}].$$

*Scalar multiple* is also defined componentwise:

$$t\,\mathbf{A} = [ta_{ij}].$$

*Matrix product* $\mathbf{AB}$ of an $m \times n$ matrix $\mathbf{A}$ by an $n \times k$ matrix $\mathbf{B}$ is the following $m \times k$ matrix:

$$\mathbf{AB} = [c_{ij}], \quad \text{where} \quad c_{ij} = \sum_{s=1}^{n} a_{is} b_{sj}.$$

In other words, the $(i, j)$th position of the matrix $\mathbf{AB}$ is the *inner product* of the $i$th row of $\mathbf{A}$ with the $j$th column of $\mathbf{B}$, where the inner product of two vectors $\mathbf{a}$ and $\mathbf{b}$ of $F^n$ is the scalar defined by

$$\mathbf{a} \cdot \mathbf{b} = a_1 b_1 + a_2 b_2 + \cdots + a_n b_n.$$

In particular, the product of a matrix $\mathbf{A}$ by a row is just the linear combination of the row vectors $\mathbf{a}_1, \ldots, \mathbf{a}_m$ of $\mathbf{A}$:

$$[t_1 t_2 \ldots t_m] \mathbf{A} = t_1 \mathbf{a}_1 + t_2 \mathbf{a}_2 + \cdots + t_m \mathbf{a}_m. \tag{7.6.1}$$

Analogously, the product of a matrix $\mathbf{A}$ by a column is just the linear combination of the column vectors of $\mathbf{A}$:

$$\mathbf{A} \begin{bmatrix} s_1 \\ s_2 \\ \vdots \\ s_n \end{bmatrix} = s_1 \begin{bmatrix} a_{11} \\ a_{21} \\ \vdots \\ a_{m1} \end{bmatrix} + s_2 \begin{bmatrix} a_{12} \\ a_{22} \\ \vdots \\ a_{m2} \end{bmatrix} + \cdots + s_n \begin{bmatrix} a_{1n} \\ a_{2n} \\ \vdots \\ a_{mn} \end{bmatrix}. \tag{7.6.2}$$

*Transpose* of an $m \times n$ matrix $\mathbf{A}$ is the $n \times m$ matrix $\mathbf{A}^{\mathrm{tr}}$ obtained from $\mathbf{A}$ by writing the columns as rows, i.e.,

$$\mathbf{A}^{\mathrm{tr}} = [a_{ji}].$$

In particular, the transpose of a vector $\mathbf{a}$ of the linear space $F^n$ (considered to be a one-row matrix $\mathbf{a} = [\begin{array}{cccc} a_1 & a_2 & \cdots & a_n \end{array}]$) is the one-column matrix

$$\mathbf{a}^{\mathrm{tr}} = \begin{bmatrix} a_1 \\ a_2 \\ \vdots \\ a_n \end{bmatrix}.$$

Returning to the system of linear equations in Figure 2, we see that it takes the following matrix form:

$$\begin{bmatrix} a_{11} & a_{12} & \cdots & a_{1n} \\ a_{21} & a_{22} & \cdots & a_{2n} \\ \multicolumn{4}{c}{\dotfill} \\ a_{m1} & a_{m2} & \cdots & a_{mn} \end{bmatrix} \begin{bmatrix} x_1 \\ x_2 \\ \vdots \\ x_n \end{bmatrix} = \begin{bmatrix} 0 \\ 0 \\ \vdots \\ 0 \end{bmatrix}.$$

Or, more succinctly,

$$\mathbf{A} \mathbf{x}^{\mathrm{tr}} = \mathbf{0}^{\mathrm{tr}}. \tag{7.6.3}$$

where $\mathbf{x}$ denotes the vector of unknowns.

An $n \times n$ matrix is called a *square matrix*. A square matrix whose terms are given by

$$a_{ij} = \begin{cases} 1 & \text{if } i = j, \\ 0 & \text{else,} \end{cases}$$

is called an *identity matrix*, and is denoted by **I**. For example, if $n = 3$, then

$$\mathbf{I} = \begin{bmatrix} 1 & 0 & 0 \\ 0 & 1 & 0 \\ 0 & 0 & 1 \end{bmatrix}.$$

The name stems from the fact that whenever the matrix product with **I** is defined, then **I** acts as a unit: $\mathbf{AI} = \mathbf{A}$ and $\mathbf{IB} = \mathbf{B}$.

Let **A** be a square matrix. **A** is said to be *regular* if it has linearly independent rows. Then **A** has an *inverse matrix*, i.e., a matrix $\mathbf{A}^{-1}$ such that

$$\mathbf{AA}^{-1} = \mathbf{A}^{-1}\mathbf{A} = \mathbf{I}.$$

In fact, $\mathbf{A}^{-1}$ can be found as follows: denote by $\begin{bmatrix} \mathbf{A} \mid \mathbf{I} \end{bmatrix}$ the $n$ by $2n$ matrix obtained by adjoining the identity matrix to the right of the matrix **A**. Perform the elementary row operations on the matrix $\begin{bmatrix} \mathbf{A} \mid \mathbf{I} \end{bmatrix}$ in order to obtain a matrix of the form $\begin{bmatrix} \mathbf{I} \mid \mathbf{B} \end{bmatrix}$. Then $\mathbf{B} = \mathbf{A}^{-1}$.

**Remark.** Let us consider a nonhomogenous system of linear equations:

$$\begin{aligned}
a_{11}x_1 + \cdots + a_{1n}x_n &= d_1, \\
a_{21}x_2 + \cdots + a_{2n}x_n &= d_2, \\
&\cdots\cdots\cdots\cdots\cdots\cdots\cdots\cdots \\
a_{m1}x_1 + \cdots + a_{mn}x_n &= d_m.
\end{aligned} \tag{7.6.4}$$

Or, in the matrix form:

$$\mathbf{Ax}^{\text{tr}} = \mathbf{d}^{\text{tr}}.$$

(1) If **A** is a regular square matrix $(m = n)$, then the above system has a unique solution, viz., $\mathbf{x}^{\text{tr}} = \mathbf{A}^{-1}\mathbf{d}^{\text{tr}}$. Let us remark that every square matrix **A** with linearly independent columns is regular (by Theorem 7.5 applied to $\mathbf{A}^{\text{tr}}$: since $\mathbf{A}^{\text{tr}}$ has linearly independent columns, **A** has linearly independent rows).

(2) More in general, if **A** has linearly independent rows (i.e., if it has rank $m$), then the above equations (7.6.4) have at least one solution.

In fact, by Theorem 7.5, **A** has $m$ linearly independent columns. If, for example, the first $m$ columns are linearly independent, than we can choose $x_i = 0$ for $i = m + 1, \ldots, n$ and solve the following equations

$$\begin{aligned}
a_{11}x_1 + \cdots + a_{1m}x_m &= d_1, \\
&\cdots\cdots\cdots\cdots\cdots\cdots\cdots\cdots \\
a_{m1}x_1 + \cdots + a_{mm}x_m &= d_m.
\end{aligned}$$

They have a unique solution [by (1)], and by adding the $n - m$ zeros, we get a solution of the system above. In the case that columns of another $m$-tuple are linearly independent, we proceed in the same way, putting $x_i = 0$ for all $i$'s except in the $m$ chosen columns.

## 7.7   Orthogonal Complement

**Remark.**   (1) Recall from 7.6 the concept of an inner product in the linear space $F^n$:

$$\mathbf{a} \cdot \mathbf{b} = a_1 b_1 + \cdots + a_n b_n.$$

Observe the following properties of the inner product:

(a) $\mathbf{a} \cdot \mathbf{b} = \mathbf{b} \cdot \mathbf{a}$ for all vectors $\mathbf{a}$ and $\mathbf{b}$,

(b) $\mathbf{a} \cdot (\mathbf{b} + \mathbf{c}) = \mathbf{a} \cdot \mathbf{b} + \mathbf{a} \cdot \mathbf{c}$ for all vectors $\mathbf{a}$, $\mathbf{b}$, and $\mathbf{c}$,

(c) $\mathbf{a} \cdot (t\,\mathbf{b}) = t\,(\mathbf{a} \cdot \mathbf{b})$ for all vectors $\mathbf{a}$ and $\mathbf{b}$ and all scalars $t$.

**Definition.**   (1) *Two vectors of $F^n$ are said to be* orthogonal *if their inner product is equal to zero.*

(2) *Let $L$ be a linear subspace of $F^n$. By the* orthogonal complement *of $L$ is meant the set of all vectors orthogonal to each vector in $L$. This is denoted by $L^\perp$:*

$$L^\perp = \{\, \mathbf{a} \in F^n \mid \mathbf{a} \cdot \mathbf{b} = 0 \quad \text{for all } \mathbf{b} \in L \,\}.$$

**Examples**

(1) If $L$ is a line in the plane $\mathbf{R}^2$, then $L^\perp$ is the perpendicular line passing through the origin. For example, the orthogonal complement of the $x$-axis is the $y$-axis.

(2) The orthogonal complement of the even-parity code $K$ is the repetition code of the same length. In fact, since each code word $\mathbf{a}$ fulfils $a_1 + \cdots + a_n = 0$, both $000\ldots00$ and $111\ldots11$ are orthogonal to every code word of $K$. Conversely, if a word $\mathbf{c} = c_1 c_2 \ldots c_n$ is orthogonal to every code word, then $c_i = c_j$ for all indices $i$, $j$. (For $i \neq j$, consider the word $\mathbf{a}$ which has 1 precisely on the $i$th and $j$th positions. Then $\mathbf{a}$ is a code word of $K$; thus, $\mathbf{a} \cdot \mathbf{c} = c_i + c_j = 0$.)

**Remark.**   (2) In the theory of real vector spaces, an important fact concerning orthogonal complements is that a linear space and its orthogonal complement have only the zero vector $\mathbf{0}$ in common: $K \cap K^\perp = \{\mathbf{0}\}$.

This is not true in general over finite fields. In fact, there are linear spaces which coincide with their orthogonal complements (e.g., the repetition code of length 2).

**Proposition.** *Let $K$ be a linear subspace of $F^n$.*

(1) *The orthogonal complement $K^\perp$ is also a linear subspace of $F^n$.*

(2) *If $K$ is spanned by vectors $a_1, \ldots, a_m$, then every vector orthogonal to each $a_i$, $i = 1, \ldots, m$, lies in $K^\perp$.*

**PROOF.** (1) Follows immediately from the linearity properties (b) and (c) in Remark (1) above.

(2) Let **b** be orthogonal to each $a_i$. Every vector of $K$ is a linear combination $a = \sum_{i=1}^{m} t_i a_i$ of the given vectors, and from the above linearity properties, we get

$$\mathbf{b} \cdot \mathbf{a} = \sum_{i=1}^{m} \mathbf{b} \cdot (t_i a_i) = \sum_{i=1}^{m} t_i (\mathbf{b} \cdot a_i) = \sum_{i=1}^{m} t_i 0 = 0.$$

Thus, **b** lies in $K^\perp$. □

**Example.** (3) Every solution of a system of linear homogenous equations (see Figure 2 of 7.5) is orthogonal to all rows of the corresponding matrix **A**. Thus, it is orthogonal to all vectors of the row space $L$ of **A**. Conversely, every vector in the orthogonal complement $L^\perp$ is a solution of the system of equations.

Thus, we see that all solutions of a system of equations with the coefficient matrix **A** form precisely the orthogonal complement of the row space of **A**.

**Theorem.** *The orthogonal complement of a $k$-dimensional subspace of the linear space $F^n$ has dimension $n - k$. In symbols,*

$$\dim L^\perp = n - \dim L.$$

**PROOF.** Let $a_1, \ldots, a_k$ be a basis of a linear subspace $L$ of $F^n$. Those vectors, written as rows, form a $k \times n$ matrix **A**. A vector **b** lies in the orthogonal complement of $L$ if and only if $\mathbf{Ab}^{\mathrm{tr}} = \mathbf{0}^{\mathrm{tr}}$.

Since **A** has rank $k$, it has $k$ linearly independent columns (see Theorem 7.5). The length of the columns is $k$, and thus it follows from Corollary (4) in 7.4 that the columns span the linear space $F^k$ (provided that we write vectors of $F^k$ as columns). Thus, every vector **v** in $F^k$ is a linear combination of the columns of $\mathbf{A}$; in other words, $\mathbf{v}$ has the form $\mathbf{v} = \mathbf{Aw}^{tr}$ for some vector $\mathbf{w}$ in $F^n$ [see formula (7.6.2)].

Let $r$ denote the dimension of $L^\perp$. We choose a basis $\mathbf{b}_1, \ldots, \mathbf{b}_r$ of $L^\perp$ and we complete it to a basis $\mathbf{b}_1, \ldots, \mathbf{b}_r, \mathbf{c}_{r+1}, \ldots, \mathbf{c}_n$ of the space $F^n$ (see Theorem 7.4). We are going to show that the $n - r$ vectors

$$\mathbf{Ac}_{r+1}^{tr}, \ldots, \mathbf{Ac}_n^{tr}$$

form a basis of the space $F^k$. This will prove that $k = n - r$; thus, $r = n - k$, whereby the proof will be finished.

(1) The vectors above span $F^k$. In fact, every vector $\mathbf{v}$ of $F^k$ has the form $\mathbf{v} = \mathbf{Aw}^{tr}$. We can express the vector $\mathbf{w}$ as a linear combination $\mathbf{w} = \sum_{i=1}^r t_i \mathbf{b}_i + \sum_{j=r+1}^n s_j \mathbf{c}_j$, and then $\mathbf{Ab}_i^{tr} = 0$ implies

$$\mathbf{v} = \mathbf{A}\left(\sum_{i=1}^r t_i \mathbf{b}_i^{tr} + \sum_{j=r+1}^n s_j \mathbf{c}_j^{tr}\right) = \sum_{j=r+1}^n s_j \mathbf{Ac}_j^{tr}.$$

(2) The vectors above are linearly independent. In fact, consider a linear combination $\sum_{j=r+1}^n t_j \mathbf{Ac}_j^{tr} = \mathbf{0}^{tr}$ [see Remark (1) in 7.4]. The vector $\mathbf{c} = \sum_{j=r+1}^n t_j \mathbf{c}_j$ then fulfils $\mathbf{Ac}^{tr} = \mathbf{0}^{tr}$; i.e., $\mathbf{c}$ lies in $L^\perp$. Thus, $\mathbf{c}$ is a linear combination of the vectors $\mathbf{b}_1, \ldots, \mathbf{b}_r$ (forming a basis of $L^\perp$) as well as a linear combination of the vectors $\mathbf{c}_{r+1}, \ldots, \mathbf{c}_n$. Since $\mathbf{b}_1, \ldots, \mathbf{b}_r, \mathbf{c}_{r+1}, \ldots, \mathbf{c}_n$ form a basis of $F^n$, Proposition 7.4 implies that $\mathbf{c} = 0$. Now, by the linear independence of $\mathbf{c}_{r+1}, \ldots, \mathbf{c}_n$, we conclude that $t_i = 0$ for all $i$, which proves the linear independence of $\mathbf{Ac}_{r+1}^{tr}, \ldots, \mathbf{Ac}_n^{tr}$.                    □

**Corollary.** *For an arbitrary subspace $L$ of the linear space $F^n$, we have*

$$\left(L^\perp\right)^\perp = L.$$

In fact, $L^\perp = K$ implies that $L$ is a subspace of $K^\perp$ (since each vector in $L$ is orthogonal to all vectors of $K = L^\perp$). If $\dim L = k$, then $\dim K = n - k$ and, hence, $\dim K^\perp = n - (n - k) = k$. Thus, $L$ and $K^\perp$ have the same dimension. By Corollary (4) of 7.5, $L = K^\perp$.                    □

**Remarks**

(3) If a system of linear homogenous equations in $n$ unknowns has matrix of rank $k$, then all solutions form a linear space of dimension $n - k$. This follows from the above Theorem and Example (3).

(4) Every linear subspace $L$ of the space $F^n$ can be described by a system of linear homogenous equations. That is, there exists a system as in

Figure 2 of 7.5 such that $L$ is precisely the set of all solutions. In fact, let $a_1, \ldots, a_m$ be a basis of the orthogonal complement of $L$, and let $A$ be the matrix whose rows are $a_1, \ldots, a_m$. Then vectors $\mathbf{x}$ of $(L^{\perp})^{\perp}$ are precisely the solutions of the system $A\mathbf{x}^{tr} = 0^{tr}$, and $(L^{\perp})^{\perp} = L$.

# Exercises

**7A** Prove that multiplication in every ring has a unique neutral element.

**7B** Verify that in every field, $(x^{-1})^{-1} = x$ for all $x \neq 0$.

**7C** Prove that in every ring, all elements $x$, for which $x^{-1}$ exists, form a group under multiplication. Apply this to $\mathbf{Z}_{12}$.

**7D** Write down the operation tables of the field $\mathbf{Z}_5$. Find $x^{-1}$ for each $x \neq 0$.

**7E** Is $\mathbf{Z}_4$ a field? Can you re-define the multiplication (leaving the addition) to obtain a field?

**7F** Verify that the following tables

| + | 0 | 1 | $p$ | $q$ |
|---|---|---|---|---|
| 0 | 0 | 1 | $p$ | $q$ |
| 1 | 1 | 0 | $q$ | $p$ |
| $p$ | $p$ | $q$ | 0 | 1 |
| $q$ | $q$ | $p$ | 1 | 0 |

| $\cdot$ | 0 | 1 | $p$ | $q$ |
|---|---|---|---|---|
| 0 | 0 | 0 | 0 | 0 |
| 1 | 0 | 1 | $p$ | $q$ |
| $p$ | 0 | $p$ | $q$ | 1 |
| $q$ | 0 | $q$ | 1 | $p$ |

define a four-element field $F = \{0, 1, p, q\}$.

**7G** How many vectors are there in the linear space $\mathbf{Z}_2^n$? In $\mathbf{Z}_3^n$?

**7H** Verify that the linear space $F^n$ over an $r$-element field $F$ has precisely

(1) $r^n - 1$ linear subspaces of dimension 1. [Hint: the number of all vectors, including 0, is $r^n$.]

(2) $r^n - 1$ linear subspaces of dimension $n - 1$. [Hint: apply (1) to the orthogonal complement.]

**7I**    Prove that the set of all $n \times m$ matrices with the addition and scalar multiplication of 7.6 form a linear space. What is its dimension?

**7J**    Prove that the linear space of Example (4) in 7.4 is not finite-dimensional.

**7K**    Find a row-echelon form of the following matrix

$$\begin{bmatrix} 1 & 0 & 1 & 0 & 1 & 0 & 1 \\ 1 & 1 & 0 & 0 & 1 & 1 & 0 \\ 0 & 1 & 1 & 0 & 0 & 1 & 1 \end{bmatrix}$$

(1) over the field $Z_2$,

(2) over the field $Z_3$.

In both cases, determine the rank.

**7L**    Find all solutions of the following system of equations over $Z_2$ and over $Z_3$:

$$\begin{aligned} x_1 + x_2 + x_4 &= 0, \\ x_3 + x_4 + x_5 &= 0, \\ x_1 + x_3 + x_5 &= 0. \end{aligned}$$

**7M**    Find an inverse matrix to the following matrix

$$\begin{bmatrix} 1 & 0 & 1 \\ 1 & 1 & 1 \\ 0 & 1 & 0 \end{bmatrix}$$

(1) over the field $Z_2$,

(2) over the field $Z_3$.

**7N**    Find an inverse matrix of the following matrix

$$A = \begin{bmatrix} 1 & 0 & 1 & 1 \\ 1 & 1 & 0 & 1 \\ 1 & 1 & 1 & 0 \\ 0 & 0 & 1 & 1 \end{bmatrix}$$

(1) over the field $Z_2$,

(2) over the field $Z_3$.

In both cases, discuss the solutions of the system of equation $\mathbf{A}\mathbf{x}^{tr} = \mathbf{b}^{tr}$, where $\mathbf{b} = 1100$.

**7O** Given a solution $\mathbf{a} = a_1 \ldots a_n$ of a nonhomogenous system of linear equations $\mathbf{A}\mathbf{x}^{tr} = \mathbf{d}^{tr}$ (see Remark 7.6), prove that all solutions of that system have the form $\mathbf{a} + \mathbf{b}$, where $\mathbf{b}$ solves the corresponding homogenous system (i.e., $\mathbf{A}\mathbf{b}^{tr} = \mathbf{0}^{tr}$). In other words, the collection of all solutions is the coset (6.2)

$$\mathbf{a} + K^\perp$$

modulo the linear space $K^\perp$ which is the orthogonal complement of the row space $K$ of the matrix $\mathbf{A}$.

**7P** Find all solutions of the following system of equations over $Z_5$:

$$\begin{aligned} x_1 + 3x_2 + 2x_3 &= 1, \\ x_1 + 2x_2 + x_3 &= 2. \end{aligned}$$

**7Q** Find the orthogonal complement of the Hamming code of length 7 (see 5.5).

**7R** What property of the field $F$ of real numbers guarantees that for each linear subspace $L$ of $F^n$, one has $L \cap L^\perp = \{\,0\,\}$? Does any of the fields $Z_p$ have this property? Do you know any other field which does?

**7S** Let $\mathbf{A}$ be an $m \times n$ matrix of rank $m$. Prove the following:

(1) A row-echelon form of $\mathbf{A}$ has 1's in the main diagonal ($a_{ii} = 1$) and zeros under it.

(2) If $m = n$, then it is possible to find elementary row operations which transform $\mathbf{A}$ into an identity matrix. [Hint: use (1) and start the operations on the row-echelon form from the bottom up.]

**7T** Prove the following generalization of Theorem 7.2: each number $i = 0, 1, \ldots, n-1$ relatively prime with $n$ has an inverse element in the ring $Z_n$; i.e., there exists $j$ with $ij \equiv 1 \pmod{n}$. [Hint: The proof is analogous to that in 7.2. Whenever $i$ is relatively prime with $n$, then the remainder of the integer division $n : i$ is also relatively prime with $n$.]

**7U**   Prove that if a matrix $\mathbf{A}$ is obtained by concatenating matrices $\mathbf{A}_1$ and $\mathbf{A}_2$ row by row (notation: $\mathbf{A} = \begin{bmatrix} \mathbf{A}_1 \mid \mathbf{A}_2 \end{bmatrix}$) and a matrix $\mathbf{B}$ is obtained by concatenating matrices $\mathbf{B}_1$ and $\mathbf{B}_2$ column by column (notation: $\mathbf{B} = \begin{bmatrix} \mathbf{B}_1 \\ \hline \mathbf{B}_2 \end{bmatrix}$), then for the matrix product, the following formula holds:

$$\mathbf{AB} = \begin{bmatrix} \mathbf{A}_1 \mid \mathbf{A}_2 \end{bmatrix} \begin{bmatrix} \mathbf{B}_1 \\ \hline \mathbf{B}_2 \end{bmatrix} = \mathbf{A}_1\mathbf{B}_1 + \mathbf{A}_2\mathbf{B}_2,$$

whenever the number of rows of $\mathbf{A}_i$ is equal to the number of columns of $\mathbf{B}_i$ for $i = 1, 2$.

## Notes

This chapter is just a brief presentation of standard linear algebra; for more information, the interested reader can consult a number of good textbooks, e.g., Birkhoff and MacLane (1953).

# Chapter 8

# Linear Codes

We now extend the concepts of generator matrix, parity check matrix, and syndrome decoding from binary codes to codes over an arbitrary alphabet. Then we turn to modifications of a given code: extension, puncturing, augmentation, and expurgation. This chapter prepares ground for the introduction of important classes of codes in subsequent chapters.

## 8.1  Generator Matrix

Linear codes over the binary field $Z_2$ were introduced in 5.3. We now generalize the concept to any finite field $F$. This means that our code alphabet carries the structure of addition and multiplication of a field; this somewhat restricts the code alphabet we can choose, but it has the advantage of structuring block codes in order to obtain good error control.

**Definition.** *Let $F$ be a finite field. By a* linear code *is meant a linear subspace of the linear space $F^n$ of all words of length $n$ ($n = 1, 2, 3, \ldots$). In more detail, a $k$-dimensional linear subspace of $F^n$ is called a linear $(n, k)$-code in the alphabet $F$.*

**Remarks**

(1) Thus, a linear code of length $n$ is a set of words of length $n$ such that

    (a) if **a** and **b** are code words, then $\mathbf{a} + \mathbf{b}$ is a code word

and

    (b) if **a** is a code word, then each scalar multiple $t\,\mathbf{a}$ is a code word.

115

Observe that every linear code contains the all-zero word $\mathbf{0} = 0\mathbf{a}$.

(2) A linear $(n,k)$-code has $k$ information symbols (4.2) and $n-k$ check symbols. In fact, let $K$ be a $k$-dimensional subspace of $F^n$, and let

$$\mathbf{e}_1, \mathbf{e}_2, \ldots, \mathbf{e}_k$$

be a basis of $K$. Then every code word $\mathbf{v}$ has the form

$$\mathbf{v} = \sum_{i=1}^{k} u_i \mathbf{e}_i \tag{8.1.1}$$

for a unique $k$-tuple of scalars $u_i$ (see Proposition 7.4). In other words, the $k$ information symbols $u_1 u_2 \ldots u_k$ determine a code word uniquely by (8.1.1), and, conversely, every code word (8.1.1) determines the $k$ information symbols uniquely.

(3) Observe that if the code alphabet $F$ has $r$ symbols, then there are $r^k$ code words in $K$.

**Definition.** *Let $K$ be a linear code with a basis $\mathbf{e}_1, \mathbf{e}_2, \ldots, \mathbf{e}_k$. The $k \times n$ matrix $\mathbf{G}$ with the rows $\mathbf{e}_1, \ldots, \mathbf{e}_k$:*

$$\mathbf{G} = \begin{pmatrix} \mathbf{e}_1 \\ \mathbf{e}_2 \\ \vdots \\ \mathbf{e}_k \end{pmatrix}$$

*is called a* generator matrix *of the code $K$.*

**Examples**

(1) The Hamming $(7,4)$-code [see Example (1) of 5.5] has the following generator matrix:

$$\mathbf{G} = \begin{bmatrix} 1 & 0 & 0 & 0 & 0 & 1 & 1 \\ 0 & 1 & 0 & 0 & 1 & 0 & 1 \\ 0 & 0 & 1 & 0 & 1 & 1 & 0 \\ 0 & 0 & 0 & 1 & 1 & 1 & 1 \end{bmatrix}.$$

In fact, each row of the matrix $\mathbf{G}$ is a code word, since we can find it in Figure 3 of 5.5. The first four columns of $\mathbf{G}$ form an identity matrix, thus, $\mathbf{G}$ is of rank 4. The dimension of the code is also 4, therefore, it is spanned by the rows of $\mathbf{G}$.

(2) The even-parity code of length 4 has the following generator matrix [see Example (3) of 7.4]:

$$G = \begin{bmatrix} 1 & 1 & 0 & 0 \\ 1 & 0 & 1 & 0 \\ 1 & 0 & 0 & 1 \end{bmatrix}.$$

Every matrix obtained from **G** by elementary row operations (7.5) is a generator matrix of the same code. For example, the following matrix (in row-echelon form)

$$G' = \begin{bmatrix} 1 & 0 & 0 & 1 \\ 0 & 1 & 0 & 1 \\ 0 & 0 & 1 & 1 \end{bmatrix}$$

is a generator matrix.

(3) The following matrix over the field $\mathbf{Z}_3$

$$G = \begin{bmatrix} 1 & 1 & 0 & 0 & 0 & 0 \\ 0 & 0 & 2 & 2 & 0 & 0 \\ 1 & 1 & 1 & 1 & 1 & 1 \end{bmatrix}$$

is a generator matrix of a linear $(6,3)$-code. If we put it into row-echelon form, we get

$$G' = \begin{bmatrix} 1 & 1 & 0 & 0 & 0 & 0 \\ 0 & 0 & 1 & 1 & 0 & 0 \\ 0 & 0 & 0 & 0 & 1 & 1 \end{bmatrix}.$$

We see that this is the "stammering" code of all words in which each symbol is repeated twice.

**Remark.** (4) If **G** is a generator matrix of a code, then the above rule (8.1.1), assigning to the information bits $\mathbf{u} = u_1 u_2 \dots u_k$ the code words $\mathbf{v}$, can be put into matrix form

$$\mathbf{v} = \mathbf{uG},$$

see formula (7.6.1). This, then, is the encoding rule of the code: from the information symbols **u**, we obtain the code word **uG**.

By changing the generator matrix (i.e., the basis), we change the encoding rule.

The most convenient encoding rule is writing down the information symbols and supplementing them by the check symbol. That is, given information symbols $u_1 u_2 \dots u_k$, we send a code word $u_1 u_2 \dots u_k v_{k+1} \dots v_n$. This corresponds to the generator matrices of the form

$$G = [\,\mathbf{I}\,|\,\mathbf{B}\,],$$

where $\mathbf{I}$ is the identity $k \times k$ matrix, and $\mathbf{B}$ is a $k$ by $n - k$ matrix.

**Definition.**  (1) *A linear code is called* systematic *provided that it has a generator matrix of the form* $\mathbf{G} = \begin{bmatrix} \mathbf{I} \mid \mathbf{B} \end{bmatrix}$, *where* $\mathbf{I}$ *is an identity matrix.*

(2) *Two linear codes $K$ and $K'$ of the same length n are said to be* equivalent *provided that they differ only in the ordering of symbols in a code word, i.e., provided that there exists a permutation $(p_1, p_2, \ldots, p_n)$ of the numbers $1, 2, \ldots, n$ such that for each word $v_1 v_2 \ldots v_n$, we have:*

$$v_1 v_2 \ldots v_n \text{ is a code word in } K \iff v_{p_1} v_{p_2} \ldots v_{p_n} \text{ is a code word in } K'.$$

**Example.**  (4) The Hamming $(7, 4)$-code in Example (1) is systematic. The even-parity code of length 4 is also systematic since the generator matrix $\mathbf{G}'$ above has the required form

$$\mathbf{G}' = \begin{bmatrix} 1 & 0 & 0 & 1 \\ 0 & 1 & 0 & 1 \\ 0 & 0 & 1 & 1 \end{bmatrix}.$$

In contrast, the stammering code $K$ above is not systematic. However, the following equivalent code $K^*$ is systematic: switch the second and the fourth symbols, and switch the third and the sixth symbols. That is, use the permutation $(1, 4, 6, 2, 5, 3)$. From the generator matrix $\mathbf{G}'$, this permutation yields

$$\mathbf{G}^* = \begin{bmatrix} 1 & 0 & 0 & 1 & 0 & 0 \\ 0 & 1 & 0 & 0 & 0 & 1 \\ 0 & 0 & 1 & 0 & 1 & 0 \end{bmatrix}.$$

**Proposition.** *Every linear code is equivalent to a systematic linear code.*

**Proof.**  The generator matrix $\mathbf{G}$ of a linear $(n, k)$-code $K$ has rank $k$; thus, it has $k$ linearly independent columns (Theorem 7.5).

I. Suppose that the first $k$ columns of $\mathbf{G}$ are linearly independent. That is, $\mathbf{G} = \begin{bmatrix} \mathbf{A} \mid \mathbf{B} \end{bmatrix}$, where $\mathbf{A}$ is a regular $n \times n$ matrix. There is a succession of elementary row operations which transform $\mathbf{A}$ into an identity matrix $\mathbf{I}$ (see Exercise 7S). If the same elementary row operations are performed on $\mathbf{G}$, we get a matrix $\mathbf{G}' = \begin{bmatrix} \mathbf{I} \mid \mathbf{B}' \end{bmatrix}$. Since $\mathbf{G}'$ is also a generator matrix of the code $K$, it follows that $K$ is systematic.

II. In general, given $k$ independent columns of $\mathbf{G}$, let $(p_1, p_2, \ldots, p_n)$ be a permutation which shifts them into the first $k$ positions. From the matrix $\mathbf{G}$, we obtain another matrix $\mathbf{G}^*$. Let $K^*$ be the linear code with $\mathbf{G}^*$ as a generator matrix. Then $K$ and $K^*$ are equivalent, and $K^*$ is systematic by I above.                                                                  $\square$

## 8.2 Parity Check Matrix

The concept of a parity check matrix is a direct generalization of the binary case (5.4):

**Definition.** *Let $K$ be a linear code of length $n$ over a field $F$. An $n$-column matrix $\mathbf{H}$ over $F$ is called a* parity check matrix *for $K$ provided that the following holds for words $\mathbf{v} = v_1 v_2 \ldots v_n$ in $F^n$: $\mathbf{v}$ is a code word of $K$ if and only if $\mathbf{H}\mathbf{v}^{\mathrm{tr}} = \mathbf{0}^{\mathrm{tr}}$; shortly:*

$$\mathbf{v} \text{ lies in } K \iff \mathbf{H}\begin{bmatrix} v_1 \\ v_2 \\ \vdots \\ v_n \end{bmatrix} = \begin{bmatrix} 0 \\ 0 \\ \vdots \\ 0 \end{bmatrix}.$$

**Proposition.** *A systematic code with a generator matrix*

$$\mathbf{G} = \begin{bmatrix} \mathbf{I} \mid \mathbf{B} \end{bmatrix}, \qquad \text{where } \mathbf{I} \text{ is an identity matrix,}$$

*has the following parity check matrix:*

$$\mathbf{H} = \begin{bmatrix} -\mathbf{B}^{\mathrm{tr}} \mid \mathbf{I}' \end{bmatrix}, \qquad \text{where } \mathbf{I}' \text{ is an identity matrix.}$$

PROOF. Let $K$ be an $(n, k)$-code with the above generator matrix (where $\mathbf{I}$ is the $k \times k$ identity matrix). If $L$ denotes the row space of the matrix $\mathbf{H}$ above, then it is our task to show that $K$ is the orthogonal complement of $L$. First, observe that the rank of the matrix $\mathbf{H}$ is $n - k$, since $\mathbf{I}'$ is an identity matrix. Consequently, the dimension of $L^\perp$ is $n - (n - k) = k$ (by Theorem 7.7), the same as the dimension of $K$. Thus, it is sufficient to show that every row $\mathbf{g}$ of the matrix $\mathbf{G}$ fulfils $\mathbf{H}\mathbf{g}^{\mathrm{tr}} = \mathbf{0}^{\mathrm{tr}}$: it then follows that every code word $\mathbf{v}$ of $K$ also fulfils $\mathbf{H}\mathbf{v}^{\mathrm{tr}} = \mathbf{0}^{\mathrm{tr}}$, i.e., that $K$ is a subspace of $L^\perp$. The equality of dimensions then implies that $K = L^\perp$ [by Corollary (4) in 7.4].

Thus, we want to prove that $\mathbf{H}\mathbf{G}^{\mathrm{tr}}$ is the all-zero matrix $\mathbf{0}$. This is an easy application of the formula in Exercise 7U:

$$\begin{aligned} \mathbf{H}\mathbf{G}^{\mathrm{tr}} &= \begin{bmatrix} -\mathbf{B}^{\mathrm{tr}} \mid \mathbf{I}' \end{bmatrix} \begin{bmatrix} \mathbf{I} \\ \hline \mathbf{B}^{\mathrm{tr}} \end{bmatrix} \\ &= -\mathbf{B}^{\mathrm{tr}}\mathbf{I} + \mathbf{I}'\mathbf{B}^{\mathrm{tr}} \\ &= -\mathbf{B}^{\mathrm{tr}} + \mathbf{B}^{\mathrm{tr}} = \mathbf{0}. \end{aligned}$$

$\square$

**Corollary.** *Every linear* $(n, k)$*-code has an* $n - k$ *by* $n$ *parity check matrix of rank* $n - k$.

In fact, this has been shown for each systematic code $K$ in the proposition above, and for an equivalent code (see Proposition 8.1), it is sufficient to perform the given permutation on the columns of the parity check matrix of $K$.                                                                               □

**Example.**   (1) Let us find a parity check matrix of the code $K$ of Example (3) in 8.1. First, let $K^*$ be the equivalent code of Example (4) in 8.1:

$$\mathbf{G}^* = \begin{bmatrix} 1 & 0 & 0 & 1 & 0 & 0 \\ 0 & 1 & 0 & 0 & 0 & 1 \\ 0 & 0 & 1 & 0 & 1 & 0 \end{bmatrix}.$$

By the above proposition, the following is a parity check matrix of $K^*$:

$$\mathbf{H}^* = \begin{bmatrix} -1 & 0 & 0 & 1 & 0 & 0 \\ 0 & 0 & -1 & 0 & 1 & 0 \\ 0 & -1 & 0 & 0 & 0 & 1 \end{bmatrix} = \begin{bmatrix} 2 & 0 & 0 & 1 & 0 & 0 \\ 0 & 0 & 2 & 0 & 1 & 0 \\ 0 & 2 & 0 & 0 & 0 & 1 \end{bmatrix}.$$

We now perform the inverse permutation on the columns of $\mathbf{H}^*$ in order to get a parity check matrix of the original code $K$:

$$\mathbf{H} = \begin{bmatrix} 2 & 1 & 0 & 0 & 0 & 0 \\ 0 & 0 & 0 & 0 & 1 & 2 \\ 0 & 0 & 1 & 2 & 0 & 0 \end{bmatrix}.$$

**Definition.** *By the* dual code *of a linear code* $K$ *is meant the code* $K^\perp$ *of all words orthogonal to all code words of* $K$. *(That is, the dual code is just another name for the orthogonal complement, see 7.7)*

Observe that the generator matrix of a code $K$ is the parity check matrix of the dual code $K^\perp$ (and vice versa).

**Examples.**

(2) The dual of the even-parity code is the repetition code. In fact, the generator matrix of the latter is $[111\ldots1]$, and this is a parity check matrix of the former (Example 5.4).

(3) The dual of the Hamming $(7, 4)$-code of Example (1) in 5.5 is the $(7, 3)$-code with the following generator matrix:

$$\mathbf{G} = \begin{bmatrix} 0 & 0 & 0 & 1 & 1 & 1 & 1 \\ 0 & 1 & 1 & 0 & 0 & 1 & 1 \\ 1 & 0 & 1 & 0 & 1 & 0 & 1 \end{bmatrix}.$$

It has minimum weight 4. In fact, each row of **G** has even weight and thus each code word (a linear combination of the rows) also has even weight. The weight cannot be equal to 2 because we know that the parity check matrix of our code is the matrix **G** of Example (1) in 8.1. By inspection, we see that its rows are nonzero and pairwise distinct and thus (by Proposition 5.5), $d \geq 3$. Since $d$ is even, $d \geq 4$.

(4) Dual codes of binary Hamming codes are called *simplex codes*. Thus, for each $m = 2, 3, 4, \ldots$, we have a binary $(2^m - 1, m)$ simplex code.

**Remark.** We know that a linear code of minimum distance $d$ detects $d - 1$ errors and corrects less than $d/2$ errors (see 4.5). The minimum distance is equal to the minimum weight—the proof is the same as that of Proposition 5.3. Thus, a linear code

(a) detects $t$ errors if and only if its minimum weight is $\geq t + 1$,

(b) corrects $t$ errors if and only if its minimum weight is $\geq 2t + 1$.

We see that the theory of error-control codes is *not* just a linear algebra: the crucial question we ask is that of the minimum weight.

# 8.3 Syndrome

Recall from 5.3 that the difference between the received word **w** and the code word **v** is called the *error pattern* and is denoted by **e**:

$$\mathbf{e} = \mathbf{w} - \mathbf{v}.$$

We know only what we have received, and our task is to guess the error pattern, from which we then deduce what was sent: $\mathbf{v} = \mathbf{w} - \mathbf{e}$. Since we use the maximum likelihood decoding (4.4), we always look for the error pattern **e** of the smallest Hamming weight—this yields a code word **v**, which is the most likely.

An important piece of information about the error pattern which we can derive directly from the received word is the syndrome:

**Definition.** *Let $K$ be a linear code with a specified $m \times n$ parity check matrix* **H**. *By the* syndrome *of each word* **w** *of length $n$, we understand the word* $\mathbf{s} = s_1 s_2 \ldots s_m$ *defined by* $\mathbf{s}^{tr} = \mathbf{H}\mathbf{w}^{tr}$, *i.e.,*

$$\begin{bmatrix} s_1 \\ s_2 \\ \vdots \\ s_m \end{bmatrix} = \mathbf{H} \begin{bmatrix} w_1 \\ w_2 \\ \vdots \\ w_n \end{bmatrix}.$$

**Example.** In Example (1) of 5.5, we have used syndromes for decoding: each code word **w** has the syndrome **s** = 000, each word with the first bit corrupted has the syndrome **s** = 001, etc.

**Proposition.** *The error pattern has the same syndrome as the received word. That is, for each code word* **v** *and each (error-pattern) word* **e**, *the word* **w** = **v** + **e** *fulfils*

$$\mathbf{H}\mathbf{e}^{tr} = \mathbf{H}\mathbf{w}^{tr}.$$

**PROOF.** Since the code word **v** fulfils $\mathbf{H}\mathbf{v}^{tr} = \mathbf{0}^{tr}$, we have

$$
\begin{aligned}
\mathbf{H}\mathbf{w}^{tr} &= \mathbf{H}(\mathbf{v}^{tr} + \mathbf{e}^{tr}) \\
&= \mathbf{H}\mathbf{v}^{tr} + \mathbf{H}\mathbf{e}^{tr} \\
&= \mathbf{0}^{tr} + \mathbf{H}\mathbf{e}^{tr} \\
&= \mathbf{H}\mathbf{e}^{tr}.
\end{aligned}
$$

$\square$

**Remark.** No matter how trivial this proposition is, it forms the basis of most of the decoding techniques introduced below: We receive a word, find its syndrome, and try to find a word with a small Hamming weight having that syndrome.

## 8.4   Detection and Correction of Errors

So far we have just moved in the realm of linear algebra: a linear code is simply a linear space, the dual code is the orthogonal complement, etc. However, the theory of error-control codes is only interested in linear codes with good properties for error detection and error correction.

Recall that a code $K$ detects $t$ errors if and only if it has minimum weight larger than $t$. Thus, a "good" linear code is a linear space with a large minimum weight $d$ and, of course, a large number $k$ of information bits. Unfortunately, these two requirements are contradictory:

**Proposition.** *The minimum weight $d$ of a linear $(n, k)$-code satisfies*

$$d \leq n - k + 1.$$

**PROOF.**   I. Let $K$ be a systematic linear $(n, k)$-code. Then we can choose the first $k$ symbols in every code word arbitrarily. Let **v** be the code word obtained by choosing 1 followed by $k - 1$ zeros:

$$\mathbf{v} = 1000\ldots0v_{k+1}v_{k+2}\ldots v_n.$$

Then $\mathbf{v} \neq \mathbf{0}$ and the weight of **v** is at most $n - k + 1$. Thus, $d \leq n - k + 1$.

II. Let $K$ be an arbitrary linear code, and let $K'$ be an equivalent systematic linear code (see Proposition 8.1. Then $K$ and $K'$ have the same parameters $n$, $k$, and $d$. Thus, from I, we get the required inequality again. ☐

Concerning error correction, we know that a linear code corrects $t$ errors if and only if $d \geq 2t + 1$ (4.6). However, more can be said: in Chapter 6, we saw a thorough decoding technique based on cosets. Since every linear code $K$ is a subgroup of the additive group $F^n$, we can generalize (and simplify) the procedure of 6.3 as follows:

*Syndrome Decoding.* Let $K$ be a linear $(n, k)$-code. Let us fix a parity check matrix $\mathbf{H}$ with linearly independent rows (see in Corollary 8.2). For each word e of length $n$, we form the coset

$$e + K = \{\, e + v \mid v \text{ a code word}\,\},$$

which we interpret as the set of all possible received words $\mathbf{w} = e + v$ when a code word $v$ is sent and the channel noise adds the error pattern e. All words in the coset have the same syndrome (Proposition 8.3).

Conversely, for each syndrome, i.e., each word s of length $n - k$, we now want to choose a *coset leader*, i.e., a word e of the smallest Hamming weight has the syndrome s. That is, we solve the system

$$\mathbf{H}e^{\mathrm{tr}} = s^{\mathrm{tr}}$$

of linear equations (which has a solution since the rows of $\mathbf{H}$ are linearly independent, see Remark 7.6). We choose one of the solutions with the smallest Hamming weight and call it the coset leader of the coset of syndrome s. This leads to the following decoding procedure:

(a) When receiving a word $\mathbf{w}$, compute the syndrome s: $\mathbf{H}\mathbf{w}^{\mathrm{tr}} = s^{\mathrm{tr}}$.

(b) Find the coset leader e of the coset with syndrome s.

(c) Assume that the code word sent is $v = \mathbf{w} - e$.

In the binary case, this is a simplification of the decoding by a standard array (see 6.3). The decoding is correct if and only if the actual error pattern is one of the chosen coset leaders. (Prove it!)

**Examples**

(2) In Example (2) of 6.3, we introduced a binary code $K_5$ by a system of equations with the following matrix coefficients:

$$\mathbf{H} = \begin{bmatrix} 1 & 1 & 0 & 1 & 0 \\ 1 & 1 & 1 & 1 & 1 \end{bmatrix}.$$

Instead of the standard array of Figure 4 in 6.3, we can use syndrome decoding, see Figure 1.  Suppose we receive 11111 [see Example (3)

| Syndrome | Coset Leader |
|----------|--------------|
| 00       | 00000        |
| 11       | 10000        |
| 01       | 00001        |
| 10       | 10001        |

**Figure 1:** Choice of coset leaders

of 6.3]. We find the syndrome

$$\begin{bmatrix} 1 & 1 & 0 & 1 & 0 \\ 1 & 1 & 1 & 1 & 1 \end{bmatrix} \begin{bmatrix} 1 \\ 1 \\ 1 \\ 1 \\ 1 \end{bmatrix} = \begin{bmatrix} 1 \\ 1 \end{bmatrix}$$

and so we decide that the error pattern is $e = 10000$. Thus, the code word

$$v = w - e = 01111$$

has been sent.

(3) Let us construct a coset decoding for the code over the field $Z_3$ given by the following parity check matrix:

$$H = \begin{bmatrix} 1 & 0 & 2 & 1 & 0 \\ 0 & 1 & 2 & 1 & 2 \end{bmatrix}.$$

Syndromes are words of length 2; in the alphabet $Z_3$, this means nine words. For the syndrome 00, we choose the coset leader 00000. Next, we choose coset leaders of Hamming weight 1. For example, all the words with a single symbol 1 have pairwise different syndromes (see Figure 2), thus, we can choose them as coset leaders. The next word of Hamming weight 1 is 20000, and its syndrome is a new word; in contrast, 02000 has the same syndrome as 00001, etc. Thus, after 20000, we have to choose two coset leaders of Hamming weight 2. By choosing 10001 and 20002, we complete the list of all syndromes in Figure 2.

| Syndrome | Coset Leader |
|:--------:|:------------:|
| 00 | 00000 |
| 10 | 10000 |
| 01 | 01000 |
| 22 | 00100 |
| 11 | 00010 |
| 02 | 00001 |
| 20 | 20000 |
| 12 | 10001 |
| 21 | 20002 |

**Figure 2:** Choice of coset leaders

Suppose we send the code word 21122 and receive  11122.  The syndrome is

$$\begin{bmatrix} 1 & 0 & 2 & 1 & 0 \\ 0 & 1 & 2 & 1 & 2 \end{bmatrix} \begin{bmatrix} 1 \\ 1 \\ 1 \\ 2 \\ 2 \end{bmatrix} = \begin{bmatrix} 2 \\ 2 \end{bmatrix}.$$

thus, $e = 20000$, and we decode

$$v = w - e = 11122 - 20000 = 21122.$$

The decoding is correct beacause the error pattern made was one of the chosen coset leaders.

# 8.5   Extended Codes and Other Modifications

It is often impossible to use a good code simply because of some restrictions imposed, e.g., on the code word length or on the information rate, which have to be respected.  Here we introduce some simple modifications of linear codes: extension, puncturing, augmentation, and expurgation.

**Definition.** *By the* extension *of a linear* $(n, k)$-*code* $K$ *is meant the linear* $(n + 1, k)$-*code* $K^*$ *obtained from* $K$ *by concatenating to each code word* $\mathbf{x} = x_1 x_2 \ldots x_n$ *a new symbol* $x_{n+1}$ *in such a way that* $\sum_{i=1}^{n+1} x_i = 0$.

**Remark.**  (1) If the code $K$ has a parity check matrix $\mathbf{H}$, then the extended code $K^*$ has the following parity check matrix

$$
\mathbf{H}^* = \left[\begin{array}{ccc|c}
 & & & 0 \\
 & \mathbf{H} & & 0 \\
 & & & \vdots \\
 & & & 0 \\
\hline
1 \quad 1 \quad 1 & \cdots & 1 \quad 1 & 1
\end{array}\right].
$$

In fact, the last line expresses the equation $\sum_{i=1}^{n+1} x_i = 1$, and we keep all the parity equations expressed by the rows of $\mathbf{H}$ (without the unknown $x_{n+1}$; thus, the last entry of these rows of $\mathbf{H}^*$ is 0).

### Examples

(1) The extended Hamming code is the $(2^m, 2^m - m - 1)$-code of all words $x_1 x_2 \ldots x_{2^m}$ of even parity whose first $2^m - 1$ symbols form a code word in the Hamming code.

For example, by extending the Hamming $(7, 4)$-code of Example (1) in 5.5, we obtain the $(8, 4)$-code $K^*$ with the following parity check matrix:

$$
\mathbf{H}^* = \left[\begin{array}{ccccccc|c}
0 & 0 & 0 & 1 & 1 & 1 & 1 & 0 \\
0 & 1 & 1 & 0 & 0 & 1 & 1 & 0 \\
1 & 0 & 1 & 0 & 1 & 0 & 1 & 0 \\
\hline
1 & 1 & 1 & 1 & 1 & 1 & 1 & 1
\end{array}\right].
$$

By inspecting Figure 6 of 5.5 [containing all the code words of the Hamming $(7, 4)$-code], we conclude that every row of the above matrix $\mathbf{H}^*$ is a code word of the extended Hamming code $K^*$. Since $\mathbf{H}^*$ has rank 4 (and $k = 4$), it follows that $\mathbf{H}^*$ is also a generator matrix of $K^*$. This means that the extended Hamming $(8, 4)$-code is self-dual.

(2) The linear space $\mathbf{Z}_2^n$ is itself an (uninteresting) code of length $n$. Its extension is the even parity code of length $n + 1$.

**Remark.**  (2) If a binary linear code $K$ has an odd minimum weight $d$, then the extended code has the minimum weight $d + 1$. In fact, let $\mathbf{x}$ be a code word of $K$ of the Hamming weight $d$. Then $\sum_{i=1}^{n} x_i = 1$, thus, $x_{n+1} = 1$. The word $x_1 x_2 \ldots x_n 1$ is a code word of the extended code of the minimum weight (which is $d + 1$).

For example, the extended Hamming codes have minimum distance 4. The importance of these codes will be seen in the next section.

**Definition.** *Let $K$ be a linear code of length $n$.*

(1) *By the* puncturing *of $K$ is meant the linear code $\overline{K}$ of length $n - 1$ obtained by deleting the last symbol from each code word.*

(2) *By the* augmentation *of $K$ is meant the expansion of $K$ by the all-ones code word, i.e., the code of all words*

$$v_1 v_2 \ldots v_n \qquad and \qquad (111 \ldots 11) + (v_1 v_2 \ldots v_n),$$

*where $v_1 v_2 \ldots v_n$ is a code word of $K$.*

(3) *By the* expurgation *of $K$ is meant the code whose code words are precisely the even-weight code words of $K$.*

**Remarks.**

(3) Puncturing is the reverse process to extension. Thus, the puncturing of the extended Hamming $(8, 4)$-code is the Hamming $(7, 4)$-code.

(4) Augmenting a binary code means that we get new code words by reversing, in each code word, 0's to 1's and vice versa.

**Proposition.** *Every linear code either has all code words of even weight or it has the same number of even-weight and odd-weight code words.*

PROOF. Let $K$ be a linear code with a word $v_1$ of odd weight. Let $v_1$, $\ldots$, $v_r$ be all code words of $K$. Then $v_1 + v_1$, $v_1 + v_2$, $\ldots$, $v_1 + v_r$ are code words (by linearity) which are pairwise distinct (since $v_1 + v_i = v_1 + v_j$ implies $v_i = v_j$). In other words, these are all the code words of $K$. Now whenever a code word $v_i$ has even weight, then $v_1 + v_i$ has an odd weight, and vice versa. Consequently, the addition of $v_1$ is a binary correspondence between all even-weight code words and all odd-weight ones, which proves the proposition. $\qquad\square$

**Corollary.** *The expurgation of a linear code $K$ is either $K$ itself or a code of half the size of $K$.*

**Example.** (3) By expurgating the Hamming $(7, 4)$-code in Figure 6 in 5.5, we obtain the code in Figure 3. Conversely, the Hamming $(7, 4)$-code is the augmentation of the code in Figure 3.

|              |              |
|--------------|--------------|
| 0000000      | 0110011      |
| 0001111      | 1101001      |
| 1100110      | 1011010      |
| 1010101      | 0111100      |

**Figure 3:** Expurgated Hamming $(7, 4)$-code

## 8.6   Simultaneous Correction and Detection of Errors

Let us start with an example. The Hamming $(7, 4)$-code has minimum distance $d = 3$ (see 5.5); thus, it can either correct single errors or detect double errors. However, it cannot do both simultaneously. In other words, whenever the Hamming code is used as an error-correcting code, double errors escape undetected. Example: we send 0000000 and receive 1010000. The syndrome is 010, i.e., we correct the second bit, and assume (incorrectly) that 1110000 has been sent. However, it is frequently required that a code correct single errors and detect double errors simultaneously. This means, of course, that each code word $\mathbf{v}$ has the following property: whenever a word $\mathbf{w}$ (the word received) has Hamming distance $d(\mathbf{w}, \mathbf{v}) \leq 2$ from $\mathbf{v}$, then the Hamming distance of $\mathbf{w}$ to all other code words is greater than 1. In fact, we then proceed as follows when receiving a word $\mathbf{w}$: we find the nearest code word $\mathbf{v}$; if $d(\mathbf{v}, \mathbf{w}) \leq 1$, then we correct $\mathbf{w}$ to $\mathbf{v}$, whereas if $d(\mathbf{v}, \mathbf{w}) > 1$, we announce a large error (i.e., double error, or worse). More in general:

**Definition.** *A block code $K$ is said to* correct $t$ errors *and* detect $s$ errors *simultaneously provided that every code word $\mathbf{v}$ has the following property: each word $\mathbf{w}$ of Hamming distance $d(\mathbf{w}, \mathbf{v}) \leq s$ has Hamming distance greater than $t$ from all code words different from $\mathbf{v}$.*

**Remark.** If a code $K$ has the property of this definition, then the simultaneous correction and detection are performed as follows: when receiving a word $\mathbf{w}$, find the nearest code word $\mathbf{v}$ (in the sense of Hamming distance). If $d(\mathbf{w}, \mathbf{v}) \leq t$, then correct the received word to the code word $\mathbf{v}$. If $d(\mathbf{w}, \mathbf{v}) > t$, announce that at least $s$ symbols are incorrect.

This really works: if at most $t$ symbols have been corrupted, we know that $d(\mathbf{w}, \mathbf{v}) \leq t$, while $d(\mathbf{w}, \mathbf{v}') > t$ for any code word $\mathbf{v}' \neq \mathbf{v}$ (see the definition). Thus, we announce nothing and correctly guess the sent word $\mathbf{v}$. If more than $t$ symbols, but no more than $s$ symbols, have been corrupted, we know that $d(\mathbf{w}, \mathbf{v}) > t$, and so our announcement of a "big error" warns the user correctly.

**Proposition.** *A code corrects $t$ errors and detects $s$ errors simultaneously if and only if its minimum distance fulfils*

$$d \geq t + s + 1.$$

**PROOF.** I. Suppose $d \geq t + s + 1$. Let $\mathbf{v}$ be a code word and $\mathbf{w}$ be a word with $d(\mathbf{v}, \mathbf{w}) \leq s$. For every code word $\mathbf{v}' \neq \mathbf{v}$, we have $d(\mathbf{v}, \mathbf{v}') \geq d \geq t + s + 1$. Thus, from the triangle inequality (4.4)

$$d(\mathbf{v}, \mathbf{w}) + d(\mathbf{w}, \mathbf{v}') \geq d(\mathbf{v}, \mathbf{v}') \geq t + s + 1$$

we conclude

$$d(\mathbf{w}, \mathbf{v}') \geq t + s + 1 - d(\mathbf{v}, \mathbf{w}) \geq t + s + 1 - s = t + 1.$$

Therefore, the condition of the above definition is satisfied.

II. Suppose $d < t + s + 1$. Let $\mathbf{v}$ and $\mathbf{v}'$ be two different code words of Hamming distance $d(\mathbf{v}, \mathbf{v}') = d \leq t + s$. Let $\mathbf{w}$ be the word obtained from $\mathbf{v}$ by changing the first $s$ symbols in which it differs from the word $\mathbf{v}'$ to their values in $\mathbf{v}'$. Then $d(\mathbf{v}, \mathbf{w}) = s$ and

$$d(\mathbf{v}', \mathbf{w}) \leq t + s - s = t,$$

which contradicts the condition of the definition above. $\qquad\square$

### Examples

(1) Extended Hamming codes correct single errors and detect double errors simultaneously. The algorithm is simple: receiving a word $w_1 \dots w_n$ ($n = 2^m$), compute the syndrome $s$ of the shortened word $w_1 \dots w_{n-1}$ using the parity check matrix of the Hamming code.

    (a) If $s = 0$, then either we received a code word or we received a word of odd parity, in which case $w_n$ must be corrected.

    (b) If $s \neq 0$, then in case $\mathbf{w}$ has even parity, announce that at least two bits are corrupted, and in case of odd parity, correct the $i$th bit $w_i$, where $i$ has the binary expansion $s$.

(2) The repetition code of length 7 can either

> correct 3 errors, or
> detect 6 errors, or
> correct 2 errors and detect 4 errors simultaneously.

## 8.7   MacWilliams Identity

We have seen in 5.6 how the error-detection probability of a binary code can be computed from the weight enumerator

$$A(x) = \sum_{i=0}^{n} A_i x^i,$$

where $A_i$ is the number of code words of Hamming weight $i$.  We now prove a surprising result which makes it possible to compute the weight enumerator $A_{K^\perp}(x)$ of the dual $K^\perp$ of a linear code directly from the weight enumerator $A_K(x)$ of $K$:

**Theorem.** *For each linear* $(n, k)$-*code the following* MacWilliams identity *holds:*

$$A_{K^\perp}(x) = \frac{(1+x)^n}{2^k} A_K \left( \frac{1-x}{1+x} \right). \tag{8.7.1}$$

**Remark.** Some authors use a different concept of weight enumerator, viz., the following polynomial of two indeterminates:

$$B(x, y) = \sum_{i=0}^{n} A_i x^i y^{n-i}.$$

In this notation, the MacWilliams identity is nicer:

$$B_{K^\perp}(x, y) = \frac{1}{2^k} B_K(y - x, y + x). \tag{8.7.2}$$

[Since $A(x) = B(x, 1)$ and, conversely, $B(x, y) = y^n A\left(\frac{x}{y}\right)$, it is easy to derive (8.7.1) from (8.7.2), and vice versa.]

**PROOF of Theorem.** I. We first show that for each word $\mathbf{w}$ of length $n$, the scalar products $\mathbf{v} \cdot \mathbf{w}$ with all code words $\mathbf{v}$ of $K$ have the following property:

$$\frac{1}{2^k} \sum_{\mathbf{v} \in K} (-1)^{\mathbf{v} \cdot \mathbf{w}} = \begin{cases} 1 & \text{if } \mathbf{w} \text{ lies in } K^\perp, \\ 0 & \text{else.} \end{cases}$$

The case of $\mathbf{w}$ in $K^{\perp}$ is clear: for each code word $\mathbf{v}$ of $K$, we have $(-1)^{\mathbf{v} \cdot \mathbf{w}} = (-1)^0 = 1$, thus, the above sum is equal to the number of code words of $K$, which is $2^k$.

Suppose $\mathbf{w}$ does not lie in $K^{\perp}$, i.e., some code word $\mathbf{v}_0$ of $K$ fulfils $\mathbf{v}_0 \cdot \mathbf{w} = 1$. Then we will show that the number of all code words of $K$ orthogonal to $\mathbf{w}$ is equal to the number of those nonorthogonal to $\mathbf{w}$—thus, the above sum is 0. Let $\mathbf{v}_1, \ldots, \mathbf{v}_r$ be precisely all the code words of $K$ orthogonal to $\mathbf{w}$. Then we claim that $\mathbf{v}_1 + \mathbf{v}_0, \ldots, \mathbf{v}_r + \mathbf{v}_0$ are precisely all the code words which are not orthogonal to $\mathbf{w}$:

(a) for each $i = 1, \ldots, r$, we have $(\mathbf{v}_i + \mathbf{v}_0) \cdot \mathbf{w} = \mathbf{v}_i \cdot \mathbf{w} + \mathbf{v}_0 \cdot \mathbf{w} = 0 + 1 = 1$;

(b) whenever a code word $\mathbf{v}$ of $K$ fulfils $\mathbf{v} \cdot \mathbf{w} = 1$, then $\mathbf{v} - \mathbf{v}_0$ is a code word orthogonal to $\mathbf{w}$, and, thus, $\mathbf{v} - \mathbf{v}_0 = \mathbf{v}_i$ for (precisely one) $i$.

II. We are going to verify (8.7.2). The weight enumerator $B(x, y)$ can be expressed by means of the Hamming weight $|\mathbf{v}|$ of code words as follows:

$$B_K(x, y) = \sum_{i=0}^{n} A_i x^i y^{n-i} = \sum_{\mathbf{v} \in K} x^{|\mathbf{v}|} y^{n-|\mathbf{v}|}.$$

Consequently, the right-hand side of the MacWilliams identity is

$$B_K(y - x, y + x) = \sum_{\mathbf{v} \in K} (y - x)^{|\mathbf{v}|} (x + y)^{n-|\mathbf{v}|}$$

$$= \sum_{\mathbf{v} \in K} \prod_{i=1}^{n} [y + (-1)^{v_i} x].$$

Analogously, the left-hand side can be expressed as

$$B_{K^{\perp}}(x, y) = \sum_{\mathbf{w} \in K^{\perp}} x^{|\mathbf{w}|} y^{n-|\mathbf{w}|}.$$

Using I, we can rewrite the last sum as follows:

$$B_{K^{\perp}}(x, y) = \sum_{\mathbf{w} \in \mathbb{Z}_2^n} \left[ \frac{1}{2^k} \sum_{\mathbf{v} \in K} (-1)^{\mathbf{v} \cdot \mathbf{w}} \right] x^{|\mathbf{w}|} y^{n-|\mathbf{w}|}.$$

In fact, the expression in the brackets is 0 for all words $\mathbf{w}$ which do not lie in $K^{\perp}$. Thus,

$$B_{K^{\perp}}(x, y) = \frac{1}{2^k} \sum_{\mathbf{v} \in K} \sum_{\mathbf{w} \in \mathbb{Z}_2^n} (-1)^{\mathbf{v} \cdot \mathbf{w}} x^{|\mathbf{w}|} y^{n-|\mathbf{w}|}.$$

Now, the inner sum ranges over all binary words $\mathbf{w}$. We can arrange the summands by the Hamming weight of $\mathbf{w}$: for $\mathbf{w} = 0$, the summand is $y^n$; for the $n$ words $\mathbf{w}$ of weight 1, we get $[(-1)^{v_1} + (-1)^{v_2} + \cdots + (-1)^{v_n}]xy^n$, etc.; finally, for the weight $n$, we get $[(-1)^{v_1} + \cdots + (-1)^{v_n}]x^n$. The sum of all these summands $\sum [(-1)^{v_{i_1}} + \cdots + (-1)^{v_{i_k}}]x^k y^{n-k}$ is easily seen to be equal to $[y + (-1)^{v_1}x][y + (-1)^{v_2}x] \cdots [y + (-1)^{v_n}x] = \prod_{i=1}^{n}[y + (-1)^{v_i}x]$. Thus,

$$B_{K^\perp}(x,y) = \frac{1}{2^k} \sum_{v \in K} \prod_{i=1}^{n} [y + (-1)^{v_i}x] = \frac{1}{2^k} B_K(y - x, y + x).$$

This proves (8.7.2), and (8.7.1) follows. $\qquad\qquad\qquad\qquad\qquad\qquad\qquad$ □

**Examples**

(1) Let us find the weight enumerator of the even-parity code $K$ of even length $n$. The dual code $K^\perp$ is the repetition code [Example (2) of 8.2] and its weight enumerator is, of course,

$$A_{K^\perp}(x) = 1 + x^n.$$

From the MacWilliams identity,

$$\begin{aligned}
A_K(x) &= \frac{(1+x)^n}{2}\left[1 + \left(\frac{1-x}{1+x}\right)^n\right] = \frac{(1+x)^n + (1-x)^n}{2}. \\
&= 1 + \binom{n}{2}x^2 + \binom{n}{4}x^4 + \cdots + x^n.
\end{aligned}$$

(2) The weight enumerator of the Hamming $(7, 4)$-code $K$ is

$$A_K(x) = 1 + 7x^3 + 7x^4 + x^7$$

[Example (2) in 5.6]. The dual code has the weight enumerator

$$A_{K^\perp}(x) = \frac{(1+x)^7}{2^4}\left[1 + 7\left(\frac{1-x}{1+x}\right)^3 + 7\left(\frac{1-x}{1+x}\right)^4 + \left(\frac{1-x}{1+x}\right)^7\right].$$

It easy to see that this expression can be simplified to

$$A_{K^\perp}(x) = 1 + 7x^4.$$

Thus, the dual code [Example (3) of 8.2] has the remarkable property that all nonzero code words have Hamming weight 4.

# Exercises

**8A**  A linear code over $\mathbf{Z}_5$ has the following generator matrix:

$$\mathbf{G} = \begin{bmatrix} 1 & 2 & 3 & 1 & 2 \\ 2 & 2 & 4 & 1 & 0 \\ 1 & 1 & 2 & 2 & 1 \end{bmatrix}.$$

Find the parity check matrix.

**8B**  Perform 8A in $\mathbf{Z}_7$.

**8C**  Find out whether or not the following binary linear code is systematic:

$$\mathbf{G} = \begin{bmatrix} 1 & 1 & 0 & 0 & 0 & 0 \\ 0 & 0 & 1 & 1 & 1 & 1 \\ 0 & 0 & 0 & 0 & 1 & 1 \end{bmatrix}.$$

If not, find a systematic equivalent code.

**8D**  Encode the information bits 101 in both of the codes of Exercise 8C.

**8E**  Find a generator matrix of a binary code with the following parity check matrix:

$$\mathbf{H} = \begin{bmatrix} 1 & 0 & 1 & 1 & 0 & 0 & 0 \\ 1 & 1 & 1 & 0 & 1 & 0 & 0 \\ 1 & 1 & 0 & 0 & 0 & 1 & 0 \\ 0 & 0 & 1 & 0 & 0 & 0 & 1 \end{bmatrix}.$$

**8F**  Prove the converse of Proposition 8.2: whenever a linear code has a parity check matrix $\mathbf{H} = \begin{bmatrix} \mathbf{A} \,|\, \mathbf{I}' \end{bmatrix}$, where $\mathbf{I}'$ is an identity matrix, then $\mathbf{G} = \begin{bmatrix} \mathbf{I} \,|\, -\mathbf{A} \end{bmatrix}$ is a generator matrix. Which linear codes have such a parity check matrix?

**8G**  Which extended Hamming codes are self-dual?

**8H**  Describe the dual of the binary $(6, 3)$-code described by the following equations:

$$\begin{aligned} x_1 &= x_4, \\ x_2 &= x_5, \\ x_3 &= x_6. \end{aligned}$$

**8I**    Construct a table of syndrome decoding for

  (1)  the repetition code of length 7,

  (2)  the Hamming code of length 7,

  (3)  the code of 8H,

  (4)  the code over $\mathbf{Z}_3$ with the following generator matrix:

$$\mathbf{G} = \begin{bmatrix} 1 & 0 & 0 & 2 & 2 \\ 0 & 1 & 0 & 0 & 1 \\ 0 & 0 & 1 & 1 & 0 \end{bmatrix}.$$

**8J**    Describe the extension and the puncturing of the code in 8H.

**8K**    Describe the augmentation and the expurgation of the following binary code:

$$\mathbf{G} = \begin{bmatrix} 1 & 1 & 1 & 0 & 0 \\ 0 & 0 & 1 & 1 & 1 \\ 1 & 1 & 1 & 1 & 0 \end{bmatrix}.$$

**8L**    *Nonbinary Hamming codes.*  (1) Generalize Proposition 5.5 to the following: a linear code corrects single errors if and only if every parity check matrix has the property that no column is a scalar multiple of a different column.

    By a *Hamming code* is meant a code with a parity check matrix $\mathbf{H}$ such that

  (a)  no column of $\mathbf{H}$ is a scalar multiple of a different column,

  (b)  $\mathbf{H}$ is maximal w.r.t. (a), i.e., every word of length $m$ is a scalar multiple of some column of $\mathbf{H}$.

Prove that condition (a) can be safeguarded by choosing as columns all words with the leading term (i.e., the first nonzero term) equal to 1.

    (2) Verify that the following is a parity check matrix of a Hamming code over $\mathbf{Z}_3$:

$$\mathbf{H} = \begin{bmatrix} 0 & 1 & 1 & 1 \\ 1 & 0 & 1 & 2 \end{bmatrix}.$$

Find a table of syndrome decoding that code.

(3) Find a parity check matrix of $m = 3$ rows for a Hamming code over $\mathbf{Z}_3$.

(4) Prove that for each $m$, there is a Hamming $\left(\frac{3^m-1}{2}, \frac{3^m-1}{2} - m\right)$-code over $\mathbf{Z}_3$.

(5) Generalize (4) to any finite field.

**8M** Describe how the repetition code of length 7 corrects two errors and detects four errors simultaneously. What number of errors can it detect while correcting single errors?

**8N** Find the minimum distance of the $(15, 4)$-simplex code [Example (4) of 8.2].

**8O** Prove that syndrome decoding is optimal in the sense that no other decoding of a linear code $K$ can correct a larger collection of error patterns. More precisely: suppose a decoding $d$ of $K$ is given [i.e., a rule assigning to each word $\mathbf{w}$ of the considered length a code word $d(\mathbf{w})$] which corrects all error patterns corrected by a syndrome decoding [i.e., for each code word $\mathbf{v}$ and each of the chosen coset leaders $\mathbf{e}$, we have $d(\mathbf{v} + \mathbf{e}) = \mathbf{v}$]. Then $d$ does not correct any other error pattern [i.e., whenever $\mathbf{e}$ is not a coset leader, then there is a code word $\mathbf{v}$ with $d(\mathbf{v} + \mathbf{e}) \neq \mathbf{v}$].

## Notes

The theory of linear error-correcting codes was first restricted to the binary case (as in Chapter 5), but the extension of all the basic ideas to any finite field is rather obvious.

The identity of 8.5 is due to MacWilliams (1963).

# Chapter 9

# Reed-Muller Codes: Weak Codes with Easy Decoding

We now introduce an interesting class of multiple-error-correcting binary codes whose prime importance lies in an easily implementable decoding technique: the Reed-Muller codes. Their parameters are listed in Figure 1.

| | |
|---|---|
| Length: | $n = 2^m$ |
| Information symbols: | $k = \sum_{i=0}^{r} \binom{n}{i}$ |
| Minimum distance: | $d = 2^{m-r}$ |
| Error-control capacity: | Corrects $2^{m-r-1} - 1$ errors by a technique based on majority logic which is easy to implement |

**Figure 1:** Parameters of the Reed-Muller code $\mathcal{R}(r, m)$

There are closely related punctured Reed-Muller codes, the parameters of which are presented in Figure 2.

One of these codes, the Reed-Muller code $\mathcal{R}(1, 5)$, was used by the 1969 Mariner to transmit pictures of the Moon. The code $\mathcal{R}(1, 5)$ has

137

| Length: | $n = 2^m - 1$ |
|---|---|
| Information symbols: | $k = \sum_{i=0}^{r} \binom{n}{i}$ |
| Minimum distance: | $d = 2^{m-r} - 1$ |
| Error-control capacity: | Corrects errors as $\mathcal{R}(r, m)$ does, but has a better information rate and is a cyclic code |

**Figure 2:** Parameters of the punctured Reed-Muller code

length 32 with 6 information bits and it corrects 7 errors. Each dot of the transmited picture was assigned one of $2^6 = 64$ degrees of greyness, and these 6 information bits were then encoded into a word of length 32.

We introduce Reed-Muller codes by means of Boolean polynomials, which we first discuss in some detail. To understand the decoding of Reed-Muller codes, it is more convenient to work with finite geometries, where code words become characteristic functions of flats.

## 9.1  Boolean Functions

Reed-Muller codes are best described by means of Boolean polynomials. We first show how binary words translate to Boolean functions and Boolean polynomials. Then we introduce the codes and present their basic properties. However, the decoding is better explained in a different, geometrical, presentation of binary words, which we introduce later.

**Definition.** *A Boolean function* $\mathbf{f} = f(x_0, x_1, \ldots, x_{m-1})$ *of m variables is a rule which assigns to each m-tuple* $(x_0, x_1, \ldots, x_{m-1})$ *of 0's and 1's a value* $f(x_0, x_1, \ldots, x_{m-1}) = 0$ *or 1. In other words,* $\mathbf{f}$ *is a function from* $\mathbf{Z}_2^m$ *to* $\mathbf{Z}_2$.

*Truth Table.* A simple way of presenting a Boolean function is to list all of its values. That is, we write down all the $2^m$ combinations of the values of all variables $x_0, x_1, \ldots, x_{m-1}$, and then to each combination, we assign the value $f(x_0, x_1, \ldots, x_{m-1})$. For notational convenience, we proceed in such a way that the columns form binary expansions of the numbers 0, 1, 2, ... (from the first row downward). This presentation is called the truth table of the function f.

An example of a truth table of a Boolean function of three variables is presented in Figure 3. Observe that a truth table of a Boolean function

| $x_0$ | 0 | 1 | 0 | 1 | 0 | 1 | 0 | 1 |
|-------|---|---|---|---|---|---|---|---|
| $x_1$ | 0 | 0 | 1 | 1 | 0 | 0 | 1 | 1 |
| $x_2$ | 0 | 0 | 0 | 0 | 1 | 1 | 1 | 1 |
| **f** | 0 | 1 | 1 | 0 | 1 | 1 | 1 | 0 |

**Figure 3:** An example of a Boolean function of three variables

of three variables yields a binary word of length 8, and, conversely, every binary word of length 8 is the truth table of some Boolean function. We thus can (and will) identify Boolean function of three variables with binary words of length 8. For example, the word 01101110 is the same as the Boolean function in Figure 3.

More in general, every binary word **f** of length $2^m$ is considered as a Boolean function of $m$ variables. If we write the indices starting with zero, then the binary word

$$\mathbf{f} = f_0 f_1 \ldots f_{2^m - 1}$$

is the Boolean function with

$$\mathbf{f}(0, 0, \ldots, 0, 0) = f_0,$$
$$\mathbf{f}(0, 0, \ldots, 0, 1) = f_1,$$
$$\mathbf{f}(0, 0, \ldots, 1, 0) = f_2,$$
$$\vdots$$
$$\mathbf{f}(1, 1, \ldots, 1, 1) = f_{2^m - 1}.$$

In general,

$$f_i = \mathbf{f}(i_{m-1}, \ldots, i_1, i_0),$$

where the number $i$ has the binary expansion $i_{m-1} \ldots i_1 i_0$ (i.e., $i = \sum_{k=0}^{2^m - 1} i_k 2^k$).

**Examples**

(1) There are two constant Boolean functions

$$\mathbf{1} = 11 \ldots 11 \quad \text{and} \quad \mathbf{0} = 00 \ldots 00.$$

(2) Every variable is a Boolean function. For example, $x_0$ is the Boolean function which assigns to each $m$-tuple $(x_0, x_1, \ldots, x_{m-1})$ the first co-ordinate value $x_0$. Thus, the value is 0 for all even numbers and 1 for all odd ones:

$$\mathbf{x_0} = 0101010\ldots1.$$

(See Figure 3 for the case $m = 3$.) In general,

$x_i$ is the binary word whose $k$th position equals 1 precisely when the binary expansion of $k$ has 1 in the $i$th position $(k = 0, 1, \ldots, 2^m - 1)$.

This follows from the way we are writing the truth tables. For example, $\mathbf{x_1} = 00110011\ldots0011$, and

$$\mathbf{x_{m-1}} = \underbrace{000\ldots00}_{2^{m-1}}\underbrace{111\ldots11}_{2^{m-1}}.$$

For $m = 4$, the four variables are shown on Figure 4.

| | | | | | | | | | | | | | | | | |
|-------|---|---|---|---|---|---|---|---|---|---|---|---|---|---|---|---|
| $x_0$ | 0 | 1 | 0 | 1 | 0 | 1 | 0 | 1 | 0 | 1 | 0 | 1 | 0 | 1 | 0 | 1 |
| $x_1$ | 0 | 0 | 1 | 1 | 0 | 0 | 1 | 1 | 0 | 0 | 1 | 1 | 0 | 0 | 1 | 1 |
| $x_2$ | 0 | 0 | 0 | 0 | 1 | 1 | 1 | 1 | 0 | 0 | 0 | 0 | 1 | 1 | 1 | 1 |
| $x_3$ | 0 | 0 | 0 | 0 | 0 | 0 | 0 | 0 | 1 | 1 | 1 | 1 | 1 | 1 | 1 | 1 |

**Figure 4:** The four variables as Boolean functions ($m = 4$)

## 9.2 Boolean Polynomials

We now introduce the basic logical operations on Boolean functions of $m$ variables. If f is a Boolean function, we denote by $f_i$ $(i = 0, 1, \ldots, 2^m - 1)$ the $i$th position of its truth table.

*The logical sum* (also called "exclusive or") of Boolean functions **f** and **g** is the function

$$\mathbf{f + g},$$

whose value is 1 precisely when either **f** or **g** has value 1, but not both. That is, the $i$th coordinate of $\mathbf{f + g}$ is $f_i + g_i$ (addition modulo 2). The logical sum is nothing new: it is just the usual addition in the linear space $\mathbf{Z}_2^n$, where $n = 2^m$.

*The logical product* (also called "and") of Boolean functions **f** and **g** is the function

$$\mathbf{fg},$$

whose value is 1 precisely when both **f** and **g** have value 1. That is, the *i*th coordinate of **fg** is $f_i g_i$ (multiplication modulo 2). This is a new operation imposed on $\mathbf{Z}_2^n$ for $n = 2^m$, viz., the coordinatewise multiplication

$$(f_{2^m-1} \ldots f_1 f_0)(g_{2^m-1} \ldots g_1 g_0) = (f_{2^m-1} g_{2^m-1}) \cdots (f_1 g_1)(f_0 g_0).$$

**Remarks**

(1) Observe that the logical product fulfils

$$\mathbf{f\,f = f}.$$

Thus, no exponents higher then 1 are ever needed.

(2) There are other natural operations which, however, can be expressed by means of the logical sum and logical product. For example, the *negation* $\overline{\mathbf{f}}$ (which has value 1 precisely when **f** has value 0) is simply expressed as a sum with the constant function $1 = 11 \ldots 11$:

$$\overline{\mathbf{f}} = 1 + \mathbf{f}.$$

The operation "or" (**f** or **g**), whose value is 1 precisely when **f** or **g** (or both) have value 1, can be expressed as

$$\mathbf{f} \text{ or } \mathbf{g} = \mathbf{f} + \mathbf{g} + \mathbf{fg}.$$

(3) We have seen that **1** and each variable $\mathbf{x}_i$ are Boolean functions. Other Boolean functions can be obtained by addition and multiplication. For example: $\mathbf{x}_i \mathbf{x}_j$, $1 + \mathbf{x}_i + \mathbf{x}_j$, etc. These are called Boolean polynomials:

**Definition.** *By a Boolean polynomial in m indeterminates is meant a sum of (some of the) following Boolean functions:* $1, \mathbf{x}_i, \mathbf{x}_i \mathbf{x}_j, \ldots, \mathbf{x}_{i_1} \mathbf{x}_{i_2} \ldots \mathbf{x}_{i_k}$ *(where the indices range over* $0, 1, \ldots, m-1$*). The zero function* **0** *is called a Boolean polynomial of degree* $-1$*, the function* **1** *is called a Boolean polynomial of degree* 0*, and a Boolean polynomial* **f** *has degree* $k \geq 1$ *provided that k is a maximum number of factors in a summand of* **f** *(i.e.,* **f** *has a summand* $\mathbf{x}_{i_1} \mathbf{x}_{i_2} \ldots \mathbf{x}_{i_k}$*, and no summand has more than k factors).*

**Examples**

(1) The Boolean polynomial $1 + \mathbf{x}_1 \mathbf{x}_2$ of three indeterminates has degree 2. It is the negation of the polynomial

$$\mathbf{x}_1 \mathbf{x}_2 = (01010101)(00110011) = 00010001.$$

Thus,

$$1 + x_1 x_2 = 11101110.$$

The Boolean polynomial $1 + x_1 x_2$ considered as a function of four indeterminates is the word

$$1110111011101110.$$

(2) The polynomial $x_i x_j$ $(i \neq j)$ is the binary word whose $k$th position is 1 precisely when $k$ has 1 in positions $i$ and $j$. The number of such $k$'s is $2^{m-2}$ (because we can choose the $m - 2$ remaining positions of $k$ arbitrarily). Thus, the binary word $x_i x_j$ has Hamming weight $2^{m-2}$.

Analogously, $x_i x_j x_k$ has Hamming weight $2^{m-3}$, and, in general,

$$x_{i_1} x_{i_2} \ldots x_{i_s} \text{ has Hamming weight } 2^{m-s}$$

for arbitrary pairwise distinct indices $i_1, \ldots, i_s$ chosen between 0 and $m - 1$.

**Remark.** (4) A Boolean polynomial never uses exponents, simply because $x_i^2 = x_i$. Thus, there are just four Boolean polynomial of one indeterminate $x$, viz.: $x$, $x + 1$, 0, and 1.

We will later introduce (non-Boolean) polynomials of one indeterminate—those are fundamentally different from the Boolean polynomials since all the information is checked by the exponents.

*Translation between words and Boolean polynomials.* Every Boolean polynomial of $m$-variables yields a binary word of length $2^m$: for a single indeterminate, see Example (2) in 9.1, and, further, we perform the required additions and multiplications.

Conversely, every binary word $\mathbf{f} = f_0 f_1 \ldots f_{2^m - 1}$ can be translated into a Boolean polynomial as follows. First, observe that the last indeterminate $x_{m-1}$ is the word

$$x_{m-1} = 00 \ldots 0011 \ldots 11,$$

whose first half is the constant function $\mathbf{0}$ and the other half is the constant function $\mathbf{1}$ (now both considered in $m - 1$ indeterminates, i.e., in the length $\frac{1}{2} 2^m = 2^{m-1}$). As a consequence, we see that for each Boolean function $f(x_0, x_1, \ldots, x_{m-1})$, the first half of the corresponding word $\mathbf{f}$ is $f(x_0, x_1, \ldots, x_{m-2}, 0)$ and the other half is $f(x_0, x_1, \ldots, x_{m-2}, 1)$ (both considered as functions of $m - 1$ indeterminates).

The following trivial proposition, applied recursively, then yields an algorithm for converting a word into a Boolean polynomial:

**Proposition.** *Every Boolean function* **f** *of m variables can be expressed* [*by means of the two halves* $f(x_0, \ldots, x_{m-2}, 0)$ *and* $f(x_0, \ldots, x_{m-2}, 1)$ *of the corresponding binary word*] *as follows:*

$$f(x_0, \ldots, x_{m-2}, x_{m-1}) =$$
$$f(x_0, \ldots, x_{m-2}, 0) + [f(x_0, \ldots, x_{m-2}, 0) + f(x_0, \ldots, x_{m-2}, 1)] x_{m-1}.$$

PROOF. Since $x_{m-1}$ can only take one of the two possible values, 0 or 1, it is sufficient to verify that the identity holds for both of them. For $x_{m-1} = 0$, the identity is clear, and for $x_{m-1} = 1$, we get

$$f(x_0, \ldots, x_{m-2}, 1) = f(x_0, \ldots, x_{m-2}, 0)$$
$$+ [f(x_0, \ldots, x_{m-2}, 0) + f(x_1, \ldots, x_{m-2}, 1)].$$

$\square$

**Example.** (3) Let us translate **f** = 01101110 into a Boolean polynomial (of three variables). We apply the preceding proposition:

$$\mathbf{f} = 0110 + [0110 + 1110]x_2$$
$$= 0110 + 1000x_2.$$

Next we apply the same proposition to the two words 0110 and 1000 (of two indeterminates):

$$\mathbf{f} = (01 + [01 + 10]x_1) + (10 + [10 + 00]x_1)x_2$$
$$= 01 + 11x_1 + 10x_2 + 10x_1x_2.$$

Finally, an application of the proposition to the words of length 2 (in the indeterminate $x_0$) yields:

$$\mathbf{f} = (0 + [0 + 1]x_0) + (1 + [1 + 1]x_0)x_1 + (1 + [1 + 0]x_0)x_2$$
$$+ (1 + [1 + 0]x_0)x_1x_0$$
$$= x_0 + x_1 + x_2 + x_0x_2 + x_1x_2 + x_0x_1x_2.$$

**Theorem.** *The linear space* $\mathbf{Z}_2^n$, *where* $n = 2^m$, *has a basis formed by all one-summand Boolean polynomials, i.e., by the following polynomials*

$$1,$$
$$x_i \qquad (i = 0, 1, \ldots, m-1),$$
$$x_i x_j \qquad (i, j = 0, 1, \ldots, m-1 \text{ and } i \neq j),$$
$$\vdots$$
$$x_0 x_1 \ldots x_{m-1}.$$

PROOF. Every word of length $n = 2^m$ is a Boolean function of $m$ indeterminates, and, hence, can be expressed as a Boolean polynomial. It follows that the one-summand Boolean polynomials span the whole space $\mathbb{Z}_2^n$. In order to prove that they form a basis, it is sufficient to show that their number is $n = 2^m$, the dimension of the space. In fact, we have 1 polynomial of degree 0, $m$ polynomials of degree 1, $\binom{m}{2}$ polynomials of degree 2, etc. For each $k = 0, 1, \ldots, m-1$, there are $\binom{m}{k}$ one-summand polynomials of degree $k$, and, thus, the total number of the one-summand polynomials is

$$\sum_{k=0}^{m} \binom{m}{k} = 2^m. \tag{9.2.1}$$

[The last equation is easily derived from the binomial theorem applied to $(1+1)^m$.]  □

## 9.3   Reed-Muller Codes

**Definition.** *By the* Reed-Muller code *of length* $n = 2^m$ *and degree* $r$ $(= 0, 1, \ldots, m)$ *is meant the binary code* $\mathcal{R}(r, m)$ *of all binary words of length* $n$, *which have, as Boolean polynomials, degree at most* $r$.

**Examples**

(1) $\mathcal{R}(0, m)$ consists of the polynomials of degree at most 0, i.e., of 0 and 1. Thus, $\mathcal{R}(0, m)$ is the repetition code of length $2^m$.

(2) $\mathcal{R}(1, m)$ has basis 1, $x_0$, ..., $x_{m-1}$. In fact, each polynomial of degree at most 1 is a sum of (some of) those $m + 1$ polynomials, and they are linearly independent by Theorem 9.2. Thus, $\mathcal{R}(1, m)$ is a $(2^m, m+1)$-code.

For example, $\mathcal{R}(1, 3)$ has the following generator matrix:

$$G = \begin{bmatrix} 1 \\ x_0 \\ x_1 \\ x_2 \end{bmatrix} = \begin{bmatrix} 1 & 1 & 1 & 1 & 1 & 1 & 1 & 1 \\ 0 & 1 & 0 & 1 & 0 & 1 & 0 & 1 \\ 0 & 0 & 1 & 1 & 0 & 0 & 1 & 1 \\ 0 & 0 & 0 & 0 & 1 & 1 & 1 & 1 \end{bmatrix}.$$

We will see that $\mathcal{R}(1, 3)$ is the extended Hamming code (see 8.5). $\mathcal{R}(1, 4)$ is a $(16, 5)$-code and $\mathcal{R}(1, 5)$ is a $(32, 6)$-code, which was used by the 1969 Mariner, as mentioned in the introduction.

(3) $\mathcal{R}(2, m)$ has basis 1, $x_0$, ..., $x_{m-1}$, $x_0 x_1$, $x_0 x_2$, ..., $x_{m-2} x_{m-1}$. Thus, this is a $\left(2^m, \binom{m}{2} + m + 1\right)$-code. For example, $\mathcal{R}(2, 3)$ is a $(8, 7)$-code.

It is easy to see that this is just the even-parity code of length 8. $\mathcal{R}(2,4)$ is a $(16,11)$-code. We will see that $\mathcal{R}(2,4)$ is the extended Hamming code.

(4) $\mathcal{R}(m-1,m)$ is the even-parity code of length $2^m$. In fact, every code word of $\mathcal{R}(m-1,m)$ is a sum of the polynomials $x_{i_1}x_{i_2}\ldots x_{i_s}$, where $s \leq m-1$. Each of these polynomials has an even Hamming weight [see Example (2) of 9.2]. Thus, $\mathcal{R}(m-1,m)$ is a subspace of the even-parity code. Moreover, $\mathcal{R}(m-1,m)$ has dimension $2^m-1$, because it contains all of the basis polynomials in Theorem 9.2 except the last one, $x_0x_1\ldots x_{m-1}$. Since the even-parity code also has dimension $2^m-1$, the two codes are identical by Corollary (4) of 7.4.

**Theorem.** *The Reed-Muller code $\mathcal{R}(r,m)$ has*

$$k = \sum_{i=0}^{r} \binom{m}{i}$$

*information symbols, and its dual code is $\mathcal{R}(m-r-1,m)$.*

**PROOF.** I. The space $\mathcal{R}(r,m)$ is spanned by all the polynomials $x_{i_1}\ldots x_{i_s}$, where $0 \leq s \leq r$, and for a given $s$, we have $\binom{m}{s}$ such polynomials. By Theorem 9.2, all these polynomials are linearly independent, thus, they form a basis of $\mathcal{R}(r,m)$. We conclude that $\mathcal{R}(r,m)$ has dimension $\sum_{s=0}^{r} \binom{m}{s}$.

II. The dimension of $\mathcal{R}(r,m)^{\perp}$ is $2^m - \sum_{s=0}^{r} \binom{m}{s}$ (by Theorem 7.7). Using Equation (9.2.1) and the well-known identity

$$\binom{m}{s} = \binom{m}{m-s},$$

we see that the dimension of $\mathcal{R}(r,m)^{\perp}$ can be re-written as follows:

$$
\begin{aligned}
\dim \mathcal{R}(r,m)^{\perp} &= \sum_{s=0}^{m} \binom{m}{s} - \sum_{s=0}^{r} \binom{m}{s} \\
&= \sum_{s=r+1}^{m} \binom{m}{s} \\
&= \sum_{s=r+1}^{m} \binom{m}{m-s} \\
&= \sum_{i=0}^{m-s-1} \binom{m}{i}.
\end{aligned}
$$

We conclude that linear spaces $\mathcal{R}(r, m)^{\perp}$ and $\mathcal{R}(m - r - 1, m)$ have the same dimension. By Corollary (4) of 7.4, it is now sufficient to show that $\mathcal{R}(m - r - 1, m)$ is a subspace of the space $\mathcal{R}(r, m)^{\perp}$.

Thus, it is our task to verify that each Boolean polynomial $\mathbf{f}$ of degree $p \leq m - r - 1$ is orthogonal to all Boolean polynomials $\mathbf{g}$ of degree $q \leq r$ [and, thus, $\mathbf{f}$ lies in $\mathcal{R}(r, m)^{\perp}$]. Since the scalar product $\mathbf{f} \cdot \mathbf{g}$ is the sum of the coordinates $f_i g_i$ of the logical product $\mathbf{fg}$, we just have to show that $\mathbf{fg}$, represented as a binary word, has an even Hamming weight. The degree of the polynomial $\mathbf{fg}$ is at most $p + q \leq m - r - 1 + r = m - 1$ (see Exercise 9A). Thus, $\mathbf{fg}$ is a code word of $\mathcal{R}(m - 1, m)$, which by Example (4) above implies that $\mathbf{fg}$ has an even Hamming weight.　　　　　　　　　　　　　□

**Example.**　(5) $\mathcal{R}(m - 2, m)$ is the extended Hamming code of length $2^m$ (see 8.5). In fact, the dual code is

$$\mathcal{R}(m - 2, m)^{\perp} = \mathcal{R}(1, m)$$

and, thus, $\mathcal{R}(m - 2, m)$ has the following parity check matrix:

$$\mathbf{H} = \begin{bmatrix} \mathbf{1} \\ \mathbf{x}_0 \\ \mathbf{x}_1 \\ \vdots \\ \mathbf{x}_m \end{bmatrix} = \begin{bmatrix} 1 & 1 & 1 & 1 & \cdots & 1 & 1 & 1 & 1 \\ 0 & 1 & 0 & 1 & \cdots & 0 & 1 & 0 & 1 \\ 0 & 0 & 1 & 1 & \cdots & 0 & 0 & 1 & 1 \\ \multicolumn{9}{c}{\dotfill} \\ 0 & 0 & 0 & 0 & \cdots & 1 & 1 & 1 & 1 \end{bmatrix}.$$

We can add the first row to all the other rows, and then interchange it with the last row. This yields another parity check matrix:

$$\mathbf{H} \sim \begin{bmatrix} 1 & 0 & 1 & 0 & \cdots & 1 & 0 & 1 & 0 \\ 1 & 1 & 0 & 0 & \cdots & 1 & 1 & 0 & 0 \\ \multicolumn{9}{c}{\dotfill} \\ 1 & 1 & 1 & 1 & \cdots & 0 & 0 & 0 & 0 \\ 1 & 1 & 1 & 1 & \cdots & 1 & 1 & 1 & 1 \end{bmatrix}.$$

By deleting the last column and the last row from the new matrix, we obtain a $2^m - 1$ by $m$ matrix $\mathbf{H}_0$ with pairwise distinct, nonzero columns. Thus, $\mathbf{H}_0$ is a parity check matrix of the Hamming code. Consequently, our matrix

$$\mathbf{H} \sim \begin{bmatrix} & & & & 0 \\ & & \mathbf{H}_0 & & 0 \\ & & & & \vdots \\ & & & & 0 \\ \hline 1 & 1 & 1 & 1 & \cdots & 1 & 1 & 1 & 1 \end{bmatrix}$$

is a parity check matrix of the extended Hamming code.

**Remarks**

(1) Encoding of the Reed-Muller codes can be performed in the usual way by multiplying the information word by the generator matrix [see Remark (4) of 8.1]. In other words, the information bits become the coefficients of the corresponding Boolean polynomial. For example, in $\mathcal{R}(1, m)$, we encode the $m + 1$ information bits as follows:

$$[u_1, u_2, \ldots, u_{m+1}] \begin{bmatrix} 1 \\ x_0 \\ x_1 \\ \vdots \\ x_{m-1} \end{bmatrix} = u_1 + u_2 x_0 + \cdots + u_{m+1} x_{m-1}.$$

(2) The minimum weight of the Reed-Muller code $\mathcal{R}(r, m)$ is

$$d = 2^{m-r}.$$

In fact, the code word $x_0 x_1 \ldots x_{r-1}$ has a Hamming weight $2^{m-r}$ [see Example (2) of 9.2], thus, $d \leq 2^{m-r}$. Since $\mathcal{R}(r, m)$ is a subspace of the even-parity code $\mathcal{R}(m-1, m)$, we know that $d$ is even. In 9.6, we will see that $\mathcal{R}(r, m)$ can correct $2^{m-r-1} - 1$ errors. Thus, by Proposition 4.6, $d > 2(2^{m-r-1} - 1)$, and we conclude that

$$2^{m-r} \leq d < 2^{m-r} - 2.$$

Since $d$ is even, this proves $d = 2^{m-r}$.

(3) In some respect, it is more suitable to work with the *punctured Reed-Muller codes* $\overline{\mathcal{R}}(r, m)$ (see 8.6). This means that in $\mathcal{R}(r, m)$, we delete the last symbol from each code word. The resulting code $\overline{\mathcal{R}}(r, m)$ has length $2^m - 1$, and the number of information symbols can be shown to be equal to that in $\mathcal{R}(r, m)$. The minimum Hamming distance of $\overline{\mathcal{R}}(r, m)$ is $2^{m-r} - 1$ and, thus, it can correct $2^{m-r-1} - 1$ errors, the same number as the original code can. We list all punctured Reed-Muller codes of lengths 7, ..., 127 in Appendix B.

For example, $\overline{\mathcal{R}}(0, m)$ is the repetition code of length $2^m - 1$ and $\overline{\mathcal{R}}(m-1, m)$ is the Hamming code of that length.

# 9.4 Geometric Interpretation: Three-Dimensional Case

In order to explain the decoding of Reed-Muller codes, it is convenient to introduce a new interpretation: instead of with Boolean functions, we work with flats (or affine subspaces). We first present the case of the three-dimensional geometry, which corresponds to the codes of length 8, and then the general geometry of $\mathbf{Z}_2^m$.

Recall that the conventional three-dimensional Euclidean geometry operates within the linear space $\mathbf{R}^3$, whose points (or vectors) are triples $\mathbf{a} = a_1 a_2 a_3$ of real numbers. We have lines in $\mathbf{R}^3$, which can be described as follows:

$$\mathbf{a} + t\,\mathbf{b} \qquad\qquad (\mathbf{a}, \mathbf{b} \text{ in } \mathbf{R}^3, \mathbf{b} \neq 0).$$

Here $t$ denotes a real parameter, thus, the line $\mathbf{a} + t\,\mathbf{b}$ is the set of all points $\{\mathbf{a} + t\,\mathbf{b} \mid t \in \mathbf{R}\}$. Further, we have planes in $\mathbf{R}^3$:

$$\mathbf{a} + t\,\mathbf{b} + s\,\mathbf{c} \qquad\qquad (\mathbf{a}, \mathbf{b}, \mathbf{c} \text{ in } \mathbf{R}^3, \mathbf{b} \text{ and } \mathbf{c} \text{ linearly independent}).$$

Here, again, $t$ and $s$ are real parameters.

Now, the *binary Euclidean three-dimensional geometry* can be introduced quite analogously. Its *points* are the vectors of the linear space $\mathbf{Z}_2^3$. In contrast to the real case above, there are precisely eight points. We can enumerate them by the corresponding binary expansions of their indices: $\mathbf{p}_0 = 000$, $\mathbf{p}_1 = 001$, etc., see Figure 5.

| Point | Characteristic Function |
|---|---|
| $\mathbf{p}_0 = 000$ | 00000001 |
| $\mathbf{p}_1 = 001$ | 00000010 |
| $\mathbf{p}_2 = 010$ | 00000100 |
| $\mathbf{p}_3 = 011$ | 00001000 |
| $\mathbf{p}_4 = 100$ | 00010000 |
| $\mathbf{p}_5 = 101$ | 00100000 |
| $\mathbf{p}_6 = 110$ | 01000000 |
| $\mathbf{p}_7 = 111$ | 10000000 |

**Figure 5:** Points of the binary three-dimensional Euclidean geometry

*Lines* of the Euclidean geometry can be described as follows:

$$\mathbf{a} + t\,\mathbf{b} \qquad\qquad (\mathbf{a}, \mathbf{b} \text{ in } \mathbf{Z}_2^3, \mathbf{b} \neq 0),$$

where $t$ is a binary parameter, $t = 0, 1$. Thus, the line has precisely two points: $\mathbf{a}$ and $\mathbf{a} + \mathbf{b}$. Conversely, every pair $\mathbf{a}, \mathbf{a}'$ of points constitutes a line, viz.,

$$\mathbf{a} + t(\mathbf{a}' - \mathbf{a}).$$

It follows that lines are just all two-point subsets:

$$\{ p_0, p_1 \}, \ \{ p_0, p_2 \}, \ \ldots, \ \{ p_6, p_7 \}.$$

The number of lines is

$$\binom{8}{2} = 27,$$

since a line is just a choice of an (unordered) pair from among the eight points.

Finally, *planes* of the Euclidean geometry are described as

$$\mathbf{a} + t_1 \mathbf{b}_1 + t_2 \mathbf{b}_2 \qquad (\mathbf{a}, \mathbf{b}_1, \mathbf{b}_2 \text{ in } \mathbf{Z}_2^3; \ \mathbf{b}_1, \mathbf{b}_2 \text{ linearly independent}),$$

where $t_1$ and $t_2$ are binary parameters. The plane, then, consists of the following four points: $\mathbf{a}$, $\mathbf{a} + \mathbf{b}_1$, $\mathbf{a} + \mathbf{b}_2$, and $\mathbf{a} + \mathbf{b}_1 + \mathbf{b}_2$. All planes are listed in Figure 6.

| Plane | Characteristic Function | Boolean Polynomial |
|-------|------------------------|---------------------|
| $\{ p_1, p_3, p_5, p_7 \}$ | 10101010 | $x_0$ |
| $\{ p_2, p_3, p_6, p_7 \}$ | 11001100 | $x_1$ |
| $\{ p_4, p_5, p_6, p_7 \}$ | 11110000 | $x_2$ |
| $\{ p_0, p_2, p_4, p_6 \}$ | 01010101 | $1 + x_0$ |
| $\{ p_0, p_1, p_4, p_5 \}$ | 00110011 | $1 + x_1$ |
| $\{ p_0, p_1, p_2, p_3 \}$ | 00001111 | $1 + x_2$ |
| $\{ p_1, p_2, p_5, p_6 \}$ | 01100110 | $x_0 + x_1$ |
| $\{ p_1, p_3, p_4, p_6 \}$ | 01011010 | $x_0 + x_2$ |
| $\{ p_2, p_3, p_4, p_5 \}$ | 00111100 | $x_1 + x_2$ |
| $\{ p_1, p_2, p_4, p_7 \}$ | 10010110 | $x_0 + x_1 + x_2$ |
| $\{ p_0, p_3, p_4, p_7 \}$ | 10011001 | $1 + x_0 + x_1$ |
| $\{ p_0, p_2, p_5, p_7 \}$ | 10100101 | $1 + x_0 + x_2$ |
| $\{ p_0, p_1, p_6, p_7 \}$ | 11000011 | $1 + x_1 + x_2$ |
| $\{ p_0, p_3, p_5, p_6 \}$ | 01101001 | $1 + x_0 + x_1 + x_2$ |

**Figure 6:** Planes in the binary three-dimensional Euclidean geometry

Observe that the planes passing through the origin ($\mathbf{a} = 0$) are precisely those which can be described by a homogenous equation

$$h_0 x_0 + h_1 x_1 + h_2 x_2 = 0.$$

In fact, such a plane is precisely a two-dimensional subspace of $\mathbb{Z}_2^3$, now see Remark (4) of 7.7. It follows that a general plane can always be described by a (possibly nonhomogenous) equation

$$h_0 x_0 + h_1 x_1 + h_2 x_2 = c.$$

(Given a plane $\mathbf{a} + t_1 \mathbf{b}_1 + t_2 \mathbf{b}_2$ and describing the parallel plane $t_1 \mathbf{b}_1 + t_2 \mathbf{b}_2$ by the equation $h_0 x_0 + h_1 x_1 + h_2 x_2 = 0$, put $c = h_0 a_0 + h_1 a_1 + h_2 a_2$, where $\mathbf{a} = a_0 a_1 a_2$.)

Furthermore, every line can be described by a pair of nonhomogenous equations

$$\begin{aligned} h_0 x_0 + h_1 x_1 + h_2 x_2 &= c, \\ h_0' x_0 + h_1' x_1 + h_2' x_2 &= c'. \end{aligned}$$

This follows from the fact that every line $\mathbf{a} + t\,\mathbf{b}$ is an intersection of two planes: choose a basis $\mathbf{b}$, $\mathbf{d}$, $\mathbf{d}'$ of the space $\mathbb{Z}_2^3$ and consider the planes $\mathbf{a} + t\,\mathbf{b} + s\,\mathbf{d}$ and $\mathbf{a} + t\,\mathbf{b} + s'\,\mathbf{d}'$.

Lines and planes are examples of *flats* (also called *affine spaces*). A *flat* in the space $\mathbb{Z}_2^3$ is a coset (6.2) of a linear subspace of the space $\mathbb{Z}_2^3$. That is, a flat has the form

$$\mathbf{a} + K = \{\, \mathbf{a} + \mathbf{b} \mid \mathbf{b} \text{ is a point of } K \,\},$$

where $\mathbf{a}$ is a point of $\mathbb{Z}_2^3$, and $K$ is a linear subspace. If the dimension of $K$ is $s$, we call the coset an $s$-flat. Thus, lines are preisely the 1-flats, and planes are the 2-flats. For each point $\mathbf{p}_i$, we have a 0-flat $\{\, \mathbf{p}_i \,\}$, and there is precisely one 3-flat, viz., the whole space $\mathbb{Z}_2^3$.

Every flat $L$ can be described by the binary word $\mathbf{f}_L = f_7 \ldots f_1 f_0$ defined by

$$f_i = \begin{cases} 1 & \text{if the point } \mathbf{p}_i \text{ lies in } L, \\ 0 & \text{otherwise.} \end{cases}$$

The word $\mathbf{f}_L$ (or the correspondig Boolean function of three variables) is called the *characteristic function* of the flat $L$. (For 1-flats and 2-flats, see the above figures.)

Given flats $L$ and $L'$, their intersection $L \cap L'$ is obviously characterized by the logical product $\mathbf{f}_L \mathbf{f}_{L'}$. For example, the first two planes in Figure 6 intersect in the line $\{\, \mathbf{p}_3, \mathbf{p}_7 \,\}$. The logical product of their characteristic functions is

$$\mathbf{x}_0 \mathbf{x}_1 = 10001000,$$

which is indeed the characteristic function of $\{\, \mathbf{p}_3, \mathbf{p}_7 \,\}$.

**Remark.** The Reed-Muller code $\mathcal{R}(1,3)$ is spanned by the characteristic functions of all planes. In fact, we see in Figure 6 that the characteristic functions of planes are precisely all Boolean polynomials of degree 1 in three variables.

The Reed-Muller code $\mathcal{R}(2,3)$ is spanned by the characteristic functions of all planes and all lines. In fact, every line $L$ is an intersection of two planes. Hence, the characteristic function $f_L$ is a product of two Boolean polynomials of degree 1, which is a Boolean polynomial of degree 2—a code word of $\mathcal{R}(2,3)$.

# 9.5  Geometric Interpretation: General Case

We now pass to the Euclidean geometry of the $m$-dimensional binary linear space $\mathbf{Z}_2^m$. The points, or vectors, of $\mathbf{Z}_2^m$ can, again, be ordered by the binary expansions of the numbers $0, 1, \ldots, 2^m - 1$. That is, we put $\mathbf{Z}_2^m = \{\, p_0, p_1, p_2, \ldots, p_{2^m-1} \,\}$, where

$$
\begin{aligned}
p_0 &= 000\ldots00, \\
p_1 &= 000\ldots01, \\
p_2 &= 000\ldots10, \\
&\vdots \\
p_{2^m-1} &= 111\ldots11.
\end{aligned}
$$

**Definition.** *Let $K$ be an $r$-dimensional linear subspace of the space $\mathbf{Z}_2^m$. Every coset*

$$
a + K = \{\, a + b \mid b \text{ lies in } K \,\}
$$

*of $K$ is called an $r$-flat in the binary $m$-dimensional Euclidean geometry.*
*An $(m-1)$-flat is also called a* hyperplane.

*Notation.* Given a basis $b_1, \ldots, b_r$ of the subspace $K$, the $r$-flat $a + K$ is also denoted by

$$
a + t_1 b_1 + \cdots + t_r b_r.
$$

It has $2^r$ points (given by the $r$ choices $t_i = 0, 1$ for $i = 1, \ldots, r$).

Another notation of the $r$-flat $a + K$ is by means of a nonhomogenous system of linear equations: whenever the space $K$ is described by equations $Hx^{tr} = 0^{tr}$ [see Remark (4) of 7.7], then the $r$-flat $a + K$ is described by the following equations:

$$
Hx^{tr} = c^{tr}, \qquad \text{where} \quad c^{tr} = Ha^{tr}.
$$

The number of these equations is $m - r$. For example, each hyperplane is described by a single equation:

$$h_0 x_0 + h_1 x_1 + \cdots + h_{m-1} x_{m-1} = c.$$

**Examples**

(1) Every 0-flat is a one-point set. Thus, there are $2^m$ different 0-flats, viz., $\{\mathbf{p}_0\}, \ldots, \{\mathbf{p}_{2^m-1}\}$.

(2) Every 1-flat (or line) is a two-point set,

$$\mathbf{a} + t\mathbf{b} \equiv \{\mathbf{a}, \mathbf{a} + \mathbf{b}\},$$

and, conversely, every two-point set is a 1-flat. Therefore, there are $\binom{2^m}{2}$ 1-flats.

(3) Let $P_i$ denote the flat described by the equation $x_i = 1$. That is, $P_i$ is the set of all points $\mathbf{p}_k$ which have a 1 in the $i$th position. For example, $P_0 = \{\mathbf{p}_1, \mathbf{p}_3, \mathbf{p}_5, \ldots, \mathbf{p}_{2^m-1}\}$.

Each $P_i$ is a hyperplane. In fact, the point $\mathbf{p}_{2^i}$ has precisely one nonzero position (the $i$th one), and, thus,

$$P_i \equiv \mathbf{p}_{2^i} + K,$$

where $K$ is the linear space determined by the equation $k_i = 0$. It is clear that the dimension of $K$ is $m - 1$.

The number of all hyperplanes is $2(2^m - 1)$. In fact, the space $\mathbf{Z}_2^m$ has precisely $2^m - 1$ subspaces $K$ of dimension $m - 1$ (see Exercise 7H). Each of these subspaces $K$ has $2^{m-1}$ points and, thus, by Remark 6.2, there are $2^m/2^{m-1}$ cosets modulo $K$.

(4) For $i \neq j$, the intersection $P_i \cap P_j$ (i.e., the set of all points with a 1 in the $i$th and $j$th positions) is an $(m - 2)$-flat. In fact, for the point $\mathbf{a} = \mathbf{p}_{2^i+2^j}$ (with 1's just on the $i$th and $j$th positions), we have

$$P_i \cap P_j \equiv \mathbf{a} + K,$$

where $K$ is determined by the equation $k_i = k_j = 0$. The dimension of $K$ is $m - 2$.

**Definition.** *By the* characteristic function *of an $r$-flat $L$ is meant the binary word $\mathbf{f}_L = f_{2^m-1} \ldots f_1 f_0$ defined by*

$$f_j = \begin{cases} 1 & \text{if the point } \mathbf{p}_j \text{ lies in } L, \\ 0 & \text{otherwise.} \end{cases}$$

**Remark.** The characteristic function $f_L$ can be interpreted as a Boolean polynomial $f_L(x_0, x_1, \ldots, x_{m-1})$. It follows from 9.1 that $L$ consists of precisely those points $p_i = x_0 x_1 \ldots x_{m-1}$ which satisfy $f_L(x_0, x_1, \ldots, x_{m-1}) = 1$. Shortly:

$$x_0 x_1 \ldots x_{m-1} \text{ lies in } L \iff f_L(x_0, x_1, \ldots, x_{m-1}) = 1.$$

**Examples**

(5) The only $m$-flat, i.e., the space $\mathbf{Z}_2^m$, has the characteristic function $1 = 111 \ldots 11$. For the hyperplane $P_i$ above $f_{P_i} = x_i$.

(6) Every hyperplane has a characteristic function which is a Boolean polynomial of degree 1: if the hyperplane $L$ is described by the equation

$$h_0 x_0 + h_1 x_1 + \cdots + h_{m-1} x_{m-1} = c,$$

then

$$f_L(x_0, \ldots, x_{m-1}) = h_0 x_0 + h_1 x_1 + \cdots + h_{m-1} x_{m-1} + c + 1.$$

In fact, a point $x_0 x_1 \ldots x_{m-1}$ lies in the hyperplane precisely when $h_0 x_0 + \cdots + h_{m-1} x_{m-1} = c$, i.e., when $f_L(x_0, x_1, \ldots, x_{m-1}) = 1$.

(7) For two flats $L$ and $L'$, the function $f_L f_{L'}$ is the characteristic function of the intersection $L \cap L'$.

For example, the polynomial $x_i x_j$ is the characteristic function of the $(m-2)$-flat, which is the intersection of the hyperplanes $P_i$ and $P_j$. More in general: the Boolean polynomial

$$\mathbf{x}_{i_1} \mathbf{x}_{i_2} \ldots \mathbf{x}_{i_s}$$

is the characteristic function of an $(m-s)$-flat.

**Theorem.** *The characteristic function of an $r$-flat is a Boolean polynomial of degree $m - r$.*

**Proof.** In the notation above we have described each $r$-flat $L$ by $m - r$ equations $H x^{tr} = c^{tr}$, or

$$\sum_{j=0}^{m-1} h_{ij} x_j = c_i \qquad \text{for } i = 1, 2, \ldots, m - r.$$

We can rewrite the equations as follows:

$$\sum_{j=0}^{m-1} (h_{ij} x_j + c_i + 1) = 1 \qquad \text{for } i = 1, 2, \ldots, m - r.$$

Then the following Boolean polynomial of degree $m - r$

$$f(x_1, \ldots, x_{m-1}) = \prod_{i=1}^{m-r} \sum_{j=0}^{m-1} (h_{ij} x_j + c_i + 1)$$

is the characteristic function of $L$: the equation $f(x_0, \ldots, x_{m-1}) = 1$ holds precisely when $\sum_{j=0}^{m-1} (h_{ij} x_j + c_i + 1) = 1$ for each $i = 1, \ldots, m - r$.   □

**Corollary.** (1) *Reed-Muller codes can be characterized geometrically as follows:* $\mathcal{R}(r, m)$ *is spanned by all characteristic functions of flats of dimension at least* $m - r$ *in the binary m-dimensional geometry over* $\mathbb{Z}_2$.

   (2) *Every characteristic function of an* $(r+1)$*-flat lies in the dual code of* $\mathcal{R}(r, m)$.

   In fact, $\mathcal{R}(r, m)$ contains all characteristic functions of $s$-flats, $s \geq m - r$, by the preceding theorem. That those functions span the space $\mathcal{R}(r, m)$ follows from Example (7). Thus, (1) is true, and (2) follows from Theorem 9.3.   □

## 9.6   Decoding Reed-Muller Codes

We now present an interesting and easily implementable decoding technique for the code $\mathcal{R}(r, m)$. It is based on majority logic, and it can correct $2^{m-r-1} - 1$ errors. In contrast to other decoding techniques, the present method does not use syndromes, rather it directly computes the corrupted bits from the properties of the received word. The idea is as follows. We receive a binary word $\mathbf{w} = w_{2^m - 1} \ldots w_1 w_0$ of length $2^m$. Assuming that less then $2^{m-r-1}$ bits are corrupted, we want to determine, for each $i = 0, \ldots, 2^m - 1$, whether or not $w_i$ should be corrected. This can be reformulated by asking whether the position of $\mathbf{w}$ corresponding to the 0-flat $\{ \mathbf{p}_i \}$ should be corrected.

   Instead of answering this question directly, we take a broader point of view: for each $s$-flat $L$, where $s = 0, 1, \ldots, r+1$, we determine whether the positions of the received word $\mathbf{w}$ corresponding to the points of $L$ (i.e., those bits $w_i$ such that the point $\mathbf{p}_i$ lies in $L$) are corrupted or not. Well, not exactly. We just distinguish between "even" and "odd" $s$-flats: an $s$-flat $L$ is called *even* if the number of all corrupted positions $w_i$ corresponding to points $\mathbf{p}_i$ of $L$ is even, otherwise $L$ is *odd*. If we are able to determine the parity of each $s$-flat $L$, the decoding is clear: we correct a bit $w_i$ if and only if the 0-flat $\{ \mathbf{p}_i \}$ has odd parity. The trick is that we start with $s = r + 1$ and then proceed to the lower dimensions.

Thus, the first step of decoding the word $\mathbf{w}$ is to determine, for each $(r+1)$-flat $L$, whether $L$ is odd or even. This is performed by computing the scalar product of $\mathbf{w}$ with the characteristic function $\mathbf{f}_L$:

$$L \text{ is even} \iff \mathbf{w} \cdot \mathbf{f}_L = 0.$$

In fact: if $\mathbf{w}$ is a code word, then $\mathbf{w} \cdot \mathbf{f}_L = 0$ by Corollary (2) in 9.5. Now, if precisely two of the bits of $\mathbf{w}$ corresponding to points of $L$ are corrupted, the value $\mathbf{w} \cdot \mathbf{f}_L$ will not be changed. Analogously with 4, 6, ... bits. But if an odd number of bits of $\mathbf{w}$ corresponding to points of $L$ are corrupted, then the received word fulfils $\mathbf{w} \cdot \mathbf{f}_L = 1$.

For $s$-flats $L$, where $s \leq r$, we proceed by majority logic: suppose we already know the parity of every $(s+1)$-flat containing $L$, then we say that $L$ is odd if a majority of these $(s+1)$-flats is odd, and $L$ is even if a majority of them is even. The reason why this procedure works is that each $s$-flat is contained in a large number of $(s+1)$-flats:

**Theorem.** *Every $s$-flat $L$ in the binary $m$-dimensional geometry is contained in exactly $2^{m-s} - 1$ different $(s+1)$-flats. Furthermore, each point outside of $L$ lies in precisely one of these $(s+1)$-flats.*

PROOF. I. We prove first that every $s$-dimensional linear subspace $K$ of $\mathbf{Z}_2^m$ is contained in precisely $2^{m-s} - 1$ different subspaces of dimension $s+1$.

Every $(s+1)$-dimensional space $\overline{K}$ containing $K$ has the form $\overline{K} = K + t\mathbf{b}$ for some point $\mathbf{b}$ outside of $K$, where

$$K + t\mathbf{b} \equiv \{ \mathbf{a} + t\mathbf{b} \mid \mathbf{a} \in K \text{ and } t = 0, 1 \}.$$

This follows immediately from the fact that every basis of $K$ can be extended (by a single vector) to a basis of $\overline{K}$—see Theorem 7.4.

Next observe that for two points $\mathbf{b}$, $\mathbf{b}'$ outside of $K$, the linear subspaces $K + t\mathbf{b}$ and $K + t\mathbf{b}'$ coincide if and only if $\mathbf{b}$ and $\mathbf{b}'$ lie in the same coset modulo $K$ (6.2). In fact, if $K + t\mathbf{b} = K + t\mathbf{b}'$, then $\mathbf{b}$ can be expressed as $\mathbf{a} + t\mathbf{b}'$, where $\mathbf{a}$ lies in $K$—thus, $t \neq 0$ and we get

$$\mathbf{b} - \mathbf{b}' = \mathbf{a} \in K.$$

By Proposition 6.2, $\mathbf{b}$ and $\mathbf{b}'$ lie in the same coset. Conversely, if $\mathbf{b} - \mathbf{b}' = \mathbf{a}$ is a point of $K$, then $\mathbf{b} = \mathbf{a} + \mathbf{b}'$ lies in $K + t\mathbf{b}'$, and $\mathbf{b}' = -\mathbf{a} + \mathbf{b}$ lies in $K + t\mathbf{b}$; thus, $K + t\mathbf{b} = K + t\mathbf{b}'$. By Remark 6.2, there are $2^m/2^s$ cosets modulo $K$. One of them is $K$ itself, and all other cosets contain only points outside of $K$. Consequently, there are $2^{m-s} - 1$ different spaces $K + t\mathbf{b}$ for $\mathbf{b}$ outside of $K$.

II. Every $s$-flat

$$L \equiv \mathbf{a} + K \qquad (\dim K = s)$$

is contained in $2^{m-s} - 1$ different $(s+1)$-flats $\mathbf{a} + K'$, where $K'$ is an $(s+1)$-dimensional space containing $K$ (this follows from I.). It remains to prove that every $(s+1)$-flat $\mathbf{a}' + K'$ containing $L$ has the mentioned form. That is, we want to show that $\mathbf{a} + K' = \mathbf{a}' + K'$. In fact, since $\mathbf{a}$ lies in $\mathbf{a}' + K'$, the difference $\mathbf{a} - \mathbf{a}'$ is in $K'$ and, hence, the points $\mathbf{a}$ and $\mathbf{a}'$ lie in the same coset modulo $K$.

III. Every point $\mathbf{b}$ outside of the $s$-flat $L = \mathbf{a} + K$ lies in an $(s+1)$-flat containing $L$, viz., the flat $\mathbf{a} + K'$, where $K' = K + t(\mathbf{b} - \mathbf{a})$. In fact, $\mathbf{b}$ lies in $\mathbf{a} + [K + t(\mathbf{b} - \mathbf{a})]$ because by choosing $t = 1$ and $0 \in K$, we have

$$\mathbf{b} = \mathbf{a} + [0 + (\mathbf{b} - \mathbf{a})].$$

To verify that $K'$ has dimension $s + 1$, it is sufficient to show that $\mathbf{b} - \mathbf{a}$ lies outside of $K$: in fact, if $\mathbf{b} - \mathbf{a}$ lies in $K$, then $\mathbf{a} + (\mathbf{b} - \mathbf{a}) = \mathbf{b}$ lies in $L$.

Finally, we prove that the $(s + 1)$-flat is unique. Every $(s + 1)$-flat containing $\mathbf{a} + K$ has the form $\mathbf{a} + K'$, where $K'$ is an $(s + 1)$-dimensional linear space containing $K$. If $\mathbf{b}$ lies in such a flat $\mathbf{a} + K'$, then $\mathbf{b} - \mathbf{a}$ is also a point of $K'$; thus, $K'$ contains the linear space $K + (\mathbf{b} - \mathbf{a})$. The last two spaces have both dimensions $s + 1$, hence, they coincide. $\qquad \square$

**Corollary.** *If the number of errors in a received word is less then $2^{m-r-1}$, then for each $s$-flat $L$, $0 \leq s \leq r$, the majority of $(s + 1)$-flats containing $L$ have the same parity of errors as $L$.*

In fact, let $t < 2^{m-r-1}$ bits of the received word $\mathbf{w}$ be corrupted. We know that $L$ is contained in

$$2^{m-r} - 1 > 2t$$

$(s+1)$-flats $L'$, and each such flat $L'$ is determined by one point outside of $L$. Let us begin with all points $\mathbf{p}_i$ outside of $L$ such that $w_i$ is a corrupted bit. There are at most $t$ corresponding $(s+1)$-flats $L'$. All the remaining flats $L'$ have the property that they contain no point $\mathbf{p}_i$ outside of $L$ such that $w_i$ is incorrect. Thus, $L'$ has the same error parity as $L$. The number of the latter flats is at least $(2^{m-r} - 1) - t > t$; thus, they form a majority. $\qquad \square$

**Decoding Algorithm for the Reed-Muller Code $\mathcal{R}(r, m)$**

*First step*: Receiving a word $\mathbf{w}$, call each $(r + 1)$-flat $L$ odd if the scalar product of its characteristic function $\mathbf{f}_L$ with $\mathbf{w}$ is 1, otherwise call $L$ even. That is, for $(r + 1)$-flats $L$:

$$L \text{ is } \begin{cases} \text{odd if } \mathbf{w} \cdot \mathbf{f}_L = 1, \\ \text{even if } \mathbf{w} \cdot \mathbf{f}_L = 0. \end{cases}$$

*Recursive steps*: For all $s = r,\ r - 1,\ \ldots,\ 0$ such that each $(s + 1)$-flat has already been called odd or even, call an $s$-flat $L$ odd if a majority of $(s + 1)$-flats containing $L$ is odd, otherwise call $L$ even.

*Last step*: Correct the $i$th bit of $\mathbf{w}$ if and only if the 0-flat $\{\, \mathbf{p}_i \,\}$ has been called odd.

**Example.** Working with $\mathcal{R}(1, 3)$, we have received

$$11101010.$$

The first step is to decide which planes (see Figure 6 in 9.4) are odd and which are even. For example, the plane $L = \{\, \mathbf{p}_1, \mathbf{p}_3, \mathbf{p}_5, \mathbf{p}_7 \,\}$ is even since $\mathbf{w} \cdot \mathbf{f}_L = 11101010 \cdot 10101010 = 0$. See Figure 7.    Next we must decide,

| Plane | Parity | Plane | Parity |
|-------|--------|-------|--------|
| $\{\mathbf{p}_1, \mathbf{p}_3, \mathbf{p}_5, \mathbf{p}_7\}$ | even | $\{\mathbf{p}_1, \mathbf{p}_3, \mathbf{p}_4, \mathbf{p}_6\}$ | odd |
| $\{\mathbf{p}_2, \mathbf{p}_3, \mathbf{p}_6, \mathbf{p}_7\}$ | odd | $\{\mathbf{p}_2, \mathbf{p}_3, \mathbf{p}_4, \mathbf{p}_5\}$ | even |
| $\{\mathbf{p}_4, \mathbf{p}_5, \mathbf{p}_6, \mathbf{p}_7\}$ | odd | $\{\mathbf{p}_0, \mathbf{p}_3, \mathbf{p}_4, \mathbf{p}_7\}$ | even |
| $\{\mathbf{p}_0, \mathbf{p}_2, \mathbf{p}_4, \mathbf{p}_6\}$ | odd | $\{\mathbf{p}_0, \mathbf{p}_2, \mathbf{p}_5, \mathbf{p}_7\}$ | even |
| $\{\mathbf{p}_0, \mathbf{p}_1, \mathbf{p}_4, \mathbf{p}_5\}$ | even | $\{\mathbf{p}_0, \mathbf{p}_1, \mathbf{p}_6, \mathbf{p}_7\}$ | odd |
| $\{\mathbf{p}_0, \mathbf{p}_1, \mathbf{p}_2, \mathbf{p}_3\}$ | even | $\{\mathbf{p}_1, \mathbf{p}_2, \mathbf{p}_4, \mathbf{p}_7\}$ | even |
| $\{\mathbf{p}_1, \mathbf{p}_2, \mathbf{p}_5, \mathbf{p}_6\}$ | odd | $\{\mathbf{p}_0, \mathbf{p}_3, \mathbf{p}_5, \mathbf{p}_6\}$ | odd |

Figure 7: First step of decoding 11101010

for each line $L$, whether $L$ is odd or even. For example, the line $\{\, \mathbf{p}_0, \mathbf{p}_1 \,\}$ is contained in three planes (see Figure 6 of 9.4):

$$\begin{aligned} \{\mathbf{p}_0, \mathbf{p}_1, \mathbf{p}_4, \mathbf{p}_5\} \quad &- \quad \text{even,} \\ \{\mathbf{p}_0, \mathbf{p}_1, \mathbf{p}_2, \mathbf{p}_3\} \quad &- \quad \text{even,} \\ \{\mathbf{p}_0, \mathbf{p}_1, \mathbf{p}_6, \mathbf{p}_7\} \quad &- \quad \text{odd.} \end{aligned}$$

| Line | Parity | Line | Parity |
|------|--------|------|--------|
| $\{p_0, p_1\}$ | even | $\{p_2, p_4\}$ | even |
| $\{p_0, p_2\}$ | even | $\{p_2, p_5\}$ | even |
| $\{p_0, p_3\}$ | even | $\{p_2, p_6\}$ | odd |
| $\{p_0, p_4\}$ | even | $\{p_2, p_7\}$ | even |
| $\{p_0, p_5\}$ | even | $\{p_3, p_4\}$ | even |
| $\{p_0, p_6\}$ | odd | $\{p_3, p_5\}$ | even |
| $\{p_0, p_7\}$ | even | $\{p_3, p_6\}$ | odd |
| $\{p_1, p_2\}$ | even | $\{p_3, p_7\}$ | even |
| $\{p_1, p_3\}$ | even | $\{p_4, p_5\}$ | even |
| $\{p_1, p_4\}$ | even | $\{p_4, p_6\}$ | odd |
| $\{p_1, p_5\}$ | even | $\{p_4, p_7\}$ | even |
| $\{p_1, p_6\}$ | even | $\{p_5, p_6\}$ | odd |
| $\{p_1, p_7\}$ | even | $\{p_5, p_7\}$ | even |
| $\{p_2, p_3\}$ | even | $\{p_6, p_7\}$ | odd |

**Figure 8:** Second step of decoding 11101010

By majority vote, the line $\{p_0, p_1\}$ is even. We must go through all the lines and perform such a majority vote. The result is seen in Figure 8.

Finaly, we are prepared to correct the individual bits. The point $p_0$ is contained in seven lines, one odd and six even; thus $w_0$ will not be corrected. Also $p_1$ is contained in one odd and six even lines, etc. The only bit to correct is $w_6$ because $p_6$ is contained in seven odd lines. The word sent is

$$10101010$$

[which is the polynomial $1 + x_1$, a code word of $\mathcal{R}(1, 3)$].

**Concluding Remark.** We have presented a method by which the Reed-Muller code $\mathcal{R}(r, m)$ can correct $2^{m-r-1} - 1$ errors. As explained in Remark (1) of 9.3, this proves that the minimum distance is $2^{m-r}$.

For example, the code $\mathcal{R}(1, 5)$ is a $(32, 6)$-code [see Example (1) in 9.3], which corrects $2^{5-1-1} - 1 = 7$ errors, as mentioned in the introduction.

# Exercises

**9A** Prove the following about degrees of Boolean polynomials:

(1) For nonzero Boolean polynomials **f** and **g**, the degree of **fg** is the sum of the degrees of **f** and **g**.

(2) The degree of **f** + **g** is the maximum of the degrees of **f** and **g**.

**9B** Find a binary $(15, 5)$-code correcting triple errors. (Hint: use a punctured Reed-Muller code.)

**9C** When using $\mathcal{R}(1, 3)$, decode 01111100. Verify the correctness of your decoding. Encode information bits 1011.

**9D** When using $\mathcal{R}(2, 3)$, decode 0111100.

**9E** When using $\mathcal{R}(2, 4)$, decode 1111111011111111.

**9F** What Boolean polynomial has the truth table

(1) 10100110?

(2) 1010011010100110?

**9G** Find the truth table of the Boolean polynomial $1 + x_0 + x_1 x_2$

(1) as a function of three variables,

(2) as a function of four variables.

**9H** What is the relationship between simplex codes $(8.2)$ and the Reed-Muller codes $\mathcal{R}(1, m)$?

**9I** Compute the number of 2-flats in the Euclidean geometry in $\mathbf{Z}_2^m$.

**9J** Prove that each hyperplane $L$ in the Euclidean geometry in $\mathbf{Z}_2^m$ has the property that its complement $\mathbf{Z}_2^m - L$ is a hyperplane too. (Hint: see the proof of Theorem 9.6.)

**9K** Is every Boolean function a characteristic function of some flat? Characterize such functions! (Hint: express each flat as an intersection of hyperplanes.)

## Notes

Reed-Muller codes are named after Reed (1954) and Muller (1954). The former paper is the source of the decoding method.

# Chapter 10

# Cyclic Codes

The search for efficient error-correcting codes has been very successful within the class of linear codes satisfying the additional requirement that a cyclic shift of a code word be a code word. Such codes are called cyclic. It turns out that a strong algebraic structure is added to all cyclic codes: besides the addition and scalar multiplication, we have an important operation of multiplication, which is best understood if code words are regarded as (coefficients of) polynomials.

We introduce polynomials and show how they are used for a succint presentation of a cyclic code. Then we present encoding and decoding methods specific for cyclic codes (in particular, for the fundamental Golay code). We further introduce correction of bursts of errors, and we construct good cyclic burst-error-correcting codes called Fire codes.

Additional important properties of polynomials will be treated in Chapter 11.

## 10.1  Generator Polynomial

**Definition.** *A linear code is called cyclic if for each code word $v_0v_1 \ldots v_{n-1}$, the cyclic shift $v_{n-1}v_0v_1 \ldots v_{n-2}$ is also a code word.*

**Examples.** The even-weight code is a cyclic code, and so is the repetition code. In contrast, the Hamming code with the parity check matrix in 5.5 is not a cyclic code: whereas 1110000 is a code word, 0111000 is not.

Although the definition of cyclic codes is very simple, the property of being cyclic is of prime importance both for the theory and for implementation.

161

We use indices starting from 0 rather than 1 (as in $v_0 v_1 \ldots v_{n-1}$) because we are going to use a description of words via polynomials. For example, instead of 101200 we, write $1 + x^2 + 2x^3$. The advantage is that the cyclic shift, 010120, is now expressed by a product with the indeterminate: $(1 + x^2 + 2x^3)x$. Analogously, the second shift 001012 is $(1 + x^2 + 2x^3)x^2$.

**Definition.** *By a* polynomial *in one indeterminate $x$ over a field $F$ is meant an expression of the form*

$$a_0 + a_1 x + a_2 x^2 + \cdots + a_k x^k,$$

*where $a_0, \ldots, a_k$ are elements of $F$; the summands $a_i x^i$ with $a_i = 0$ can be omitted from the expression.*

*The polynomial is said to have* degree *$k$ if $a_k \neq 0$; the polynomial 0 is said to have degree $-1$. If $a_k = 1$, then the polynomial is called* monic.

**Caution!** A polynomial is *not a function* of the form $f(x) = a_0 + a_1 x + \cdots + a_k x^k$. For example, the following polynomials over $\mathbf{Z}_2$

$$1 + x + x^2 \qquad \text{and} \qquad 1 + x^2 + x^4$$

are certainly different (in fact, their degrees are different). Nevertheless, they define the same function, viz., the constant function of value 1.

A polynomial can be understood as a word over $F$, $a_0 a_1 \ldots a_k$, except that the length of the word is not specified: the same polynomial corresponds to the words $a_0 \ldots a_k 0$, $a_0 \ldots a_k 00$, etc. However, whenever the length $n$ of words is given, then polynomials of degree at most $n - 1$ can be identified with words by the bijective correspondence

$$a_0 a_1 \ldots a_{n-1} \longleftrightarrow a_0 + a_1 x + \cdots + a_{n-1} x^{n-1}.$$

From now on, polynomials and words will be freely interchanged, provided the word length is given.

*Operation on polynomials.* Given polynomials $a(x) = a_0 + a_1 x + \cdots + a_n x^n$ and $b(x) = b_0 + b_1 x + \cdots + b_m x^m$ over a field, we define:

(1) *Addition* by

$$a(x) + b(x) = (a_0 + b_0) + (a_1 + b_1)x + (a_2 + b_2)x^2 + \cdots,$$

i.e., $a(x) + b(x) = c(x)$, where $c_i = a_i + b_i$ $[i = 1, 2, \ldots, \max(n, m)]$. This is precisely the addition of words introduced in 7.3. For example, if $a(x) = 1 + x + 2x^4$ and $b(x) = 1 + 2x + x^2$ over $\mathbf{Z}_3$, then

$$a(x) + b(x) = 2 + x^2 + 2x^4.$$

(In another notation: $11002 + 12100 = 20102$.)

(2) *Multiplication* by

$$a(x)b(x) = a_0b_0 + (a_1b_0 + a_0b_1)x + (a_2b_0 + a_1b_1 + a_0b_2)x^2 + \cdots,$$

i.e., $a(x)b(x) = c(x)$, where

$$c_i = a_ib_0 + a_{i-1}b_1 + \cdots + a_1b_{i-1} + a_0b_i \qquad \text{for} \quad i = 0, 1, \ldots, nm.$$

For example, if $a(x) = 1 + x + 2x^4$ and $b(x) = 1 + 2x + x^2$ over $\mathbf{Z}_3$, then

$$a(x)b(x) = 1 + x^3 + 2x^4 + x^5 + 2x^6.$$

Observe that, in particular, the product $xa(x)$ corresponds to the shift of the word $a(x)$ to the right.

(3) *Division* of $a(x)$ by $b(x)$, provided that $b(x) \neq 0$, as the following pair of polynomials $q(x)$ (the *quotient*) and $r(x)$ (the *remainder*):

$$a(x) = q(x)b(x) + r(x) \qquad \text{and} \qquad \text{degree } r(x) < \text{degree } b(x) \qquad (10.1.1)$$

It is not difficult to verify that (10.1.1) determines both the quotient and the remainder uniquely, see Excercises 10A and 10B. Let us perform the long division on the polynomials $a(x) = 1 + x + 2x^4$ and $b(x) = 1 + 2x + x^2$ over $\mathbf{Z}_3$:

$$
\begin{array}{r}
2x^2 + 2x \phantom{+ x + 1} = q(x) \\
\hline
x^2 + 2x + 1) \overline{\smash{\big)}\, 2x^4 \phantom{+ x^3 + 2x^2} + x + 1} \\
2x^4 + x^3 + 2x^2 \phantom{+ x + 1} \\
\hline
2x^3 + x^2 + x + 1 \\
2x^3 + x^2 + 2x \phantom{+ 1} \\
\hline
x + 1 = r(x)
\end{array}
$$

**Remarks**

(1) For two nonzero polynomials $a(x)$ and $b(x)$, the degree of $a(x)b(x)$ is the sum of the degrees of $a(x)$ and $b(x)$. In fact, let $a(x)$ have degree $n$ and $b(x)$ degree $m$. Then for $c_i = a_ib_0 + \cdots + a_0b_i$, we see that

$$
\begin{aligned}
c_{n+m} &= (a_{n+m}b_0 + \cdots + a_{n+1}b_{m-1}) + a_nb_m \\
&\quad + (a_{n-1}b_{m+1} + \cdots + a_0b_{m+n}),
\end{aligned}
$$

where the summands in the first set of paretheses are 0 because $a_i = 0$ for all $i > n$, and those in the second set of parentheses are 0 because $b_j = 0$ for all $j > m$. Thus,

$$c_{m+m} = a_nb_m \neq 0 \qquad \text{(since } a_n \neq 0 \neq b_m\text{)}.$$

For each $k > n + m$, the summands of

$$c_k = (a_k b_0 + \cdots + a_{n+1} b_{k-n-1}) + (a_n b_{k-n} + \cdots + a_0 b_k)$$

are all zeros. Thus, $c(x)$ has degree $n + m$.

(2) Polynomials can be cancelled:

$$a(x)c(x) = b(x)c(x) \quad \text{implies} \quad a(x) = b(x), \qquad \text{whenever } c(x) \neq 0.$$

In fact, $[a(x) - b(x)]c(x) = 0$ has degree $-1$. If $c(x) \neq 0$ and $a(x) - b(x) \neq 0$, then, by (1), the degree could not be negative. Thus, $a(x) - b(x) = 0$.

**Proposition.** *Every cyclic code $K$ of length $n$ has the following property:*

$$g(x) \text{ lies in } K \Rightarrow q(x)g(x) \text{ lies in } K$$

*for all polynomials $q(x)$ such that the degree of $q(x)g(x)$ is smaller than $n$.*

PROOF. Let $s$ be the degree of $g(x)$. If $s = -1$, there is nothing to prove: $q(x)g(x) = 0$ lies in $K$. Suppose $s \geq 0$, then the degree $r$ of $q(x)$ satisfies $r < n - s$. Put $g(x) = g_0 + g_1 x + \cdots + g_s x^s$. For each $i < n - s$, the polynomial $x^i g(x) = g_0 x^i + g_1 x^{i+1} + \cdots + g_s x^{s+i}$ corresponds to the word of length $n$ obtained by $i$ cyclic shifts of the word $g_0 g_1 \ldots g_s$ to the right. Since our code is cyclic, $x^i g(x)$ is a code word. Consequently, any linear combination of those code words is a code word. It follows that

$$q(x)g(x) = q_0 g(x) + q_1 x g(x) + \cdots + q_r x^r g(x)$$

is a code word.                                                               □

It turns out that the whole cyclic code can be described by means of a single polynomial. Recall that the code $\{0\}$ is called trivial.

**Theorem.** *Every nontrivial cyclic $(n, k)$-code contains a code word $g(x)$ of degree $n - k$. Then code words are precisely all the multiples $q(x)g(x)$, where $q(x)$ is any polynomial of degree smaller than $k$. The code has the following generator matrix:*

$$G = \begin{bmatrix} g(x) \\ xg(x) \\ \vdots \\ x^{k-1}g(x) \end{bmatrix}$$

$$= \begin{bmatrix} g_0 & g_1 & g_2 & \cdots & g_{n-k} & 0 & 0 & \cdots & 0 & 0 & 0 \\ 0 & g_0 & g_1 & g_2 & \cdots & g_{n-k} & 0 & \cdots & 0 & 0 & 0 \\ 0 & 0 & g_0 & g_1 & g_2 & \cdots & & g_{n-k} & \cdots & 0 & 0 & 0 \\ \multicolumn{12}{c}{\cdots\cdots\cdots\cdots\cdots\cdots\cdots\cdots\cdots\cdots\cdots\cdots\cdots\cdots\cdots\cdots} \\ 0 & 0 & 0 & 0 & 0 & \cdots & g_0 & & g_1 & g_2 & \cdots & g_{n-k} \end{bmatrix}$$

PROOF. Let $g(x)$ be the nonzero code word of the smallest degree $s$. We will prove that $s = n - k$.

(1) By the preceding proposition, all the multiples $q(x)g(x)$ are code words. Conversely, we will prove that every code word $w(x)$ is a multiple of $g(x)$ by a polynomial of degree smaller than $n - s$. Dividing $w(x)$ by $g(x)$, we obtain the quotient $q(x)$ and the remainder $r(x)$ such that

$$w(x) = q(x)g(x) + r(x) \quad \text{and} \quad \text{degree } r(x) < s.$$

Since both $w(x)$ and $q(x)g(x)$ are code words, their difference $r(x) = w(x) - q(x)g(x)$ is also a code word. But the degree of $r(x)$ is smaller than $s$, the smallest degree of a nonzero code word. Thus, $r(x) = 0$. Consequently, $w(x) = q(x)g(x)$. By Remark (1), the degree of $q(x)$ is either $-1$, or it is equal to the difference $\deg w(x) - \deg g(x)$, which is smaller than $n - s$ [since the code word $w(x)$ has degree smaller than $n$].

(2) The $n - s$ code words $g(x), xg(x), \ldots, x^{n-s-1}g(x)$ form a basis of the code: by (1) every code word is a linear combination of those words. By Remark (2), those words are linearly independent, since every linear combination has the form $q(x)g(x)$ [where $q(x)$ is a polynomial], and $q(x)g(x) = 0$ implies $q(x) = 0$.

(3) Thus, we see that the dimension of the code is $k = n - s$, in other words, $s = n - k$. By substituting $n - k$ for $s$ above, we conclude the proof of the theorem. $\square$

Definition. *By a* generating polynomial *of a nontrivial cyclic $(n, k)$-code is meant a code word of degree $n - k$.*

Examples

(1) The even-parity code of length $n$ is cyclic. The code word of degree

$n - k = 1$ is just one: $1 + x$. The generator matrix is

$$\mathbf{G} = \begin{bmatrix} 1 & 1 & 0 & 0 & 0 & \cdots & & 0 \\ 0 & 1 & 1 & 0 & 0 & \cdots & & 0 \\ 0 & 0 & 1 & 1 & 0 & \cdots & & 0 \\ 0 & 0 & 0 & & \cdots & 0 & 1 & 1 \end{bmatrix}.$$

(2)  The repetition code is a cyclic code whose generator polynomial is
$g(x) = 1 + x + x^2 + \cdots + x^{n-1}$.

(3)  Consider the binary cyclic code $K$ of length 7 with the generator polynomial $g(x) = 1 + x + x^3$. It has the following generator matrix:

$$\mathbf{G} = \begin{bmatrix} 1 & 1 & 0 & 1 & 0 & 0 & 0 \\ 0 & 1 & 1 & 0 & 1 & 0 & 0 \\ 0 & 0 & 1 & 1 & 0 & 1 & 0 \\ 0 & 0 & 0 & 1 & 1 & 0 & 1 \end{bmatrix}.$$

It is easy to find a parity check matrix:

$$\mathbf{H} = \begin{bmatrix} 1 & 0 & 1 & 1 & 1 & 0 & 0 \\ 1 & 1 & 1 & 0 & 0 & 1 & 0 \\ 0 & 1 & 1 & 1 & 0 & 0 & 1 \end{bmatrix}.$$

Since the columns are pairwise distinct and nonzero, we see that $K$
is a Hamming $(7, 4)$-code. Thus, a different ordering of the columns
of $\mathbf{H}$ from that used in 5.5 leads to an (equivalent) cyclic code. Cyclic
Hamming codes are systematically presented in 12.1.

(4)  Consider a cyclic code of length 6 in the alphabet $\mathbf{Z}_3$ with the generator
polynomial $g(x) = 2 + x^2$. It has the following generator matrix:

$$\mathbf{G} = \begin{bmatrix} 2 & 0 & 1 & 0 & 0 & 0 \\ 0 & 2 & 0 & 1 & 0 & 0 \\ 0 & 0 & 2 & 0 & 1 & 0 \\ 0 & 0 & 0 & 2 & 0 & 1 \end{bmatrix}.$$

This is a $(6, 4)$-code.

**Remark.**  (3) We see that every cyclic code can be described by a single
polynomial, the generator polynomial $g(x)$, substituting the generator matrix. Later we will find another polynomial, substituting the parity check
matrix.

Observe that the generator polynomial is unique up to a scalar multiple. More precisely: every cyclic code has a unique monic generator polynomial $g(x)$ [and all other generator polynomials are precisely the scalar multiples $tg(x)$ for $t \neq 0$]. In fact, if $g(x)$ is a code word of degree $n - k$, then so is $tg(x)$. On the other hand, two generating polynomials of the same code have the same degree, and one is a multiple of the other one (by the theorem above), thus, one must be a scalar multiple of the other one.

From now on, generator polynomials are supposed to be monic.

## 10.2 Encoding Cyclic Codes

One of the important properties of cyclic codes is the simplicity of encoding information symbols. There are two encoding methods: one, more direct but nonsystematic, is based on multiplication by the generator polynomial, and the other one, which is systematic, is based on division by that polynomial.

*Nonsystematic encoding.* This is just a special case of the general encoding method: multiply the information symbols $u_0 u_1 \ldots u_{k-1}$ by the generator matrix (see Theorem 10.1):

$$[u_0 u_1 \ldots u_{k-1}] \begin{bmatrix} g(x) \\ xg(x) \\ \vdots \\ x^{k-1}g(x) \end{bmatrix} = (u_0 + u_1 x + \cdots + u_{k-1}x^{k-1})g(x).$$

In other words the $k$ information symbols are used as coefficients of the polynomial $u(x) = u_0 + u_1 x + \cdots + u_{k-1}x^{k-1}$, and then the code word $u(x)g(x)$ is sent.

The operation of multiplication by a given polynomial $g(x)$ can be realized by a simple shift-register circuit. Observe that in the case $g(x) = g_i x^i$, the multiplication of a polynomial $u(x)$ by $g(x)$ is just the scalar multiplication by $g_i$ followed by $i$ shifts to the right. For $g(x) = \sum_{i=0}^{n-k} g_i x^i$, these operations are simply added. A multiply-by-$g(x)$ circuit is shown in Figure 1, where $\rightarrow\Box\rightarrow$ denotes a shift-register stage, and

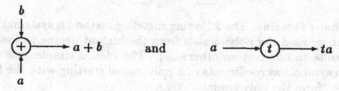

denote the adder and scaler (in the field under consideration), respectively.

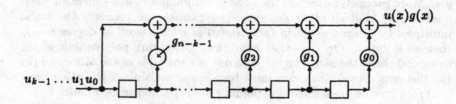

**Figure 1:** A circuit for multiplication $u(x) \mapsto u(x)g(x)$

## Examples

(1) The Hamming cyclic code with the generator polynomial $g(x) = 1 + x + x^3$ [see Example (3) of 10.1] has the following encoder:

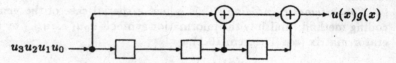

The information bits 1001 are encoded as follows:

$$u(x)g(x) = (1 + x^3)(1 + x + x^3) = 1 + x + x^4 + x^6.$$

The code word 1100101 is sent; this encoding is not systematic.

(2) The cyclic code over $\mathbf{Z}_3$ with the generator polynomial $g(x) = 2 + x^2$ [see Example (4) of 10.1] has the following encoder:

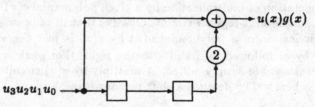

*Systematic encoding.* The following encoding method is systematic, provided that we read the polynomials from the highest degree to the lowest one (opposite to our custom otherwise). The idea is simple: use the information symbols as coefficients of a polynomial starting with the highest degree; i.e., form the polynomial

$$u(x) = u_{n-1}x^{n-1} + u_{n-2}x^{n-2} + \cdots + u_{n-k}x^{n-k}.$$

Divide $u(x)$ by the generator polynomial $g(x)$, and denote by $q(x)$ the quotient (which is not used) and by $r(x)$ the remainder:

$$u(x) = q(x)g(x) + r(x) \qquad \text{and} \qquad \text{degree } r(x) < n - k.$$

Then send the polynomial

$$u(x) - r(x).$$

This is a code word, since it is a multiple of $g(x)$:

$$u(x) - r(x) = q(x)g(x)$$

(see Theorem 10.1).

For example, if we use the above Hamming code with $g(x) = 1 + x + x^3$, then the information bits 1001 are encoded as follows: divide $u(x) = x^6 + x^3$ by $g(x)$:

$$
\begin{array}{r}
x^3 \qquad\ + x \ = \quad q(x) \\[2pt]
\hline
x^3 + x + 1 \overline{)\ \ x^6 \qquad + x^3 \qquad\quad} \\[2pt]
x^6 + x^4 + x^3 \\[2pt]
\hline
x^4 \qquad\qquad\quad \\[2pt]
x^4 \qquad + x^2 + x \\[2pt]
\hline
x^2 + x \ = \quad r(x)
\end{array}
$$

The remainder is $r(x) = x^2 + x$. Thus, we send the polynomial

$$u(x) - r(x) = x^6 + x^3 + x^2 + x,$$

or the word 1001110 (provided that we read polynomials from degree 6).

Observe that whereas the highest coefficient of the remainder is at $x^{n-k-1}$ [since $r(x)$ has degree smaller than $n - k$], the lowest coefficient of the polynomial $u(x)$ is that at $x^{n-k}$. Thus, the two polynomials $u(x)$ and $r(x)$ are not mixed at all, and this explains why the encoding is systematic.

Fortunately, digital circuits (unlike human beings) divide by a given polynomial as easily as they multiply. A divide-by-$g(x)$ feedback circuit, based on the long division of polynomials, is shown in Figure 2. It takes $n$ shifts for the quotient to pass out of the shift register; at that moment, the contents of the shift register are the coefficients of the remainder $r(x) = r_0 + r_1 x + \cdots + r_{n-k-1} x^{n-k-1}$. By using this idea (and the fact that we do not need the quotient), a simple encoding circuit for cyclic codes can be constructed. For example, a systematic encoder for the Hamming code of length 7 [with $g(x) = 1 + x + x^3$] is shown in Figure 3: for the first 4 shifts, the information bits $u_6 u_5 u_4 u_3$ are sent both to the channel and the

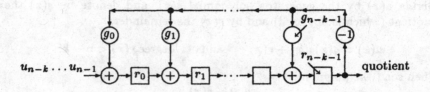

**Figure 2:** A circuit for division $u(x) \mapsto u(x) : g(x)$

divide-by-$g(x)$ circuit, and since at that moment the shift register contains the remainder (i.e., the check bits $u_2 u_1 u_1$), we disconnect the feedback by opening the gate and send the contents of the shift register to the channel.

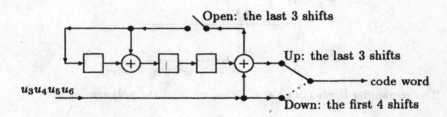

**Figure 3:** A systematic encoder for the Hamming code

**Example.** (3) Jumping ahead a little, we consider a double-error-correcting code which belongs to the important class of BCH codes studied in Chapter 12. The following polynomial

$$g(x) = 1 + x^4 + x^6 + x^7 + x^8$$

generates a linear cyclic $(15, 7)$-code. We prove later that the code has minimum distance 5, and thus corrects double errors. (Compare this code with the single-error-correcting Hamming code with 11 information bits, and the shortened triple-error-correcting Reed-Muller code $\overline{\mathcal{R}}(1, 4)$ with 5 information bits.)

An encoder for this code is shown in Figure 4.

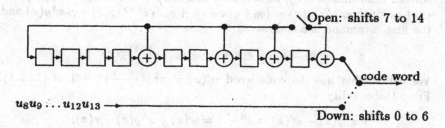

$u_8 u_9 \ldots u_{12} u_{13} \longrightarrow$

**Figure 4:** An encoder for the $(15, 7)$-BCH code correcting double errors

## 10.3 Parity Check Polynomial

We have defined the generator polynomial of a cyclic code, and now we show which polynomials can serve as generator polynomials, and how the parity check matrix can be substituted by a polynomial.

Observe first that if $g(x) = g_0 + g_1 x + \cdots + g_{n-k-1} x^{n-k-1} + x^{n-k}$ is a monic generator polynomial [see Remark (3) of 10.1] of a cyclic code $K$, then $g(x)$, $xg(x)$, $\ldots$, $x^{k-1}g(x)$ are code words of $K$, in fact, cyclic shifts of the word $g(x)$. However, $x^k g(x)$ is not a code word (since its degree is not smaller than $n$). In order to "produce" a code word we have to shift the highest-degree summand of $x^k g(x)$, which is $x^n$, to the lowest-degree position; in other words, we have to subtract $x^n$ and add 1. Thus,

$$x^k g(x) - x^n + 1 = 100\ldots00g_0g_1\ldots g_{n-k-1} \qquad (10.3.1)$$

is a code word of $K$.

**Theorem.** *Every generator polynomial of a cyclic code of length $n$ divides $x^n - 1$. Conversely, every proper divisor of $x^n - 1$ generates a cyclic code of length $n$.*

**PROOF.** I. Let $g(x)$ be a monic generator polynomial of a cyclic code [see Remark (3) of 10.1]. The degree of $g(x)$ is $n - k$ (with $k > 0$, since a cyclic code is nontrivial), and when dividing $x^n - 1$ by $g(x)$, we get

$$x^n - 1 = q(x)g(x) + r(x) \qquad \text{and} \qquad \text{degree } r(x) < n - k.$$

In order to prove that $r(x) = 0$, it is sufficient to verify that $r(x)$ is a code word: by Theorem 10.1, $r(x)$ is a multiple of $g(x)$, but since it has a degree smaller than that of $g(x)$, we conclude that $r(x) = 0$. Put $q(x) = q_0 + q_1 x + \cdots + q_k x^k$, then $q(x)g(x) = (q_0 + q_1 x + \cdots + q_{k-1} x^{k-1})g(x) + q_k x^k g(x)$ and the first summand is a code word

$$w(x) = (q_0 + q_1 x + \cdots + q_{k-1} x^{k-1})g(x).$$

We will further use the code word $w'(x) = x^k g(x) - x^n + 1$ of (10.3.1). From the equality

$$x^k g(x) - w'(x) = x^n - 1 = w(x) + x^k g(x) + r(x),$$

we get

$$r(x) = -w'(x) - w(x).$$

Since $-w(x)$ and $-w'(x)$ are code words, it follows that $r(x)$ is a code word—hence, $r(x) = 0$.

II. Let $g(x)$ be a divisor of $x^n - 1$ of degree $s < n$. The code $K$ of all multiples $q(x)g(x)$, where $q(x)$ is any polynomial of degree smaller then $n - s$, is easily seen to be linear. To prove that $K$ is cyclic, consider a code word $w(x) = q(x)g(x)$:

(a) If the degree of $q(x)$ is smaller than $n - s - 1$, then the cyclic shift of $w(x)$ to the right is $xw(x) = [xq(x)]g(x)$, which is a code word.

(b) If the degree of $q(x)$ is $n - s - 1$, then the cyclic shift $\widetilde{w}(x)$ of $w(x)$ to the right is obtained from $xq(x)g(x)$ by shifting the highest coefficient $a_n x^n$ to the lowest position:

$$\widetilde{w}(x) = xq(x)g(x) - a_n x^n + a_n = xq(x)g(x) - a_n(x^n - 1).$$

Since $g(x)$ divides $x^n - 1$, we can write $x^n - 1 = h(x)g(x)$ and we obtain

$$\widetilde{w}(x) = [xq(x) - a_n x^n h(x)]g(x),$$

which is a code word.

Thus, $K$ is a cyclic code with basis $g(x)$, $xg(x)$, $\ldots$, $x^{n-s-1}g(x)$. It follows that the dimension of $K$ is $k = n - s$. Therefore, the degree of $g(x)$ is $n - k$. Hence, $g(x)$ is a generator polynomial of $K$.                                          □

**Definition.** *For each cyclic code of length $n$ with generator polynomial $g(x)$, we call the polynomial*

$$h(x) = \frac{x^n - 1}{g(x)}$$

*a* parity check polynomial *of the code.*

**Example.** (1) We are going to list all binary cyclic codes of length 7. Since the generator polynomials are precisely the divisors of $x^7 - 1$ (except of $x^7 - 1$ itself), we first decompose that polynomial:

$$x^7 - 1 = (x+1)(x^3 + x + 1)(x^3 + x^2 + 1).$$

It is not difficult to verify that no further decomposition of the polynomials $x^3 + x + 1$ and $x^3 + x^2 + 1$ in the field $\mathbf{Z}_2$ is possible. Thus, the generator polynomials are precisely all the combinations of the polynomials decomposing $x^7 - 1$—their number is $2^3 - 1 = 7$. See Figure 5.

| Generator Polynomial | Parity Check Polynomial | Name of the Code |
|---|---|---|
| $x + 1$ | $(x^3 + x + 1)(x^3 + x^2 + 1)$ | Even-parity code [Ex. (1) in 10.1] |
| $x^3 + x + 1$ | $(x + 1)(x^3 + x^2 + 1)$ | Hamming code [Ex. (3) in 10.1] |
| $x^3 + x^2 + 1$ | $(x + 1)(x^3 + x + 1)$ | Hamming code [Exercise 10C] |
| $(x + 1)(x^3 + x + 1)$ | $x^3 + x^2 + 1$ | Simplex code [Exercise 10C] |
| $(x + 1)(x^3 + x^2 + 1)$ | $x^3 + x + 1$ | Simplex code |
| $(x^3 + x + 1)$ $\times (x^3 + x^2 + 1)$ | $x + 1$ | Repetition code [Ex. (4) of 10.1] |
| $1$ | $x^7 - 1$ | All of $\mathbf{Z}_2^7$ |

**Figure 5:** All binary cyclic codes of length 7

**Remark.** (1) The parity check polynomial is a monic polynomial (provided that, as agreed, we restrict ourselves to monic generator polynomials) of degree $k$.

**Proposition.** *A cyclic code with the parity check polynomial $h(x) = h_0 + h_1 x + \cdots + h_{k-1} x^{k-1} + x^k$ has the following parity check matrix:*

$$\mathbf{H} = \begin{bmatrix} 0 & 0 & \cdots & 0 & 0 & 0 & 1 & h_{k-1} & \cdots & h_2 & h_1 & h_0 \\ 0 & 0 & \cdots & 0 & 0 & 1 & h_{k-1} & \cdots & & h_2 & h_1 & h_0 & 0 \\ 0 & 0 & \cdots & 0 & 1 & h_{k-1} & \cdots & & h_2 & h_1 & h_0 & 0 & 0 \\ & & & & & \cdots & & & & & & & \\ 1 & h_{k-1} & \cdots & h_2 & h_1 & h_0 & 0 & 0 & \cdots & 0 & 0 & 0 \end{bmatrix}.$$

PROOF. The above matrix $\mathbf{H}$ has, obviously, $n - k$ linearly independent rows. Thus, its rank is $n - k$, and the linear space $L$ of all vectors $\mathbf{w}$ satisfying $\mathbf{Hw}^{\mathrm{tr}} = \mathbf{0}^{\mathrm{tr}}$ has dimension $n - (n - k) = k$, see Theorem 7.7. It is our aim to prove that the code $K$ with the parity check polynomial $h(x)$ is equal to $L$. Since the two linear spaces have the same dimension, it is sufficient to prove that $K$ is a subspace of $L$ [by Corollary (4) of 7.7].

We first observe that the generator polynomial $g(x)$ lies in the space $L$, i.e., that $\mathbf{Hg}^{\mathrm{tr}} = \mathbf{0}^{\mathrm{tr}}$. In fact, the inner product of the first row of $\mathbf{H}$ with $\mathbf{g}$ is $\sum_{i=0}^{n-1} h_i g_{n-1-i}$. This is the coefficient of the polynomial $h(x)g(x)$ at $x^{n-1}$, which is zero because $h(x)g(x) = x^n - 1$. The inner product of the second row with $\mathbf{g}$ is $\sum_{i=0}^{n-1} h_i g_{n-2-i}$, i.e., the coefficient of $h(x)g(x)$ at $x^{n-2}$, which is also zero, etc. Thus, $g(x)$ lies in $L$. For the same reason, the shifts $xg(x)$, $x^2 g(x)$, $\ldots$, $x^{k-1}g(x)$ of the generator polynomial lie in $L$. Therefore, $L$ contains a basis of the linear space $K$. It follows that $L$ contains $K$, hence, $K = L$.                                                      $\square$

## Examples

(2) The Hamming cyclic code of length 7 with the generator polynomial $g(x) = 1 + x + x^3$ has the parity check polynomial $h(x) = (x^7 - 1) \div (x^3 + x + 1) = x^4 + x^2 + x + 1$. Thus, it has the following parity check matrix:

$$\mathbf{H} = \begin{bmatrix} 0 & 0 & 1 & 0 & 1 & 1 & 1 \\ 0 & 1 & 0 & 1 & 1 & 1 & 0 \\ 1 & 0 & 1 & 1 & 1 & 0 & 0 \end{bmatrix}.$$

A different parity check matrix was found in Example (3) of 10.1.

(3) The polynomial $1 + x + x^4$ divides $x^{15} - 1$ in the field $\mathbf{Z}_2$:

$$x^{15} - 1 = (1 + x + x^4)(1 + x + x^2 + x^3 + x^5 + x^7 + x^8 + x^{11}).$$

Thus, there is a cyclic code of length 15 with the parity check polynomial $h(x) = 1 + x + x^2 + x^3 + x^5 + x^7 + x^8 + x^{11}$. The code has the following parity check matrix:

$$\mathbf{H} = \begin{bmatrix} 0 & 0 & 0 & 1 & 0 & 0 & 1 & 1 & 0 & 1 & 0 & 1 & 1 & 1 & 1 \\ 0 & 0 & 1 & 0 & 0 & 1 & 1 & 0 & 1 & 0 & 1 & 1 & 1 & 1 & 0 \\ 0 & 1 & 0 & 0 & 1 & 1 & 0 & 1 & 0 & 1 & 1 & 1 & 1 & 0 & 0 \\ 1 & 0 & 0 & 1 & 1 & 0 & 1 & 0 & 1 & 1 & 1 & 1 & 0 & 0 & 0 \end{bmatrix}.$$

Since the $2^4 - 1$ columns of $\mathbf{H}$ are nonzero and pairwise distinct, this is a Hamming $(15, 11)$-code.

**Remarks**

(2) In the preceding examples, we have seen two Hamming codes as cyclic codes. This is no coincidence, as is explained in 12.1.

(3) The dual of a cyclic code $K$ is a cyclic code. The generator polynomial of $K^\perp$ is the parity check polynomial of $K$ "read backwards" (i.e., from the highest-degree position to the lowest one). More precisely, let $h(x)$ be the parity check polynomial of $K$, $h(x) = h_0 + h_1 x + \cdots + h_k x^k$. Then the dual code $K^\perp$ has the generator polynomial $g^*(x) = h_k + h_{k-1} x + \cdots + h_0 x^k$.

In fact, the polynomial $h(x)$ generates a cyclic $(n, n-k)$-code $\overline{K}$ (since it divides $x^n - 1$, and has degree $k$). It is then obvious that the above polynomial $g^*(x)$ generates the cyclic code $K^*$ of all words in $\overline{K}$ read backwards. This code $K^*$ is also an $(n, n-k)$-code, and from the above proposition, we see that any code word of $K^*$ lies in $K^\perp$. Since $K^*$ and $K^\perp$ have the same dimension $n - k$, we conclude that they are equal (see 7.7).

**Example.** (4) In order to obtain a $(15, 4)$-simplex code as a cyclic code, we use the polynomial $h(x)$ of Example (3) above, and read it backwards: the following polynomial

$$g^*(x) = 1 + x^3 + x^4 + x^6 + x^9 + x^{10} + x^{11}$$

generates a simplex code.

# 10.4 Decoding Cyclic Codes

We have seen in 8.3 that an important piece of information about the error pattern, obtainable directly from the received word, is the syndrome. In the case of cyclic codes it is often more convenient to work with the syndrome polynomial:

**Definition.** *Let $K$ be a cyclic code of length $n$ with a generator polynomial $g(x)$. By the syndrome polynomial $s(x)$ of a (received) word $\mathbf{w}$ of length $n$ is meant the remainder of the division of the corresponding polynomial $w(x)$ by $g(x)$.*

**Remarks**

(1) Analogously to the situation with syndrome words (8.3), the received word has the same syndrome polynomial as the error-pattern word. In more detail: we send a code word $q(x)g(x)$ and receive

$$w(x) = q(x)g(x) + e(x)$$

[where $e(x)$ is the error pattern]. Then the remainders of the divisions of $w(x)$ and $e(x)$, respectively, by the polynomial $g(x)$ are the same, since $w(x) - e(x)$ is divisible by $g(x)$.

(2) The syndrome decoding that we saw in 8.3 can be realized by means of polynomials: the syndromes are precisely all polynomials of degrees smaller than $n - k$, and to each syndrome $s(x)$, we choose an error pattern $e(x)$ of the smallest Hamming weight which has that syndrome. Fortunately, the algebraic structure of cyclic codes can be used to obtain a much more efficient decoding method. We first illustrate the syndrome decoding on a simple example.

**Example.** (1) Let $K$ be the Hamming code of length 7 with the generator polynomial $g(x) = 1 + x + x^3$. The syndrome of $\mathbf{w} = 1011001$ is the remainder of $(x^6 + x^3 + x^2 + 1) \div (x^3 + x + 1)$, which is $s(x) = x + 1$. We know that Hamming codes correct single errors, thus, it is worthwhile to find the syndromes of all the corresponding error patterns $e(x) = x^i$, see Figure 6. Since $x + 1$ is the syndrome of $e(x) = x^3$, we conclude that the third bit is corrupted, and we decode

$$w(x) - e(x) = 1011001 - 0001000 = 1010001.$$

| Error-Pattern Polynomial | Syndrome Polynomial |
|:---:|:---:|
| 0 | 0 |
| 1 | 1 |
| $x$ | $x$ |
| $x^2$ | $x^2$ |
| $x^3$ | $x + 1$ |
| $x^4$ | $x^2 + x$ |
| $x^5$ | $x^2 + x + 1$ |
| $x^6$ | $x^2 \quad + 1$ |

**Figure 6:** Syndrome decoding for the cyclic Hamming code of length 7

The computation of the syndrome can be realized by a circuit analogous to the encoding circuit of 10.2, see Figure 7.

*Meggitt decoder.* The most complicated part of syndrome decoding is listing of error patterns corresponding to the syndromes, and searching this list every time a word is received. A substantial simplification can be achieved by using the cyclic character of the code: We can concentrate on

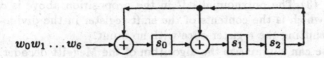

**Figure 7:** Syndrome computing circuit for the cyclic Hamming code

the last (i.e., highest-degree) position of each received word **w**, which we correct or not, according to its syndrome. Then we make a cyclic shift of **w**, and again study the last position, etc. After $n$ cyclic shifts, all positions will have been corrected.

The advantage of this decoding method, discovered by Meggitt in 1960, is that we only list syndromes of those correctable error patterns which have degree exactly $n - 1$. (For example, of the seven syndromes of the Hamming code in Figure 6 only one has the degree 6.) The computation of syndromes need not be repeated for each shift: we just compute the syndrome **s** of the received word **w**, and by the cyclic shift of **s** within the divide-by-$g(x)$ circuit, we obtain the syndrome of the cyclic shift of **w**. This follows from the next proposition.

**Proposition.** *If a word* **w** *has a syndrome polynomial* $s(x)$, *then the cyclic shift of* **w** *has the syndrome polynomial* $s^{(1)}(x)$, *which is the remainder of the division of* $xs(x)$ *by the generator polynomial* $g(x)$.

PROOF. The syndrome polynomial $s(x)$ fulfils

$$w(x) = s(x) + q(x)g(x),$$

where $q(x)$ is the quotient of the division of $w(x)$ by $g(x)$. The cyclic shift of $w(x)$ is obtained from the (noncyclic) shift $xw(x)$ by shifting the highest-degree summand $w_{n-1}x^n$ to the first position, i.e., the cyclic shift is

$$
\begin{aligned}
w^{(1)}(x) &= xw(x) - w_{n-1}x^n + w_{n-1} \\
&= xw(x) - w_{n-1}(x^n - 1) \\
&= xw(x) - w_{n-1}g(x)h(x) \\
&= xs(x) + xq(x)g(x) - w_{n-1}g(x)h(x) \\
&= xs(x) + g(x)\big[xq(x) - w_{n-1}h(x)\big].
\end{aligned}
$$

It follows that the remainders of the division of $w^{(1)}(x)$ and $xs(x)$ by the polynomial $g(x)$ are the same.                                              □

**Remark.** (3) The polynomial $s^{(1)}$ in the proposition above is obtained from $s(x)$ [which is the contents of the shift register in the divide-by-$g(x)$ circuit] by shifting the register once with no input.

Thus, we can summarize the algorithm of the Meggitt decoder (for binary codes, just to simplify the presentation) as follows:

*Meggitt decoding algorithm for binary cyclic $(n, k)$)-codes*

Step 1. Make a list of all syndromes whose chosen coset leader has 1 in the rightmost position (i.e., the coset leader is an error-pattern polynomial of degree $n - k - 1$).

Step 2. When receiving a word $w(x)$, feed it into the divide-by-$g(x)$ circuit (in $n$ clock times).

Step 3. If the resulting syndrome is on the list above, correct the rightmost bit of the received word.

Step 4. Shift cyclically both the received word and the contents of the divide-by-$g(x)$ circuit, and repeat step 3. After $n - 1$ such cyclic shifts, all bits of the received word are corrected; a final cyclic shift of the received word concludes the decoding.

**Example.** (2) The Meggitt decoder of the Hamming code of Example (1) proceeds as follows.

Step 1. The only syndrome on our list is $x^2 + 1$.

Step 2. When receiving, say, $\mathbf{w} = 1011001$, feed it into the circuit in Figure 7: in 7 clock times, one obtains the syndrome 110:

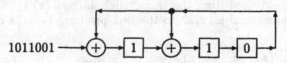

Step 3. Do not correct $w_6$, since the syndrome 110 is not on our list.

Step 4. Shift the received word to $w_6 w_0 w_1 \ldots w_5 = 1101100$ and the contents of the above shift register with no input:

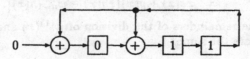

The syndrome is, again, not on our list. Thus, $w_5$ will not be corrected, etc. The contents of the shift register during steps 7 to 13 are listed in Figure 8. It follows that the only bit to correct is $w_3$ because the tenth step of decoding is the only one for which the shift-register contents is 100 (i.e., $1 + x^2$), which is on our list. Finally, make the last cyclic shift, and obtain the decoded word 1010001 [as in Example (1)].

| Step of Decoding | Bit Considered | Syndrome |
|:---:|:---:|:---:|
| 7 | $w_6$ | 110 |
| 8 | $w_5$ | 011 |
| 9 | $w_4$ | 111 |
| 10 | $w_3$ | 101 |
| 11 | $w_2$ | 100 |
| 12 | $w_1$ | 010 |
| 13 | $w_0$ | 001 |

**Figure 8:** Decoding the word 1011001

**Example.** (3) Consider the double-error-correcting $(15, 7)$-code of Example (3) in 10.2. We can correct double errors either by the syndrome-decoding technique [which requires listing syndromes for all error patterns of weight 0, 1, 2, the number of which is $1 + 15 + \binom{15}{2} = 121$] or by the Meggitt decoder. Observe that there are just 15 syndromes to be listed for the latter, viz., the syndromes of $e(x) = x^{14}$ and $e(x) = x^i + x^{14}$ for $i = 0, 1, \ldots, 13$. The table of syndromes is shown in Figure 9. Thus, receiving a word **w** of length 15, we compute its syndrome, and if it can be found among the syndromes of Figure 9, we correct the last bit, $w_{14}$. Then we shift cyclically the received word and correct bits $w_{13}, w_{12}, \ldots, w_0$.

**Remark.** Observe that in the last example, the encoding is not complete: the Meggitt decoder will correct all single errors and all double errors, which (together with the no-error pattern) means 121 error patterns. However, the code $K$ has $2^7$ code words, and thus there are $2^{15}/2^7 = 256$ classes modulo $K$, see Remark 6.2. This is a typical situation: for codes correcting $t$ errors, we want to find a simple decoder correcting all error patterns of Hamming weight at most $t$, ignoring the possibility of other corrections. Well, it would actually be best to have no other correctable errors, but, unfortunately, this is a very rare property of codes, as will be seen in 10.6.

| Error-Pattern Polynomial | Syndrome Polynomial |
|---|---|
| $x^{14}$ | $x^7 + x^6 + x^5 \qquad + x^3$ |
| $1 + x^{14}$ | $x^7 + x^6 + x^5 \qquad + x^3 \qquad\qquad + 1$ |
| $x + x^{14}$ | $x^7 + x^6 + x^5 \qquad + x^3 \qquad + x$ |
| $x^2 + x^{14}$ | $x^7 + x^6 + x^5 \qquad + x^3 + x^2$ |
| $x^3 + x^{14}$ | $x^7 + x^6 + x^5$ |
| $x^4 + x^{14}$ | $x^7 + x^6 + x^5 + x^4 + x^3$ |
| $x^5 + x^{14}$ | $x^7 + x^6 \qquad\qquad + x^3$ |
| $x^6 + x^{14}$ | $x^7 \qquad + x^5 \qquad + x^3$ |
| $x^7 + x^{14}$ | $x^6 + x^5 \qquad + x^3$ |
| $x^8 + x^{14}$ | $x^5 + x^4 + x^3 \qquad\qquad + 1$ |
| $x^9 + x^{14}$ | $x^7 \qquad\qquad + x^4 + x^3 \qquad + x + 1$ |
| $x^{10} + x^{14}$ | $x^3 + x^2 + x$ |
| $x^{11} + x^{14}$ | $x^7 + x^6 + x^5 + x^4 \qquad + x^2 + x$ |
| $x^{12} + x^{14}$ | $x^7 + x^6 \qquad + x^4 \qquad\qquad + x$ |
| $x^{13} + x^{14}$ | $x^7 \qquad\qquad + x^4 + x^3 + x^2$ |

**Figure 9:** Syndrome list for the Meggitt decoder of a double-error-correcting code with $g(x) = 1 + x^4 + x^6 + x^7 + x^8$

In the following section, we present a better decoder of the BCH code under study.

## 10.5   Error-Trapping Decoding

A powerful decoding method, particularly useful for single-error- and double-error-correcting codes (and, as we will see later, for burst-error corrections) is based on the possibility of "trapping" all errors within the syndrome circuit.

Let $K$ be a cyclic $(n, k)$-code capable of correcting $t$ errors. The error-trapping decoding we are going to describe corrects $t$ errors whenever they are confined to $n - k$ consecutive positions (including end-around). We first make the last concept precise, and then we prove the basic proposition which shows how error trapping works.

**Definition.** (1) *By a (cyclic)* burst-error pattern *of length $l$ is meant a nonzero word $e_0 e_1 \ldots e_{n-1}$ such that all nonzero components are confined* to $l$ consecutive positions in the cyclic sense, i.e., they are among $e_{i+1}$, $e_{i+2}$, ..., $e_{i+l}$ for some $i = 0, 1, \ldots, n-1$, with modulo $n$ addition in the indices.

(2) If a word $\mathbf{v}$ is sent and a word $\mathbf{w}$ is received, we say that errors are confined to $l$ consecutive positions provided that the error pattern $\mathbf{e} = \mathbf{w} - \mathbf{v}$ is a burst-error pattern of length $l$.

**Proposition.** Let $\mathbf{w}$ be a word received when a cyclic $(n, k)$-code is used, and assume that at most $t$ symbols have been corrupted.

(1) If the syndrome polynomial has Hamming weight at most $t$, then the error-pattern polynomial is equal to the syndrome polynomial.

(2) Whenever the errors are confined to $n - k$ consecutive positions, then some cyclic shift of $\mathbf{w}$ has the syndrome polynomial of Hamming weight at most $t$.

**PROOF.** (1) The syndrome polynomial $s(x)$ is the remainder of the division of the error-pattern polynomial $e(x)$ by the generator polynomial $g(x)$. Thus,

$$e(x) = q(x)g(x) + s(x).$$

By hypothesis, $e(x)$ has Hamming weight at most $t$ (since at most $t$ symbols are corrupted), and $e(x) - s(x) = q(x)g(x)$ is a code word of $K$. Whenever $s$ has Hamming weight at most $t$, then the code word $e(x) - s(x)$ has Hamming weight at most $2t$. However, since $K$ corrects $t$ errors, the minimum distance of $K$ is $2t + 1$ or more. Thus, no nonzero code word has Hamming weight smaller than $2t + 1$ —consequently, $e(x) - s(x) = 0$.

(2) It is obvious that whenever the word $\mathbf{w}$ has errors confined to $n - k$ consecutive positions, then some cyclic shift $\mathbf{w}'$ has errors confined to the first $n-k$ consecutive positions (i.e., to the positions $w'_0, \ldots, w'_{n-k-1}$). This implies that the error pattern $\mathbf{e}$ shifted cyclically in the same manner yields a word $\mathbf{e}'$ with $e'_i = 0$ for all $i \geq n - k$. In other words, the corresponding polynomial $e'(x)$, which is the error-pattern polynomial of the word $\mathbf{w}'$, has degree at most $n - k - 1$. The syndrome of $w'$ is the remainder $s'(x)$ of the division of $e'(x)$ by the generator polynomial $g(x)$. Since the degree of $e'(x)$ is smaller than that of $g(x)$, it follows that the remainder is $e'(x)$; i.e., $s'(x) = e'(x)$. Thus, $s'$ has Hamming weight at most $t$.  □

*Error-trapping decoding algorithm.* Let $K$ be a cyclic code correcting $t$ errors. When receiving a word $\mathbf{w}$, find its syndrome $\mathbf{s}$, and if the Hamming weight of $\mathbf{s}$ is smaller or equal to $t$, decode as $\mathbf{w} - \mathbf{s}$. If $\mathbf{s}$ has Hamming weight larger than $t$, shift cyclically $\mathbf{w}$ (to the right) and find the syndrome $\mathbf{s}^{(1)}$ of the shifted word $\mathbf{w}^{(1)}$. If the Hamming weight of $\mathbf{s}^{(1)}$ is smaller than $t$, then decode the word as $w^{(1)} - s^{(1)}$ shifted cyclically to the left. If $s^{(1)}$ has Hamming weight larger than $t$, shift cyclically the word $w^{(1)}$ to $w^{(2)}$, etc.

This algorithm corrects $t$ errors whenever they are confined to $n - k$ consecutive positions. In fact, by (2) in the above proposition, one of the shifted words $w^{(i)}$ has syndrome $s^{(i)}$ of Hamming weight at most $t$. Then by (1) of that proposition, $s^{(i)}$ is the $i$th shift of the error pattern.

**Examples**

(1) Error trapping is an optimal decoding method for Hamming codes. The received word $w$ is either a code word or we shift it until a syndrome of weight 1 is found. The unique 1 in that syndrome then indicates which bit should be corrected.

For example, let us have another look at Example (2) of 10.4. In Figure 8, we see that at the eleventh step of decoding (when the received word $w = 1011001$ has been shifted to $w_3 w_4 \ldots w_7 w_0 w_1 w_2 = 1001101$) the syndrome has Hamming weight 1. Thus, the syndrome 100 is the error pattern, therefore, the bit $w_3$ must be corrected.

(2) Error trapping is also very suitable for the double-error-correcting BCH code of Example (3) in 10.2. Observe that whenever two symbols are corrupted (say, $w_i$ and $w_j$, $j > i$), then errors are confined to $n - k = 8$ consecutive positions. In fact:

  (a) if $i + 7 \geq j$, then errors are confined to the eight positions $i$, $i + 1$, ..., $i + 7$, and

  (b) if $i + 7 < j$, then errors are confined to the eight positions $j$, $j + 1$, ..., 14, 0, 1, ..., $i$.

Thus, we compute the syndromes of all 15 cyclic shifts of the received word, and whenever we find a syndrome of Hamming weight 1 or 2, we know which bit, or pair of bits, to correct.

# 10.6   Golay Code: A Perfect Code for Triple Errors

In this section, we introduce one of the most fascinating error-correcting codes: a triple-error-correcting binary $(23, 12)$-code, discovered by Golay in 1949. This is a code important both for practical applications and in theory, since it has a rich algebraic and combinatorical structure. Besides, it is the only perfect code we have not yet introduced. We first turn to the concept of "perfectness".

What is the perfect solution to the problem of finding a code of length $n$ which corrects $t$ errors? The best code would correct $t$ errors and nothing else, since then it would have the least redundancy necessary for the task required. In other words, in syndrome decoding (6.3), it would have as coset leaders precisely all words of Hamming weights at most $t$. This is equivalent to the following property: every word of length $n$ has distance at most $t$ from precisely one code word.

**Definition.** *A linear code of length $n$ is called* perfect for $t$ errors *provided that for every word* **w** *of length $n$, there exists precisely one code word of Hamming distance $t$ or less from* **w**.

**Remarks**

(1) A perfect code for $t$ errors has minimum distance $2t+1$; thus, it corrects $t$ errors.

(2) If a binary $(n, k)$-code is perfect for $t$ errors, then

$$2^{n-k} = \sum_{i=0}^{t} \binom{n}{i}.$$

In fact, the left-hand side is the number of cosets modulo $K$ (see Remark 6.2), and the right-hand side is the number of coset leaders, i.e., words of Hamming weight $i = 0, 1, \ldots, t$. [The number of words of weight $i$ is just the number of combinations of order $i$ among the (bit) numbers $1, 2, \ldots, n$, which is $\binom{n}{i}$.]

(3) Conversely, every $t$-error-correcting binary $(n, k)$-code such that $2^{n-k} = \sum_{i=0}^{t} \binom{n}{i}$ is perfect. In fact, since the code corrects $t$ errors, we can choose all words of Hamming weight at most $t$ as coset leaders. And these will be all the coset leaders beause their number is equal to the number of cosets, which is $2^{n-k}$.

**Examples**

(1) The binary repetition code of length $2t + 1$ is perfect for $t$ errors. In fact, every word has either a majority of 0's (and then its Hamming distance from $00\ldots0$ is at most $t$) or a majority of 1's (and then its Hamming distance from $11\ldots1$ is at most $t$).

(2) Hamming codes are perfect for single errors, see Remark (2) of 5.5.

(3) The double-error-correcting BCH code of Example (3) in 10.2 is not perfect: it corrects, in addition to all double errors, also a lot (but

by no means all) of error patterns of three errors. This follows from the fact that this $(15, 7)$-code has $2^{15-7} = 256$ coset leaders of which only $\sum_{i=0}^{2} \binom{15}{i} = 121$ have Hamming weight at most 2. (In contrast, a triple-error-correcting code must have at least $\sum_{i=0}^{3} \binom{15}{i} = 451$ coset leaders.)

**Definition.** *The binary cyclic code of length 23 with the generator polynomial $g(x) = 1 + x^2 + x^4 + x^5 + x^6 + x^{10} + x^{11}$ is called* Golay code.

**Theorem.** *The Golay code has minimum distance 7.*

The proof, which is very technical, is omitted. The interested reader can find it in Blahut (1983).

**Corollary.** *The Golay code is a $(23, 12)$-code which is perfect for triple errors.*

In fact, since the generator polynomial has degree 11, the code has $k = 23 - 11 = 12$ information bits. It is easy to verify that

$$2^{23-12} = 2048 = \binom{23}{0} + \binom{23}{1} + \binom{23}{2} + \binom{23}{3}.$$

Thus, the Golay code is perfect for triple errors by Remark (3) above.

*Decoder for the Golay code.* The following decoder is a variation on error-trapping decoding (10.5). Suppose we send a code word and at most three bits are corrupted. If all the errors are confined to 11 consecutive positions, then we can trap them: some cyclic shift of the received word has syndrome of Hamming weight at most 3, and the syndrome is then equal to the error pattern (which we correct). Next suppose that errors are not confined to 11 consecutive positions. Then if we happen to correct one "suitable" bit, we can achieve that the remaining errors (at most two) are confined to 11 consecutive positions. More precisely, if the corrupted bits are $w_i$, $w_j$, and $w_k$, then one of the pairs, $(w_i, w_j)$, $(w_j, w_k)$, or $(w_i, w_k)$, is confined to 11 consecutive positions. This suggests the following algorithm:

Step 1: Compute the syndrome of the received word **w**.

Step 2: Find the syndrome $s^{(i)}$ of the cyclic shifts $\mathbf{w}^i$ of the received word (to the right) for $i = 0, 1, \ldots, 22$. If the Hamming weight of some $s^{(i)}$ is at most 3, the decoded word is the $i$th cyclic shift of $\mathbf{w}^{(i)} - s^{(i)}$ to the left.

Step 3: If all the syndromes in step 2 have Hamming weight larger than 3, change one bit of the received word, say, the bit $w_0$. Repeat step 2, searching for a syndrome of Hamming weight at most 2. If such a syndrome is found, the decoding is finished: the syndrome plus the bit $w_0$ form the error pattern to be corrected. If no syndrome of weight at most 2 is found, then $w_0$ is correct. Reset it to its original value, and repeat step 3 with other bits changed.

**Remarks**

(4) One of the deepest results of coding theory is the following theorem proved by Tietäväinen (1974) and Van Lint (1975): Every perfect binary code is either a repetition code (of odd length), or a Hamming code (of length $2^m - 1$), or a code equivalent to the Golay code (of length 23).

(5) The situation in the three-element alphabet $Z_3$ is analogous. Every perfect ternary code is either a repetition code, or a Hamming code, or a code equivalent to the *ternary Golay code*, which is a perfect triple-error-correcting $(11, 6)$-code.

(6) In alphabets of more than three elements, the situation is even simpler: the only perfect codes are the repetition codes and the Hamming codes.

# 10.7   Burst Errors

We usually assume that the corrupted symbols in a transmitted code word are distributed randomly (white noise). In some applications, however, errors are typically grouped in bursts. This is the case, for example, of telephone lines disturbed by a stroke of lightening, and of mechanical disturbances of floppy discs, etc. Codes designed for protection against white noise are less effective in combatting burst errors than codes specifically designed for burst-error detection or burst-error correction. The most efficient burst-error control codes have been found among cyclic codes, and we thus restrict our attention to those. For this reason, we also extend the concept of burst error to include the end-around case (as defined in 10.5).

**Remarks**

(1) A linear code is said to *detect burst errors of length l* provided that no burst-error pattern (10.5) of length $l$ is a code word. This means, then, that if we send a code word $\mathbf{v}$ and receive a word $\mathbf{w} = \mathbf{v} + \mathbf{e}$, where the error pattern $\mathbf{e}$ is a burst of length $l$, then $\mathbf{w}$ is not a code word. (If it were, $\mathbf{e} = \mathbf{w} - \mathbf{v}$ would also be a code word!) Thus, we detect the error.

(2) If a linear $(n,k)$-code detects burst errors of length $l$, then it must have at least $l$ parity check symbols:

$$n - k \geq l.$$

In fact, in the given $r$-symbol alphabet, there are precisely $r^l$ words, all with nonzero components confined to the first $l$ positions. No two of these words lie in the same coset modulo the code (6.2) because their difference is a burst of length $l$ (which is not a code word). Thus, the number $r^{n-k}$ of classes modulo the code (see Remark 6.2) is larger or equal to $r^l$. Hence, $n - k \geq l$.

The following proposition thus shows that all cyclic codes are very effective in detecting burst errors:

**Proposition.** *Every cyclic $(n,k)$-code detects burst errors of length $n - k$.*

PROOF. Every burst $e(x)$ of length $n - k$ can be obtained by a cyclic shift (to the right) of a burst which has all nonzero components confined to the first $n - k$ positions, i.e.,

$$e(x) = x^i a(x), \qquad \text{degree } a(x) < n - k.$$

Since $a(x)$ is a nonzero polynomial of degree smaller than that of the generator polynomial, it follows that $a(x)$ is not a code word. Then neither is $e(x)$, because $a(x)$ can be obtained by a cyclic shift from $e(x)$.          □

**Example.**  (1) The cyclic Hamming $(7,4)$-code detects burst errors of length 3. Recall that it detects two (random) errors.

**Remarks**

(3) A linear code is said to *correct burst errors of length $l$* provided that two different bursts of length $l$ always lie in different cosets modulo the code (6.2). We can then correct analogously as in 6.3 by forming an array in which all bursts of length $l$ are chosen as coset leaders. (Conversely, if two bursts, $e_1$ and $e_2$, lie in the same coset, then $v = e_1 - e_2$ is a code word. If we send $v$ and receive $w = v + e_2 = e_1$, we cannot correct this error: we do not know whether $v$ or $0$ was sent.)

(4) If a linear $(n,k)$-code corrects burst errors of length $l$, then it must have at least $2l$ parity check symbols:

$$n - k \geq 2l.$$

In fact, no burst of length $2l$ can be a code word. Thus, the number of cosets is at least $r^{2l}$ [compare Remark (2)].

## Examples

(2) The expurgated cyclic Hamming $(7,3)$-code corrects burst errors of length 2. This cyclic code [consisting of the even-parity code words of the cyclic Hamming $(7,4)$-code] has the following generator polynomial:

$$g(x) = (x^3 + x + 1)(x - 1) = x^4 + x^3 + x^2 + 1.$$

The minimum distance of this code is 4. Thus, in order to verify that no two bursts of length 2 lie in the same coset, it is sufficient to show that none of the following words

$$1100000 - 0011000 = 1111000,$$
$$1100000 - 0001100 = 1101100,$$
$$1100000 - 0000110 = 1100110,$$
$$1100000 - 0000011 = 1100011,$$

is a code word. (In fact, all the other cases yielding a word of Hamming weight 4 can be obtained by cyclic shifts of some of the four cases.) The verification that these four words are no code words can be performed mechanically.

(3) A number of good binary burst-error-correcting codes have been found by computer search. Some are listed in Figure 10.

| Length $n$ | Information Symbols $k$ | Corrects Bursts $l$ | Generator Polynomial |
|:---:|:---:|:---:|:---|
| 15 | 10 | 2 | $x^5 + x^4 + x^2 + 1$ |
| 15 | 9 | 3 | $x^6 + x^5 + x^4 + x^3 + 1$ |
| 31 | 25 | 2 | $x^6 + x^5 + x^4 + 1$ |
| 63 | 56 | 2 | $x^7 + x^6 + x^5 + x^3 + x^2 + 1$ |
| 63 | 55 | 3 | $x^8 + x^7 + x^6 + x^3 + 1$ |

**Figure 10:** Some binary burst-error-correcting codes

*Interleaving* is a simple but powerful technique for creating new cyclic burst-error-correcting codes from a given one. For each $(n, k)$-code $K$, we form a $(jn, jk)$-code by taking $j$ arbitrary code words in $K$ and merging them to a word of length $jn$ by alternating the symbols. If the original code $K$ corrects burst errors of length $l$, then the new code will, obviously, correct burst errors of length $jl$. For example, the expurgated Hamming code yields a $(14, 6)$-code correcting bursts of length 4, a $(21, 9)$-code correcting bursts of length 6, etc.

The interleaving of a cyclic code $K$ produces a cyclic code: if we interleave the code words $v_1$, $v_2$, ..., $v_j$ and then make a cyclic shift to the right, we get the same result as when interleaving the words $v_j^*$, $v_1^*$, ..., $v_{j-1}^*$, where the asterisk denotes the cyclic shift to the right. The generator polynomial of the new code is $g(x^j)$: it is obtained by interleaving $g(x) = g_0 g_1 \ldots g_{n-k} 00 \ldots 0$ and $j - 1$ zero words. The result is $g_0 00 \ldots 0 g_1 00 \ldots 0 \ldots 0 g_2 \ldots g_{n-k} 00 \ldots 0 = g(x^j)$.

**Example.** By interleaving the expurgated Hamming code above we obtain a cyclic $(14, 6)$-code correcting burst errors of length 4 with the generator polynomial

$$g(x) = x^8 + x^6 + x^4 + 1.$$

*Decoding.* Burst-error-correcting cyclic codes are efficiently decoded by the error trapping described in 10.5.

## 10.8   Fire Codes: High-Rate Codes for Burst Errors

Besides the burst-error-correcting codes found by computer search and interleaving, some analytic methods have also been developed for a construction of good codes for burst errors. Here we introduce the Fire codes, see Figure 11, and in 12.4, we will see the class of Reed-Solomon codes.

| | |
|---|---|
| Specified: | By an irreducible polynomial $p(x)$ of degree $t$ |
| Length: | $n = LCM(\tilde{n}, 2t - 1)$, where $\tilde{n}$ is the period of $p(x)$ |
| Information symbols: | $k = n - 3t + 1$ |
| Generator polynomial: | $g(x) = (x^{2t-1} - 1) p(x)$ |
| Error-control capability: | Corrects burst errors of length $t$ |

**Figure 11:** Properties of Fire codes

We first present an interesting concept concerning polynomials:

**Definition.** *A polynomial $p(x)$ over a field is said to have* period $n$ *provided that $n$ is the smallest number such that $p(x)$ divides $x^n - 1$ [i.e., such that $p(x)$ generates a cyclic code of length $n$].*

**Example.** (1) The binary polynomial $x^2 + x + 1$ has period 3; the binary polynomial $x^3 + x + 1$ has period 7. The binary polynomial $x^2$ does not have a period.

**Remarks**

(1) If $p(x)$ is a polynomial of period $n$, then $p(x)$ divides $x^k - 1$ if and only if $n$ divides the number $k$. In fact:

   (a) If $n$ divides $k$, then $x^n - 1$ divides $x^k - 1$:

$$x^k - 1 = (x^n - 1)\left(1 + x^n + x^{2n} + \cdots + x^{\frac{k}{n}}\right).$$

   Thus, $p(x)$ divides $x^k - 1$.

   (b) Let $p(x)$ divide $x^k - 1$. Then $k \geq n$, and we prove that $k$ is divisible by $n$ by induction on $k$. The case $k = n$ is clear. Suppose $k > n$. We know that $p(x)$ divides both

$$x^n - 1 = (x - 1)(1 + x + \cdots + x^{n-1})$$

   and

$$x^k - 1 = (x - 1)(1 + x + \cdots + x^{k-1}).$$

   Since $p(x)$ is irreducible, it divides both $1 + x + \cdots + x^{n-1}$ and $1 + x + \cdots + x^{k-1}$; thus, it also divides the difference of the last two polynomials, $x^n(1 + x + \cdots + x^{n-k-1})$. It follows that $p(x)$ divides $1 + x + \cdots + x^{n-k-1}$; finally, $p(x)$ also divides

$$x^{k-n} - 1 = (x - 1)(1 + x + \cdots + x^{n-k-1}).$$

   By the induction hypothesis, $n$ divides $k - n$; consequently, $n$ divides $k$.

(2) In particular, since $p(x) = x^n - 1$ has period $n$, we conclude that

$$x^n - 1 \text{ divides } x^k - 1 \iff n \text{ divides } k.$$

**Definition.** *A* Fire code *is a cyclic code with a generator polynomial*

$$g(x) = \left(x^{2t-1} - 1\right)p(x)$$

*for some irreducible polynomial $p(x)$ of degree at least $t$ and of period not divisible by $2t - 1$. The length of the code is the period of $g(x)$.*

**Remark.** (3) If $p(x)$ has period $\tilde{n}$, then the length of the Fire code is the least common multiple of $\tilde{n}$ and $2t - 1$:

$$n = LCM(\tilde{n}, 2t - 1).$$

In fact, the period of $g(x)$ is a multiple of both $\tilde{n}$ and $2t - 1$ [by Remarks (1) and (2)]. Thus, it is a multiple of $n$. Conversely, $x^n - 1$ is divisible both by $x^{2t-1} - 1$ and by $p(x)$. Since $2t - 1$ does not divide $\tilde{n}$, the polynomials $x^{2t-1} - 1$ and $p(x)$ are relatively prime. Therefore, $x^n - 1$ is divisible by their product, i.e., by $g(x)$. It follows that the period of $g(x)$ is $n$.

## Examples

(2) The irreducible binary polynomial $p(x) = x^2 + x + 1$ of period $\tilde{n} = 3$ does not allow the choice $t = 2$ (since $2t - 1 = 3$ divides $\tilde{n}$), and for $t = 1$, we get the repetition code of length 3.

(3) The irreducible binary polynomial $p(x) = x^3 + x + 1$ of period 7 defines a Fire code generated by

$$g(x) = (x^5 - 1)(x^3 + x + 1).$$

Its length is $n = 7 \times 5 = 35$. This $(35, 28)$-code corrects burst errors of length 3, as we presently prove.

**Theorem.** *The Fire code generated by $g(x) = (x^{2t-1} - 1)p(x)$ corrects burst errors of length $t$.*

PROOF. We are going to prove that whenever two bursts, $e_1(x)$ and $e_2(x)$, of length $t$ lie in the same coset modulo the Fire code, then $e_1(x) = e_2(x)$.

By a certain number $r$ of cyclic shifts, we can turn $e_1(x)$ into the position in which the first (lowest-degree) component is nonzero and all the nonzero components are confined to the first $t$ positions. Then $e_1(x) = x^r a(x)$, where

$$\text{degree } a(x) < t \quad \text{and} \quad a_0 \neq 0, \tag{10.8.1}$$

Analogously, $e_2(x) = x^s b(x)$ for some polynomial $b(x)$ with

$$\text{degree } b(x) < t \quad \text{and} \quad b_0 \neq 0. \tag{10.8.2}$$

It is our task to show that if $e_1(x) - e_2(x)$ is a code word, then it must be 0. We can restrict ourselves to the case $r = 0$ because the Fire code is a cyclic code (and the general case is obtained by $r$ cyclic shifts to the right from the special case). Thus, our task is to prove the following implication:

$$a(x) - x^s b(x) \text{ is a code word} \implies a(x) = x^s b(x) \tag{10.8.3}$$

Let us divide $s$ through $2t - 1$:

$$s = q(2t-1) + r \quad \text{and} \quad r < 2t - 1. \quad (10.8.4)$$

It follows that

$$a(x) - x^s b(x) = a(x) - x^r b(x) - x^r b(x)\big(x^{q(2t-1)} - 1\big).$$

The code word $a(x) - x^s b(x)$ is a multiple of the generator polynomial $g(x)$. Hence, $x^{2t-1} - 1$ divides the polynomial $a(x) - x^s b(x)$. It also divides $x^{q(2t-1)} - 1$ [by Remark (2)]; thus, the difference

$$a(x) - x^r b(x) = \big[a(x) - x^s b(x)\big] - x^r b(x)\big(x^{q(2t-1)} - 1\big)$$

is also divisible by $x^{2t-1} - 1$.

We now prove that

$$a(x) = x^r b(x). \quad (10.8.5)$$

As observed above, we can write

$$a(x) - x^r b(x) = d(x)\big(x^{2t-1} - 1\big) \quad (10.8.6)$$

for some polynomial $d(x)$ of degree $k$. Suppose that Equation (10.8.5) is false, i.e., $k \geq 0$. We will derive a contradiction. The right-hand side of (10.8.6) has degree $2t - 1 + k$. This is larger or equal to $t$, and since by (10.8.1), the degree of $a(x)$ is smaller than $t$, it follows that the degree of the left-hand side of (10.8.6) is determined by the summand $x^r b(x)$ alone. By (10.8.2), we conclude that $r + t > 2t - 1 + k$; thus,

$$r \geq t + k. \quad (10.8.7)$$

This implies that the degree of $a(x)$ is smaller than $t \leq r$. We conclude that the coefficient of the left-hand side of (10.8.6) at $x^r$ is $b_0$. Recall that $b_0 \neq 0$ [see (10.8.2)]; thus, the right-hand side also contains $x^r$. However, from (10.8.7) and (10.8.4), we see that $r$ fulfils $k < r < 2t - 1$; consequently, neither the polynomial $d(x)x^{2t-1}$ nor $-d(x)$ has nonzero coefficients at $x^r$— a contradiction. This proves (10.8.5).

Since $a_0 \neq 0$, see (10.8.1), Equation (10.8.5) can hold only if $r = 0$ and $a(x) = b(x)$. It remains to prove that $s = 0$. The code word of (10.8.3) has the form

$$a(x) - x^s b(x) = -b(x)(x^s - 1).$$

Every code word is divisible by $g(x)$, hence, by $p(x)$. The irreducible polynomial $p(x)$ has degree at least $t > \text{degree}\,[-b(x)]$; thus, $p(x)$ must divide $x^s - 1$. It follows from Remark (1) that $s$ is a multiple of the period $\tilde{n}$ of $p(x)$. Since $r = 0$ in (10.8.4), $s$ is also a multiple of $2t - 1$. Thus, $s$ is a multiple of $n = LCM(\tilde{n}, 2t - 1)$. However, $s$ is one of the numbers $0, 1, \ldots, n-1$. This proves $s = 0$, whereby the proof of (10.8.3) is concluded. $\quad\square$

**Example.** (4) To construct a binary Fire code correcting burst errors of length 4, we consider an irreducible polynomial of degree 4, e.g., $p(x) = x^4 + x + 1$. Its period is 15 (not divisible by 7); thus, we get a Fire code with the generator polynomial

$$g(x) = (x^7 - 1)(x^4 + x + 1)$$

and of length $n = 7 \times 15 = 105$. This $(105, 94)$-code corrects burst errors of length 4.

**Remark.** (3) Fire codes typically have high information rates. Some examples of binary Fire codes are listed in Figure 12.

| Length | Information Symbols | Corrects Bursts of Length |
|--------|---------------------|---------------------------|
| 35     | 27                  | 3                         |
| 105    | 94                  | 4                         |
| 297    | 265                 | 5                         |
| 693    | 676                 | 6                         |
| 1651   | 1631                | 7                         |

Figure 12: Parameters of binary Fire codes

# Exercises

**10A**   Verify that the division of a polynomial $a(x)$ by a polynomial $b(x) \neq 0$ can be performed by the following algorithm:

(a) If $b(x)$ has a degree larger than $a(x)$, then the quotient is 0, and the remainder is $a(x)$.

(b) If $b(x)$ has a degree smaller or equal to that of $a(x)$, divide the leading coefficient $a_n$ of $a(x)$ by the leading coefficient $b_m$ of $b(x)$. The result $q_{n-m} = a_n \div b_m$ is the coefficient of the quotient at the power $x^{n-m}$.

(c) Put $a(x) := a(x) - q_{n-m} x^{n-m} b(x)$ and perform recursively steps (a), (b), and (c). [Observe that the new polynomial $a(x)$ has a smaller degree than the original one. Thus, the algorithm stops after $n$ repetitions of steps (a), (b), and (c).]

**10B**  Prove that polynomial division is unique, i.e., given polynomials $a(x)$ and $b(x) \neq 0$, then whenever

$$a(x) = b(x)q(x) + r(x) = b(x)q'(x) + r'(x)$$

and the degrees of $r(x)$, $r'(x)$ are both smaller than that of $b(x)$, then $q(x) = q'(x)$ and $r(x) = r'(x)$. [Hint. Since the polynomial $r'(x) - r(x) = b(x)[q(x) - q'(x)]$ has degree smaller than that of $b(x)$, it follows that $q(x) - q'(x) = 0$; see Remark (1) in 10.1.]

**10C**  Verify that the binary cyclic code of length 7 with the generator polynomial $g(x) = 1 + x^2 + x^3$ is a Hamming code, and conclude that the code with the generator polynomial $(x^7 - 1):g(x) = x^4 + x^3 + x^2 + 1$ is the dual (simplex) code (8.2). [Hint: use remark (3) of 10.3 and the fact that by reading a Hamming code backwards one obtains another Hamming code.]

**10D**  Find all binary cyclic codes of length 5. Find all cyclic codes of length 5 over $\mathbf{Z}_3$.

**10E**  Describe the dual code of the binary cyclic code of length 5 with the generator polynomial $g(x) = x^3 + 2x^2 + 3x + 1$.

**10F**  In systematic coding, encode the information bits 1101 into a code word of the cyclic binary code of length 7 with the generator polynomial $g(x) = 1 + x^2 + x^3$.

**10G**  Describe the Meggitt decoder for the binary code of length 7 with the generator polynomial $g(x) = (1 + x^2 + x^3)(x + 1)$. Can you decode by error trapping?

**10H**  Prove that every double-error-correcting $(n, k)$-code with $n \geq 2k$ can be corrected by error trapping. What about the case $n < 2k$?

**10I**  What is the smallest length of a binary code with the generator polynomial $g(x) = x^4 + x^3 + x^2 + 1$? Design an encoder and decoder for the code. How many errors does it correct? Can error-trapping decoding be used?

**10J**  Can error-trapping decoding be used for the Golay code? Design an encoder and decoder for that code.

**10K**  Find a modification of the error-trapping decoding which can decode the double-error-correcting binary code of length 31 with the generator polynomial $g(x) = x^{10} + x^9 + x^8 + x^6 + x^5 + x^3 + 1$.

**10L**  Prove that whenever a cyclic code detects an error pattern e, then it also detects all error patterns obtained by cyclic shifts of e.

**10M**  Design an encoder for the Hamming $(15, 11)$-code of Example (3) in 10.3.

**10N**  Are the linear binary codes with the following generator matrices cyclic?

$$
\begin{bmatrix}
1 & 0 & 1 & 1 & 1 & 0 & 0 \\
1 & 1 & 0 & 1 & 0 & 0 & 0 \\
1 & 1 & 0 & 0 & 1 & 0 & 1 \\
0 & 0 & 1 & 0 & 1 & 1 & 1
\end{bmatrix}
\qquad
\begin{bmatrix}
1 & 1 & 1 & 1 & 0 & 0 & 0 \\
0 & 1 & 1 & 1 & 1 & 0 & 0 \\
0 & 0 & 1 & 1 & 1 & 1 & 0 \\
0 & 0 & 0 & 1 & 1 & 1 & 1
\end{bmatrix}
$$

**10O**  If the generator polynomial of a binary code is divisible by $x + 1$, verify that all code words have even weight. Does the converse hold?

**10P**  What is the necessary and sufficient condition on a generator polynomial of a cyclic code of odd length in order that $111\ldots 11$ be a code word?

**10Q**  Describe the generator polynomial of the expurgation of a given cyclic code.

**10R**  If $g(x)$ generates a cyclic $(n, k)$-code, verify that $g(x^i)$ generates a cyclic $(in, ik)$-code. Describe the code for $g(x) = x+1$ and $g(x) = x^3+x+1$ with $n = 7$.

**10S**  Verify that the intersection of two cyclic codes of the same length is a cyclic code. What generator polynomial does it have?

## Notes

Cyclic codes were introduced by Prange (1957), who discovered their rich algebraic structure and prepared ground for the major development of coding theory in the early 1960s. The Golay code is one of the first known error-correcting codes, see Golay (1949). The Meggitt decoder was described by Meggitt (1960), and the origin of error trapping is usually connected with Prange. The decoder of the Golay code in 10.6 is based on an idea of Kasami (1964).

# Chapter 11

# Polynomials and Finite Fields

In this chapter, we introduce further properties of polynomials and fields needed for the presentation of the most important class of error-correcting codes, the BCH codes. The reader may decide to skip a part of this chapter (in particular the later sections which are rather abstract) and to return to some topics whenever necessary. However, the material presented in the early sections is indispensable for understanding the BCH codes, which are defined by means of zeros of polynomials (found in algebraic extensions of the code alphabet).

The crucial idea of the theory of finite fields is that each polynomial over a field $F$ has a zero either in $F$ or in some field $F^*$ extending $F$. Conversely, given an extension $F^*$ of the given field, then every element $a$ of $F^*$ is a zero of some polynomial with coefficients in $F$. The smallest-degree polynomial with that property is called the minimal polynomial of $a$. Using these ideas, it is possible to present a full description of all finite fields: each finite field $F$ can be obtained by extending the field $Z_p$ for some prime $p$. The extension is performed via the minimal polynomial of a primitive element of $F$.

## 11.1  Zeros of Polynomials

Recall that a polynomial over a field $F$ is a formal expression

$$f(x) = f_0 + f_1 x + \cdots + f_m x^m.$$

Although $f(x)$ cannot be identified with a function on the field $F$, it certainly does define a function: the function assigning to each element $a$ of

197

the field $F$ the element $f(a) = f_0 + f_1 a + \cdots + f_m a^m$. Here

$$a^m = a \times a \times \cdots \times a \qquad (m \text{ factors});$$

we also define, for each nonzero element $a$,

$$a^0 = 1.$$

Observe that in a finite field, there always exist infinitely many polynomials defining the same function.

An element $a$ of the field $F$ is called a *zero* of the polynomial $f(x)$ provided that $f(a) = 0$.

**Proposition.** *An element $a$ is a zero of a polynomial $f(x)$ if and only if the polynomial $x - a$ is a divisor of $f(x)$.*

**PROOF.**  I. Let $a$ be a zero of $f(x)$. Dividing $f(x)$ by the polynomial $x - a$, we obtain a quotient $q(x)$ and a remainder $r$, the latter of degree smaller than 1 (i.e., a constant $r$), such that $f(x) = q(x)(x-a)+r$. Substituting $a$ for $x$, we get $0 = q(a) \times 0 + r = r$. Thus, $f(x) = q(x)(x - a)$, which proves that $x - a$ divides $f(x)$.

II. Let $x - a$ be a divisor of $f(x)$, i.e., $f(x) = q(x)(x - a)$. By substituting $a$ for $x$, we get $f(a) = q(a) \times 0 = 0$. □

**Corollary.** *Every polynomial with pairwise distinct zeros, $a_1, a_2, \ldots, a_n$, is divisible by the polynomial $(x - a_1)(x - a_2)\cdots(x - a_n)$.*

In fact, $f(x)$ is divisible by $x - a_1$, i.e., $f(x) = \overline{f}(x)(x - a_1)$. Since $f(a_2) = 0 = \overline{f}(a_2)(a_2 - a_1)$ implies that $a_2$ is a zero of $\overline{f}(x)$, we see that $\overline{f}(x)$ is divisible by $x - a_2$. Thus, $f(x)$ is divisible by $(x - a_1)(x - a_2)$, etc. □

**Remark.**  (1) A polynomial of degree $n$ has at most $n$ pairwise distinct zeros. This follows directly from the above corollary.

**Examples**

(1)  The polynomial $x^3 + 1$ has a zero in 1 in the field $\mathbf{Z}_2$. Thus, $x^3 + 1$ can be divided by $x + 1$:

$$x^3 + 1 = (x + 1)(x^2 + x + 1).$$

This is a complete factorization of $x^3 + 1$: since $x^2 + x + 1$ has no zero, it cannot be factored into a product of polynomials of degree 1.

(2) The same polynomial $x^3 + 1$ over the field $\mathbf{Z}_3$ has a zero in 2; thus, it can be divided by $x - 2 = x + 1$. In fact, in that field, we have

$$x^3 + 1 = (x + 1)^3.$$

We conclude that factorization of a polynomial depends on the field under consideration.

**Definition.** *A polynomial $f(x)$ over a given field is called* irreducible *provided that it cannot be factored as a product of two polynomials of degrees smaller than that of $f(x)$.*

**Remarks**

(2) Every linear polynomial is irreducible. For polynomials $f(x)$ of degree 2 or more, the above proposition tells us that

$$\text{irreducible} \implies \text{no zeros.}$$

The reverse implication is false in general. For example, the polynomial $f(x) = (x^2 + x + 1)^2$ is certainly reducible, but it has no zeros in $\mathbf{Z}_2$. [Observe that the degree of $f(x)$ is 4, and the reverse implication *is* true for polynomials of degree 2 or 3: such a polynomial is irreducible if and only if it has no zeros.]

(3) In the field $\mathbf{R}$ of real numbers, $x^2 + 1$ is irreducible. However, no polynomial $f(x)$ of degree $n \geq 3$ is irreducible over $\mathbf{R}$: if $n$ is odd, then $f(x)$ has a zero; if $n$ is even, then $f(x)$ has either a real zero or two complex zeros $a \pm ib$. In the latter case, by the above corollary $f(x)$ can be divided by

$$[x - (a + ib)][x - (a - ib)] = (x - a)^2 + b^2,$$

which is a real polynomial of degree 2.

(4) In the field of complex numbers, the fundamental theorem of algebra tells us that no polynomial of degree at least 2 is irreducible.

In a sharp contrast to the two last examples, we will later see that every finite field has the property that irreducible polynomials of all degrees exist.

The following result is analogous to the well-known factorization theorem for natural numbers as products of primes:

**Unique Factorization Theorem.** *Every nonzero polynomial $f(x)$ has a factorization*

$$f(x) = af_1(x)f_2(x)\ldots f_s(x),$$

*where $a$ is a scalar, and $f_i(x)$ are monic irreducible polynomials of positive degrees. The factorization is unique up to the order of the factors.*

PROOF.   I. Existence. Let $f(x)$ be a nonzero polynomial with leading coefficient $a$. Then $f(x) = a\overline{f}(x)$, where $\overline{f}(x) = a^{-1}f(x)$ is a monic polynomial. We will find a factorization of $\overline{f}(x)$ into a product of monic irreducible polynomials by induction on the degree $n$ of $\overline{f}(x)$.

If $n = 0$, then $\overline{f}(x) = 1$ is irreducible.

Let $n > 0$, and suppose that a factorization exists for all polynomials of smaller degrees. If $\overline{f}(x)$ is irreducible, then the factorization of $f(x)$ is $f(x) = a\overline{f}(x)$. In the case $\overline{f}(x) = g(x)h(x)$, where $g(x)$ and $h(x)$ are monic polynomials of degrees smaller than $n$, we use the induction hypothesis on both $g(x)$ and $h(x)$: there are monic irreducible polynomials $f_1(x)$, $\ldots$, $f_n(x)$, $f_{n+1}(x)$, $\ldots$, $f_m(x)$ with $g(x) = f_1(x)\ldots f_n(x)$ and $h(x) = f_{n+1}(x)\ldots f_m(x)$. Then the required factorization is

$$f(x) = af_1(x)\ldots f_n(x)f_{n+1}(x)\ldots f_m(x).$$

II. Uniqueness. It is certainly sufficient to restrict ourselves to monic polynomials [since for any polynomial $f(x)$, there is a unique monic polynomial $\overline{f}(x)$ and a unique scalar $a$ with $f(x) = a\overline{f}(x)$: in fact, $a$ must be the leading coefficient of $f(x)$ and $\overline{f}(x) = a^{-1}f(x)$]. Let $f(x)$ be a monic polynomial of degree $n$. We will prove that $f(x)$ has at most one factorization into irreducible factors.

If $n = 0$, then $f(x) = 1$ has no nontrivial factorization.

Let $n > 0$, and suppose that $f(x)$ has the following two factorizations into monic, irreducible factors:

$$f_1(x)\ldots f_s(x) = g_1(x)\ldots g_t(x). \tag{11.1.1}$$

We will first prove that $f_1(x)$ can be found on the right-hand side, i.e., $f_1(x) = g_i(x)$ for some $i$. We can assume that $f_1(x)$ has degree smaller or equal to the degree of $g_1(x)$ [since else we just interchange the two sides of (11.1.1)]. If $f_1(x) = g_1(x)$, put $i = 1$. In case $f_1(x) \neq g_1(x)$, divide $g_1(x)$ by $f_1(x)$ to get a quotient $q(x)$ and a remainder $r(x)$ such that

$$g_1(x) = q(x)f_1(x) + r(x) \quad \text{and} \quad \text{degree } r(x) < \text{degree } f_1(x) \leq \text{degree } g_1(x).$$

Since $g_1(x)$ is irreducible, $r(x)$ is a nonzero polynomial, and because both $f_1(x)$ and $g_1(x)$ are monic [thus, the quotient $q(x)$ is monic too], we conclude that $r(x) = g_1(x) - q(x)f_1(x)$ is also monic. We can substitute for $g_1(x)$ in (11.1.1) to get

$$f_1(x)f_2(x)\ldots f_s(x) = q(x)f_1(x)g_2(x)\ldots g_t(x) + r(x)g_2(x)\ldots g_t(x).$$

Consequently,

$$f_1(x)[f_2(x)\ldots f_s(x) - q(x)g_2(x)\ldots g_t(x)] = r(x)g_2(x)\ldots g_t(x).$$

By I, the bracket on the left-hand side has a factorization into monic irreducible factors $h_1(x) \ldots h_m(x)$. Thus,

$$f_1(x)h_1(x) \ldots h_m(x) = r(x)g_2(x) \ldots g_t(x). \tag{11.1.2}$$

We now apply the induction hypothesis to the polynomial whose two factorizations are expressed by (11.1.2). That polynomial has degree smaller than $n$ because $r(x)$ has degree smaller than $g_1(x)$ [and the polynomial $f(x) = g_1(x)g_2(x) \ldots g_t(x)$ has degree $n$]. Consequently, the polynomial of (11.1.2) has a unique factorization. In particular, $f_1(x)$ can be found on the right-hand side of (11.1.2). Since $f_1(x)$ cannot be equal to $r(x)$ [because the latter polynomial has degree smaller then that of $f_1(x)$], we conclude that $f_1(x) = g_i(x)$ for some $i = 2, \ldots, t$.

Thus, we can cancel $f_1(x)$ from both sides of (11.1.1) and we get two factorizations of a polynomial of degree smaller than $n$ as follows:

$$f_2(x) \ldots f_s(x) = g_1(x) \ldots g_{i-1}(x)g_{i+1}(x) \ldots g_t(x).$$

By applying the induction hypothesis again, we conclude that the two sides of the last equation differ only in the order of their factors. Consequently, the same is true about (11.1.1). □

## 11.2 Algebraic Extensions of a Field

The idea of algebraic extension is well known from the case of the field **R** of real numbers: the polynomial $x^2 + 1$ has no zero in that field, but we can extend the field by a new element $i$, which is a zero of $x^2 + 1$, and we "obtain" the field of complex numbers. (A side remark: do you really know what complex numbers are? One approach of introducing this fundamental concept is to say that we adjoin the element $i = \sqrt{-1}$ to the reals. Well, this is too obscure to be a reasonable way to introduce a mathematical object! Another approach is to say, quite formally, that complex numbers are pairs of reals which instead of $(a, b)$ are denoted by $a + ib$. Then formal addition and formal multiplication are introduced. Well, this is too formal to be a reasonable way of explaining complex numbers—for example, why, then, do we not multiply them coordinatewise? In the present section, although our prime aim is different, we will find a precise and suggestive way of introducing complex numbers.)

**Example.** (1) We want to extend the field $\mathbf{Z}_2$ by a zero of the polynomial $p(x) = x^2 + x + 1$. This new zero, say, $\alpha$, will satisfy $\alpha^2 + \alpha + 1 = 0$, i.e.,

$$\alpha^2 = \alpha + 1.$$

Thus, we have to add at least two new elements: $\alpha$ and $\alpha + 1$. Denote the latter by $\beta$, i.e., $\beta = \alpha + 1$. Then we get four elements, 0, 1, $\alpha$, and $\beta$, and this is all we need. In fact:

(a) Addition is clear because in any extension of $\mathbf{Z}_2$, we have $x + x = 0$ for each $x$ (since $1 + 1 = 0$, and this equation can be multipled by $x$). Thus,

$$\alpha + \beta = \alpha + \alpha + 1 = 1, \qquad \beta + 1 = \alpha + 1 + 1 = \alpha, \qquad \text{etc.}$$

(b) Multiplication follows from $\alpha^2 = \alpha + 1 = \beta$: we have

$$\alpha\beta = \alpha(\alpha + 1) = \beta + \alpha = 1,$$
$$\beta^2 = (\alpha + 1)(\alpha + 1) = \beta + \alpha + \alpha + 1 = \beta + 1 = \alpha,$$

etc. The tables of addition and multiplication are shown in Figure 1.

| + | 0 | 1 | $\alpha$ | $\beta$ |   | $\times$ | 0 | 1 | $\alpha$ | $\beta$ |
|---|---|---|----------|---------|---|----------|---|---|----------|---------|
| 0 | 0 | 1 | $\alpha$ | $\beta$ |   | 0 | 0 | 0 | 0 | 0 |
| 1 | $\beta$ | 0 | 1 | $\alpha$ |   | 1 | 0 | 1 | $\alpha$ | $\beta$ |
| $\alpha$ | $\alpha$ | $\beta$ | 0 | 1 |   | $\alpha$ | 0 | $\alpha$ | $\beta$ | 1 |
| $\beta$ | 1 | $\alpha$ | $\beta$ | 0 |   | $\beta$ | 0 | $\beta$ | 1 | $\alpha$ |

**Figure 1:** Extension of $\mathbf{Z}_2$ by a zero of $p(x) = x^2 + x + 1$

Still on the informal level, let us consider a polynomial

$$p(x) = p_0 + p_1 x + \cdots + p_m x^m \qquad (p_m \neq 0)$$

over a field $F$. Suppose we want to "extend" the field $F$ by a zero $\alpha$ of the polynomial $p(x)$. Thus, in the extended field, we have $p(\alpha) = 0$. Now, $p(\alpha)$ is just the same polynomial, but with a new name for the indeterminate. The equation $p(\alpha) = 0$ implies, of course, that each polynomial $q(x)$, which is a multiple of $p(x)$, also fulfils $q(\alpha) = 0$. Now recall that all polynomials form a ring $F[x]$ (10D) and that $p(x)$ is an element of that ring. Thus, we can consider the ring $F[x]/\operatorname{mod} p(x)$ of all coset leaders modulo $p(x)$ (see 7.2).

Observe that if two polynomials $q(x)$ and $q'(x)$ lie in the same coset modulo $p(x)$ [i.e., if their diference $q(x) - q'(x)$ is a multiple of $p(x)$, see 6.2], then $q(\alpha) = q'(\alpha)$. In fact, $q(\alpha) - q'(\alpha)$ is a multiple of $p(\alpha) = 0$. Thus, it is not surprising that a formalization of the idea of "creating a zero of $p(x)$" can be realized by the ring $F[x]/\bmod p(x)$ of coset leaders modulo $p(x)$. In Example (1), the coset leaders were $0$, $1$, $x$, and $x + 1$. In general, there is always a canonical choice of the coset leaders:

**Proposition.** *Let $p(x)$ be a polynomial of degree $m \geq 0$ over a field. All polynomials of degrees smaller than $m$ are coset leaders modulo $p(x)$. That is, every polynomial $f(x)$ over the field lies in the coset of precisely one polynomial of degree smaller than $m$, viz., the remainder of the division of $f(x)$ by $p(x)$.*

**PROOF.** The above division is expressed by

$$f(x) = q(x)p(x) + r(x), \qquad \text{degree } r(x) < m.$$

Then $f(x)$ and $r(x)$ lie in the same coset modulo $p(x)$ because $f(x) - r(x)$ is a multiple of $p(x)$, see Proposition 6.2.

It remains to prove that such a polynomial is unique, i.e., if $r(x)$ and $r'(x)$ are two polynomials of the same coset and having degrees smaller than $m$, then $r(x) = r'(x)$. In fact, by Proposition 6.2, we have

$$r(x) - r'(x) = q(x)p(x)$$

for some polynomial $q(x)$. In the last equation, the degree of the left-hand side is smaller than that of $p(x)$. Consequently, $q(x) = 0$ [see Remark (1) of 10.1]. Thus, $r(x) = r'(x)$. □

**Definition.** *By an* algebraic extension *of a field $F$ is meant the ring*

$$F[x]/\bmod p(x),$$

*where $p(x)$ is a polynomial of degree $m \geq 1$. The elements of the extension are all polynomials $f(\alpha)$ of degree less than $m$ in indeterminate $\alpha$ over $F$. The algebraic operations are defined as follows: the addition is the usual addition of polynomials:*

$$f(\alpha) + g(\alpha) = h(\alpha) \iff f(x) + g(x) = h(x),$$

*and the multiplication is given by*

$$f(\alpha)g(\alpha) = h(\alpha) \iff h(x) \text{ is the remainder of} \\ \text{the division of } f(x)g(x) \text{ by } p(x).$$

**Examples**

(1) The algebraic extension of the field $\mathbf{Z}_2$ by the polynomial $p(x) = x^2 + x + 1$ is the ring

$$\mathbf{Z}_2[x]/\operatorname{mod} x^2 + x + 1.$$

Its elements are

$$0, 1, \alpha, \alpha + 1 \; (\overset{\text{def}}{=} \beta).$$

The addition and multiplication are presented in Figure 1. Observe that we have (finally!) obtained a four-element field: here $1^{-1} = 1$, $\alpha^{-1} = \beta$, and $\beta^{-1} = \alpha$.

(2) The algebraic extension of $\mathbf{Z}_2$ by $p(x) = x^2 + 1$ also has four elements, $0, 1, \alpha$, and $\alpha + 1 = \beta$. The table of addition is the same as in Figure 1. However, multiplication is different: since $\alpha^2 + 1 = 0$, we see that

$$
\begin{aligned}
\alpha^2 &= 1, \\
\alpha\beta &= \alpha(\alpha + 1) = \alpha^2 + \alpha = 1 + \alpha = \beta, \\
\beta^2 &= (\alpha + 1)^2 = 1 + 1 = 0, \qquad \text{etc.}
\end{aligned}
$$

From the last equation, we conclude, of course, that this extension is not a field.

(3) The algebraic extension of the field $\mathbf{R}$ of real numbers by the polynomial $p(x) = x^2 + 1$ consists of all real polynomials of degree at most 1 in an indeterminate which (rather then by $\alpha$) is traditionally denoted by $i$. That is, the elements of $\mathbf{R}[x]/\operatorname{mod} x^2 + 1$ are all polynomials $a + bi$, addition is componentwise as usual, and multiplication is determined by $i^2 + 1 = 0$, i.e., $i^2 = -1$.

We see that the algebraic extension of $\mathbf{R}$ by a zero of $x^2 + 1$ is just the field of complex numbers. This definition of complex numbers is both precise and suggestive.

**Remarks**

(2) The algebraic extension $F[x]/\operatorname{mod} p(x)$ actually does extend the field $F$: all elements of $F$ are contained in the extension (as the polynomials of degrees $-1$ and 0), and the addition and multiplication of those elements are the same in $F$ and in $F[x]/\operatorname{mod} p(x)$.

(3) We have seen above that the algebraic extension is sometimes, but not always, a field. Whenever the polynomial $p(x)$ under consideration can be factorized as $p(x) = a(x)b(x)$, where the degrees of $a(x)$ and $b(x)$ are smaller than that of $p(x)$, then the extension $F[x]/\operatorname{mod} p(x)$ cannot be

a field. In fact, the nonzero elements $a(\alpha)$ and $b(\alpha)$ of the extension fulfil

$$a(\alpha)b(\alpha) = 0,$$

which cannot happen in a field. Conversely, in analogy to Theorem 7.2, we have the following:

**Theorem.** *For each irreducible polynomial $p(x)$ over a field $F$, the algebraic extension $F[x]/\bmod p(x)$ is a field.*

PROOF. Let $m$ be the degree of $p(x)$. We will prove by induction on $k = 0, 1, \ldots, m - 1$ that every element $a(\alpha)$ of degree $k$ in the extension $F[x]/\bmod p(x)$ has an inverse element.

If $k = 0$, then $a(\alpha)$ lies in $F$, and it has an inverse there.

Let $k > 0$ and suppose that all nonzero elements of smaller degrees have inverse elements. Divide $p(x)$ by $a(x)$ to get a quotient $q(x)$ and a remainder $r(x)$. The latter has degree smaller than $k$ and, since $p(x)$ is irreducible, it is nonzero. Thus, the element $r(\alpha)$ has an inverse element in $F[x]/\bmod p(x)$; i.e., there is a polynomial $s(x)$ such that $s(\alpha)r(\alpha) = 1$. In other words, the product $s(x)r(x)$ has remainder 1 when divided by $p(x)$:

$$s(x)r(x) = t(x)p(x) + 1 \qquad \text{for some } t(x).$$

When multiplying the equation $p(x) = q(x)a(x) + r(x)$ by the polynomial $s(x)$, we get

$$s(x)p(x) = s(x)q(x)a(x) + t(x)p(x) + 1.$$

Thus,

$$\left[-s(x)q(x)\right]a(x) = 1 + p(x)\left[t(x) - s(x)\right].$$

Consequently, the remainder of the right-hand side polynomial divided by $p(x)$ is 1; hence, the same is true of the left-hand side:

$$\left[-s(\alpha)q(\alpha)\right]a(\alpha) = 1 \qquad \text{in} \quad F[x]/\bmod p(x).$$

We conclude that $-s(\alpha)q(\alpha)$ is an inverse element of $a(\alpha)$. $\qquad\square$

**Concluding Remark.** Every polynomial $p(x)$ over a field $F$ defines a ring

$$F[x]/\bmod p(x)$$

of cosets of polynomials modulo $p(x)$. Two polynomials, $f(x)$ and $g(x)$, lie in the same coset precisely when their difference $f(x) - g(x)$ is divisible by $p(x)$. In notation:

$$f(x) \equiv g(x) \pmod{p(x)}.$$

In particular, every polynomial $f(x)$ lies in the same coset as the remainder of the division of $f(x)$ by $p(x)$. Consequently, all polynomials of degrees smaller than that of $p(x)$ can be chosen as coset leaders.

For irreducible polynomials $p(x)$, the resulting extension of $F$ is a field. When extending the field $F = \mathbf{Z}_p$ in this way, we obtain the important Galois fields studied in the next section.

## 11.3    Galois Fields

**Definition.** *An algebraic extension of the field $\mathbf{Z}_p$ by an irreducible polynomial of degree $m$ is called a* Galois field, *and is denoted by $GF(p^m)$.*

**Examples**

(1) We have constructed the field $GF(4)$ in 11.2, see Figure 1.

(2) $GF(8)$ is obtained by extending the field $\mathbf{Z}_2$ by an irreducible polynomial of degree 3, for example, by $p(x) = x^3 + x + 1$. Thus, the new zero $\alpha$ of $p(x)$ fulfils

$$\alpha^3 = \alpha + 1.$$

It follows that

$$
\begin{aligned}
\alpha^4 &= \alpha^2 + \alpha, \\
\alpha^5 &= \alpha^3 + \alpha^2 = \alpha^2 + \alpha + 1, \\
\alpha^6 &= \alpha^4 + \alpha^3 = \alpha^2 + 1, \\
\alpha^7 &= \alpha^5 + \alpha^4 = 1.
\end{aligned}
$$

Consequently, all nonzero elements of $GF(8)$ can be expressed as powers of $\alpha$, see Figure 2. Observe that the double expression of each nonzero

| 0 | 1 | $\alpha$ | $1+\alpha$ | $\alpha^2$ | $\alpha^2+1$ | $\alpha^2+\alpha$ | $\alpha^2+\alpha+1$ |
|---|---|---|---|---|---|---|---|
| – | $\alpha^0 = \alpha^7$ | $\alpha^1$ | $\alpha^3$ | $\alpha^2$ | $\alpha^6$ | $\alpha^4$ | $\alpha^5$ |

Figure 2: Galois field $GF(8) = \mathbf{Z}_2/\mathrm{mod}\, x^3 + x + 1$

element (as a polynomial in $\alpha$ and as a power of $\alpha$) yields a complete and simple description of the field. In fact, the upper row of Figure 2 tells us how to add, and the lower row how to multiply. For example:

$$(\alpha^2 + 1)(\alpha^2 + \alpha + 1) = \alpha^4 \alpha^5 = \alpha^9 = \alpha^2 \alpha^7 = \alpha^2.$$

(3) The Galois field $GF(9)$ is obtained by extending the field $\mathbf{Z}_3$ by an irreducible polynomial of degree 2, e.g., by $p(x) = x^2 + x + 2$. Then $\alpha^2 + \alpha + 2 = 0$ implies

$$
\begin{aligned}
\alpha^2 &= 2\alpha + 1, \\
\alpha^3 &= 2\alpha^2 + \alpha = 2\alpha + 2, \\
\alpha^4 &= 2\alpha^2 + a\alpha = 2, \\
\alpha^5 &= 2\alpha, \\
\alpha^6 &= 2\alpha^2 = \alpha + 2, \\
\alpha^7 &= \alpha^2 + 2\alpha = \alpha + 1, \\
\alpha^8 &= \alpha^2 + \alpha = 12.
\end{aligned}
$$

A complete description of $GF(9)$ is presented in Figure 3.

| 0 | 1 | 2 | $\alpha$ | $2\alpha$ | $\alpha+1$ | $\alpha+2$ | $2\alpha+1$ | $2\alpha+2$ |
|---|---|---|---|---|---|---|---|---|
| – | $\alpha^0 = \alpha^8$ | $\alpha^4$ | $\alpha^1$ | $\alpha^5$ | $\alpha^7$ | $\alpha^6$ | $\alpha^2$ | $\alpha^3$ |

**Figure 3:** Galois field $GF(9) = \mathbf{Z}_3[x]/\operatorname{mod} x^2 + x + 2$

**Remarks**

(1) All Galois fields up to $GF(32)$ are listed in Appendix A.

(2) The Galois field $GF(p^m)$ has $p^m$ elements: this is the number of all polynomials $a_0 + a_1\alpha + \cdots + a_{n-1}\alpha^{n-1}$, where each $a_i$ has $p$ possible values.

Later we will see that irreducible polynomials of all degrees exist over $\mathbf{Z}_p$ for any prime $p$. Therefore, a field of $p^m$ elements exists for any prime $p$ and any $m$. (Conversely, every finite field has a number of elements which is a power of some prime.)

(3) The presentation of the fields $GF(8)$ and $GF(9)$ above is based on the fact that all nonzero elements are powers of a "special" element. In the next section, we will see that such an element exists in every finite field.

# 11.4 Primitive Elements

We have seen in the above examples of fields the importance of finding an element $\alpha$ whose powers cover all the field except 0. Such elements are called primitive, and we will now prove that they can be found in each finite field. The characteristic property of a primitive element $\alpha$ is that the equation $\alpha^n = 1$ does not hold for "small" $n$. We thus first pay attention to this type of equation:

**Definition.** *An element $a$ of a field is said to have* order $n = 1, 2, 3, \ldots$ *provided that $a^n = 1$ while $a^k \neq 1$ for all $k = 1, 2, \ldots, n-1$.*

**Examples**

(1) In the field $\mathbf{Z}_5$, the element 2 has order 4: $2^2 = 4$, $2^3 = 3$, and $2^4 = 1$. The element 4 has order 2, and the element 1 has, of course, order 1. The order of 0 is undefined.

(2) In the field of real numbers, 1 has order 1, and $-1$ has order 2. All other orders are undefined.

**Proposition.** *In a finite field, every nonzero element $a$ has an order $n = 1, 2, 3, \ldots$. Then the elements $a, a^2, \ldots, a^n$ are pairwise distinct, and*

$$a^k = 1 \quad \text{if and only if $n$ is a divisor of $k$.}$$

PROOF. Let $a$ be a nonzero element. Since the elements $a, a^2, a^3, \ldots$ cannot be pairwise distinct in a finite field, we can choose the smallest $n = 1, 2, 3, \ldots$ for which $a^{i+n} = a^i$ (for some $i$). We can divide the equation by $a^i$ ($\neq 0$), and we get $a^n = 1$. It follows that $a, a^2, \ldots, a^n$ are pairwise distinct elements, hence, $n$ is the order of $a$.

Whenever $n$ is a divisor of $k$, i.e., $k = in$, then $a^k = (a^n)^i = 1^i = 1$. Conversely, suppose that $a^k = 1$. Performing the integer division of $k$ by $n$, we get a quotient $q$ and a remainder $r < n$ such that $k = qn + r$. Then $a^{qn} = 1$ implies

$$1 = a^k = a^{qn} a^r = a^r.$$

Since $r < n$, we conclude that $r = 0$.                                      □

**Definition.** *An element $a$ of a field is said to be* primitive *provided that every nonzero element is equal to some power of $a$.*

**Example.** (3) The number 2 is primitive in $\mathbf{Z}_5$ because it has order 4, thus, all the four nonzero elements of $\mathbf{Z}_5$ are powers of 2:

$$2 = 2^1, \quad 3 = 2^3, \quad 4 = 2^2, \quad \text{and} \quad 1 = 2^4.$$

**Remark.** (1) Let $F$ be a finite field of $r$ elements. Then an element is primitive if and only if it has order $r - 1$.

In fact, if $a$ has order $r-1$, then we have nonzero, pairwise distinct elements $a, a^2, \ldots, a^{r-1}$—these must be all the nonzero elements. Conversely, if $a$ is primitive, then we can express 1 as $1 = a^n$. The smallest such $n$ is the order of $a$. The number of all powers of $a$ is $n$ (because $a^{n+1} = a$, $a^{n+2} = a^2$, etc.), thus, $n = r-1$.

**Theorem.** *Every finite field has a primitive element.*

PROOF. Let $F$ be a field of $r$ elements. We can choose an element $a$ of the largest order, say, $n$. It is clear that $n \leq r-1$ because the $n$ elements, $a, a^2$, $\ldots, a^n$, are nonzero and pairwise distinct (see Proposition above) and there are just $r-1$ nonzero elements. It is our task to prove that $n \geq r-1$; then $a$ is primitive by Remark (1) above. We will show that for each nonzero element $b$, the order of $b$ is a divisor of $n$. This will conclude the proof: by Proposition above, $b$ is then a zero of the polynomial $x^n - 1$, and, thus, $x^n - 1$ is a polynomial of degree $n$ with $r-1$ zeros. By Corollary 11.1, this proves $n \geq r-1$.

Let $s$ be the order of $b$. Consider the prime factorization of $s$:

$$s = p^i q^j \ldots \qquad (p, q, \ldots \text{ primes}).$$

We will prove that $p^i$ is a divisor of $n$. By symmetry, also $q^j$ (and all the other prime-power factors of $s$) are divisors of $n$, which proves that $s$ is also a divisor of $n$.

The number $n$ can be factored as

$$n = p^t n',$$

where $n'$ is a number not divisible by $p$ (and $t$ can possibly be zero). It is sufficient to find an element $c$ of order

$$m = p^i n'.$$

In fact, since $n = p^t n'$ is the largest order, we then have $p^i n' \leq p^t n'$, which proves $i \leq t$, hence, $p^i$ is a divisor of $n = p^t n'$.

Put $s' = s/p^i$ (i.e., $s = p^i s'$); we will prove that the following element

$$c = a^{p^t} b^{s'}$$

has order $m$. Firstly, $c^m = 1$ is demonstrated by a simple computation:

$$
\begin{aligned}
c^m &= a^{p^t m} b^{s' m} \\
&= a^{p^t n' p^i} b^{p^i s' n'} \\
&= (a^n)^{p^i} (b^s)^{n'} \\
&= (1^{p^i})(1^{n'}) \\
&= 1.
\end{aligned}
$$

Secondly, whenever $c^{m'} = 1$, we are to prove that $m' \geq m$. It is sufficient to verify that both $p^i$ and $n'$ are divisors of $m'$: since the two divisors are relatively prime (recall that the prime $p$ does not divide $n'$), it then follows that their product $m = p^i n'$ is also a divisor of $m'$. The trick is to compute the powers of $c^{m'}$ ($= 1$) to $n'$ and to $p^i$:

$$1 = \left(c^{m'}\right)^{n'} = a^{p^i n' m'} b^{s'm'} = \left(a^n\right)^{m'} b^{s'm'} = b^{s'm'}.$$

By Proposition above, the order $s = p^i s'$ of $b$ divides $s'm'$; thus, $p^i$ divides $m'$. Next:

$$1 = \left(c^{m'}\right)^{p^i} = a^{p^i p^i m'} b^{p^i s' m'} = a^{p^i p^i m'} \left(b^s\right)^{m'} = a^{p^i p^i m'}.$$

We see that the order $n = p^i n'$ of $a$ divides $p^i p^i m'$; thus, $n'$ divides $p^i m'$. $\quad\square$

**Remark.** (2) Given an element $a$ of order $n$, we can factor $x^n - 1$ as follows:

$$x^n - 1 = (x - a)(x - a^2)\ldots(x - a^n).$$

In fact, each $a^i$ is a zero of $x^n - 1$, and since the zeros $a$, $a^2$, $\ldots$, $a^n$ are pairwise distinct (by Proposition above), the right-hand side polynomial divides $x^n - 1$, see Corollary 11.1. The equality now follows from the fact that both of the polynomials considered are monic and have degree $n$.

**Corollary** (Fermat's Theorem). *In a field $F$ of $r$ elements, every element is a zero of $x^r - x$; thus,*

$$x^r - x = \prod_{a \in F}(x - a) \tag{11.4.1}$$

*and*

$$x^{r-1} - 1 = \prod_{a \in F, a \neq 0}(x - a). \tag{11.4.2}$$

In fact, let $b$ be a primitive element. By Remark (2),

$$x^{r-1} - 1 = (x - b)(x - b^2)\cdots(x - b^{r-1}) = \prod_{a \in F, a \neq 0}(x - a).$$

Multiplying the last equation by $x$, we obtain (11.4.1); thus, $a^r - a = 0$.

**Example.** In $\mathbf{Z}_3$, we have

$$x^3 - x = x(x - 1)(x - 2) = \prod_{a \in \mathbf{Z}_3}(x - a).$$

**Remark.** (3) Several theorems bear the name of Pierre Fermat. (For example, the famous theorem on the nonsolvability of $x^n + y^n = z^n$ for $n \geq 3$, which is not yet known to be true.) In this book, only the corollary above is called Fermat's Theorem.

# 11.5   The Characteristic of a Field

In a finite field the elements $1, 1+1, 1+1+1, \ldots$ cannot be pairwise distinct — thus, for some number $p$ of summands we have $1+1+\cdots+1 = 0$. The smallest such $p$ is an important feature of the field, since the field then is an extension of $Z_p$. It is called the characteristic:

**Definition.** *The characteristic of a field is the smallest number $n$ of summands in the equation $1 + 1 + \cdots + 1 = 0$; if no such number exists, the field is said to have characteristic $\infty$.**

### Examples

(1) $Z_2$ has characteristic 2. All extensions of $Z_2$, e.g., $GF(4)$ (see Figure 1 in 11.2), have characteristic 2.

(2) $Z_3$ and all of its extensions have characteristic 3.

(3) **R** has characteristic $\infty$.

**Proposition.** *Every finite field has a characteristic which is a prime number.*

PROOF. Since the elements $a_i = 1+1+\cdots+1$ ($i$ summands) cannot be pairwise distinct, let $p$ be the smallest number such that $a_i = a_{i+p}$ for some $i$. It follows that $a_p = a_{i+p} - a_i = 0$. Thus, the field has characteristic $p$.

To prove that $p$ is a prime, consider a factorization $p = st$: we will prove that if $s < p$, then $s = 1$ and $t = p$. Obviously,

$$0 = a_{st} = a_s + a_s + \cdots + a_s \qquad (t \text{ summands}).$$

Since $s < p$, we know that $a_s \neq 0$. Dividing the last equation by $a_s$, we get $0 = 1 + 1 + \cdots + 1 = a_t$. Thus, $t = p$.   $\square$

### Remarks

(1) Every field $F$ of characteristic $p$ is an extension of the field $Z_p$: the elements

$$0,$$
$$1,$$
$$2 = 1 + 1,$$
$$\vdots$$
$$p - 1 = 1 + 1 + \cdots + 1 \qquad (p - 1 \text{ summands})$$

---

*Some authors say, instead of $\infty$, that the characteristic is zero.

of $F$ are pairwise distinct, and they are added as in $\mathbf{Z}_p$ because $(p-1)+1 = 1+1+\cdots+1 = 0$. They are also multiplied as in $\mathbf{Z}_p$ because from a product of two elements of the type above we can always substract $p$ summands 1. Thus, the product of two elements $nm$ of the type above is equal to the remainder of the division of the usual product $nm$ by $p$.

(2) Every binary polynomial can be regarded as a polynomial over the field $GF(2^m)$ whose coefficients happen to be restricted to 0 and 1. More in general, by (1), every polynomial over $\mathbf{Z}_p$ is also a polynomial over any field of characteristic $p$. In particular, it makes sense, given a polynomial over $\mathbf{Z}_p$, to ask about its zeros in any field of characteristic $p$.

**Theorem.** *Every field $F$ of characteristic $p$ has the following properties:*

(1) *An element $a$ fulfils $a^p = a$ precisely when $a \in \mathbf{Z}_p$.*

(2) *Arbitrary elements $a$, $b$ fulfil $(a+b)^p = a^p + b^p$.*

(3) *Given a polynomial $f(x)$ over $\mathbf{Z}_p$, which has a zero $a$ in $F$, then $a^p$, $a^{p^2}$, $a^{p^3}$, ... are also zeros of $f(x)$.*

PROOF. (1) Every element $a \in \mathbf{Z}_p$ fulfils $a^p = a$ by Fermat's Theorem (11.4.1). Since the polynomial $x^p - x$ cannot have more than $p$ zeros (see Corollary 11.1), it follows that $a^r \neq a$ for any $a \in F - \mathbf{Z}_p$.

(2) By the binomial theorem, we have $(a+b)^p = \sum_{k=0}^{p} \binom{p}{k} a^k b^{p-k}$ (see 11B). However, in a field of characteristic $p$, the element $p$ is equal to 0, and each $\binom{p}{k}$, where $0 < k < p$, is a multiple of this element, i.e., $\binom{p}{k} = 0$. Therefore,

$$(a+b)^p = \binom{p}{p} a^p + \binom{p}{0} b^p = a^p + b^p.$$

(3) Observe first that from (2), we immediately get $(a_0 + a_1 + \cdots + a_s)^p = a_0^p + a_1^p + \cdots + a_s^p$. Let $f(x) = f_0 + f_1 x + \cdots + f_s x^s$ be a polynomial with a zero in $a$. Then $f(a) = 0$ implies $[f(a)]^p = 0$, i.e.,

$$f_0^p + f_1^p a^p + \cdots + f_s^p a^{sp} = 0.$$

Now, assuming that the coefficients of $f(x)$ lie in $\mathbf{Z}_p$, we have $f_i^p = f_i$ by (1). Thus, the last equation implies $f(a^p) = \sum_{i=0}^{s} f_i a^{ip} = 0$.

By applying the same rule, we see that $f((a^p)^p) = 0$, i.e., $a^{p^2}$ is a zero of $f(x)$, etc.    □

**Example.** In $GF(2^m)$, we have $(a + b)^2 = a^2 + b^2$. Any binary polynomial $f(x)$ with a zero in $a$ has zeros in $a^2$, $a^4$, $a^8$, ... (many of which are mutually equal; e.g., $a^{2^m} = a$ by Fermat's Theorem).

**Remarks**

(4) Analogously to (2) in the above theorem, we can see that in a field of characteristic $p$,

$$(x + a)^p = x^p + a^p.$$

More in general, for every polynomial $a(x) = a_0 + a_1 x + \cdots + a_s x^s$,

$$[a(x)]^p = a_0^p + a_1^p x^p + \cdots + a_s^p x^{ps}.$$

(5) Note that by applying (2) of the above theorem twice, we get $(a+b)^{p^2} = (a^p + b^p)^p = a^{p^2} + b^{p^2}$. In general, whenever $q$ is a power of $p$, then $(a + b)^q = a^q + b^q$.

# 11.6 Minimal Polynomial

We have already remarked that a binary polynomial $f(x)$ can be regarded as a polynomial over $GF(2^m)$ and that we can study the zeros of $f(x)$ in the extended field. An important algebraic concept results from the opposite point of view: given an element $\beta$ in the extended field $GF(2^m)$, we are interested in binary polynomials having a zero in $\beta$. By Fermat's Theorem (11.4), such a polynomial always exists, e.g., $x^r - x$, where $r = 2^m$. The lowest-degree binary polynomial with a zero in $\beta$ is called the minimal polynomial of $\beta$. More in general:

**Definition.** *Let $F$ be a field and let $\beta$ be an element of some extension of $F$. By the minimal polynomial of $\beta$ (with respect to $F$) is meant the lowest-degree monic polynomial over $F$ with a zero in $\beta$.*

**Example.** (1) In the field

$$GF(8) = \mathbf{Z}_2[x]/\operatorname{mod} x^3 + x + 1,$$

the element $\alpha$ (see Figure 1 in 11.2) has the minimal polynomial $M(x) = x^3 + x + 1$. In fact, since $\alpha^3 + \alpha + 1 = 0$ in $GF(8)$, $M(x)$ has a zero in $\alpha$, and no binary polynomial of degree less than 3 has a zero in $\alpha$ (except the zero polynomial which is not monic).

By Theorem (2) of 11.5, $M(x)$ also has zeros in $\alpha^2$ and $\alpha^4$. It is clear that $M(x)$ is the minimal polynomial of both of these elements.

The element 1 has the minimal polynomial $x + 1$ and 0 has the minimal polynomial $x$.

**Remarks**

(1) Observe the importance of the requirement that the minimal polynomial be over $F$. In fact, each element $\beta$ of, say, $GF(2^m)$ is a zero of the linear polynomial $x - \beta$. But we are only interested in *binary* polynomials with a zero in $\beta$.

(2) Let us point out that the requirement that the minimal polynomial be monic excludes the zero polynomial. This requirement serves otherwise to guarantee the uniqueness.

**Proposition.** *Each element $\beta$ of a finite extension of a field $F$ has a unique minimal polynomial $M(x)$. Moreover, $M(x)$ divides each polynomial over $F$ with a zero in $\beta$.*

**PROOF.** By Fermat's Theorem (11.4), $\beta$ is a zero of $x^r - x$, which is a polynomial over $F$. Let $M(x)$ be the lowest-degree monic polynomial over $F$ with a zero in $\beta$. We will prove that whenever a polynomial $f(x)$ has a zero in $\beta$, then $M(x)$ is a divisor of $f(x)$. It is then clear that the minimal polynomial is unique (since whenever two monic polynomials divide each other, then they are equal).

We divide $f(x)$ by $M(x)$ over $F$ and obtain a quotient $q(x)$ and a remainder $r(x)$,

$$f(x) = q(x)M(x) + r(x) \qquad \text{and} \qquad \deg r(x) < \deg M(x).$$

Since $r(\beta) = f(\beta) - q(\beta)M(\beta) = 0 - q(\beta)0 = 0$, we see that $r(x)$ is a polynomial over $F$ of degree smaller than that of $M(x)$ with a zero in $\beta$. We can factor $r(x)$ as $r(x) = kr'(x)$, where $k$ is a scalar, and $r'(x)$ is a monic polynomial. If $k \neq 0$, then $r'(x)$ is a monic polynomial of degree smaller than that of $M(x)$ and with a zero in $\beta$—a contradiction. Thus, $k = 0$, and we conclude that $f(x) = q(x)M(x)$.                                □

**Corollary.** *Every minimal polynomial is irreducible.*

In fact, if $M(x) = f(x)g(x)$ is the minimal polynomial of $\beta$, then $M(\beta) = 0$ implies $f(\beta) = 0$ or $g(\beta) = 0$. Thus, $M(x)$ divides either $f(x)$ or $g(x)$, which proves that $f(x)$ and $g(x)$ cannot both have degrees smaller than that of $M(x)$.                                □

**Theorem.** *The minimal polynomial of each element $\beta$ of the Galois field $GF(p^m)$ with respect to $\mathbf{Z}_p$ can be computed as follows:*

$$M(x) = (x - \beta)(x - \beta^p)(x - \beta^{p^2}) \cdots (x - \beta^{p^i}),$$

*where $i$ is the smallest number with $\beta^{p^{i+1}} = \beta$.*

PROOF. (1) Such an $i$ exists. In fact, by Fermat's Theorem (11.4), one candidate is $i = n - 1$ since $\beta^{p^n} = \beta$.

(2) The elements $\beta$, $\beta^p$, $\beta^{p^2}$, ..., $\beta^{p^i}$ are pairwise distinct: suppose $\beta^{p^s} = \beta^{p^t}$ for some $s < t$, then we divide the equation by $\beta^{p^{s-1}}$ and get $\beta = \beta^{p^{t-s-1}}$. Thus, $t - s \geq i$; hence, $s$, $t$ cannot be among $0, 1, 2, \ldots, i$. (The only possibility would be $s = 0$, $t = i$, but $\beta \neq \beta^{p^i}$ by the choice of $i$.)

(3) $M(x)$ divides all polynomials over $\mathbf{Z}_p$ with a zero in $\beta$. This follows from Corollary 11.1 and Theorem (3) of 11.5. Thus, it remains to prove that $M(x)$ has coefficients in $\mathbf{Z}_p$. Put $M(x) = m_0 + m_1 x + \cdots + m_r x^r$. We will prove that $m_i^p = m_i$ for each $i$. Then $m_i$ lies in $\mathbf{Z}_p$ by Theorem (1) in 11.5.

Observe that the $p$th power of $M(x)$ is $M(x^p)$. In fact, by Remark (4) of 11.5,

$$
\begin{aligned}
[M(x)]^p &= (x - \beta)^p (x - \beta^p)^p \cdots (x - \beta^{p^i})^p \\
&= (x^p - \beta^p)(x^p - \beta^{p^2}) \cdots (x^p - \beta^{p^i})(x^p - \beta^{p^{i+1}}).
\end{aligned}
$$

Since $\beta^{p^{i+1}} = \beta$, we conclude (shifting the last term forward) that

$$
[M(x)]^p = (x^p - \beta)(x^p - \beta^p)(x^p - \beta^{p^2}) \cdots (x^p - \beta^{p^i}) = M(x^p).
$$

On the other hand, by Remark (4) of 11.5, we have

$$
[M(x)]^p = m_0^p + m_1^p x^p + \cdots + m_r^p x^{pr}.
$$

Consequently, $m_i^p$, the coefficient of $[M(x)]^p$ at $x^{pi}$, is equal to $m_i$, the coefficient of $M(x^p)$ at $x^{pi}$. $\qquad \square$

**Examples**

(2) Let us find the minimal polynomials of all elements of $GF(8)$ (see Figure 4). We already know them for $0, 1, \alpha, \alpha^2, \alpha^4$, see Example (1).

| Element | Minimal Polynomial |
|---|---|
| $0$ | $x$ |
| $1$ | $x + 1$ |
| $\alpha, \alpha^2, \alpha^4$ | $x^3 + x + 1$ |
| $\alpha^3, \alpha^5, \alpha^6$ | $x^3 + x^2 + 1$ |

**Figure 4:** Minimal polynomials of elements of $GF(8)$

For $\alpha^3$, we form $\left(\alpha^3\right)^2 = \alpha^6$, $\left(\alpha^6\right)^2 = \alpha^{12} = \alpha^5$, and $\left(\alpha^5\right)^2 = \alpha^{10} = \alpha^3$; thus, here the process stops. Consequently, the minimal polynomial of $\alpha^3$ (and $\alpha^6$ and $\alpha^5$) is

$$M(x) = (x - \alpha^3)(x - \alpha^6)(x - \alpha^5) = x^3 + x^2 + 1.$$

(3) Binary minimal polynomials of all elements of $GF(16)$ (see Appendix A) are listed in Figure 5.

| Element | Minimal Polynomial |
|---|---|
| 0 | $x$ |
| 1 | $x + 1$ |
| $\alpha, \alpha^2, \alpha^4, \alpha^8$ | $x^4 + x + 1$ |
| $\alpha^3, \alpha^6, \alpha^9, \alpha^{12}$ | $x^4 + x^3 + x^2 + x + 1$ |
| $\alpha^5, \alpha^{10}$ | $x^2 + x + 1$ |
| $\alpha^7, \alpha^{11}, \alpha^{13}, \alpha^{14}$ | $x^4 + x^3 + 1$ |

**Figure 5:** Minimal polynomials of elements of $GF(16)$

(4) In $GF(9)$ (see Figure 3 in 11.3), the element $\alpha$ has the minimal polynomial $x^2 + x + 2$. To find the minimal polynomial of $\alpha^2$, we compute $\left(\alpha^2\right)^3 = \alpha^6$, $\left(\alpha^6\right)^3 = \alpha^{18} = \alpha^2$; thus,

$$M(x) = \left(x - \alpha^2\right)\left(x - \alpha^6\right) = x^2 + 1.$$

## 11.7   Order

In this section, we show how to find elements of prescribed orders in finite fields.

**Proposition.** *In a field of r elements,*

  (1) *the order of each element divides $r - 1$,*

  (2) *every divisor of $r - 1$ is an order of some element.*

PROOF. Let $a$ be a primitive element (11.4) of a field of $r$ elements. Then each nonzero element has the form $a^i$, and since $\left(a^i\right)^{r-1} = \left(a^{r-1}\right)^i =$

$1^i = 1$, it follows that the order of $a^i$ is a divisor of $r - 1$ (see Proposition 11.4). Conversely, whenever $i$ is a divisor of $r - 1$, then the element $b = a^{(r-1)/i}$ has order $i$:

(1) $b^i = a^{i(r-1)/i} = a^{r-1} = 1$,

(2) $b^j \neq 1$ for all $j < i$ because $a^s \neq 1$ for all $s < r$ [in particular for $s = j(r - 1)/i$]. $\square$

**Examples**

(1) In $GF(16)$, we can find elements of orders 1, 3, 5, and 15. In fact, the primitive element $\alpha$ has order 15, $\alpha^3$ has order 5, and $\alpha^5$ has order 3.

(2) Is there an extension of $\mathbf{Z}_2$ in which some element has order 9? In other words, is there a number $n$ such that 9 divides $2^n - 1$? Sure: $n = 6$. This is so since $\varphi(9) = 6$ for the following function $\varphi$:

**Definition.** *The Euler function assigns to each number $n = 1, 2, 3, \ldots$ the number $\varphi(n)$ of all $i = 1, 2, \ldots, n - 1$ such that $n$ and $i$ are relatively prime.*

**Examples**

(3) $\varphi(p) = p - 1$ for every prime $p$ since each $i < p$ is relatively prime with $p$.

(4) $\varphi(pq) = (p - 1)(q - 1)$ for two distinct primes $p$, $q$. In fact, all $i < pq$ except $i = sq$ ($s = 1, 2, \ldots, p - 1$) and $i = pt$ ($t = 1, 2, \ldots, q - 1$) have the property that $pq$ and $i$ are relatively prime. Thus,

$$\varphi(pq) = pq - 1 - (q - 1) - (p - 1) = (p - 1)(q - 1).$$

(5) $\varphi(p^k) = p^k - p^{k-1}$ for each prime $p$. In fact, all $i < p^k$ except $i = sp$ ($s = 1, 2, \ldots, p^{k-1}$) are relatively prime with $p^k$.

Using these rules, we can compute $\varphi(n)$ for all $n \leq 11$, see Figure 6.

| $n$ | 1 | 2 | 3 | 4 | 5 | 6 | 7 | 8 | 9 | 10 | 11 |
|------|---|---|---|---|---|---|---|---|---|----|----|
| $\varphi(n)$ | 0 | 1 | 2 | 2 | 4 | 2 | 6 | 4 | 6 | 4 | 10 |

**Figure 6:** The Euler function $\varphi(n)$ for $n \leq 11$

**Euler-Fermat Theorem.** *If $q$ and $n$ are relatively prime natural numbers, then $n$ is a divisor of $q^{\varphi(n)} - 1$, i.e.,*

$$q^{\varphi(n)} \equiv 1 \pmod{n}.$$

PROOF. We will work in the ring $\mathbf{Z}_n = \mathbf{Z}/\bmod n$ of coset leaders modulo $n$ (see 7.2). Observe first that whenever a number $i$ is relatively prime with $n$, then all elements of the coset $i + n\mathbf{Z}$ are numbers $i + nk$ relatively prime with $n$. (In fact, any common divisor of $n$ and $i + nk$ divides $i = i + nk - nk$, thus, it is equal to 1.) Let $a_1, a_2, \ldots, a_{\varphi(n)}$ be all the numbers between 1 and $n - 1$ which are relatively prime with $n$. Each of the numbers $qa_i$ is, obviously, relatively prime with $n$ too. The coset $qa_i + n\mathbf{Z}$ contains a coset leader which, as observed above, must be relatively prime with $n$, i.e., is equal to $a_k$ for some $k$. Moreover, the cosets of $qa_i$ are pairwise distinct for $i = 1, \ldots, n$: suppose $qa_i$ and $qa_j$ lie in the same coset, i.e., $n$ divides $q(a_i - a_j)$. Then $n$ must divide $a_i - a_j$; however, $|a_i - a_j| < n$ —thus, $a_i = a_j$. We conclude that the cosets of the numbers $qa_1, qa_2, \ldots, qa_{\varphi(n)}$ are the same as those of the numbers $a_1, a_2, \ldots, a_{\varphi(n)}$. Consequently, the two products $b = a_1 a_2 \ldots a_{\varphi(n)}$ and $q^{\varphi(n)}b = (qa_1)(qa_2)\cdots(qa_{\varphi(n)})$ lie in the same coset:

$$q^{\varphi(n)}b \equiv b \pmod{n}.$$

That is, $n$ divides $q^{\varphi(n)}b - b = b(q^{\varphi(n)} - 1)$. However, $b$ is relatively prime with $n$; thus, $n$ divides $q^{\varphi(n)} - 1$.     □

**Corollary.** *The Galois field $GF(q^{\varphi(n)})$ contains an element of order $n$ whenever $q$ and $n$ are relatively prime.*

In fact, the field has $r = q^{\varphi(n)}$ elements and $n$ divides $r - 1$. Apply Proposition (2) above.     □

**Examples**

(6) We want to find an extension of $\mathbf{Z}_2$ with an element of order 11. Since $\varphi(11) = 10$, we can find such an element in $GF(2^{10})$.

(7) An element of order 7 exists, by the above corollary, in $GF(2^{\varphi(7)}) = GF(64)$. However, it also exists in $GF(8)$. Thus, the corollary does not always provide the best answer.

(8) No element of $GF(2^m)$ has an even order. In fact, $2^m - 1$ is odd, thus, it is not divisible by an even number. This shows that the hypothesis that $q$ and $n$ be relatively prime is essential.

## 11.8   The Structure of Finite Fields

The aim of the next two sections is to prove that every finite field is a Galois field, and that the number of elements determines essentially the field. The reader may skip the remainder of the chapter without breaking the continuity of the text.

Let us first discuss the "essential determination" of a finite field. We can always create a new field by simply re-labeling the elements (e.g., in $\mathbf{Z}_2$, we can use $\cdot$ , $—$ instead of 0, 1). By giving each element $a$ of a field $F$ a new label $\varrho(a)$, we will get another field $F'$ in which the algebraic operations are defined as in $F$, i.e.,

$$\varrho(a) + \varrho(b) = \varrho(a+b), \quad -\varrho(a) = \varrho(-a),$$
$$\varrho(a)\varrho(b) = \varrho(ab), \quad \varrho(a)^{-1} = \varrho(a^{-1}) \text{ if } a \neq 0, \qquad \text{for all } a, b \text{ in } F. \qquad (*)$$

The fields $F$ and $F'$ are essentially the same. Conversely, if we can find, for two fields $F$ and $F'$, a bijective correspondence $a \mapsto \varrho(a)$ between the elements $a$ (of $F$) and $\varrho(a)$ (of $F'$) such that the algebraic operations agree in the sense of $(*)$, the two fields can be identified.

**Definition.** *Two fields $F$ and $F'$ are said to be* isomorphic *provided that there exists a bijective function $\varrho$ from $F$ onto $F'$ satisfying $(*)$.*

**Theorem.** *Every finite field is isomorphic to a Galois field.*

**Remark.** More in detail: given a finite field $F$ of characteristic $p$, find a primitive element $a$ of $F$ and its minimal polynomial $M(x)$ (of degree $m$). Then $F$ is isomorphic to the Galois field

$$GF(p^m) = \mathbf{Z}_p[x]/\operatorname{mod} M(x).$$

PROOF (of the theorem and remark). Since $F$ has a primitive element $a$ (Theorem 11.2) and $a$ has an irreducible minimal polynomial $M(x)$ (see 11.6), the statement of the remark above makes sense. Recall that the elements of the Galois field $GF(p^m)$ are polynomials $f(\alpha)$, where $f(x)$ is a polynomial over $\mathbf{Z}_p$ of degree smaller than $m$. By computing the polynomials in the primitive element $a$, we obtain a function

$$\varrho : GF(p^m) \to F, \qquad \varrho[f(\alpha)] = f(a).$$

We will show that $\varrho$ is a bijection satisfying $(*)$.

(1) $\varrho$ is one to one since $\varrho[f(\alpha)] = \varrho[g(\alpha)]$ means that $f(a) = g(a)$, i.e., $a$ is a zero of the polynomial $f(x) - g(x)$. By Corollary 11.6, this implies that $M(x)$ divides $f(x) - g(x)$, but the degree of $f(x) - g(x)$ is smaller than $m$; thus, $f(x) - g(x) = 0$. Consequently, $f(\alpha) = g(\alpha)$.

(2) $\varrho$ is onto because each element $b$ of $F$ has the form $b = f(a)$ for some polynomial $f(x)$ over $\mathbb{Z}_p$ of degree smaller then $m$. In fact, if $b = 0$, choose $f(x) = 0$. For nonzero elements, we have $b = a^i$, since $a$ is primitive. Now the situation is clear if $i < m$: put $f(x) = x^i$. For $i = m$, use that fact that $a$ is a zero of the (monic) polynomial $M(x) = M_0 + M_1 x + \cdots + M_{m-1} x^{m-1} + x^m$:

$$a^m = -\left(M_0 + M_1 a + \cdots + M_{m-1} a^{m-1}\right).$$

Thus, for $f(x) = -\left(M_0 + M_1 x + \cdots + M_{m-1} x^{m-1}\right)$, we have $b = f(a)$. Analogously, if $i = m + 1$, we can express $a^{m+1}$ by the powers 1, $a$, $a^2$, ..., $a^{m-1}$ (using the above expression for $a^m$ twice), etc.

(3) $\varrho$ satisfies (∗). In fact, there is no problem with the addition and the opposite element, since $f(\alpha) + g(\alpha) = h(\alpha)$ holds precisely if $f(x) + g(x) = h(x)$:

$$\varrho\big[f(\alpha) + g(\alpha)\big] = f(a) + g(a) = \varrho\big[f(\alpha)\big] + \varrho\big[g(\alpha)\big],$$

$$\varrho\big[-f(\alpha)\big] = -f(a) = -\varrho\big[f(\alpha)\big].$$

For the multiplication, recall that $f(\alpha)g(\alpha) = h(\alpha)$ implies that the polynomial $M(x)$ divides $f(x)g(x) - h(x)$; say, $f(x)g(x) - h(x) = q(x)M(x)$. Then $M(a) = 0$ implies

$$
\begin{aligned}
\varrho\big[f(\alpha)\big]\varrho\big[g(\alpha)\big] &= f(a)g(a) \\
&= q(a)M(a) + h(a) \\
&= h(a) \\
&= \varrho\big[h(\alpha)\big] \\
&= \varrho\big[f(\alpha)g(\alpha)\big].
\end{aligned}
$$

Moreover, since $\varrho(1) = 1$, it follows that $\varrho\big[f(\alpha)^{-1}\big] = \varrho\big[f(\alpha)\big]^{-1}$: divide the equation $\varrho\big[f(\alpha)\big]\varrho\big[f(\alpha)\big]^{-1} = 1$ through $\varrho\big[f(\alpha)\big]$.    □

**Proposition.** *Let $F$ be a field of characteristic $p$. For each power $q$ of $p$, all elements $a$ of $F$ satisfying $a^q = a$ form a field $F_0$ whose extension is $F$. If the number of elements of $F$ is a power of $q$, then $F_0$ has precisely $q$ elements.*

PROOF. I. Denote by $F_0$ the set of all elements of $F$ satisfying $a^q = a$. We are to prove that $F_0$ forms a field whose extension is $F$, i.e., that $F_0$ is closed under the algebraic operations in $F$:

(1) Addition: given $a$, $b$ in $F_0$, then by Remark (5) of 11.5,

$$(a + b)^q = a^q + b^q = a + b.$$

Thus, $a + b$ lies in $F_0$.

(2) Opposite element: if $q$ is odd, then for $a$ in $F_0$,

$$(-a)^q = -(a^q) = -a.$$

If $q$ is even, then it is necessarily a power of 2, and there is nothing to prove, since $-a = a$.

(3) Multiplication: given $a$, $b$ in $F_0$, then

$$(ab)^q = a^q b^q = ab.$$

(4) Inverse element: $(a^{-1})^q = (a^q)^{-1} = a^{-1}$ for any $a$ in $F_0$.

II. Suppose $F$ has $q^m$ elements. Since $q - 1$ divides $q^m - 1 = (q - 1) \times (q^{m-1} + q^{m-2} + \cdots + 1)$, there is an element $c$ of order $q - 1$ in $F$ (see Proposition 11.7). Each of the elements $0, c, c^2, \ldots, c^{q-1} (= 1)$ is clearly a zero of $x^q - x$. These $q$ elements are pairwise distinct by Proposition 11.2; thus, these are all zeros of $x^q - x$. In other words,

$$F_0 = \{0, c, c^2, \ldots, c^{q-1}\}.$$

□

**Corollary.** *The Galois field $GF(p^m)$ is an extension of $GF(p^k)$ whenever $k$ is a divisor of $m$.*

In fact, put $q = p^k$ in the above proposition: if $k$ divides $m$, then $p^m$ is a power of $q$. □

**Example.** $GF(16)$ extends $GF(4)$: in the table of $GF(16)$ in Appendix A the elements $0, 1, \alpha^5, \alpha^{10}$ (i.e., the zeros of $x^4 - x$) form the field $GF(4)$.

Observe that $GF(16)$ does not extend $GF(8)$: no element of $GF(16)$ has order 7.

## 11.9 Existence of Galois Fields

In the preceding section, we proved that the only finite fields are the Galois fields. We now prove that they exist:

**Theorem.** *For each prime $p$ and each number $m$, there exists a Galois field $GF(p^m)$.*

PROOF. (1) We will first prove that there exists a field $F$ of characteristic $p$ in which the polynomial $x^{p^m} - x$ factors into linear factors. We will find $F$ by approximations: $F = F_i$ for some $i$, where $F_i$ are the following fields.

Put $F_0 = \mathbf{Z}_p$ and factor $x^{p^m} - x$ in $F_0$ using the unique factorization theorem (11.1):

$$x^{p^m} - x = f_1(x)f_2(x)\ldots f_{k_0}(x).$$

If each of the irreducible polynomials, $f_i(x)$ has degree 1, then put $F = F_0$. Else, find $i$ with $f_i(x)$ of degree at least 2 and use $f_i(x)$ to extend the field $F_0$:

$$F_1 = F_0[x]/\bmod f_i(x).$$

By Theorem 11.2, $F_1$ is a field extending $F_0$. Therefore, we can factor $x^{p^m} - x$ over $F_1$ using the unique factorization theorem again:

$$x^{p^m} - x = g_1(x)g_2(x)\ldots g_{k_1}(x).$$

Observe that every linear factor $f_j(x) = x - a$ of the above factorization in $F_0$ appears again in the factorization in $F_1$ (because this means precisely that $a$ is a zero of $x^{p^m} - x$). The number $k_1$ of factors is now strictly larger than the previous number $k_0$ because the above polynomial $f_i(x)$ has a zero $\alpha$ in $F_1$; thus, $x^{p^m} - x$ has a new linear factor: $x - \alpha$. Now continue in the same manner: if each of the irreducible polynomial $g_j(x)$ has degree 1, put $F = F_1$, else $F_2 = F_1[x]/\bmod g_j(x)$, etc. Since the number of factors is strictly increasing, after at most $p^m$ steps, we will find $i$ such that the field $F = F_i$ has the required property.

(2) The polynomial $x^{p^m} - x$ has no multiple zeros (11D) in any field of characteristic $p$ because its formal derivative

$$\left(x^{p^m} - x\right)' = p^m x^{p^m - 1} - 1 = -1$$

has no zero. Thus, in the field $F$ constructed in (1), the polynomial $x^{p^m} - x$ has $p^m$ distinct zeros. By Proposition 11.8, these zeros form a field of $p^m$ elements. That field is isomorphic to $GF(p^m)$ by Theorem 11.8. $\quad\square$

**Corollary.** *For each prime $p$, there exist irreducible polynomials of all degrees over $\mathbf{Z}_p$.*

## Concluding Remarks

(1) For each power of a prime $q = p^m$, there exists an essentially unique field of $q$ elements: the Galois field $GF(q)$. It can be constructed by finding an irreducible polynomial $r(x)$ over $\mathbf{Z}_p$ of degree $m$: $GF(q) = \mathbf{Z}_p[x]/\bmod r(x)$.

(2) Each Galois field $GF(q^k)$ is an extension of $GF(q)$ [see Corollary 11.8].

(3) For each finite field $F$ and each number $n$ relatively prime with the number of elements of $F$, some extension of $F$ contains an element of order $n$. [In fact, $F = GF(q)$ for some $q$ and then such an element can be found, by Corollary 11.7, in $GF(q^{\varphi(n)})$, which is an extension of $GF(q)$.]

(4) Given an element $\beta$ of some extension of a finite field $F$, there exists a unique minimal polynomial $M(x)$ of $\beta$. In case $\beta$ has order $n$, the minimal polynomial is a divisor of $x^n - 1$. [In fact, $x^n - 1$ is a polynomial over $F$ with a zero in $\beta$. It follows that $M(x)$ divides it, see Proposition 11.6.]

# Exercises

**11A**  Let $F$ be a field of characteristic $p$. For each natural number $n$, denote

$$n = 1 + 1 + \cdots + 1 \qquad (n \text{ summands}).$$

In particular, in $F$, we have $p = 0$, $p + 1 = 1$, etc.

Verify that for all $n = 0, 1, \ldots, p \, (= 0)$, we can define *binomial coeficients* in $F$ in the usual manner:

$$\binom{n}{k} = \frac{n(n-1)\cdots(n-k+1)}{k(k-1)\cdots 1} = n(n-1)\cdots(n-k+1)[k(k-1)\cdots 1]^{-1}$$

if $0 < k < p$, and

$$\binom{n}{0} = 1, \qquad \binom{p}{p} = 1.$$

Verify that the following well-known formula is valid:

$$\binom{n}{k} + \binom{n}{k-1} = \binom{n+1}{k}.$$

**11B**  Prove that a field of characteristic $p$ has the following properties.

(1) The usual *binomial theorem*:

$$(a + b)^n = \sum_{k=0}^{n} \binom{n}{k} a^k b^{n-k}$$

holds for all $n = 1, 2, \ldots, p$ and arbitrary elements $a$, $b$; beware that the exponents are interpreted as ordinary natural numbers, not as field elements: $a^i = a \times a \times \cdots \times a$ ($i$ factors). [Hint: use mathematical induction on $n$, applying the formula in 11A.]

(2) For each polynomial $f(x)$ over $\mathbf{Z}_p$ we have

$$f(x^p) = [f(x)]^p.$$

[Hint: analogous to 11B (1).]

**11C**    *The formal derivative* of a polynomial $a(x) = a_0 + a_1 x + a_2 x^2 + \cdots + a_n x^n$ is defined by $a'(x) = a_1 + 2a_2 x + 3a_3 x^2 + \cdots + na_n x^{n-1}$ (where $2 = 1 + 1$, etc.). Prove that the "usual" formulas for derivatives are true:

(1) $[a(x) + b(x)]' = a'(x) + b'(x)$,

(2) $[a(x)b(x)]' = a'(x)b(x) + a(x)b'(x)$.

**11D**    *Multiple zeros.* An element $a$ is called a multiple zero of a polynomial $f(x)$ provided that $(x - a)^k$ divides $f(x)$ for some $k \geq 2$.

(1) Prove that each multiple zero of $f(x)$ is a zero of the formal derivative $f'(x)$.

(2) Find a polynomial over $\mathbf{Z}_2$ with no multiple zeros whose derivative has a zero.

(3) Prove that every common zero of $f(x)$ and $f'(x)$ is a multiple zero of $f(x)$.

**11E**    Prove that in a field of characteristic 2:

(1) Every element has a square root (i.e., for each $a$, there exists $b$ with $a = b^2$). [Hint: if $c$ is primitive in $GF(2^m)$, then $c^{2^m} = c$; thus, $c$ has the square root $c^{2^{m-1}}$, and then each $c^i$ has a square root too.]

(2) The formal derivative of every polynomial is a perfect square (i.e., for each polynomial $f(x)$, there exists a polynomial $g(x)$ with $f'(x) = [g(x)]^2$). [Hint: since $(x^n)' = nx^{n-1} = 0$ for $n$ even, the formal derivative has only even powers. Using (1), write $f'(x) = f_0^2 + f_2^2 x^2 + f_4^2 x^4 + \cdots$ and then put $g(x) = f_0 + f_2 x + f_4 x^2 + \cdots$.]

**11F**    Verify that orders of elements of $GF(2^m)$ are always odd numbers. More in general: if a field of $q$ elements has the property that some of its extensions contain an element of order $n$, verify that $q$ and $n$ are relatively prime. Compare with Corollary 11.7.

**11G**    *Formal power series.* Just as (finite) words can be expressed by polynomials, infinite words correspond to a so-called formal power series. In other words, given a field $F$, a formal power series over $F$ in one indeterminate $x$ is an expression of the form $\sum_{i=0}^{\infty} a_i x^i$, where $a_0, a_1, a_2, \ldots$ are elements of $F$. The summands $a_i x^i$ with $a_i = 0$ can be omitted from the expression. (Thus, in particular, every polynomial is a formal power series.) The question of convergence, discussed so much in the case $F = \mathbf{R}$, never arises in finite fields; thus, a formal power series is *not* a function.

(1) Verify that all formal power series form a ring under the usual addition

$$\sum_{i=0}^{\infty} a_i x^i + \sum_{i=0}^{\infty} b_i x^i = \sum_{i=0}^{\infty} (a_i + b_i) x^i$$

and multiplication

$$\left( \sum_{i=0}^{\infty} a_i x^i \right) \left( \sum_{i=0}^{\infty} b_i x^i \right) = \sum_{i=0}^{\infty} (a_i b_0 + a_{i-1} b_1 + \cdots + a_0 b_i) x^i.$$

(2) A remarkable fact: the well-known formula for the *sum of a geometric series* is valid even in the formal setting: for each element $a$,

$$\sum_{i=0}^{\infty} a^i x^i = \frac{1}{1 - ax}.$$

More precisely, the product of the power series $\sum a^i x^i$ and $1 - ax$ is 1. Prove it. [Hint: multiply $\sum a^i x^i (1 - ax) = \sum a^i x^i - \sum a^{i+1} x^{i+1}$.]

**11H**    Prove that polynomials over any field have the following properties:

(1) The following formula

$$x^{km} - 1 = (x^m - 1) \sum_{i=0}^{k-1} (x^m)^i$$

holds. Therefore,

$$m \text{ divides } n \quad \Longrightarrow \quad x^m - 1 \text{ divides } x^n - 1.$$

(2) Conversely, whenever $x^m - 1$ divides $x^n - 1$, prove that $m$ divides $n$. [Hint: given $x^n - 1 = (x^m - 1)q(x) = (x^m - 1)(q_0 + q_1 x + \cdots + q_r x^r)$, multipy out the last product.]

**11I** Let $f(x)$ be an irreducible polynomial over a field $F$. Prove that $f(x)$ is the minimal polynomial (with respect to $F$) of any zero $f(x)$ has in any extension of $F$. Use this fact to describe the minimal polynomials of all elements of $GF(16)$ w.r.t. $GF(4)$. Can you apply Theorem 11.6?

**11J** Prove the following:

(1) $x^8 - 1$ factors as the product of all binary irreducible polynomials whose degree divides 3 (see Figure 4 of 11.6).

(2) More in general, the product of all binary irreducible polynomials whose degree divides $n$ is equal to $x^{2^n} - 1$. [Hint: if $\alpha$ is a primitive element of $GF(2^n)$, then $x^{2^n} - x$ factors as $x(x - \alpha)(x - \alpha^2) \cdots (x - \alpha^{2^n - 1})$ by Fermat's Theorem. Use the fact that minimal polynomials are irreducible and vice versa, and apply Theorem 11.6.]

(3) Generalize (2) from $\mathbf{Z}_2$ to any finite field.

**11K** Find a primitive element of $\mathbf{Z}_3[x]/x^2 + 1$.

**11L** What is an algebraic extension $F[x]/\bmod p(x)$ in the case $p(x)$ has degree 1?

**11M** Prove that in a field of characteristic $p$, no element has an order divisible by $p$.

**11N** Prove that in a field of characteristic $p$, every polynomial $f(x)$ fulfils

$$[f(x)]^{p^m} = f_0^{p^m} + f_1^{p^m} x^{p^m} + \cdots + f_n^{p^m} x^{np^m}.$$

Conclude that for polynomials $f(x)$ over $\mathbf{Z}_p$,

$$[f(x)]^{p^m} = f(x^{p^m}).$$

**11O** Find an extension of $\mathbf{Z}_2$ in which $x^9 - 1$ factors into linear factors.

**11P** Prove that if $GF(2^k)$ extends $GF(2^n)$, then $k$ is divisible by $n$. Find all fields which are extended by $GF(16)$.

**11Q** Show that the polynomial $x^2 - 1$ has more than two zeros in $\mathbf{Z}_{15}$. Compare this with Remark (1) in 11.1.

**11R** What are the orders of all elements of $GF(27)$ and $GF(32)$?

**11S** An irreducible polynomial $p(x)$ over a field $F$ is called *primitive* if the indeterminate $\alpha$ is a primitive element of $F[x]/\operatorname{mod} p(x)$.

(1) Find a nonprimitive irreducible polynomial of degree 2 over $\mathbf{Z}_3$, and find a primitive polynomial of degree 2 over $\mathbf{Z}_3$.

(2) Prove that every finite field has primitive polynomials of all degrees. [Hint: use Theorems 11.2 and 11.9.]

**11T** Construct $GF(16)$ as an algebraic extension of $GF(4)$.

## Notes

Many textbooks on modern algebra contain material concerning finite fields. A good reference is, e.g., Berlekamp (1968), Chapter 4.

# Chapter 12

# BCH Codes: Strong Codes Correcting Multiple Errors

In this chapter, we introduce an important class of cyclic codes: the Bose-Chaudhuri-Hocquenghem codes (BCH codes). Their properties are summarized in Figure 1. The main distinctive feature of the BCH codes is the possibility of choosing the number of errors they are to correct. In the next chapter, we present a fast decoder of BCH codes.

| | |
|---|---|
| Specified: | By zeros $\beta$, $\beta^2$, ..., $\beta^{2t}$ of all code words |
| Length: | $n$ = order of $\beta$ |
| Minimum distance: | $d \geq 2t + 1$ |
| Generator polynomial: | Least common multiple of the minimal polynomials of $\beta$, $\beta^2$, ..., $\beta^{2t}$ |
| Information symbols: | $k = n -$ degree $g(x)$ |
| Error-control capability: | Corrects $t$ errors; a fast decoder is presented in Chapter 13 |

**Figure 1:** Properties of BCH codes

229

The most important BCH codes are, undoubtadly, the binary codes. However, the nonbinary Reed-Solomon codes, which are BCH codes of length $n$ such that the code alphabet has $n + 1$ letters, are tools for a construction of good burst-error correcting binary codes. We also present a class of codes generalizing BCH codes, the Goppa codes, which have interesting theoretical properties, and are used in cryptography, as will be explained in 15.3 below.

We first revisit Hamming codes, which turn out to be special BCH codes, then we present the double-error-correcting BCH codes, and, finally, we turn to the general BCH codes. We also introduce nonbinary BCH codes, called Reed-Solomon codes, from which important binary burst-error-correcting codes are derived. The last section is devoted to Goppa codes, a generalization of BCH codes used, e.g., in cryptography.

## 12.1  Hamming Codes as Cyclic Codes

We presented Hamming codes in 5.5 via binary expansions of numbers as columns of the parity check matrix. Those codes are not cyclic. We now introduce (equivalent) cyclic codes via a prescribed zero of polynomials. This is both an important view of Hamming codes and a prelude to BCH codes, which are defined by zeros.

Suppose that a fixed element $\beta$ of some extension of the field $\mathbf{Z}_2$ is given. If the order of $\beta$ is $n$, we can consider all binary words $w_0 w_1 \ldots w_{n-1}$ of length $n$ characterized by the equation

$$w(\beta) = 0,$$

i.e, all binary polynomials of degree smaller than $n$ with $\beta$ as a zero. All these words form a cyclic code. In fact:

(1) Let $M(x)$ be the minimal polynomial of $\beta$. Then $M(x)$ is a divisor of $x^n - 1$. (Proof: since $\beta^n = 1$, $\beta$ is a zero of $x^n - 1$, thus, $M(x)$ divides $x^n - 1$ by Proposition 11.6.)

(2) $M(x)$ generates a cyclic code of length $n$—see Theorem 10.3.

(3) A binary polynomial of degree smaller than $n$ has $\beta$ as a zero if and only if it is a multiple of $M(x)$.

Consequently, the binary code determined by $\beta$ is the cyclic code of length $n$ whose generator polynomial is $M(x)$.

In particular, if $\beta$ is a primitive element of $GF(2^m)$, we get a binary cyclic code of length $2^m - 1$. Nothing new:

**Proposition.** *Let $\beta$ be a primitive element of $GF(2^m)$. Then the binary cyclic code of length $2^m - 1$ given by the equation $w(\beta) = 0$ is a Hamming code.*

PROOF. The equation determining the code is $w_0 + w_1\beta + \cdots + w_{n-1}\beta^{n-1} = 0$ (where $n = 2^m - 1$). In matrix form,

$$\begin{bmatrix} 1 & \beta & \beta^2 & \cdots & \beta^{n-1} \end{bmatrix} \begin{bmatrix} w_0 \\ w_1 \\ w_2 \\ \vdots \\ w_{n-1} \end{bmatrix} = 0.$$

Thus, the one-row matrix

$$\mathbf{H} = \begin{bmatrix} 1 & \beta & \beta^2 & \cdots & \beta^{n-1} \end{bmatrix}$$

could be called a parity check matrix of the code, except that this is a matrix over $GF(2^m)$, not a binary matrix. However, we can translate $\mathbf{H}$ into binary: each element of $GF(2^m)$ is a binary polynomial $f(\alpha) = f_0 + f_1\alpha + \cdots + f_{m-1}\alpha^{m-1}$ of degree smaller than $m$, which we can identify with the binary column of its coefficients:

$$f(\alpha) \longleftrightarrow \begin{pmatrix} f_0 \\ f_1 \\ \vdots \\ f_{m-1} \end{pmatrix}.$$

If each $\beta^i$ in the matrix $\mathbf{H}$ is translated in this manner, we obtain an $m \times n$ binary matrix which is the parity check matrix of the given code. Now the columns $\beta^i$ of that matrix are nonzero and pairwise distinct (see Proposition 11.2); thus, our code is a Hamming code by definition (5.5). $\square$

**Examples**

(1) Let $\alpha$ be a primitive element of $GF(8)$ in Figure 2 of 11.3. The binary cyclic code of length 7 given by the equation $w(\alpha) = 0$ has the following parity check matrix:

$$\mathbf{H} = \begin{bmatrix} 1 & \alpha & \alpha^2 & \alpha^3 & \alpha^4 & \alpha^5 & \alpha^6 \end{bmatrix}.$$

In binary: 1 is the polynomial $1 + 0 \times \alpha + 0 \times \alpha^2$ or the column

$$1 \longleftrightarrow \begin{pmatrix} 1 \\ 0 \\ 0 \end{pmatrix}.$$

Analogously, $\alpha = 0 + 1 \times \alpha + 0 \times \alpha^2$ is the column

$$\alpha \longmapsto \begin{pmatrix} 0 \\ 1 \\ 0 \end{pmatrix},$$

etc. The translation of $\mathbf{H}$ into binary is the following matrix:

$$\mathbf{H} = \begin{bmatrix} 1 & 0 & 0 & 1 & 0 & 1 & 1 \\ 0 & 1 & 0 & 1 & 1 & 1 & 0 \\ 0 & 0 & 1 & 0 & 1 & 1 & 1 \end{bmatrix}.$$

Another presentation of the same cyclic Hamming code is by means of its generator polynomial: $g(x)$ is the minimal polynomial of $\alpha$, which (by 11.7) is

$$g(x) = x^3 + x + 1.$$

(2) The primitive element $\alpha$ of $GF(16)$ in Appendix A determines the binary cyclic code of the parity check matrix:

$$\mathbf{H} = \begin{bmatrix} 1 & \alpha & \alpha^2 & \cdots & \alpha^{13} & \alpha^{14} \end{bmatrix}$$

$$= \begin{bmatrix} 1 & 0 & 0 & 0 & 1 & 0 & 0 & 1 & 1 & 0 & 1 & 0 & 1 & 1 & 1 \\ 0 & 1 & 0 & 0 & 1 & 1 & 0 & 1 & 0 & 1 & 1 & 1 & 1 & 0 & 0 \\ 0 & 0 & 1 & 0 & 0 & 1 & 1 & 0 & 1 & 0 & 1 & 1 & 1 & 1 & 0 \\ 0 & 0 & 0 & 1 & 0 & 0 & 1 & 1 & 0 & 1 & 0 & 1 & 1 & 1 & 1 \end{bmatrix}.$$

The generator polynomial (see Figure 5 of 11.7) is

$$g(x) = x^4 + x + 1.$$

# 12.2 Double-Error-Correcting BCH Codes

Before introducing BCH codes in general, we present an important special case (with an important special decoding technique): the binary BCH codes correcting double errors. Observe that (except for the repetition code of length 5) no double-error-correcting codes have been introduced so far.

In 12.1, we saw that one zero $\beta$ determines the (perfect) single-error-correcting Hamming code. With some optimism, we can expect that two zeros (say, two different powers of the element $\beta$) will determine a double-error-correctig code. This is indeed the case. However, the second zero cannot be $\beta^2$: we know that every binary polynomial with $\beta$ as a zero also has $\beta^2$ as a zero (Theorem 11.5). The next element to try is $\beta^3$. We now show that this works.

**Definition.** *By the binary double-error-correcting BCH code is meant the code of all binary words* **w** *of length n satisfying*

$$w(\beta) = w(\beta^3) = 0,$$

*where $\beta$ is an element of order n in some algebraic extension of the field $\mathbf{Z}_2$.*

**Remarks**

(1) The name "double-error-correcting BCH code" naturally requires justification: we have to prove that the code corrects double errors. We will do this below by presenting a powerful decoding algorithm.

(2) The BCH code is cyclic. This is proved exactly as in 12.1 for the Hamming codes: if $M_1(x)$ is the minimal polynomial of $\beta$ and $M_3(x)$ the minimal polynomial of $\beta^3$, then $g(x) = M_1(x)M_3(x)$ is a generator polynomial of the BCH code.

(3) The length $n$ of the BCH code can be any odd number: by Corollary 11.7, an element of order $n$ exists in some $GF(2^m)$.

**Example.** (1) Let $\beta = \alpha$ be the primitive element of $GF(16)$ in Appendix A. The binary code of length 15 given by the equations

$$w(\alpha) = w(\alpha^3) = 0$$

can equivalently be described by the matrix equation

$$\begin{bmatrix} 1 & \alpha & \alpha^2 & \alpha^3 & \cdots & \alpha^{13} & \alpha^{14} \\ 1 & \alpha^3 & (\alpha^3)^2 & (\alpha^3)^3 & \cdots & (\alpha^3)^{13} & (\alpha^3)^{14} \end{bmatrix} \begin{bmatrix} w_0 \\ w_1 \\ w_2 \\ \vdots \\ w_{13} \\ w_{14} \end{bmatrix} = \begin{bmatrix} 0 \\ 0 \end{bmatrix}.$$

Thus, we have the parity check matrix

$$\mathbf{H} = \begin{bmatrix} 1 & \alpha & \alpha^2 & \alpha^3 & \cdots & \alpha^{13} & \alpha^{14} \\ 1 & \alpha^3 & \alpha^6 & \alpha^9 & \cdots & \alpha^{39} & \alpha^{42} \end{bmatrix}.$$

This can be translated into binary as we saw in 12.1: each element $\alpha^i$ of $GF(16)$ is a binary column of its four coefficients (when considered as a polynomial in $\alpha$ of degree smaller then 4). Thus:

$$\mathbf{H} = \left[\begin{array}{cccccccccccccccc} 1 & 0 & 0 & 0 & 1 & 0 & 0 & 1 & 1 & 0 & 1 & 0 & 1 & 1 & 1 \\ 0 & 1 & 0 & 0 & 1 & 1 & 0 & 1 & 0 & 1 & 1 & 1 & 1 & 0 & 0 \\ 0 & 0 & 1 & 0 & 0 & 1 & 1 & 0 & 1 & 0 & 1 & 1 & 1 & 1 & 0 \\ 0 & 0 & 0 & 1 & 0 & 0 & 1 & 1 & 0 & 1 & 0 & 1 & 1 & 1 & 1 \\ \hline 1 & 0 & 0 & 0 & 1 & 1 & 0 & 0 & 0 & 1 & 1 & 0 & 0 & 0 & 1 \\ 0 & 0 & 0 & 1 & 1 & 0 & 0 & 0 & 1 & 1 & 0 & 0 & 0 & 1 & 1 \\ 0 & 0 & 1 & 0 & 1 & 0 & 0 & 1 & 0 & 1 & 0 & 0 & 1 & 0 & 1 \\ 0 & 1 & 1 & 1 & 1 & 0 & 1 & 1 & 1 & 1 & 0 & 1 & 1 & 1 & 1 \end{array}\right].$$

This BCH code is a $(15,7)$-code, because the last matrix $\mathbf{H}$ has linearly independent rows.

Since $\alpha$ has the minimal polynomial $M_1(x) = x^4 + x + 1$, and $\alpha^3$ the minimal polynomial $M_3(x) = x^4 + x^3 + x^2 + x + 1$ (see Figure 5 of 11.7), it follows that every code word is a polynomial $w(x)$ divisible by both $M_1(x)$ and $M_3(x)$. The latter polynomials are irreducible; thus, $w(x)$ must be divisible by $M_1(x)M_3(x)$ (by the unique factorization theorem 11.1). Consequently, the lowest-degree nonzero code word (= the generator polynomial) is

$$\begin{aligned} g(x) &= M_1(x)M_3(x) \\ &= (x^4 + x + 1)(x^4 + x^3 + x^2 + x + 1) \\ &= x^8 + x^7 + x^6 + x^4 + 1. \end{aligned}$$

All code words of the BCH code are the multiples $q(x)g(x)$ of the generator polynomial $g(x) = x^8 + x^7 + x^6 + x^4 + 1$ by a polynomial $q(x)$ of degree lower than 7.

*Decoding.* Suppose that we receive a word $\mathbf{w} = w_0 w_1 \ldots w_{n-1}$ and that at most two positions are corrupted, say, the positions $w_i$ and $w_j$. We compute the syndrome based on the parity check matrix

$$\mathbf{H} = \left[\begin{array}{cccccc} 1 & \beta & \beta^2 & \beta^3 & \cdots & \beta^{n-1} \\ 1 & \beta^3 & (\beta^3)^2 & (\beta^3)^3 & \cdots & (\beta^3)^{n-1} \end{array}\right].$$

That is, we compute

$$\mathbf{H}\left[\begin{array}{c} w_0 \\ w_1 \\ \vdots \\ w_{n-1} \end{array}\right] = \left[\begin{array}{c} w_0 + w_1\beta + \cdots + w_{n-1}\beta^{n-1} \\ w_0 + w_1\beta^3 + \cdots + w_{n-1}(\beta^3)^{n-1} \end{array}\right]$$

$$= \left[\begin{array}{c} w(\beta) \\ w(\beta^3) \end{array}\right] = \left[\begin{array}{c} s_1 \\ s_3 \end{array}\right].$$

The error-pattern word $e(x) = x^i + x^j$ has the same syndrome (see Proposition 8.3):

$$\begin{bmatrix} s_1 \\ s_3 \end{bmatrix} = \begin{bmatrix} e(\beta) \\ e(\beta^3) \end{bmatrix} = \begin{bmatrix} \beta^i + \beta^j \\ \beta^{3i} + \beta^{3j} \end{bmatrix}.$$

Thus, it is our task to compute the unknown elements $\beta^i$ and $\beta^j$ (from which $i$ and $j$ are easily determined) from the known syndrome $(s_1, s_3)$ using the following equations

$$\beta^i + \beta^j = s_1,$$
$$\beta^{3i} + \beta^{3j} = s_3.$$

To solve these equations, we consider the third power of the first one:

$$\begin{aligned} s_1^3 &= \beta^{3i} + 3\beta^{2i}\beta^j + 3\beta^i\beta^{2j} + \beta^{3j} \\ &= (\beta^{3i} + \beta^{3j}) + 3\beta^i\beta^j(\beta^i + \beta^j) \\ &= s_3 + \beta^i\beta^j s_1. \end{aligned}$$

Thus, we know both the sum of the unknown elements: $\beta^i + \beta^j = s_1$, and their product:

$$\beta^i\beta^j = \frac{s_1^3 - s_3}{s_1} = s_1^2 + s_3 s_1^{-1}.$$

The sum and the product of two unknown numbers allow us to write a quadratic equation for those numbers:

$$x^2 - (\beta^i + \beta^j)x + \beta^i\beta^j = 0.$$

That is,

$$x^2 + s_1 x + (s_1^2 + s_3 s_1^{-1}) = 0.$$

This leads to the following

*Decoding algorithm*

**Step I:** Compute the syndrome $s_1 = w(\beta)$ and $s_3 = w(\beta^3)$. If $s_1 = s_3 = 0$, the received word $\mathbf{w}$ is a code word.

**Step II:** If $s_1 = 0 \neq s_3$, announce that more than two bits are corrupted. If $s_1 \neq 0$, solve the quadratic equation

$$x^2 + s_1 x + s_1^2 + s_3 s_1^{-1} = 0.$$

(The solutions can be found by brute force: try all $\beta^i$, $i = 0, 1, \ldots, n-1$.)

**Step III:** If the quadratic equation has roots $\beta^i$ and $\beta^j$, correct $w_i$ and $w_j$. If it has roots 0 and $\beta^i$, correct $w_i$. If it has no roots, announce that more than 2 bits are corrupted.

The proof of correctness of the above algorithm has essentially been performed above. There are four possibilities:

(1) Two different bits $w_i$ and $w_j$ have been corrupted. Then, as we have seen, $\beta^i$ and $\beta^j$ are the roots of the above quadratic equation.

(2) One bit has been corrupted. Then $s_1 = e(\beta) = \beta^i$ and $s_3 = e(\beta^3) = \beta^{3i}$. Thus, $s_1^2 + s_3 s_1^{-1} = 0$, and the quadratic equation takes the form

$$x^2 + s_1 x = 0.$$

It has roots 0 and $s_1 = \beta^i$, and we must correct $w_i$.

(3) No bit has been corrupted, i.e., $s_1 = s_3 = 0$.

(4) More than two bits have been corrupted—this takes place precisely when none of (1)–(3) does.

**Examples**

(1) (continued) When receiving

$$\mathbf{w} = 0000000111000000 = x^6 + x^7 + x^8,$$

we decode as follows:

**Step I:** The syndrome is

$$
\begin{aligned}
s_1 &= \alpha^6 + \alpha^7 + \alpha^8 = \alpha, \\
s_3 &= \alpha^{18} + \alpha^{21} + \alpha^{24} = \alpha^3 + \alpha^6 + \alpha^9 = \alpha^{11}.
\end{aligned}
$$

**Step II:** Since $s_1^2 + s_3 s_1^{-1} = \alpha^2 + \alpha^{10} = \alpha^4$, solve the equation

$$x^2 + \alpha x + \alpha^4 = 0.$$

Its roots are found by inserting $x = 1, \alpha, \alpha^2, \dots$ : they are

$$x_1 = 1 \qquad \text{and} \qquad x_2 = \alpha^4.$$

**Step III:** Correct $w_0$ (since $x_1 = \alpha^0$) and $w_4$ and obtain

$$\mathbf{v} = 100010111000000.$$

It is easy to verify that $v(\alpha) = v(\alpha^3) = 0$. Thus, the decoding is correct: $\mathbf{v}$ is a code word of Hamming distance 2 from the received word.

(2) Let us construct the double-error BCH code of length 9. We must find an element of order 9 in some extension of $Z_2$. Since $\varphi(9) = 6$ (see Figure 6 of 11.7), such an element can be found in $GF(2^6) = GF(64)$. In fact, the primitive element $\alpha$ in Appendix A has order $63 = 9 \times 7$; thus, $\beta = \alpha^7$ has order 9. The BCH code is therefore determined by the zeros $\beta$ and $\beta^3$. We compute the minimal polynomials by means of Theorem 11.6. For $\beta = \alpha^7$, we have

$$M_1(x) = (x - \alpha^7)(x - \alpha^{14})(x - \alpha^{28})(x - \alpha^{56})(x - \alpha^{112})(x - \alpha^{224}),$$

since $\alpha^{224} = \alpha^{35}$ and $(\alpha^{35})^2 = \alpha^7$. For $\beta^3 = \alpha^{21}$, we have

$$M_3(x) = (x - \alpha^{21})(x - \alpha^{42}),$$

since $(\alpha^{42})^2 = \alpha^{21}$. We conclude that the generator polynomial

$$g(x) = M_1(x)M_3(x)$$

has degree 8. Thus, this BCH code is simply the repetition code of length 9.

(3) For the length $n = 31$, we choose the primitive element $\beta = \alpha$ of $GF(32)$ in Appendix A. Then $\alpha$ has, obviously, the minimal polynomial

$$M_1(x) = x^5 + x^2 + 1$$

[used for defining $GF(32)$], and $\alpha^3$ has the minimal polynomial

$$
\begin{aligned}
M_3(x) &= (x - \alpha^3)(x - \alpha^6)(x - \alpha^{12})(x - \alpha^{24})(x - \alpha^{17}) \\
&= x^5 + x^4 + x^3 + x^2 + 1.
\end{aligned}
$$

Thus, we obtain a cyclic $(31, 21)$-code with the generator polynomial

$$g(x) = (x^5 + x^2 + 1)(x^5 + x^4 + x^3 + x^2 + 1).$$

The definition of double-error-correcting BCH codes contains some uncertainty. In which extension of $Z_2$ are we working? Which element $\beta$ are we choosing? We will now show that the answers to such questions are irrelevant:

**Independence Theorem.** *The double-error-correcting BCH code does not depend, up to equivalence, on the choice of the element $\beta$. That is, if $\beta$ and $\overline{\beta}$ are two elements of order n in two extensions of $Z_2$, then the two corresponding BCH codes: $K$, defined by the zeros $\beta$ and $\beta^3$, and $\overline{K}$, defined by the zeros $\overline{\beta}$ and $\overline{\beta}^3$, are equivalent.*

PROOF. If $\beta$ lies in $GF(2^m)$ and $\overline{\beta}$ lies in $GF(2^{\overline{m}})$, then for $k = m\overline{m}$, the field $GF(2^k)$ is a common extension of $GF(2^m)$ and $GF(2^{\overline{m}})$, see Corollary 11.8. Thus, both $\beta$ and $\overline{\beta}$ lie in $GF(2^k)$. In that field, $x^n - 1$ factors as follows:

$$x^n - 1 = (x - \beta)(x - \beta^2) \cdots (x - \beta^n),$$

see Remark (1) in 11.4. Therefore, each element of order $n$ is a power of $\beta$; in particular, $\overline{\beta} = \beta^i$.

We will prove that the following numbers $\pi_k = 0, 1, \ldots, n$

$$\pi_k \equiv ik \pmod{n} \qquad \text{for } k = 0, 1, \ldots, n$$

form a permutation such that a word $v_0 \ldots v_{n-1}$ is a code word of $K$ if and only if the word $v_{\pi_0} \ldots v_{\pi_{n-1}}$ is a code word of $\overline{K}$. In fact, to show that $\pi_0, \ldots, \pi_{n-1}$ is a permutation, it is sufficient to verify that the numbers $\pi_k$ are pairwise distinct. If $\pi_k = \pi_l$, then $ik - il$ is divisible by $n$, hence, $\beta^{ik-il} = 1$. This means $(\beta^i)^k = (\beta^i)^l$, i.e., $\overline{\beta}^k = \overline{\beta}^l$. Since $\overline{\beta}$ has order $n$, it follows that $k = l$ (see Proposition 11.4). Therefore, $\pi_0, \pi_1, \ldots, \pi_{n-1}$ is a permutation of the numbers $0, 1, \ldots, n - 1$. We conclude the proof by showing that for each word $\mathbf{v}$,

$$v_0 v_1 \ldots v_{n-1} \quad \text{lies in } K \iff v_{\pi_0} v_{\pi_1} \ldots v_{\pi_{n-1}} \quad \text{lies in } \overline{K}.$$

In fact, $\mathbf{v}$ lies in $K$ precisely when $\sum v_i \beta^i = \sum v_i \beta^{3i} = 0$. The index $i$ can be substituted by $\pi_i$, and these equations read $\sum v_{\pi_i} \beta^{\pi_i} = \sum v_{\pi_i} \beta^{3\pi_i} = 0$. Since $\beta^{\pi_i} = \beta^{ik} = \overline{\beta}^k$, the last equations can be written as $\sum v_{\pi_i} \overline{\beta}^i = \sum v_{\pi_i} \overline{\beta}^{3i} = 0$. Those characterize the code words $v_{\pi_0} v_{\pi_1} \ldots v_{\pi_{n-1}}$ of $\overline{K}$. $\square$

## Concluding Remarks

(1) For every odd number $n$, there is a binary double-error-correcting BCH code of legth $n$. It is determined by choosing an element $\beta$ of order $n$ in some Galois field $GF(2^m)$ and requiring that $\beta$ and $\overline{\beta}$ be zeros of code words. The concrete choice of $\beta$ is irrelevant: different choices give equivalent codes.

(2) The BCH code is determined either by its generator polynomial $g(x) = M_1(x)M_3(x)$ [where $M_i(x)$ is the minimal polynomial of $\beta^i$] or by the parity check matrix

$$\mathbf{H} = \begin{bmatrix} 1 & \beta & \beta^2 & \cdots & \beta^{n-1} \\ 1 & \beta^3 & \beta^6 & \cdots & \beta^{3(n-1)} \end{bmatrix}.$$

(3) The code corrects double errors by solving a specific quadratic equation. It follows that its minimum distance is at least 5. It can be larger: for length 9, the BCH code is just the repetition code with $d = 9$.

(4) Consider the extended double-error-correcting BCH code (see 8.5). It has minimum distance 6 (or more), thus, it can correct single errors and detect triple errors smultaneously (see 8.6). For example, the extended double-error-correcting BCH code of length 32 is a $(32, 21)$-code.

## 12.3 BCH Codes

Recall that for each $r$-element fied $F$ (which will now be the code alphabet) and each number $n$ such that $r$ and $n$ are relatively prime, there exists an element $\beta$ of order $n$ in some extension of $F$ (Corollary 11.7). Recall further that each power $\beta^i$ (in the same extension) has a minimal polynomial $M_i(x)$ which is the smallest-degree polynomial over $F$ with $\beta^i$ as a zero.

**Definition.** *Let $F$ be a finite field, and let $n$ be a number relatively prime with the number of elements of $F$. By a $t$-error-correcting BCH code of length $n$ in the alphabet $F$ is meant the cyclic code of all words $\mathbf{w}$ in $F^n$ satisfying the equations*

$$w(\beta) = w(\beta^2) = w(\beta^3) = \cdots = w(\beta^{2t}) = 0,$$

*where $\beta$ is an element of order $n$ in some algebraic extension of $F$. That is, code words are polynomials over $F$ of a degree smaller than $n$ with $\beta$, $\beta^2$, $\beta^3$, ..., $\beta^{2t}$ as zeros.*

### Examples

(1) If the alphabet $F$ is $\mathbf{Z}_2$, we can delete the even powers of $\beta$ in the above definition: any polynomial with $\beta^i$ as a zero also has $\beta^{2i}$ as a zero [by Theorem (2) in 11.5]. Thus, the case $t = 2$ reduces to

$$w(\beta) = w(\beta^3) = 0$$

studied in the previous section.

(2) A binary triple-error-correcting BCH code is given by

$$w(\beta) = w(\beta^3) = w(\beta^5) = 0.$$

For example, let $\beta = \alpha$ be the primitive element of $GF(16)$ in Appendix A. The minimal polynomials $M_i(x)$ of the elements $\alpha^i$ are listed in Figure 5 of 11.6:

$$M_1(x) = x^4 + x + 1,$$
$$M_3(x) = x^4 + x^3 + x^2 + x + 1,$$
$$M_5(x) = x^2 + x + 1.$$

A binary polynomial has $\alpha$, $\alpha^3$, $\alpha^5$ as zeros precisely when it can be divided by each of $M_1(x)$, $M_3(x)$, and $M_5(x)$. Since those three polynomials are irreducible (as are all minimal polynomials), divisibility by each of them is equivalent to divisibility by their product. Thus, the generator polynomial of the BCH code is

$$g(x) = M_1(x)M_3(x)M_5(x) = (x^4+x+1)(x^4+x^3+x^2+x+1)(x^2+x+1).$$

It has degree 10; thus, we get a cyclic $(15,5)$-code.

(3) Let $F = \mathbf{Z}_3$. A ternary double-error correcting BCH code of length 26 is obtained by choosing $\beta = \alpha$, the primitive element of $GF(27)$ in Appendix A. The equations

$$w(\alpha) = w(\alpha^2) = w(\alpha^3) = w(\alpha^4) = 0$$

can be reduced by discarding $w(\alpha^3) = 0$, since every polynomial with a zero in $\alpha$ has a zero in $\alpha^3$ [by Theorem (2) in 11.5]. Let us compute the minimal polynomials:

$$M_1(x) = (x - \alpha)(x - \alpha^3)(x - \alpha^9) = x^3 + 2x + 1,$$
$$M_2(x) = (x - \alpha^2)(x - \alpha^6)(x - \alpha^{18}) = x^3 + 2x^2 + x + 2,$$
$$M_4(x) = (x - \alpha^4)(x - \alpha^{12})(x - \alpha^{10}) = x^3 + 2x^2 + 1.$$

The code words are precisely the polynomials divisible by each of these (irreducile) polynomials, hence, divisible by their product. Thus, the generator polynomial is

$$g(x) = M_1(x)M_2(x)M_4(x) = (x^3+2+1)(x^3+2x^2+x+2)(x^3+2x^2+1).$$

We get a cyclic ternary $(26,17)$-code correcting double errors.

**Remark.** (1) Usually the best choice of the element $\beta$ determining a BCH code is a primitive element of some extension of the code alphabet. Such BCH codes are called *primitive*.

For example, primitive binary BCH codes are those of lengths $n = 2^m - 1$. Compare the primitive codes of length 15 and 31 in Examples (1) and (3) of 12.2 with the nonprimitive (repetition) code of length 9 in Example (2).

**Proposition.** *The t-error-correcting BCH code is a cyclic code of length n whose generator polynomial is the least common multiple\* of the minimal polynomials $M_i(x)$ of $\beta^i$ for $i = 1, 2, \ldots, 2t$. In short:*

$$g(x) = \text{LCM}\big[\, M_1(x), M_2(x), \ldots, M_{2t}(x) \,\big].$$

**PROOF.** The above polynomial $g(x)$ is a code word since $M_i(\beta^i) = 0$ implies $g(\beta^i) = 0$ for $i = 1, 2, \ldots, 2t$. Since the order of $\beta$ is $n$, we have $\beta^n = 1$; thus, $(\beta^i)^n = (\beta^n)^i = 1$. It follows that $\beta^i$ is a zero of $x^n - 1$; thus, $x^n - 1$ is a common multiple of all $M_i(x)$ (by Proposition 11.6). Consequently, $x^n - 1$ is a multiple of $g(x)$. This implies that $g(x)$ generates a cylic code of length $n$ (see Theorem 10.3).

Now, each multiple $w(x) = q(x)g(x)$ of $g(x)$ fulfils

$$w(\beta^i) = q(\beta^i) \times 0 = 0 \qquad \text{for } i = 1, 2, \ldots, 2t,$$

thus, $w(x)$ is a code word of the BCH code. Conversely, if $w(x)$ is a code word of the BCH code, then $w(x)$ is divisible by each $M_i(x)$ (by Proposition 11.6 again). Since all $M_i(x)$ are irreducible (see Corollary 11.6), it follows from the unique factorization theorem (11.1) that $w(x)$ is divisible by the least common multiple $g(x)$ of the polynomials $M_i(x)$. Consequently, the cyclic code generated by $g(x)$ is precisely the BCH code. $\qquad\square$

*Parity check matrix.* Analogous to the case of double-error-correcting codes in 12.2, the following matrix is a parity check matrix of the $t$-error-correcting BCH code:

$$\mathbf{H} = \begin{bmatrix} 1 & \beta & \beta^2 & \beta^3 & \cdots & \beta^{n-1} \\ 1 & \beta^2 & (\beta^2)^2 & (\beta^2)^3 & \cdots & (\beta^2)^{n-1} \\ 1 & \beta^3 & (\beta^3)^2 & (\beta^3)^3 & \cdots & (\beta^3)^{n-1} \\ \cdots\cdots\cdots\cdots\cdots\cdots\cdots\cdots\cdots\cdots\cdots \\ 1 & \beta^{2t} & (\beta^{2t})^2 & (\beta^{2t})^3 & \cdots & (\beta^{2t})^{n-1} \end{bmatrix}.$$

In fact, for each word $\mathbf{w}$ of length $n$, we have

$$\mathbf{H}\mathbf{w}^{\text{tr}} = \begin{bmatrix} w_0 + w_1\beta + w_2\beta^2 + \cdots + w_{n-1}\beta^{n-1} \\ w_0 + w_1\beta^2 + w_2(\beta^2)^2 + \cdots + w_{n-1}(\beta^2)^{n-1} \\ \cdots\cdots\cdots\cdots\cdots\cdots\cdots\cdots\cdots\cdots\cdots \\ w_0 + w_1\beta^{2t} + w_2(\beta^{2t})^2 + \cdots + w_{n-1}(\beta^{2t})^{n-1} \end{bmatrix} = \begin{bmatrix} w(\beta) \\ w(\beta^2) \\ \vdots \\ w(\beta^{2t}) \end{bmatrix}.$$

---

\*The least common multiple is, in general, the lowest-degree polynomial divisible by each of the polynomials under consideration. Since each $M_i(x)$ is irreducible, the least common multiple is simply the product of all $M_i(x)$'s from which duplicate factors are deleted.

Thus, $\mathbf{Hw^{tr}} = \mathbf{0^{tr}}$ precisely when $\mathbf{w}$ is a code word of the BCH code.

The above matrix $\mathbf{H}$ is expressed (instead of in the code alphabet $F$) in an extension of $F$. This can be translated to $F$, as explained in 12.2: suppose the algebraic extension in which $\beta$ lies is $F[x]/\mathrm{mod}\, p(x)$. The elements $\beta^i$ are then polynomials $f(\alpha)$ of degree smaller than $m = \mathrm{degree}\, p(x)$ in the indeterminate $\alpha$. Each such polynomial is substituted by the column of its coefficients:

$$\beta^i = f(\alpha) \longleftrightarrow \begin{pmatrix} f_0 \\ f_1 \\ \vdots \\ f_{m-1} \end{pmatrix}$$

This turns the $2t$ by $n$ matrix $\mathbf{H}$ above into a $2tm$ by $n$ matrix over $F$, which is a parity check matrix of the BCH code.

**Remark.** (2) In order to prove that the $t$-error-correcting BCH code does correct $t$ errors, we apply a classical result concerning determinants of matrices of the following form:

$$\begin{bmatrix} 1 & 1 & 1 & \cdots & 1 \\ a_1 & a_2 & a_3 & \cdots & a_n \\ a_1^2 & a_2^2 & a_3^2 & \cdots & a_n^2 \\ \cdots\cdots & \cdots\cdots & \cdots\cdots & \cdots & \cdots\cdots \\ a_1^{n-1} & a_2^{n-1} & a_3^{n-1} & \cdots & a_n^{n-1} \end{bmatrix}.$$

Here $a_1, a_2, \ldots, a_n$ are elments of some field, and such matrices are called *Vandermonde matrices*.

We assume here that the reader is familiar with the concept of determinant and with the Laplace expansion formula for determinants: $\det \mathbf{A} = \sum_k a_{ik}(-1)^{i+k} A_{ik}$, where $A_{ik}$ is the minor of $a_{ik}$.

Observe that for $n = 2$, the Vandermonde determinant is

$$\det \begin{bmatrix} 1 & 1 \\ a_1 & a_2 \end{bmatrix} = a_2 - a_1.$$

For $n = 3$, we have

$$\det \begin{bmatrix} 1 & 1 & 1 \\ a_1 & a_2 & a_3 \\ a_1^2 & a_2^2 & a_3^2 \end{bmatrix} = \det \begin{bmatrix} 1 & 1 & 1 \\ 0 & a_2 - a_1 & a_3 - a_1 \\ 0 & a_2^2 - a_1 a_2 & a_3^2 - a_1 a_3 \end{bmatrix},$$

where, from the second and third rows, we subtracted the scalar multiple of the preceding row by $a_1$. Thus:

$$\det \begin{bmatrix} 1 & 1 & 1 \\ a_1 & a_2 & a_3 \\ a_1^2 & a_2^2 & a_3^2 \end{bmatrix} = \det \begin{bmatrix} a_2 - a_1 & a_3 - a_1 \\ a_2^2 - a_1 a_2 & a_3^2 - a_1 a_3 \end{bmatrix}$$

$$= (a_2 - a_1)(a_3 - a_1) \det \begin{bmatrix} 1 & 1 \\ a_2 & a_3 \end{bmatrix}$$

$$= (a_2 - a_1)(a_3 - a_1)(a_3 - a_2).$$

In general, the Vandermonde determinant is

$$\det \begin{bmatrix} 1 & 1 & 1 & \cdots & 1 \\ a_1 & a_2 & a_3 & \cdots & a_n \\ a_1^2 & a_2^2 & a_3^2 & \cdots & a_n^2 \\ \cdots & \cdots & \cdots & \cdots & \cdots \\ a_1^{n-1} & a_2^{n-1} & a_3^{n-1} & \cdots & a_n^{n-1} \end{bmatrix} = \prod_{i>j}(a_i - a_j).$$

(The proof by induction on $n$ is easy; we perform the same algebraic modifications as in the above case, $n = 3$.) In particular, the Vandermonde determinant is nonzero precisely when the elements $a_1, a_2, \ldots, a_n$ are pairwise distinct.

**Theorem.** *The $t$-error-correcting BCH code has minimum distance at least $2t + 1$ (and, thus, it actually corrects $t$ errors).*

PROOF. Given a code word $\mathbf{w}$ of weight at most $2t$, we will show that $\mathbf{w} = \mathbf{0}$. We can find $2t$ indices, $i_1, i_2, \ldots, i_{2t}$, such that $w_i = 0$ for all $i \neq i_1, i_2, \ldots, i_{2t}$. (No claim is made about $w_{i_1}, w_{i_2}, \ldots, w_{i_{2t}}$.) Since $\mathbf{w}$ is a code word, for the parity check matrix $\mathbf{H}$ above, we have

$$\mathbf{H}\mathbf{w}^{\mathrm{tr}} = \mathbf{0}^{\mathrm{tr}}.$$

We can rewrite this system of equations by deleting all columns of $\mathbf{H}$ corresponding to the zeros $w_i = 0$ $(i \neq i_1, \ldots, i_{2t})$ and leaving only the columns $i_1, \ldots, i_{2t}$. Observe that the $i$th column of $\mathbf{H}$ consists of the $i$th powers of $\alpha, \alpha^2, \ldots, \alpha^{2t}$. Thus, we get

$$\begin{bmatrix} \alpha^{i_1} & \alpha^{i_2} & \cdots & \alpha^{i_{2t}} \\ (\alpha^{i_1})^2 & (\alpha^{i_2})^2 & \cdots & (\alpha^{i_{2t}})^2 \\ (\alpha^{i_1})^3 & (\alpha^{i_2})^3 & \cdots & (\alpha^{i_{2t}})^3 \\ \cdots & \cdots & \cdots & \cdots \\ (\alpha^{i_1})^{2t} & (\alpha^{i_2})^{2t} & \cdots & (\alpha^{i_{2t}})^{2t} \end{bmatrix} \begin{bmatrix} w_{i_1} \\ w_{i_2} \\ w_{i_3} \\ \vdots \\ w_{i_{2t}} \end{bmatrix} = \begin{bmatrix} 0 \\ 0 \\ 0 \\ \vdots \\ 0 \end{bmatrix}.$$

We will prove that this system of equations has a unique (all-zero) solution. It is sufficient to verify that the determinant of the matrix of that system is nonzero. We can divide the first column by $\alpha^{i_1}$, the second one by $\alpha^{i_2}$, etc., and we obtain the Vandermonde determinant:

$$
\det \begin{bmatrix}
\alpha^{i_1} & \alpha^{i_2} & \cdots & \alpha^{i_{2t}} \\
\left(\alpha^{i_1}\right)^2 & \left(\alpha^{i_2}\right)^2 & \cdots & \left(\alpha^{i_{2t}}\right)^2 \\
\left(\alpha^{i_1}\right)^3 & \left(\alpha^{i_2}\right)^3 & \cdots & \left(\alpha^{i_{2t}}\right)^3 \\
\cdots\cdots\cdots\cdots\cdots\cdots\cdots\cdots\cdots\cdots \\
\left(\alpha^{i_1}\right)^{2t} & \left(\alpha^{i_2}\right)^{2t} & \cdots & \left(\alpha^{i_{2t}}\right)^{2t}
\end{bmatrix}
$$

$$
= \alpha^{i_1}\alpha^{i_2}\ldots\alpha^{i_{2t}} \det \begin{bmatrix}
1 & 1 & \cdots & 1 \\
\alpha^{i_1} & \alpha^{i_2} & \cdots & \alpha^{i_{2t}} \\
\left(\alpha^{i_1}\right)^2 & \left(\alpha^{i_2}\right)^2 & \cdots & \left(\alpha^{i_{2t}}\right)^2 \\
\cdots\cdots\cdots\cdots\cdots\cdots\cdots\cdots\cdots\cdots \\
\left(\alpha^{i_1}\right)^{2t-1} & \left(\alpha^{i_2}\right)^{2t-1} & \cdots & \left(\alpha^{i_{2t}}\right)^{2t-1}
\end{bmatrix}
$$

$$
= \alpha^{i_1}\alpha^{i_2}\ldots\alpha^{i_{2t}} \prod_{p>q}\left(\alpha^{i_p} - \alpha^{i_q}\right).
$$

Since the elements $\alpha^{i_1}$, $\alpha^{i_2}$, ..., $\alpha^{i_{2t}}$ are pairwise distinct (see Proposition 11.1) and nonzero, we conclude that the above determinant is nonzero. Thus, $\mathbf{w} = 0$. $\qquad\square$

### Concluding Remarks

(1) Given numbers $n$ and $t$, we can construct a $t$-error-correcting BCH code of length $n$ over any finite field whose number of elements is relatively prime with $n$. The code is determined by the zeros $\beta$, $\beta^2$, ..., $\beta^{2t}$, where $\beta$ is an element of order $n$ in some extension of the code alphabet. The choice of $\beta$ is irrelevant: different choices give equivalent codes, which is proved in the same manner as the independence theorem of 12.2.

It is possible to define BCH codes more generally by using the zeros $\beta^i$, $\beta^{i+1}$, ..., $\beta^{i+2t-1}$ for an element $\beta$ of order $n$ and for some $i = 0, 1, \ldots$. We restrict our attention to $i = 1$ for simplicity.

(2) The $t$-error-correcting BCH code has minimum distance $2t+1$ or more. In Example (2) of 12.2, we saw a double-error-correcting BCH code of minimum distance 9. A fast decoder which performs the actual correction of $t$ errors will be presented in Chapter 13.

# 12.4 Reed-Solomon Codes and Derived Burst-Error-Correcting Codes

Reed-Solomon codes are special BCH codes, namely, those BCH codes for which the prescribed zeros $\beta^i$ are found in the code alphabet, not in an extension. These codes are never binary. However, important binary burst-error-correcting codes are obtained by a "translation" of Reed-Solomon codes over $GF(2^m)$.

**Definition.** *A Reed-Solomon code is a BCH code of length $n$ in a code alphabet of $n+1$ symbols.*

**Proposition.** *A $t$-error-correcting Reed-Solomon code has the generator polynomial $g(x) = (x - \beta)(x - \beta^2) \cdots (x - \beta^{2t})$ and its minimum distance is precisely $2t + 1$.*

PROOF. A Reed-Solomon code over a field $F$ is determined by the zeros $\beta, \beta^2, \ldots, \beta^{2t}$, where the order $n$ of $\beta$ is the number of the elements of $F$ minus 1—thus, $\beta$ is a primitive element of $F$. Consequently, the minimal polynomial of $\beta^i$ is $x - \beta^i$, and Proposition 12.3 implies that $g(x) = (x - \beta)(x - \beta^2) \cdots (x - \beta^{2t})$. The weight of the generator polynomial $g(x)$ is at most $2t + 1$, and since by Theorem 12.3 the minimum weight is $2t + 1$ or more, we conclude $d = 2t + 1$. $\qquad \square$

## Examples

(1) Since 3 is a primitive element of $\mathbf{Z}_7$, we can define a double-error-correcting Reed-Solomon code of length 6 over $\mathbf{Z}_7$ by the generator polynomial

$$g(x) = (x - 3)(x - 3^2)(x - 3^3)(x - 3^4) = (x - 3)(x - 2)(x - 6)(x - 4).$$

(2) Choose the primitive element $\alpha$ of $GF(8)$ in Appendix A. The following polynomial

$$g(x) = (x - \alpha)(x - \alpha^2)(x - \alpha^3)(x - \alpha^4) = \alpha^3 + \alpha x + x^2 + \alpha^3 x^3 + x^4$$

generates a double-error-correcting Reed-Solomon code of length 7 over $GF(8)$.

*Derived burst-error correcting codes.* Given a $t$-error-correcting Reed-Solomon code $K$ over $GF(2^m)$, we can form a new code by interpreting each of the nonbinary symbols $f(\alpha) = f_0 + f_1\alpha + \cdots + f_{m-1}\alpha^{m-1}$ of $GF(2^m)$ as the binary $m$-tuple $f_0 f_1 \ldots f_{m-1}$. Thus, from the nonbinary code $K$ of length

$n = 2^m - 1$, we derive a binary code $K^*$ of length $nm$ by substituting for each symbol the corresponding binary $m$-tuple.

For example, the generator polynomial of the Reed-Solomon code in Example (2) is the word $\alpha^3 \alpha 1 \alpha^3 100$ of length 7 over $GF(8)$. Since $\alpha^3 = \alpha + 1$ corresponds to 110, $\alpha$ corresponds to 010, etc., the derived binary code of length 21 contains the following word:

$$110\,010\,100\,110\,100\,000\,000.$$

From the $(7, 2)$-Reed-Solomon code over $GF(8)$, we derive a binary $(21, 6)$-code.

The importance of those derived codes lies in their capability of correcting burst errors of length $(t - 1)m + 1$. In fact, such a burst in the derived binary word can corrupt at most $t$ (adjacent) symbols of the original word over $GF(2^m)$, see Figure 2.

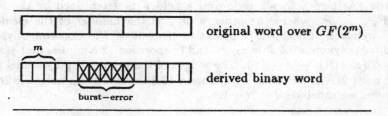

**Figure 2:** A burst error on a word derived from a Reed-Solomon code

For example, the above double-error-correcting Reed-Solomon code over $GF(8)$ yields a binary $(21, 6)$-code which corrects burst errors of length $3 + 1 = 4$: any such burst affects at most two adjacent symbols of the original word.

## 12.5   Generalized Reed-Muller Codes

Recall that puncturing (8.5) is a modification of a code consisting in deleting the last symbol from each code word. We now return to the Reed-Muller codes $\mathcal{R}(r, m)$ of length $n = 2^m$ studied in Chapter 9. Since the code $\mathcal{R}(r, m)$ has even minimum distance $d = 2^{m-r}$ (Remark 9.6), the punctured code $\overline{\mathcal{R}}(r, m)$ has the same error-correcting capacity: it corrects $2^{m-r-1} - 1$ errors. The punctured code has a better information rate and, moreover, it is cyclic.

*Notation.* For each natural number $s$, we denote by $w_q(s)$ the Hamming weight of the $q$-ary expansion of $s$. Examples: $w_2(1) = w_2(2) = 1$ and $w_2(3) = 2$.

**Theorem.** *The punctured Reed-Muller code $\overline{\mathcal{R}}(r, m)$ is a binary cyclic code consisting of all binary polynomials of degree less than $2^m - 1$ which have $\beta^s$ as zeros, where $\beta$ is a fixed primitive element of $GF(2^m)$, and $s = 1, 2, \ldots, 2^m - 1$ is any number with $w_2(s) < m - r$. In notation:*

$$w(x) \text{ lies in } \overline{\mathcal{R}}(r, m) \iff w(\beta^i) = 0 \text{ for all } i < 2^m,\ 0 < w_2(i) < m - r.$$

The proof, which is quite technical, is omitted. The reader can find it in the monograph of MacWilliams and Sloane (1981).

**Definition.** *Let $\beta$ be a primitive element of $GF(q^m)$. By a generalized Reed-Muller code of length $n = q^m - 1$ and order $r$ over the alphabet $GF(q)$ is meant the cyclic code of all polynomials with $\beta^i$ as zeros for all $i = 1, 2, \ldots, n$ such that $w_q(i) < m - r$.*

**Remark.** The case $q = 2$ leads to the punctured Reed-Muller code $\overline{\mathcal{R}}(r, m)$ by the preceding theorem. Thus, Reed-Muller codes form a subclass of the extended generalized Reed-Muller codes: $\mathcal{R}(r, m)$ is obtained from $\overline{\mathcal{R}}(r, m)$ by extension (8.5).

### Examples

(1) Take $q = 2$, $m = 4$, and $r = 2$. All the numbers $i = 1, 2, \ldots, 2^4 - 1$ with $w_2(i) < 2$ are 1, 2, 4, and 8. Thus, we obtain a cyclic binary code of length 15 with zeros at $\beta$, $\beta^2$, $\beta^4$, and $\beta^8$. Equivalently, with a zero at $\beta$. This is the Hamming $(16, 11)$-code.

(2) For $q = 2$, $m = 4$, and $r = 1$, we consider all the numbers $i = 1, 2, \ldots, 2^4 - 1$ with $w_2(i) < 3$: besides the four numbers above, these are 3, 5, 6, 9, 10, and 12. The code is determined by the zeros $\beta$, $\beta^3$, and $\beta^5$. This is the BCH $(15, 5)$-code.

(3) Take $q = 3$, $m = 3$, and $r = 1$. All the numbers $i = 1, 2, \ldots, 3^3 - 1$ with $w_3(i) < 2$ are 1, 3, and 9. The resulting ternary code of length 26 is determined by a single zero $\beta$.

**Proposition.** *The binary generalized Reed-Muller code has minimum distance at least $2^{m-r} - 1$.*

**PROOF.** It is sufficient to prove that the generalized Reed-Muller code is a subcode of the $t$-error-correcting BCH code, where $t = 2^{m-r-1} - 1$. Since the latter code has minimum distance $d \geq 2t+1$ (Theorem 12.3), it follows that the former code has this property too. Observe that the first number $i$ with $w_2(i) \geq m - r$ is $i = 2^{m-r} - 1$. Thus, each $i = 1, 2, \ldots, 2^{m-r} - 2$ satisfies $w_2(i) < m - r$. It follows that every code word $w(x)$ of the generalized Reed-Muller code has $\beta^i$ as zeros for $i = 1, 2, \ldots, 2^{m-r} - 2 = 2t$. Therefore, $w(x)$ is a code word of the $t$-error-correcting BCH code.          □

## 12.6   Goppa Codes: Asymptotically Good Codes

We now introduce a class of noncyclic binary linear codes, discovered by Goppa in 1970, which generalize binary BCH codes and contain a number of interesting codes (e.g., a double-error-correcting code of length 8). Later we will also use these codes for a construction of secret codes. Parameters of the important subclass of irreducible binary Goppa codes are listed in Figure 3.

| Specified: | By an irreducible polynomial of degree $t$ over $GF(2^m)$ |
|---|---|
| Length: | $n = 2^m$ |
| Information symbols: | $k \geq n - mt$ |
| Minimum distance: | $d \geq 2t + 1$ |
| Error-control capability: | Corrects $t$ errors by a technique analogous to that for BCH codes |

**Figure 3:** Parameters of irreducible binary Goppa codes

*Notation.* Let $r(x)$ be a fixed polynomial over a field $F$. Given an element $a$ with $r(a) \neq 0$, we denote by $\frac{1}{x-a}$ the following polynomial over $F$:

$$\frac{1}{x-a} = -\frac{r(x) - r(a)}{x-a} r(a)^{-1}.$$

(The right-hand side is well-defined: since the polynomial $r(x) - r(a)$ has $a$ as a zero, it is divisible by $x - a$, see 11.1.)

This notation expresses the fact that in the algebraic extension $F[x]/r(x)$ (see 11.2), the above polynomial $\frac{1}{x-a}$ is inverse to $x - a$:

$$(x - a)\frac{1}{x-a} = -[r(x) - r(a)]r(a)^{-1} = 1 + tr(x) \qquad [t = -r(a)^{-1}]$$

and $r(x)$ is the zero element of $F[x]/r(x)$.

**Definition.** *Let $F$ be a finite field. A Goppa code of length $n$ in the alphabet $F$ is determined by* (i) *a polynomial $r(x)$ of degree $\geq 2$ over some extension of $F$ and* (ii) *$n$ elements $a_1, \ldots, a_n$ of that extension, in none of which $r(x)$ has a zero. The code words are precisely those words $v_1 \ldots v_n$ in $F^n$ which satisfy*

$$\sum_{i=1}^{n} \frac{v_i}{x - a_i} = 0.$$

Before presenting examples, we mention an alternative definition without the notation of $\frac{1}{x-a}$. Recall that the BCH code is characterized by the condition $v(\alpha^s) = 0$ for $s = 1, 2, \ldots, 2t$; in other words, by $\sum_{i=1}^{n} v_i \alpha^{is} = 0$ for $s = 1\, 2, \ldots, 2t$. Rather analogously:

**Proposition.** *The code words of the Goppa code given by a polynomial $r(x)$ are precisely those words $v_1 \ldots v_n$ satisfying*

$$\sum_{i=1}^{n} v_i r(a_i)^{-1} a_i^s = 0 \qquad \textit{for } s = 0, 1, \ldots, [\deg r(x)] - 1.$$

**Proof.** We first compute $\frac{1}{x-a}$ explicitly. Given

$$r(x) = r_0 + r_1 x + \cdots + r_t x^t \qquad (r_t \neq 0),$$

it is easy to verify the following equation [for each element $a$ with $r(a) \neq 0$]:

$$\begin{aligned}
\frac{r(x) - r(a)}{x - a} &= r_t x^{t-1} + (ar_t + r_{t-1})x^{t-2} + (a^2 r_t + ar_{t-1} + r_{t-2})x^{t-3} \\
&\quad + \cdots + (a^{t-1}r_t + a^{t-2}r_{t-1} + \cdots + r_1).
\end{aligned}$$

Thus, the coefficient of the polynomial

$$\frac{1}{x-a} = -\frac{r(x) - r(a)}{x - a}r(a)^{-1}$$

at $x^{k-1}$ ($k = 1, \ldots, t$) is the following:

$$-r(a)^{-1}\left(a^{t-k}r_t + a^{t-k-1}r_{t-1} + \cdots + r_k\right) = -r(a)^{-1}\sum_{j=k}^{t} a^{j-k}r_j.$$

Now the characteristic equation of the Goppa code:

$$\sum_{i=1}^{n} \frac{v_i}{x - a_i} = 0$$

implies that for each $k = 1, \ldots, t$, the coefficient at $x^{k-1}$ is equal to zero. That is:

$$\sum_{i=1}^{n} v_i r(a_i)^{-1} \sum_{j=k}^{t} a^{t-j} r_j = 0 \qquad \text{for } k = 1, \ldots, t.$$

The case $k = t$ yields

$$r_t \sum_{i=1}^{n} v_i r(a_i)^{-1} = 0$$

and since $r_t \neq 0$, this is equivalent to $\sum_{i=1}^{n} v_i r(a_i) = 0$. The case $k = t + 1$ yields

$$r_t \sum_{i=1}^{n} v_i r(a_i)^{-1} a_i + r_{t-1} \sum_{i=1}^{n} v_i r(a_i)^{-1} = 0,$$

and since we already know that the second summand is zero and $r_t \neq 0$, this equation is equivalent to $\sum_{i=1}^{n} v_i r(a_i)^{-1} a_i = 0$, etc. Thus, we see that

$$\sum_{i=1}^{n} \frac{v_i}{x - a_i} = 0 \iff \sum_{i=1}^{n} v_i r(a_i)^{-1} a_i^s = 0 \quad \text{for } s = 0, 1, \ldots, t - 1.$$

□

**Corollary.** *The Goppa code determined by a polynomial $r(x)$ of degree $t$ has the following parity check matrix:*

$$\mathbf{H} = \begin{bmatrix} \frac{1}{r(a_1)} & \frac{1}{r(a_2)} & \frac{1}{r(a_3)} & \cdots & \frac{1}{r(a_n)} \\ \frac{a_1}{r(a_1)} & \frac{a_2}{r(a_2)} & \frac{a_3}{r(a_3)} & \cdots & \frac{a_n}{r(a_n)} \\ \frac{a_2^2}{r(a_1)} & \frac{a_2^2}{r(a_2)} & \frac{a_3^2}{r(a_3)} & \cdots & \frac{a_n^2}{r(a_n)} \\ \cdots\cdots\cdots\cdots\cdots\cdots\cdots\cdots\cdots\cdots\cdots\cdots \\ \frac{a_1^{t-1}}{r(a_1)} & \frac{a_2^{t-1}}{r(a_2)} & \frac{a_3^{t-1}}{r(a_3)} & \cdots & \frac{a_n^{t-1}}{r(a_n)} \end{bmatrix}.$$

**Examples**

(1) The polynomial

$$r(x) = x^2 + x + 1$$

is irreducible over the field $GF(8)$, since it has no zero (see Figure 2 of 11.3). If we choose as $a_i$'s all elements of $GF(8)$, we obtain a Goppa code of length 8 with the following parity check matrix:

$$
\mathbf{H} = \begin{bmatrix} \frac{1}{r(0)} & \frac{1}{r(1)} & \frac{1}{r(z)} & \frac{1}{r(z^2)} & \cdots & \frac{1}{r(z^6)} \\ 0 & \frac{1}{r(1)} & \frac{z}{r(z)} & \frac{z^2}{r(z^2)} & \cdots & \frac{z^6}{r(z^6)} \end{bmatrix}
$$

$$
= \begin{bmatrix} 1 & 1 & z^2 & z^4 & z^2 & z & z & z^4 \\ 0 & 1 & z^3 & z^6 & z^5 & z^5 & z^6 & z^3 \end{bmatrix}.
$$

That is, in binary:

$$
\mathbf{H} = \begin{bmatrix} 1 & 1 & 0 & 0 & 0 & 0 & 0 & 0 \\ 0 & 0 & 0 & 1 & 0 & 1 & 1 & 1 \\ 0 & 0 & 1 & 1 & 1 & 0 & 0 & 1 \\ 0 & 1 & 1 & 1 & 1 & 1 & 1 & 1 \\ 0 & 0 & 1 & 0 & 1 & 1 & 0 & 1 \\ 0 & 0 & 0 & 1 & 1 & 1 & 1 & 0 \end{bmatrix}
$$

The code has precisely four code words:

$$
\begin{aligned}
&00000000, \\
&00111111, \\
&11001011, \\
&11110100.
\end{aligned}
$$

Its minimum distance is 5. Thus, we have obtained a double-error-correcting $(8, 2)$-code. Observe that this code is not cyclic.

(2) BCH codes form a subclass of the class of Goppa codes: choose $r(x) = x^{2t}$ and as $a_i$'s, consider all the nonzero elements of some extension $F^*$ of our alphabet $F$. That is, all the elements

$$
\alpha^0, \ \alpha^{-1}, \ \alpha^{-2}, \ \ldots, \ \alpha^{-(n-1)},
$$

where $\alpha$ is a primitive element of $F^*$. The resulting Goppa code has the following parity check matrix:

$$
\mathbf{H} = \begin{bmatrix} 1 & \alpha^{2t} & \left(\alpha^2\right)^{2t} & \cdots & \left(\alpha^{n-1}\right)^{2t} \\ 1 & \alpha^{2t-1} & \left(\alpha^2\right)^{2t-1} & \cdots & \left(\alpha^{n-1}\right)^{2t-1} \\ \multicolumn{5}{c}{\cdots\cdots\cdots\cdots\cdots\cdots\cdots\cdots\cdots\cdots} \\ 1 & \alpha & \alpha^2 & \cdots & \alpha^{n-1} \end{bmatrix}.
$$

This is, up to the order of rows, the parity check matrix of the $t$-error-correcting BCH code (see 12.3).

**Remarks**

(1) The binary Goppa code of length $n$ determined by a polynomial of degree $t$ over $GF(2^m)$ has

$$k \geq n - mt$$

information symbols. In fact, the above parity check matrix has $t$ rows in $GF(2^m)$, i.e., $tm$ rows in the binary. Thus, the number $n - k$ of check symbols is smaller or equal to $mt$.

(2) Let $r(x)$ be an irreducible polynomial over some extension $F^*$ of the alphabet $F$. The Goppa code determined by $r(x)$ and *all* the elements of $F^*$ is called *irreducible*. Example (1) is an irreducible Goppa code.

(3) The minimum distance of a Goppa code determined by a polynomial of degree $t$ is at least $t + 1$. This can be proved exactly as Theorem 12.3. However, a much better result holds for the binary irreducible codes:

**Theorem.** *The irreducible binary Goppa code determined by a polynomial of degree $t$ corrects $t$ errors.*

**PROOF.** Let $r(x)$ be an irreducible polynomial of degree $t$ over some extension $F$ of $\mathbf{Z}_2$, $F = \{ a_1, \ldots, a_n \}$. We are to prove that the Hamming weight $q$ of an arbitrary nonzero coce word $v_1 \ldots v_n$ of the irreducible Goppa code fulfils $q \geq 2t + 1$. Let $v_{i_1}, v_{i_2}, \ldots, v_{i_q}$ be all the 1's of $\mathbf{v}$. Since $\mathbf{v}$ is a code word, we have

$$\sum_{i=1}^{n} \frac{v_i}{x - a_i} = \sum_{s=1}^{q} \frac{1}{x - a_{i_s}} = 0. \qquad (12.6.1)$$

The following polynomial

$$f(x) = (x - a_{i_1})(x - a_{i_2}) \cdots (x - a_{i_q}) \qquad (12.6.2)$$

is not divisible by the polynomial $r(x)$. In fact, since $r(x)$ is an irreducible polynomial of degree $t \geq 2$, this follows from the unique factorization theorem (11.1). Thus, $f(\alpha) \neq 0$ in the algebraic extension $\mathbf{Z}_2[x]/r(x)$, and since $r(x)$ is irreducible, $f(\alpha)$ has an inverse element (by Theorem 11.2). That is, there exists a polynomial $g(x)$ with

$$f(\alpha)g(\alpha) = 1 \qquad (12.6.3)$$

We can compute the formal derivative $f'(x)$, see 11D: it is, obviously, the sum of the following polynomials:

$$(x - a_{i_1}) \cdots (x - a_{i_{s-1}})(x - a_{i_{s+1}}) \cdots (x - a_{i_k}) \qquad (s = 1, \ldots, q).$$

The latter can be more succinctly written as $f(x)/x - a_{i_s}$. Thus,

$$f'(x) = \sum_{s=1}^{q} \frac{f(x)}{x - a_{i_s}}.$$

Substituting $\alpha$ for $x$ and multiplying both sides by $g(\alpha)$, we get, by (12.5.3) and (12.5.1),

$$f'(\alpha)g(\alpha) = \sum_{s=1}^{q} \frac{f(\alpha)g(\alpha)}{\alpha - a_{i_s}} = \sum_{s=1}^{q} \frac{1}{\alpha - a_{i_s}} = 0.$$

This means that $f'(x)g(x)$ is divisible by $r(x)$. Now $r(x)$ is irreducible and does not divide $g(x)$ [since $g(\alpha) \neq 0$, see (12.5.3)]. It follows that $r(x)$ divides $f'(x)$.

We know that $f'(x)$ is a perfect square, $f'(x) = b^2(x)$ (see Exercise 11E). Since $r(x)$ is an irreducible divisor of $b^2(x)$, it must be a divisor of $b(x)$ (by the unique factorization theorem again). Thus, $r^2(x)$ divides $b^2(x) = f'(x)$. Since $f'(x) \neq 0$ (in fact, the degree of $f'$ is $q-1$ and $q \geq 1$), it follows that the degree of $f'(x)$ is larger or equal to that of $r^2(x)$:

$$q - 1 \geq 2t.$$

□

**Examples**

(3) The polynomial $r(x) = x^3 + x + 1$ has three zeros in $GF(8) = \mathbf{Z}_2[x]/ \bmod$ $x^3 + x + 1$. Consequently, it has no roots in $GF(32)$ [$GF(32)$ is not an extension of $GF(8)$]. It follows that $r(x)$ is irreducible over $GF(32)$.

The corresponding irreducible Goppa code has the following parameters:

$$\begin{aligned} n &= 32, \\ k &\geq 32 - 5 \times 3 = 17 \qquad \text{(actually, } k = 17\text{)}, \\ d &\geq 7. \end{aligned}$$

This is a triple-error-correcting $(32, 17)$-code. Compare it with the $(31, 16)$ triple-error-correcting BCH code whose extension is a $(32, 17)$-code with $d = 8$.

(4) So far, we have considered only binary polynomials $r(x)$. However, $r(x)$ can have coefficients in the extended field. For example, $r(x) = x^2 + \alpha x + 1$ is an irreducible polynomial over $GF(8)$ of Figure 2 in 11.3. The

corresponding irreducible Goppa code has the following parity check matrix:

$$\mathbf{H} = \begin{bmatrix} 1 & \alpha^6 & 1 & \alpha^5 & \alpha^6 & \alpha^5 & \alpha & \alpha \\ 0 & \alpha^6 & \alpha^2 & \alpha & \alpha^2 & \alpha^2 & \alpha^6 & 1 \end{bmatrix}.$$

This is another triple-error-correcting binary $(8, 2)$-code.

## Concluding Remarks

(1) Goppa codes form a generalization of BCH codes. The decoding (which we do not describe here) can also be performed by a technique analogous to that for BCH codes. A fast decoder has been described by Patterson (1975).

(2) No short Goppa code is known today which has parameters improving those of short BCH codes (as listed in Appendix B).

(3) A remarkable property of Goppa codes is that they are "asymptotically good". Recall that Shannon's Fundamental Theorem (4.8) promises codes $K_i$ ($i = 1, 2, \dots$) with information rates $\frac{k_i}{n_i}$ converging to some positive number (the capacity) while the error probability converges to zero. Let $d_i$ denote the minimum distance of the code $K_i$. We call the sequence of codes $K_1, K_2, K_3, \dots$ *asymptotically good* provided that both $\frac{k_i}{n_i}$ and $\frac{d_i}{n_i}$ converge to positive limits (with increasing $i$). In other words, the codes $K_1, K_2, K_3, \dots$ are asymptotically good provided that, for a given information rate $R > 0$ and a given percentage $P > 0$ of correctable symbols per code word, we have $\frac{k_i}{n_i} \to R$ and $\frac{d_i}{n_i} \to P$. The proof of the following statements can be found, e.g., in MacWilliams and Sloane (1981):

   (a) BCH codes are asymptotically bad, that is, there does not exist any asymptotically good sequence of BCH codes. (Consequently, BCH codes cannot ever be used for a realization of the parameters of Shannon's Fundamental Theorem.)

   (b) Goppa codes are asymptotically good: there exists an asymptotically good sequence of irreducible binary Goppa codes.

However, the proof of (b) is purely existential. It is not known how to produce irreducible polynomials giving asymptotically good Goppa codes.

# Exercises

**12A** Using the BCH code of Example (1) in 12.2, decode the words

(1) 00000111000000,

(2) 11000100000001.

**12B** Describe the binary double-error-correcting code of length 11.

**12C** What is the information rate of the double-error-correcting BCH code of length 31

(1) over $Z_2$?

(2) over $Z_3$?

**12D** Find the generator and parity check polynomials for the binary triple-error-correcting BCH code of length

(1) 15,

(2) 31.

Encode the information word consisting of all 1's.

**12E** Prove the independence theorem (see 12.2) for the $t$-error-correcting BCH codes.

**12F** Using Reed-Solomon codes, construct a binary $(75, 28)$-code correcting burst errors of length 11 and a $(75, 40)$-code correcting burst errors of length 6.

**12G** For $r(x) = x^{2t}$, show that $\frac{1}{x-a} = \sum_{j=1}^{2t} a^{-j} x^{j-1}$. Use this to verify again that the Goppa code determined by $x^{2t}$ and all nonzero elements $\alpha^0, \alpha^{-1}, \ldots, \alpha^{-(n-1)}$ of the extension field is precisely the BCH code.

**12H** Find the minimum distance of the binary Goppa code determined by $r(x) = x^2 + 1$ and by the elements $0, z, z^2$ of $GF(4)$. Compare this with Theorem 12.5.

**12I** Find a parity check matrix of the irreducible binary $(16, 8)$-Goppa code given by $r(x) = x^2 + x + \alpha^3$, where $\alpha$ is primitive in $GF(16)$.

**12J**    Verify that the polynomial $x^2 + x + 1$ is irreducible over $GF(32)$. Find the parameters and parity check matrix of the corresponding irreducible Goppa code.

## Notes

Binary BCH codes were discovered by Bose and Ray-Chaudhuri (1960) and Hocquenhem (1959). They were generalized to other alphabets by Gorenstein and Ziegler (1961), who also observed that the codes earlier discovered by Reed and Solomon (1960) represent a special case. Goppa codes were published by Goppa (1970).

# Chapter 13

# Fast Decoding of BCH Codes

We have described two decoding techniques for the binary double-error-correcting BCH codes: error trappnig (10.5) and quadratic equations (12.2). For the general BCH codes, several decoding methods are known. We present a decoding algorithm based on the procedure of finding the greatest common divisor of two polynomials (the famous Euclidean algorithm, which we first introduce in detail). The decoder we present is fast, and of all the known fast decoders, it is the simplest one to understand. Theoretical results show that the (more complicated) Berlekamp decoder, see Chapter 7 in Berlekamp (1968), is faster for very large lengths $n$. However, the speed of the two decoders is comparable for all $n \leq 10^6$.

Throughout this chapter, we assume that a $t$-error-correcting BCH code of length $n$ over an arbitrary finite field $F$ is used. The code words are the polynomials $v(x)$ satisfying $v(\beta^i) = 0$ for $i = 1, 2, \ldots, 2t$. We send a code word $\mathbf{v}$ and receive a different word $\mathbf{w}$ of Hamming distance

$$d(\mathbf{v}, \mathbf{w}) = p \leq t.$$

In other words, the actual number $p$ of corrupted symbols lies between 1 and $t$. (The case $p = 0$ need not be considered: whenever the syndrome is $\mathbf{0}$, we stop decoding since we have received a code word.) It is our aim to find the error-pattern word

$$\mathbf{e} = \mathbf{w} - \mathbf{v}.$$

257

# 13.1   Error Location and Error Evaluation

Our task is to determine the error-pattern word **e** from the received word **w**. Since **e** has Hamming weight $p$ (= the number of actual errors made), it is characterized by its $p$ nonzero components $e_{i_1}, e_{i_2}, \ldots, e_{i_p}$. For each $k = 1, 2, \ldots, p$, put

$$a_k = \beta^{i_k} \qquad \text{(error-location number)}, \tag{13.1.1}$$

$$b_k = e_{i_k} \qquad \text{(error-evaluation number)}. \tag{13.1.2}$$

It is sufficient to determine the $2p$ elements $a_1, \ldots, a_p$ and $b_1, \ldots, b_p$: we then know the location of errors:

$$e_i \neq 0 \qquad \text{iff } \beta^i \text{ is one of } a_1, \ldots, a_p,$$

and in the case $e_i \neq 0$, we can evaluate the error:

$$e_i = b_k \qquad \text{whenever } \beta^i = a_k.$$

More succinctly:

$$e_i = \begin{cases} b_k & \text{if } \beta^i = a_k, \\ 0 & \text{if } \beta^i \neq a_1, a_2, \ldots, a_p. \end{cases} \tag{13.1.3}$$

In order to find the error-location numbers, it is sufficient to determine the following *error-location polynomial:*

$$\sigma(x) = (1 - a_1 x)(1 - a_2 x) \cdots (1 - a_p x). \tag{13.1.4}$$

It has zeros in $a_1^{-1}, a_2^{-1}, \ldots, a_p^{-1}$. Thus, once we know $\sigma(x)$, we know the error-location numbers as inverses of all the zeros of $\sigma(x)$. [Since we work within a finite field, the zeros can be found by brute force: compute all the values of $\sigma(x)$.]

Once the error-location numbers have been established, the error-evaluation numbers can be found by means of the following *error-evaluation polynomial:*

$$\omega(x) = \sum_{k=1}^{p} b_k (1 - a_1 x) \cdots (1 - a_{k-1} x)(1 - a_{k+1} x) \cdots (1 - a_p x) \tag{13.1.5}$$

In fact:

**Proposition.** *The error-evaluation numbers are given by*

$$b_j = -a_j \omega\left(a_j^{-1}\right) \left[\sigma'\left(a_j^{-1}\right)\right]^{-1}, \tag{13.1.6}$$

*where $\sigma'(x)$ is the formal derivative (11C) of $\sigma(x)$.*

PROOF. From (13.1.5), it clearly follows that for each $j = 1, 2, \ldots, p$,

$$\omega(a_j^{-1}) = b_j(1 - a_1 a_j^{-1}) \cdots (1 - a_{j-1} a_j^{-1})(1 - a_{j+1} a_j^{-1}) \cdots (1 - a_p a_j^{-1}).$$

On the other hand, the formal derivative of the polynomial in (13.1.4) is, obviously, the sum of the polynomials:

$$-a_k(1 - a_1 x)(1 - a_2 x) \cdots (1 - a_{k-1} x)(1 - a_{k+1} x) \cdots (1 - a_p x)$$

for $k = 1, 2, \ldots, p$. Thus,

$$\sigma'(a_j^{-1}) = -a_j(1 - a_1 a_j^{-1}) \cdots (1 - a_{j-1} a_j^{-1})(1 - a_{j+1} a_j^{-1}) \cdots (1 - a_p a_j^{-1}).$$

Dividing $\omega(a_j^{-1})$ by $\sigma'(a_j^{-1})$, we get (13.1.6). □

**Remark.** In subsequent sections, we will see how to compute the polynomials $\sigma(x)$ and $\omega(x)$ from the *syndrome* $s(x)$ of the received word $w(x)$ defined by

$$s(x) = s_0 + s_1 x + \cdots + s_{2t-1} x^{2t-1}, \qquad \text{where } s_i = w(\alpha^i). \qquad (13.1.7)$$

Then the decoding is easy to conclude: we find the error locations $a_k$ as inverse zeros of the polynomial $\sigma(x)$, and the error evaluations $b_k$ by (13.1.6). The error-pattern word is then given by (13.1.3).

We now list some crucial properties of the known polynomial $s(x)$ and the unknown polynomials $\sigma(x)$ and $\omega(x)$ to be used later. Recall from 11.2 that the expression

$$f(x) \equiv g(x) \pmod{x^i}$$

means that $f(x) - g(x)$ is divisible by $x^i$; in other words, that the polynomials $f(x)$ and $g(x)$ have the same coefficients at $1, x, x^2, \ldots, x^{i-1}$.

**Theorem**

(1) $\omega(x) \equiv \sigma(x) s(x) \pmod{x^{2t}}$.

(2) $\omega(x)$ has degree smaller than $t$, and $\sigma(x)$ has degree at most $t$.

(3) $s(x) \not\equiv 0 \pmod{x^t}$, i.e., $s_i \neq 0$ for some $i < t$.

PROOF. (1) The received word **w** has the same syndrome as the error-pattern word **e**: in fact, **w** − **e** is the code word sent, thus, $w(\alpha^i) - e(\alpha^i) = 0$ for $i = 1, 2, \ldots, 2t$ (by the definition of the BCH code). Therefore,

$$s_i = e(\alpha^i) = e_{i_1} \alpha^{i i_1} + \cdots + e_{i_p} \alpha^{i i_p}.$$

By (13.1.1) and (13.1.2),

$$s_i = b_1 a_1^i + \cdots + b_p a_p^i. \tag{13.1.8}$$

On the other hand, we can express the sumands of (13.1.5) as $b_k \sigma(x)/(1 - a_k x)$:

$$\omega(x) = \sum_{k=1}^{p} b_k \frac{\sigma(x)}{1 - a_k x}.$$

Using formal power series (11G), we have $1/(1 - a_k x) = \sum_{i=0}^{\infty}(a_k x)^i$, thus,

$$
\begin{aligned}
\omega(x) &= \sigma(x) \sum_{k=1}^{p} b_k \sum_{i=0}^{\infty}(a_k x)^i \\
&= \sigma(x) \sum_{i=0}^{\infty} \sum_{k=1}^{p} b_k a_k^i x^i \\
&= \sigma(x) \sum_{i=0}^{\infty}(b_1 a_1^i + b_2 a_2^i + \cdots + b_p a_p^i)x^i.
\end{aligned}
$$

Comparing the last expression with (13.1.8), we see that $\omega(x)$ and $\sigma(x)s(x)$ have the same coefficients at $x^i$ for all $i = 0, 1, \ldots, 2t - 1$. In other words, $\omega(x) \equiv \sigma(x)s(x) \pmod{x^{2t}}$.

(2) By assumption, the number $p$ of actual errors is at most $t$. The degree of $\sigma(x)$ is $p$ and that of $\omega(x)$ is $p - 1$.

(3) Suppose that, to the contrary, $s_i = 0$ for all $i = 0, 1, \ldots, t - 1$. Since $p \leq t$, we see from (13.1.8) that the following equations

$$
\begin{bmatrix}
1 & 1 & \cdots & 1 \\
a_1 & a_2 & \cdots & a_p \\
a_1^2 & a_2^2 & \cdots & a_p^2 \\
\cdots\cdots\cdots\cdots\cdots\cdots \\
a_1^{p-1} & a_2^{p-1} & \cdots & a_p^{p-1}
\end{bmatrix}
\begin{bmatrix}
b_1 \\
b_2 \\
b_3 \\
\vdots \\
b_p
\end{bmatrix}
=
\begin{bmatrix}
0 \\
0 \\
0 \\
\vdots \\
0
\end{bmatrix}
$$

hold. This is impossible since the matrix has a nonzero Vandermonde determinant [see Remark (2) in 12.3] and the $b_i$'s are nonzero.        □

## 13.2   Euclidean Algorithm

More than two thousand years ago, Euclid formulated the following algorithm for finding the greatest common divisor (GCD) of two numbers, $a_0$

and $a_1$: Suppose $a_0 \geq a_1$; perform the integer division of $a_0$ by $a_1$, and denote the quotient by $q_1$ and the remainder by $a_2$:

$$a_0 = q_1 a_1 + a_2, \quad a_2 < a_1.$$

If $a_2 = 0$, then $a_1 = \mathrm{GCD}(a_0, a_1)$. If $a_2 \neq 0$, then perform the integer division $a_1 \div a_2$ and denote the quotient by $q_2$ and the remainder by $a_3$:

$$a_1 = q_2 a_2 + a_3, \quad a_3 < a_2,$$

etc. Since $a_1 > a_2 > a_3 > \cdots$, we eventually get $a_{k+1} = 0$ for some $k$, and then $a_k = \mathrm{GCD}(a_0, a_1)$.

The same procedure can be used to find the *greatest common divisor of two nonzero polynomials*, $a_0(x)$ and $a_1(x)$, over any field. By definition, this is a polynomial of the highest degree which divides both $a_0(x)$ and $a_1(x)$. Assuming that degree $a_0(x) \geq$ degree $a_1(x)$, we can define further polynomials $a_2(x)$, $a_3(x)$, ... and $q_1(x)$, $q_2(x)$, ... by the following recursion:

$$a_{k-1}(x) = q_k(x) a_k(x) + a_{k+1}(x), \quad \deg a_{k+1}(x) < \deg a_k(x). \qquad (13.2.1)$$

In other words, $q_k(x)$ is the quotient and $a_{k+1}(x)$ is the remainder of the division of $a_{k-1}(x)$ by $a_k(x)$. Since the degrees of $a_1(x)$, $a_2(x)$, ... are decreasing, we eventually get $a_{k+1}(x) = 0$. Then $a_k(x)$ is the greatest common divisor of $a_0(x)$ and $a_1(x)$. [In fact: (1) $a_k(x)$ divides $a_{k-1}(x)$ since the remainder of that division is $a_{k+1}(x) = 0$. It follows that $a_k(x)$ divides $a_{k-2}(x) = q_{k-1}(x) a_{k-1}(x) + a_k(x)$; hence, it divides $a_{k-3}(x)$, etc. We conclude that $a_k(x)$ divides both $a_1(x)$ and $a_0(x)$. (2) Any polynomial $b(x)$ which divides both $a_0(x)$ and $a_1(x)$ divides the polynomial $a_2(x) = a_0(x) - q_1(x) a_1(x)$. Thus, $b(x)$ divides $a_3(x) = a_1(x) - q_2(x) a_2(x)$, etc. We conclude that $b(x)$ divides $a_k(x)$ and, thus, it has a degree smaller or equal to that of $a_k(x)$.]

**Example.** Find a greatest common divisor of the polynomials $x^2 + x$ and $x^2 + 2$ over $\mathbf{Z}_3$.

In the first step, we divide $a_0(x) = x^2 + x$ by $a_1(x) = x^2 + 2$ and obtain

$$q_1(x) = 1 \quad \text{and} \quad a_2(x) = x + 1.$$

Then we divide $a_1(x)$ by $a_2(x)$. The remainder is $a_3(x) = 0$; thus, $a_2(x) = x + 1$ is the greatest common divisor.

Observe that $2x + 2$ is the greatest common divisor too. (The concept of greatest common divisor is only unique up to a scalar multiple, see 13A.)

**Remarks**

(1) Define polynomials $u_k(x)$ and $v_k(x)$ by the following recursion, using the quotients $q_k(x)$ of (13.2.1):

$$u_0(x) = 0, \quad u_1(x) = 1, \quad u_{k+1}(x) = q_k(x)u_k(x) + u_{k-1}(x),$$
$$v_0(x) = 1, \quad v_1(x) = 0, \quad v_{k+1}(x) = q_k(x)v_k(x) + v_{k-1}(x). \qquad (13.2.2)$$

Then each of the steps of the Euclidean algorithm is the following linear combination of the two given polynomials $a_0(x)$ and $a_1(x)$:

$$a_k(x) = (-1)^k \left[ v_k(x)a_0(x) - u_k(x)a_1(x) \right]. \qquad (13.2.3)$$

In fact, this trivially holds for $k = 0, 1$, and for higher $k$'s, it readily follows by mathematical induction.

In the above example we have

$$
\begin{aligned}
u_0(x) &= 0, & v_0(x) &= 1, \\
u_1(x) &= 1, & v_1(x) &= 0, \\
u_2(x) &= 1, & v_2(x) &= 1, \\
u_3(x) &= x + 1, & v_3(x) &= x.
\end{aligned}
$$

It is easy to check that

$$a_2(x) = x + 1 = (-1)^2 \left[ (x^2 + x) - (x^2 + 2) \right],$$
$$a_3(x) = \quad 0 \quad = (-1)^3 \left[ x(x^2 + x) - (x + 1)(x^2 + 2) \right].$$

(2) If two polynomials $a_0(x)$ and $a_1(x)$ are relatively prime, i.e., have the greatest common divisor 1, then each polynomial can be expressed as a linear combination of those polynomials. That is, for each polynomial $f(x)$, there exist polynomials $f_0(x)$ and $f_1(x)$ with

$$f(x) = f_0(x)a_0(x) + f_1(x)a_1(x).$$

In fact, there exists $k$ such that $a_k(x)$ is a nonzero scalar [i.e., the greatest common divisor of $a_0(x)$ and $a_1(x)$, see 13A]. For this scalar, say, $c$, we have by (13.2.3) polynomials $p_0(x)$ and $p_1(x)$ with

$$c = p_0(x)a_0(x) + p_1(x)a_1(x).$$

Put $f_i(x) = c^{-1}p_i(x)f(x)$ for $i = 0, 1$.

(3) The polynomials $u_k(x)$ and $v_k(x)$ above fulfill

$$u_k(x)v_{k+1}(x) - v_k(x)u_{k+1}(x) = (-1)^{k+1}.$$

(Verify by induction.) It follows that $u_k(x)$ and $v_k(x)$ are relatively prime: every common divisor divides $(-1)^{k+1}$.

(4) The quotient $q_k(x)$ of $a_{k-1}(x) \div a_k(x)$ has the following degree:

$$\deg q_k(x) = \deg a_{k-1}(x) - \deg a_k(x).$$

It is easy to verify by induction that

$$\deg u_k(x) = \deg a_0(x) - \deg a_{k-1}(x).$$

## 13.3  The Decoding Algorithm

Using the $t$-error-correcting BCH code and receiving a word $w(x)$ which is not a code word, we correct it as follows:

**Step I.** Compute the syndrome $s_i = w(\alpha^i)$ of the received word $w(x)$. [By assumption, $s(x) \neq 0$.]

**Step II.** Perform the Euclidean algorithm with the polynomials

$$a_0(x) = x^{2t} \quad \text{and} \quad a_1(x) = s(x). \qquad (13.3.1)$$

Denote by $k$ the first index such that $a_k(x)$ has degree smaller than $t$. That is:

$$\deg a_k(x) < t \quad \text{and} \quad \deg a_{k-1}(x) \geq t. \qquad (13.3.2)$$

For this $k$, put $d = [u_k(0)]^{-1}$ and define

$$\sigma(x) = d u_k(x) \quad \text{and} \quad \omega(x) = (-1)^{k+1} d a_k(x). \qquad (13.3.3)$$

We will prove below that these are the actual error-locator and error-evaluator polynomials, respectively.

**Step III.** Correct those symbols $w_i$, $i = 0, 1, \ldots, n-1$, for which $\sigma(x)$ has a zero in $\beta^{-i}$. The correct value is

$$v_i = w_i - a_i \omega(a_i^{-1}) [\sigma'(a_i^{-1})]^{-1}.$$

[This is the necessary correction by (13.1.3) and (13.1.6).]

**Remark.** The second step requires that (1) there exists $k$ such that the degree of $a_k(x)$ is lower than $t$, and (2) $u_k(0) \neq 0$. It follows from the next theorem that both are true whenever the actual number $p$ of errors is smaller or equal to $t$. Thus, if the second step cannot be performed, we stop decoding and announce that an incorrectable error has been made.

**Theorem.** *Under our standing assumption that $p \leq t$, the polynomials of (13.3.3) are the true error-location and error-evaluation polynomials, respectively.*

PROOF. Throughout the proof, we use the symbols $\sigma(x)$ and $\omega(x)$ for the true polynomials, defined by (13.1.4) and (13.1.5), respectively. Observe that in step II such $k$ as required exists: the greatest common divisor of $x^{2t}$ and $s(x)$ certainly has the form $x^i$ for some $i$. However, $s(x)$ is not divisible by $x^t$ [see Theorem (3) in 13.1]; thus, $i < t$. In the Euclidean algorithm, the final step is the polynomial $a_{k_0}(x) = x^i$, and since $i < t$, we can choose (the largest) $k$ with degree $a_k(x) < t$. We are going to prove that there is a scalar $d$ such that

$$\sigma(x) = du_k(x) \qquad \text{and} \qquad \omega(x) = d(-1)^{k+1}a_k(x). \tag{13.3.4}$$

This will conclude the proof: it remains then to verify that $d = \left[u_k(0)\right]^{-1}$, but by inserting 0 into (13.3.4), we see that $\sigma(0) = 1 = du_k(0)$.

To prove (13.3.4), we first show that the polynomials

$$\overline{\sigma}(x) = u_k(x) \qquad \text{and} \qquad \overline{\omega}(x) = (-1)^{k+1}a_k(x)$$

have the properties (1), (2) of Theorem 13.1. In fact, (1) follows from the equation (13.2.3): we have

$$\begin{aligned} \overline{\omega}(x) &= (-1)^{k+1}(-1)^k\left[v_k(x)x^{2t} - \overline{\sigma}(x)s(x)\right] \\ &= \overline{\sigma}(x)s(x) + x^{2t}\left[-v_k(x)\right] \equiv \overline{\sigma}(x)s(x) \pmod{x^{2t}}. \end{aligned} \tag{13.3.5}$$

Concerning (2), the degree of $\overline{\omega}(x)$ is smaller than $t$ by the choice of $k$, and for $\overline{\sigma}(x)$, we use Remark (4) of 13.2:

$$\deg \overline{\sigma}(x) = 2t - \deg a_{k-1}(x).$$

By the choice of $k$, $\deg a_{k-1}(x) \geq t$; thus, $\deg \overline{\sigma}(x) \leq t$.

We conclude that

$$\sigma(x)\overline{\omega}(x) = \overline{\sigma}(x)\omega(x). \tag{13.3.6}$$

In fact, both sides are polynomials of degree smaller than $2t$, and since property (1) of Theorem 13.1 holds for both of the pairs of polynomials, we have

$$\frac{\omega(x)}{\sigma(x)} \equiv s(x) \equiv \frac{\overline{\omega}(x)}{\overline{\sigma}(x)} \pmod{x^{2t}};$$

more precisely, $\omega(x)\overline{\sigma}(x) \equiv \overline{\omega}(x)\sigma(x) \pmod{x^{2t}}$. This establishes (13.3.6). It follows that $\sigma(x)$ is a divisor of $\overline{\sigma}(x)$: in fact, $\sigma(x)$ can be factored into linear polynomials $1 - a_k x$ [see (13.1.4)] none of which divides $\omega(x)$ [because $\omega(x)$ does not have a zero in $a_k^{-1}$, see Proposition 11.1]. By the unique factorization theorem (11.1), since $\sigma(x)$ divides $\overline{\sigma}(x)\omega(x)$, it must divide $\overline{\sigma}(x)$. Put

$$b(x) = \frac{\overline{\sigma}(x)}{\sigma(x)}.$$

Then from (13.3.6), we get

$$\overline{\sigma}(x) = b(x)\sigma(x) \qquad \text{and} \qquad \overline{\omega}(x) = b(x)\omega(x).$$

The proof of (13.3.4) will be concluded when we show that $b(x)$ is actually a nonzero scalar: just let $d$ be the inverse of that scalar, then $\sigma(x) = d\,\overline{\sigma}(x)$ and $\omega(x) = d\overline{\omega}(x)$.

It is sufficient to verify that $b(x)$ divides both $u_k(x)$ and $v_k(x)$: since the latter two polynomials are relatively prime [see Remark (3) of 13.2], it follows that $b(x)$ is a scalar. The polynomial $b(x)$ certainly divides $b(x)\sigma(x) = \overline{\sigma}(x) = u_k(x)$. To prove that it also divides $v_k(x)$, use (13.3.5):

$$
\begin{aligned}
x^{2t} v_k(x) &= \overline{\sigma}(x)s(x) - \overline{\omega}(x) \\
&= \overline{\sigma}(x)s(x) - b(x)\omega(x).
\end{aligned}
$$

By Theorem (1) of 13.1, we have a polynomial $c(x)$ such that $\omega(x) = \sigma(x)s(x) + x^{2t}c(x)$. Then

$$
\begin{aligned}
x^{2t} v_k(x) &= \overline{\sigma}(x)s(x) - b(x)\sigma(x)s(x) - b(x)x^{2t}c(x) \\
&= \overline{\sigma}(x)s(x) - \overline{\sigma}(x)s(x) - b(x)x^{2t}c(x) \\
&= -b(x)x^{2t}c(x).
\end{aligned}
$$

Dividing by $x^{2t}$, we see that $v_k(x)$ is divisible by $b(x)$. Thus, $b(x)$ is a scalar.                                                                    □

**Example.** Suppose we use the binary double-error-correcting BCH code of length 15, and we receive

$$001000100000000 = x^2 + x^6.$$

**Step I.** The syndrome $s_i = w(z^i) = \alpha^{2i} + \alpha^{6i}$ is computed in $GF(16)$ (Appendix A) as follows:

$$
\begin{aligned}
s_0 &= 0, \\
s_1 &= \alpha^3, \\
s_2 &= \alpha^6, \\
s_3 &= \alpha^2.
\end{aligned}
$$

Thus,
$$s(x) = \alpha^2 x^3 + \alpha^6 x^2 + \alpha^3 x.$$

**Step II.** The Euclidean algorithm with $a_0(x) = x^4$ and $a_1(x) = s(x)$, performed until degree $a_k(x) < 2$.

The division of $a_0(x)$ by $a_1(x)$ yields

$$q_1(x) = \alpha^{13} x + \alpha^2 \qquad \text{and} \qquad a_2(x) = \alpha^{10} x^2 + \alpha^5 x.$$

Since $a_2(x)$ has degree $\geq 2$, we further divide $a_1(x)$ by $a_2(x)$:

$$q_2(x) = \alpha^7 x + \alpha^9 \qquad \text{and} \qquad a_3(x) = x.$$

Thus, in (13.3.3), we have $k = 3$. Next, we compute $u_3(x)$:

$$
\begin{aligned}
u_0(x) &= 0, \\
u_1(x) &= 1, \\
u_2(x) &= q_1(x) = \alpha^{13} x + \alpha^2, \\
u_3(x) &= u_2(x) q_2(x) + u_1(x) = \alpha^5 + x + \alpha^{12}.
\end{aligned}
$$

We see that in (13.3.3), $d = u_3(x)^{-1} = \alpha^{-12} = \alpha^3$ and the error-locator polynomial is

$$\sigma(x) = d u_3(x) = \alpha^8 x^2 + \alpha^3 x + 1.$$

**Step III.** We find the zeros of $\sigma(x)$ (by brute force): they are $\alpha^9$, $\alpha^{13}$ (or $\alpha^{-6}$, $\alpha^{-2}$). We thus correct $w_2$ and $w_6$: the word sent is $0$.

# Exercises

**13A**   Prove that if $b(x)$ is a greatest common divisor of two polynomials, then

(1) for each scalar $c \neq 0$, the multiple $cb(x)$ is also a greatest common divisor of those polynomials, and

(2) each of the greatest common divisors of those two polynomials is a scalar multiple of $b(x)$.

[Hint: As observed above, in the Euclidean algorithm, every divisor of $a_0(x)$ and $a_1(x)$ divides each $a_k(x)$.]

**13B**  Let $a_0(x)$ and $a_1(x)$ be relatively prime polynomials. Find an algorithm which produces polynomials $p_0(x)$ and $p_1(x)$ satisfying $p_0(x)a_0(x) + p_1(x)a_1(x) = 1$. [Hint: In the Euclidean algorithm above, there exists $k$ with $a_k(x)$ of degree 0. Use (13.2.3).]

**13C**  Analogously to 13B, find an algorithm which, for relatively prime numbers $a_0$ and $a_1$, produces numbers $p_0$ and $p_1$ with $p_0 a_0 + p_1 a_1 = 1$. Conclude that for each number $n$ ($= a_1$), every element of $Z_n$ relatively prime with $n$ has an inverse element which can be found by the Euclidean algorithm.

**13D**  Suppose we use the binary triple-error-correcting BCH code of length 15. Decode 101011001000000.

**13E**  Suppose we use the double-error-correcting BCH code over $Z_3$ of length 8. Decode 00120000.

## Notes

The first decoder for (the binary) BCH codes was proposed by Peterson (1960). The decoder based on the Euclidean algorithm is due to Sugiyama et al. (1975).

# Chapter 14

# Convolutional Codes

Whereas linear codes encode information symbols without memory (i.e., each code word only depends on the present $k$-tuple of information symbols), there is an important error-correcting technique based on coding with memory: the convolutional codes. A convolutional code breaks the input message into frames of length $k$ and encodes them into code frames of length $n$, but each code frame depends not only on the last information frame, but also on $m$ preceding information frames.

We first describe convolutional codes by means of generator polynomials and generator matrices, and then we present an error-correcting procedure called the Viterbi algorithm.

## 14.1 Linear Codes and Convolutional Codes

Before defining convolutional codes, let us take a new, global look at linear codes. We have so far considered a linear $(n, k)$-code locally: each word $\mathbf{u}$ of length $k$ is encoded into a code word $\mathbf{v} = \mathbf{u}G$ of length $n$. However, we can also view a linear code as a function which transforms source messages (of any length $ik$ for $i = 1, 2, 3, \ldots$ ) into code messages (of length $in$). For example, the even-parity code of length 4 is a function given as follows:

$$u_0 u_1 u_2 u_3 u_4 u_5 \ldots \quad \longmapsto \quad u_0 u_1 u_2 a_0 u_3 u_4 u_5 a_1 \ldots ,$$
$$a_0 = u_0 + u_1 + u_2, \quad a_1 = u_3 + u_4 + u_5, \ldots .$$

Such a function is best expressed by means of polynomials (because these correspond to words, except that the length is not specified). Denote by $u(x) = u_0 + u_1 x + u_2 x^2 + \cdots$ the polynomial representing the source message and by $v(x) = v_0 + v_1 x + v_2 x^2 + \cdots$ the encoded message. Then a linear

269

code is a function $C$ assigning to each polynomial $u(x)$ the encoded polynomial $v(x) = C[u(x)]$. It is obvious that this function has the following properties:

(1) $C$ is linear, i.e.,

$$C[u(x) + u'(x)] = C[u(x)] + C[u'(x)],$$
$$C[tu(x)] = tC[u(x)].$$

(2) $C$ is time-invariant, i.e., by delaying the source message for $k$ shifts [which is expressed by the polynomial $x^k u(x)$], we only delay the responce for $n$ shifts:

$$C[x^k u(x)] = x^n C[u(x)].$$

(3) $C$ has no memory, i.e., the response to a given $k$-tuple does not depend on the preceding $k$-tuples. In view of the time-invariance, this is equivalent to the following: by changing the first $k$ symbols of the source message $\mathbf{u}$, we can only change the first $n$ symbols of the response $\mathbf{v}$.

Conversely, every function $C$ on polynomials satisfying (1)–(3) expresses a linear code. In fact, denote by $v_i(x)$ the response to $x^i$ for $i = 0, 1, \ldots, k$. By (3), the degree of $v_i(x)$ is less than $n$; thus, we have $k$ words $\mathbf{v}_0$, $\mathbf{v}_1$, $\ldots$, $\mathbf{v}_{k-1}$ of length $n$. The matrix

$$\mathbf{G} = \begin{bmatrix} \mathbf{v}_0 \\ \mathbf{v}_1 \\ \vdots \\ \mathbf{v}_{k-1} \end{bmatrix}$$

defines a linear code. The usual ecoding

$$\mathbf{u} \longmapsto [u_0 u_1 \ldots u_{k-1}]\mathbf{G} = \sum_{i=0}^{k-1} u_i \mathbf{v}_i$$

corresponds to the function $C$ (applied to polynomials of degree less than $k$):

$$C[u_0 + u_1 x + \cdots + u_{k-1} x^{k-1}] = \sum_{i=0}^{k-1} u_i C[x^i] = \sum_{i=0}^{k-1} u_i v_i(x).$$

The time-invariance and linearity (of both the function $C$ and the linear code defined by the matrix $\mathbf{G}$) then guarantee that $C$ is the global description of the linear code generated by $\mathbf{G}$.

By dropping the condition (3) above, we get the concept of convolutional code:

**Definition.** *Let $F$ be a finite field (the source alphabet). By a convolutional $(n, k)$-code is meant a function $C$ assigning to each polynomial $u(x)$ over $F$ a (response) polynomial $C[u(x)]$, which is linear:*

$$C[u(x) + u'(x)] = C[u(x)] + C[u'(x)],$$
$$C[tu(x)] = tC[u(x)],$$

*and time-invariant:*

$$C[x^k u(x)] = x^n C[u(x)].$$

**Example.** (1) Consider the following-shift register sequence:

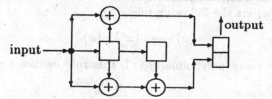

It consists of two shift registers, three binary adders, and a two-bit output buffer which emits two bits in every shift. The input-output function of this shift-register sequence is linear (because only linear elements are involved) and time-invariant: a delay of 1 shift at the input causes a delay of 2 shifts at the output. Thus, we get a convolutional $(2, 1)$-code.

The response to a single 1 is 11 at the first shift, 11 at the second shift, and 01 at the third shift (followed by $0000\dots$), thus,

$$C[1] = 111101 = 1 + x + x^2 + x^3 + x^5.$$

Consequently, by time-invariance,

$$C[01] = 00111101,$$
$$C[001] = 0000111101,$$

etc. By linearity, the single response $C[1]$ determines the whole code. For example, the response to 101 is

$$C[101] = C[1] + C[001] = 1111101101.$$

*Convolutional $(n, 1)$-codes.* In the special case $k = 1$, the whole code is determined by the single response to 1. We call

$$C[1] = g_0(x)$$

the *generator polynomial* of the convolutional $(n, 1)$-code. Observe that, by the time-invariance,

$$C[x] = x^n g_0(x),$$
$$C[x^2] = x^{2n} g_0(x),$$

etc. Thus, for each polynomial $u(x) = u_0 + u_1 x + u_2 x^2 + \cdots$, we have

$$
\begin{aligned}
C[u(x)] &= u_0 C[1] + u_1 C[x] + u_2 C[x^2] + \cdots \\
&= u_0 g_0(x) + u_1 x^n g_0(x) + u_2 x^{2n} g_0(x) + \cdots \\
&= (u_0 + u_1 x^n + u^2 x^{2n} + \cdots) g_0(x) \\
&= u(x^n) g_0(x).
\end{aligned}
$$

We conclude that a convolutional $(n, 1)$-code is determined by its generator polynomial $g_0(x)$ via the following rule:

$$u(x) \longmapsto u(x^n) g_0(x).$$

Conversely, for every polynomial $g_0(x)$, this rule defines a convolutional $(n, 1)$-code.

**Remark.** (1) Generator polynomials play here a different role from that in the realm of cyclic codes. For example, *every* polynomial $g_0(x)$ generates a convolutional $(n, 1)$-code by the rule

$$u(x) \longmapsto u(x^n) g_0(x).$$

For each polynomial $g_0(x) = a_0 + a_1 x + \cdots + a_s x^s$, there is a simple rule of how to describe a circuit which realizes the encoding. For simplicity, we will describe it just in the binary case. Use the first $n$ summands of $g_0(x)$ to decide whether the individual $n$ bits of the output buffer are connected directly with the input (if $a_i = 1$, then the $i$th output bit is connected; if $a_i = 0$, then it is not). The next $n$ summands decide whether the individual $n$ bits are connected directly with the output of the first shift-register stage, etc. Thus, we write

$$
\begin{aligned}
g_0(x) = & (a_0 + a_1 x + \cdots + a_{n-1} x^{n-1}) \\
& + (a_n x^n + a_{n+1} x^{n+1} + \cdots + a_{2n-1} x^{2n-1}) \\
& + \cdots + (a_{mn} x^{mn} + a_{mn+1} x^{mn+1} + \cdots + a_{mn+n-1} x^{mn+n-1}).
\end{aligned}
$$

The number $m + 1$ of parentheses indicates that we need a shift-register sequence of length $m$. The $(i + 1)$st set of parentheses determines the connection of the output of the $i$th shift-register stage with the individual bits of the output buffer.

## Examples

(2) Let us sketch an encoder of the convolutional $(2, 1)$-code with the generator polynomial $g(x) = 1 + x + x^2 + x^5 = (1 + x) + (x^2 + 0) + (0 + x^5)$. The first expression in parentheses, $1 + x$, means that both bits of the output buffer are directly connected with the input; the next expression in parentheses, $x^2 + 0$, tells us that only the first output bit is connected with the first memory; and, finally, from $0 + x^5$, we see that only the second output bit is connected with the second memory. See Figure 1.

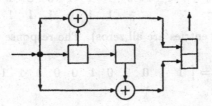

**Figure 1:** An encoder of a convolutional $(2, 1)$-code

(3) Consider the convolutional $(3, 1)$-code with $g_0(x) = 1 + x^2 + x^3 + x^5 + x^6 + x^7 + x^{12} + x^{13} + x^{14}$. We rewrite the generator polynomial as follows: $g_0(x) = (1 + 0 + x^2) + (x^3 + 0 + x^5) + (x^6 + x^7 + 0) + (x^{12} + x^{13} + x^{14})$. The encoder is shown in Figure 2.

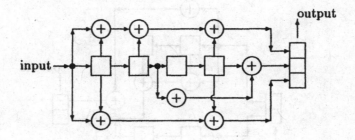

**Figure 2:** An encoder of a convolutional $(3, 1)$-code

**Remark.** From the generator polynomial, we can form a *generator matrix* analogously to the case of cyclic codes: Let **G** be the matrix whose first row is $g_0(x)$, second row is $x^n g_0(x)$ (i.e., the first row shifted $n$ times to the right), third row is $x^{2n} g_0(x)$, etc. The number of rows of $\mathbf{G}$ is not fixed: for each $i = 1, 2, 3, \ldots$, we have an $i \times n$ generator matrix serving to encode messages $\mathbf{u} = u_0 u_1 \ldots u_{i-1}$ of length $i$. The encoding rule is as usual:

$$\mathbf{u} \longmapsto \left[ u_0 u_1 \ldots u_{i-1} \right] \mathbf{G}.$$

For example, let $C$ be the binary convolutional $(3, 1)$-code with generator polynomial $g_0(x) = 1 + x + x^3 + x^4 + x^5 + x^8$. For messages of length 3, we have the following generator matrix:

$$\mathbf{G} = \begin{bmatrix} 1 & 1 & 0 & 1 & 1 & 1 & 0 & 0 & 1 & & & \\ & & & 1 & 1 & 0 & 1 & 1 & 1 & 0 & 0 & 1 & & & \\ & & & & & & 1 & 1 & 0 & 1 & 1 & 1 & 0 & 0 & 1 \end{bmatrix}$$

(where the missing entries are all zeros). The response of that code to 101 is

$$\left[\, 1 \quad 0 \quad 1 \,\right] \mathbf{G} = \left[\, 1 \quad 1 \quad 0 \quad 0 \quad 0 \quad 1 \quad 0 \quad 0 \quad 0 \quad 1 \quad 1 \quad 0 \quad 0 \quad 0 \quad 1 \,\right].$$

## 14.2   Generator Polynomials and Generator Matrices

In the preceding section, we have seen how a convolutional $(n, 1)$-code is described by its generator polynomial. We now present an analogous description of convolutional $(n, k)$-codes. Let us begin with an example.

**Example.** Consider the two shift-register sequences in Figure 3 encoding

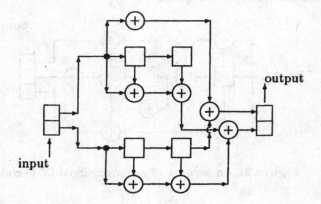

**Figure 3:** An encoder of a convolutional $(2, 2)$-code

convolutional $(2, 1)$-codes, which only share the output buffer. At each clock time, the input buffer is filled by two bits, giving the inputs to both of the shift-register sequences. The two outputs are then added, and the resulting contents of the output buffer is sent out. The input-output function of this circuit is linear and time-invariant: a delay of the input by two shifts results in a delay of the output by 2 shifts. That is, we obtain a convolutional $(2, 2)$-code.

Observe that the response to 10 is 110101 (the upper shift-register sequence is activated alone), and the response to 01 is 010111 (activating the lower sequence alone). That is,

$$C[1] = 1 + x + x^3 + x^5 = g_0(x),$$
$$C[x] = x + x^3 + x^4 + x^5 = g_1(x).$$

By the time invariance, we can compute other responses:

$$C[x^2] = x^2 g_0(x) \qquad\qquad C[x^3] = x^2 g_1(x)$$
$$C[x^4] = x^4 g_0(x) \qquad\qquad C[x^5] = x^4 g_1(x)$$
$$\vdots \qquad\qquad\qquad\qquad \vdots$$

Thus, the general response can be expressed as follows:

$$C[u_0 + u_1 x + u_2 x^2 + u_3 x^3 + u_4 x^4 + \cdots] =$$
$$= (u_0 + u_2 C[x^2] + u_4 C[x^4] + \cdots) + (u_1 + u_3 C[x^3] + u_5 C[x^5] + \cdots)$$
$$= u^{(0)}(x^2) g_0(x) + u^{(1)}(x^2) g_1(x).$$

Here $u^{(0)}(x)$ and $u^{(1)}(x)$ are the polynomials representing the even and odd symbols of the word $u_0 u_1 u_2 u_3 \ldots$, respectively:

$$u^{(0)}(x) = u_0 + u_2 x + u_4 x^2 + \cdots,$$
$$u^{(1)}(x) = u_1 + u_3 x + u_5 x^2 + \cdots.$$

More in general:

**Definition.** *For each convolutional $(n, k)$-code, the polynomials*

$$g_i(x) = C[x^i] \qquad i = 0, 1, \ldots, k - 1$$

*are called the* generator polynomials.

**Theorem.** *A convolutional $(n, k)$-code with generator polynomials $g_0(x)$, $g_1(x)$, ..., $g_{k-1}(x)$ is determined by the following formula:*

$$u(x) \longmapsto \sum_{i=0}^{k-1} u^{(i)}(x^n) g_i(x),  \qquad (14.2.1)$$

*where for each word $\mathbf{u} = u_0 u_1 u_2 \ldots$, we put*

$$\mathbf{u}^{(i)} = u_i u_{i+k} u_{i+2k} \cdots \qquad (i = 0, 1, \ldots, k-1).$$

*Conversely, given polynomials $g_0(x)$, $g_1(x)$, ..., $g_{k-1}(x)$ and a number $n$, the formula (14.2.1) determines a convolutional $(n, k)$-code.*

PROOF. We first prove the latter statement. Observe that the transformation

$$u(x) \longmapsto u^{(i)}(x^n) g_i(x)$$

is linear and $(n, k)$-time-invariant (for each $i = 0, 1, \ldots, k-1$). The former follows from the fact that the transformation is composed from linear transformations, viz.,

$$u(x) \longmapsto u^i(x),$$
$$v(x) \longmapsto v(x^n),$$

and

$$w(x) \longmapsto w(x) g_i(x).$$

To prove the time invariance, observe that for each word $\mathbf{u}$,

$$\left[x^k u(x)\right]^{(i)} = x u^{(i)}(x).$$

Thus, the response to $x^k u(x)$ in our transformations is $x^n u^i(x^n) g_0(x)$.

It follows that the formula (14.2.1) defines a linear $(n, k)$-time-invariant transformation, i.e., a convolutional $(n, k)$-code.

Next we prove that each convolutional $(n, k)$-code $C$ is equal to the transformation $C'[u(x)] = \sum u^i(x^n) g_i(x)$, provided that $g_i(x) = C[x^i]$ are the generator polynomials. Since both $C$ and $C'$ are linear, it is sufficient to prove that $C[x^r] = C'[x^r]$ for each $r = 0, 1, 2, \ldots$: we then have

$$\begin{aligned}
C[u_0 + u_1 x + u_2 x^2 + \cdots] &= \sum u_r C[x^r] \\
&= \sum u_r C'[x^r] \\
&= C'[u_0 + u_1 x + u_2 x^2 + \cdots].
\end{aligned}$$

Further, since both $C$ and $C'$ are $(n,k)$-time-invariant, we can restrict ourselves to $r \leq k - 1$. For $\mathbf{u} = x^r = 00\ldots01000\ldots$, we clearly get $\mathbf{u}^{(r)} = 1000\ldots$ and $\mathbf{u}^{(i)} = 000\ldots$ for $i \neq r$; therefore,

$$C'[x^r] = g_r(x) = C[x^r].$$

□

**Remark.** (1) Analogously to the case of $(n,1)$-codes in 14.1, the formula (14.2.1) can be expressed in matrix form: the following matrix

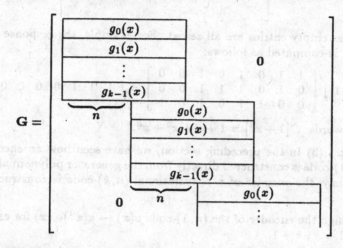

of $r$ lines (where $r$ is a fixed number) is a *generator matrix*. That is, the response of the convolutional code to a word $u_0 u_1 \ldots u_{r-1}$ of length $r$ is the word $[u_0 u_1 \ldots u_{r-1}]\mathbf{G}$.

In fact, the lines of $\mathbf{G}$ are $g_0(x)$, $g_1(x)$, $\ldots$, $g_{k-1}(x)$, $x^n g_0(x)$, $x^n g_1(x)$, $\ldots$, $x^n g_{k-1}(x)$, $x^{2n} g_0(x)$, $\ldots$; thus,

$$
\begin{aligned}
[u_0 u_1 \ldots u_{r-1}]\mathbf{G} &= u_0 g_0(x) + \cdots + u_{k-1} g_{k-1}(x) \\
&\quad + x^n [u_k g_0(x) + \cdots + u_{2k-1} g_{k-1}(x)] \\
&\quad + x^{2n} [x_{2k} g_0(x) + \cdots + u_{3k-1} g_{k-1}(x)] + \cdots \\
&= (u_0 + u_k x^n + u_{2k} x^{2n} + \cdots) g_0(x) \\
&\quad + \cdots + (u_{k-1} + u_{2k-1} x^n + u_{3k-1} x^{2n} + \cdots) g_{k-1}(x) \\
&= \sum_{i=1}^{k-1} u^{(i)}(x^n) g_i(x).
\end{aligned}
$$

**Example** (continued). The generator matrix of the above convolutional $(2,2)$-code with $g_0(x) = 1 + x + x^3 + x^5$ and $g_1(x) = x + x^3 + x^4 + x^5$ is

$$
G = \begin{bmatrix}
1 & 1 & 0 & 1 & 0 & 1 & & & & & & \\
0 & 1 & 0 & 1 & 1 & 1 & & & & & & \\
 & & 1 & 1 & 0 & 1 & 0 & 1 & & & & \\
 & & 0 & 1 & 0 & 1 & 1 & 1 & & & & \\
 & & & & 1 & 1 & 0 & 1 & 0 & 1 & & \\
 & & & & 0 & 1 & 0 & 1 & 1 & 1 & & \\
 & & & & & & & & \ddots & & &
\end{bmatrix}
$$

(where the empty entries are all zeros). For example, the response to the word 101 is computed as follows:

$$
[\,1 \quad 0 \quad 1\,]
\begin{bmatrix}
1 & 1 & 0 & 1 & 0 & 1 & 0 & 0 \\
0 & 1 & 0 & 1 & 1 & 1 & 0 & 0 \\
0 & 0 & 1 & 1 & 0 & 1 & 0 & 1
\end{bmatrix}
= [\,1 \quad 1 \quad 1 \quad 0 \quad 0 \quad 0 \quad 0 \quad 1\,].
$$

In other words, $C[1 + x^3] = 1 + x + x^3 + x^8$.

**Remark.** (3) In the preceding section, we have seen how an encoder of each $(n, 1)$-code is constructed directly from the generator polynomial $g_0(x)$. Analogously, the encoder of a convolutional $(n, k)$-code is constructed as follows:

(1) Design the encoder of the $(n, 1)$-code $u(x) \mapsto u(x^n)g_i(x)$ for each $i = 0, 1, \ldots, k - 1$.

(2) Use a common ($n$-symbol) output buffer for all the $k$ shift registers by simply adding the corresponding output symbols.

(3) Use a $k$-symbol input buffer to multiplex the input string **u** into the $k$ input strings $\mathbf{u}^{(0)}, \mathbf{u}^{(1)}, \ldots, \mathbf{u}^{(k-1)}$.

For example, let us construct an encoder for the binary convolutional $(2, 2)$-code with the generator polynomials

$$
\begin{aligned}
g_0(x) &= 1 + x + x^2 + x^4 + x^5 + x^6 + x^7, \\
g_1(x) &= x + x^3 + x^4 + x^5.
\end{aligned}
$$

We write $g_0(x) = (1+x) + (x^2+0) + (x^4+x^5) + (x^6+x^7)$; the corresponding shift-register sequence has length 3. Further, $g_1(x) = (0 + x) + (0 + x^3) + (x^4 + x^5)$, which leads to a shift-register sequence of length 2. The encoder is shown in Figure 4. Observe that this convolutional code has memory of length 3: for the computation of the present output frame, it remembers, besides the present input frame, symbols of three preceding input frames.

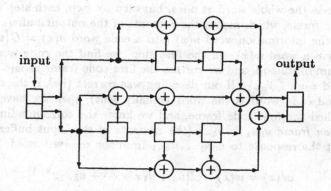

**Figure 4:** An encoder of a convolutional $(2, 2)$-code

**Definition.** *A convolutional $(n, k)$-code is said to have* memory $m$ *provided that the degrees of its generator polynomials fulfil*

$$\deg g_i(x) \leq m(n+1) \qquad for\ i = 0, 1, \ldots\ k-1.$$

*The number $m(n + 1)$ is called the* constraint length *of the code.*

From Remark 2, we see that a convolutional code of memory $m$ can be encoded by a combination of shift-register sequences of length $m$. Thus, the code remembers $m$ input frames. The constraint length is the number of output symbols, which can be changed by the change of a single input symbol.

Observe that the use of the symbols $n$ and $k$ is only partially analogous when we speak about linear $(n, k)$-codes and convolutional $(n, k)$-codes: in some respect, it is the constraint length $m(n + 1)$ which plays the role that $n$ does in case of linear codes.

# 14.3 Maximum-Likelihood Decoding of Convolutional Codes

The basic idea of decoding is the same for linear codes and convolutional codes: receiving a word, we decode it as the code word of maximum likelihood, i.e., of the minimal Hamming distance from the word received. By *code words* we understand all words which are responses of the code $C$ to information words $u(x)$, i.e., all words of the form $v(x) = C[u(x)]$. We do not decode the whole word at once, but step by step, each step correcting one *code frame*, which means the contents of the output buffer. Thus, we encode the information word $u(x)$ into a code word $v(x) = C[u(x)]$, and we receive a word $w(x)$. In the first step, we find the code word $v(x)$ of maximum likelihood, and we correct the first code frame $w_0 w_1 \ldots w_{n-1}$ to the word $v_0 v_1 \ldots v_{n-1}$. If our decoding was correct (i.e., if the maximum-likelihood code word is the word actually sent), then we have correctly established the first code frame, and we know the corresponding first *information frame* $u_0 u_1 \ldots u_{k-1}$ (the contents of the input buffer). Let us subtract the response to $u_0 u_1 \ldots u_{k-1}$ from the received word, i.e., let us define

$$w'(x) = w(x) - C[u_0 + u_1 x + \cdots + u_{k-1} x^{k-1}].$$

Then we can discard the first $n$ symbols from the word $w'(x)$, and the second step will be the same as the first one: find the maximum-likelihood word for the word $w'_n w'_{n+1} w'_{n+2} \ldots$ and correct the second code frame $w_n w_{n+1} \ldots w_{2n-1}$ to the prefix of that code word of length $n$. In fact, the above subtraction means that instead of the code word $v(x) = C[u(x)]$, we now work with

$$
\begin{aligned}
& v(x) - C[u_0 + u_1 x + \cdots + u_{k-1} x^{k-1}] \\
={} & C[u(x)] - C[u_0 + u_1 x + \cdots + u_{k-1} x^{k-1}] \\
={} & C[u_k x^k + u_{k+1} x^{k+1} + \cdots] \\
={} & C[x^k (u_k + u_{k+1} x + u_{k+2} x^2 + \cdots)] \\
={} & x^n C[u_k + u_{k+1} x + u_{k+1} x^2 + \cdots].
\end{aligned}
$$

Thus, by discarding the first $n$ zeros, we obtain the response to the information symbols $u_k u_{k+1} u_{k+2} \ldots$ . The third step is quite analogous: put

$$w''(x) = w'(x) - x^n C[u_k + u_{k+1} x + \cdots + u_{2k-1} x^{2k-1}]$$

and discard the first $2n$ symbols from $w''(x)$. Then find the maximum-likelihood code word and correct $w_{2n} w_{2n+1} \ldots w_{3n-1}$, etc.

**Example.** Consider the binary convolutional $(2, 1)$-code with the generator polynomial $g_0(x) = 1 + x + x^3$. Its code words are

$$
\begin{array}{ll}
g_0(x) & 11010000\ldots, \\
x^2 g_0(x) & 001101000\ldots, \\
(1 + x^2) g_0(x) & 111001000\ldots,
\end{array}
$$

etc. When receiving, say,

$$w = 11110001,$$

we find the maximum-likelihood code word, which is $(1 + x^2 + x^4)g_0(x) =$ 11101001. The first code frame is 11 and, thus, the first information frame is 1. Put

$$w' = w - C[1] = 11110001 - 11010000 = 00100001.$$

Discard the first two symbols of $w'$ and find the maximum-likelihood code word for 100001. It is $000\ldots 0$; thus, the second code frame is 00, and the second information frame is 0. Put

$$w'' = w' - x^2 C[0] = 00100001.$$

Discard the first four symbols of $w''$ and find the maximum-likelihood code word for 0001. It is $000\ldots$ again. Thus, we correct $w$ to

$$C[1 + 0x + 0x^2] = 11010000.$$

**Remark.** A convolutional code is said to *correct t errors* provided that the above decoding can find the code word $v(x)$ actually sent whenever the Hamming distance of $v(x)$ from the received word $w(x)$ is at most $t$. Since the subsequent steps are just repetitions of the first step (after the "dead" symbols are discarded), a convolutional code corrects $t$ errors precisely when the first decoding step is successful in all situations with at most $t$ corrupted symbols. This leads to the following analogy of the minimum distance of linear codes:

**Definition.** *By the* free distance *of a convolutional* $(n, k)$-*code $C$ is meant the smallest Hamming distance $d_{\text{free}}$ of code words $C[u(x)]$ and $C[u'(x)]$ such that the first information frames of the inputs $u(x)$ and $u'(x)$ are different. In symbols:*

$$d_{\text{free}} = \min\Big\{ \text{dist}\left(C[u(x)], C[u'(x)]\right) \;\Big|\; u_0 u_1 \ldots u_{k-1} \neq u_0' u_1' \ldots u_{k-1}' \Big\}.$$

**Remark.** Analogous to the case of linear codes (Remark 8.2), the free distance can be substituted by the minimum Hamming weight of a code word $C[u^*(x)]$ such that $u_0^* u_1^* \ldots u_{k-1}^* \neq 0$. In fact, given code words $C[u(x)]$ and $C[u'(x)]$ of the Hamming distance $d_{\text{free}}$, consider $C[u^*(x)]$, where $u^*(x) = u(x) - u'(x)$.

**Example** (continued). The above convolutional $(2, 1)$-code has

$$d_{\text{free}} = 3.$$

In fact, the code word $g_0(x)$ has Hamming weight 3, and an arbitrary code word $C[u_0 + u_1 x + \cdots]$ with $u_0 \neq 0$ has Hamming weight at least 3. Thus, that code corrects single errors, since we have the following analogy of Proposition 4.6:

**Proposition.** *A convolutional code corrects $t$ errors if and only if its free distance is greater than $2t$.*

PROOF. Suppose $d_{\text{free}} > 2t$. Receiving a word $w(x)$ with at most $t$ errors, we find the code word $v(x) = C[u(x)]$ of the smallest Hamming distance, say, $s$, from $w(x)$. It is our task to show that the first information frame $u_0 u_1 \ldots u_{k-1}$ agrees with that of the code word $v^*(x) = C[u^*(x)]$ actually sent. The Hamming distance of $w(x)$ and $v^*(x)$ is at most $t$, by assumption. Therefore, the Hamming distance of $v(x)$ and $v^*(x)$ is at most $s + t$ (by the triangle inequality, see 4.4). Since $s$ is the smallest Hamming distance, we have $s \leq t$; hence, the Hamming distance of $v(x) = C[u(x)]$ and $v^*(x) = C[u^*(x)]$ is $s + t \leq 2t < d_{\text{free}}$. It follows from the definition of the free distance that $u(x)$ and $u^*(x)$ agree in the first information frame. This proves that the first step of decoding is successful. The proof for the subsequent steps is analogous.

Conversely, suppose $d_{\text{free}} \leq 2t$, and let $v(x) = C[u(x)]$ and $v'(x) = C[u'(x)]$ be code words of Hamming distance $d_{\text{free}}$ with the first information frames different. Let $i_1, i_2, \ldots, i_{d_{\text{free}}}$ be all the indices $i$ for which $v_i \neq v_i'$. Let $w(x)$ be the following word:

$$w_i = \begin{cases} v_i & \text{whenever } v_i = v_i', \text{ or } i = i_m, \ m \text{ odd}, \\ v_i' & \text{if } i = i_m, \ m \text{ even}. \end{cases}$$

The Hamming distance of $w(x)$ and $v(x)$ is smaller or equal to the Hamming distance of $w'(x)$ and $v'(x)$, and the latter is at most $t$ (since $d_{\text{free}} \leq 2t$). Assume that $v'(x)$ is sent and $w(x)$ is received. This error, corrupting at most $t$ symbols, can be decoded incorrectly: in the first step, we choose the code word $v(x)$ as the word of maximum likelihood, and this leads to a wrong estimate of the first information frame. Thus, the code does not correct $t$ errors.                                                                    □

**Concluding Remark.** For a convolutional code, an important parameter is the free distance which specifies the number of errors correctable by the code. No analytic method of constructing good convolutional codes (comparable, say, to the BCH codes) is known. However, a number of good convolutional codes have been found by computer search. We list some of them in Figure 5.

| $n$ | $d_{\text{free}}$ | $g_0(x)$ | |
|---|---|---|---|
| 2 | 5 | 110111 | $= 1 + x + x^3 + x^4 + x^5$ |
| 2 | 6 | 11110111 | |
| 2 | 7 | 1101011011 | |
| 2 | 8 | 110111011011 | |
| 2 | 10 | 11011111001011 | |
| 2 | 10 | 111011110111 | |
| 3 | 8 | 111011111 | |
| 3 | 10 | 111011101111 | |
| 3 | 12 | 111011101011111 | |
| 4 | 10 | 111101111111 | |
| 4 | 13 | 1111011110011111 | |

**Figure 5:** Some good binary convolutional $(n, 1)$-codes

# 14.4 The Viterbi Decoding Algorithm

We now describe in detail a decoder realizing the maximum-likelihood decoding of a convolutional code. This algorithm was applied, for example, by the Voyager spacecraft in 1974 for its mission to Mars, Jupiter, and Saturn. [The spacecraft used the convolutional $(2, 1)$-code with the generator polynomial $g_0(x) = 1 + x + x^2 + x^5 + x^6 + x^7 + x^8 + x^{10} + x^{11} + x^{12}$.] In order to explain the Viterbi algorithm, we introduce another representation of a convolutional code called the trellis diagram. For the sake of simplicity, we restrict ourselves now to the binary convolutional $(n, 1)$-codes. However, the reader will have no difficulty in generalizing the Viterbi algorithm to arbitrary convolutional codes.

A *trellis diagram* depicts each *state* of the code, i.e., each state of the shift-register encoder, at each clock time. The state $S$ at the clock time $i$ is connected by an edge with two states at the clock time $i + 1$: the state $S^0$ resulting from the input 0 (at the clock time $i$) and the state $S^1$ resulting from the input 1. We draw the edges in such a way that the edge $S \to S^0$ always lies under the edge $S \to S^1$. Every edge is labeled by the output frame corresponding to the state and the input.

**Examples**

(1) The convolutional $(2, 1)$-code with the following encoder

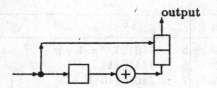

has two states: 0 and 1. In the state 0, the output is

               00     if the input is 0,
               11     if the input is 1.

In the state 1, the ouput is

               01     if the input is 0,
               10     if the input is 1.

The trellis diagram is shown in Figure 6.

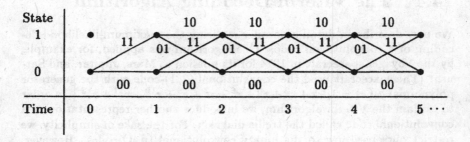

**Figure 6:** The trellis diagram of a $(2,1)$-code of memory $m = 1$

(2) The convolutional $(2,1)$-code with the encoder in Figure 7 has four states: 00, 01, 10, and 11.

From the state $S = 00$, we get to $S^0 = 00$ if the input is 0 or to $S^1 = 10$ if the input is 1. The corresponding outputs are 00 and 11, respectively. This yields the following part of the trellis diagram:

$$
\begin{array}{ccc}
 & 10 \nearrow \bullet\, 10 \\
00 \bullet \!\!\!\! \underleftarrow{\phantom{00}} \!\! \underset{00}{\phantom{0}} \bullet\, 00
\end{array}
$$

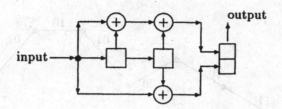

**Figure 7:** An encoder of a $(2, 1)$-code of memory $m = 2$

Analogously, if $S = 10$, then $S^0 = 01$ (input 0, output 10) and $S^1 = 11$ (input 1, output 01), etc. The whole trellis diagram is shown in Figure 8.

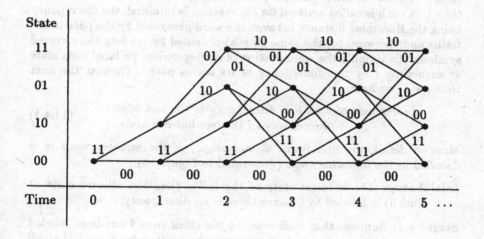

**Figure 8:** The trellis diagram of a $(2, 1)$-code of memory $m = 2$

Observe that every path through the trellis starting at time 0 yields a code word. For example, the path in Figure 9 corresponds to the code word $111000011001 = C[110110]$. Conversely, every code word represents a path in the trellis.

*Viterbi algorithm.* Receiving a word $w = w_0 w_1 w_2 \ldots$, we try to find the maximum-likelihood path through the trellis. For each time $i$ and each

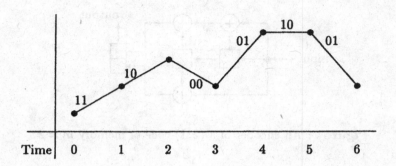

**Figure 9:** A path through the trellis

state $S$, we list the *active path* (or paths) through the trellis to the state $S$ at time $i$. A path is called active if its *discrepancy* is minimal, the discrepancy being the Hamming distance between the word generated by the path in the trellis and the word (of the same length) obtained by reading the received symbols. To simplify the computation of discrepancies, we label each state at each time $i$ by the discrepancy of its active path. Then at the next time $i + 1$, we have

$$\text{discrepancy of a path} = \text{discrepancy of the last edge} \\ + \text{discrepancy of the last-but-one state.} \qquad (14.4.1)$$

More in detail, the first frame $w_0 w_1 \ldots w_{n-1}$ of the received word **w** is decoded in the following steps (illustrated in Figure 10):

**Initial step:** The leftmost state of the trellis (i.e., the all-zero state at time 0) is labeled by 0, since there is no discrepancy.

**Step $i + 1$:** Suppose that each state at the clock time $i$ has been labeled by the discrepancy of (all) active paths leading to it, and that all active paths of length $i$ have been listed. Given a state $S$ at the clock time $i + 1$, find all active paths in the trellis leading to $S$ [using the previously listed active paths, see (14.4.1)]. Label $S$ by the discrepancy of those paths. Make a list of all active paths at the clock time $i$.

**Final step:** The procedure terminates at time $b$ provided that all the active paths at that time have the same first edge. If the label of that edge is $v_0 v_1 \ldots v_{n-1}$, then the first code frame $w_0 w_1 \ldots w_{n-1}$ is corrected to $v_0 v_1 \ldots v_{n-1}$.

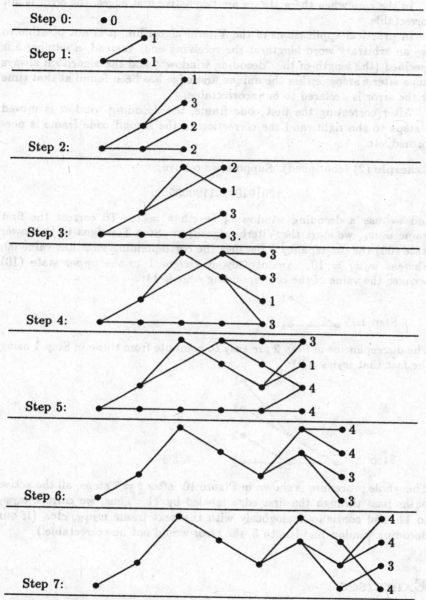

**Figure 10:**   The Viterbi algorithm for **w** = 10010100101100...
with decoding window b = 7

In the case when there always are two active first edges, the error is not correctable.

In practical applications of the Viterbi algorithm, it is not possible to use an arbitrary word length at the receiving end. Instead, a number $b$ is specified (the length of the "decoding window") and the algorithm always stops after $b$ steps: either the unique first edge has been found at that time or the error is declared to be incorrectable.

After correcting the first code frame, the decoding window is moved $n$ steps to the right, and the correction of the second code frame is performed, etc.

**Example** (2) (continued).  Suppose we receive

$$10010100101100000\ldots$$

and we use a decoding window of length $b = 7$.  To correct the first frame $w_0 w_1$, we start the Viterbi algorithm.  Step 1 assigns to the lower state (00) the discrepancy 1 because the corresponding edge has value 00, whereas $w_0 w_1 = 10$.  Analogously, it assigns 1 to the upper state (10) because the value of the corresponding edge is 11:

Step 1:

The discrepancies in Step 2 are easy to compute from those in Step 1 using the fact that $w_2 w_3 = 01$:

Step 2: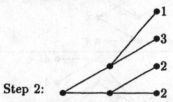

The whole procedure is shown in Figure 10: after $b = 7$ steps, all the active paths pass through the first edge labeled by 11.  Thus, we correct $w_0 w_1$ to 11, and continue analogously with the next frame $w_2 w_3$, etc.  (If our decoding window had length 5, the error would not be correctable.)

# Exercises

**14A**   Design an encoder of the binary convolutional $(2, 1)$-code with the generator polynomial $g_0(x) = 1 + x + x^3 + x^4 + x^6 + x^7 + x^9$.  Encode 110.

**14B** Find a five-row generator matrix for the code in 14A.

**14C** Design an encoder of a binary convolutional $(3,2)$-code of memory $m = 2$.

**14D** The encoder in Figure 4 in 14.2 uses five shift registers. Design an encoder of the same code using four shift register states only. [Hint: the two shift-register sequences can share the last register.]

**14E** Describe the generator polynomials of the convolutional code in Figure 11.

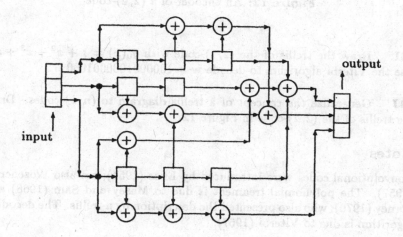

**Figure 11:** An encoder of a $(3,3)$-code

**14F** Find a five-row generator matrix for the code in 14E. Encode 11001.

**14G** Design an encoder for the $(2,3)$-code with the generator polynomials $g_0(x) = 1 + x + x^3 + x^5 + x^6$, $g_1(x) = x + x^2 + x^3 + x^4$, and $g_2(x) = 1 + x^2 + x^3 + x^5 + x^6$.

**14H** Use the Viterbi algorithnm to decode $w = 01000001000\ldots$ provided that the code of Example 2 of 14.4 is used (and $b = 7$).

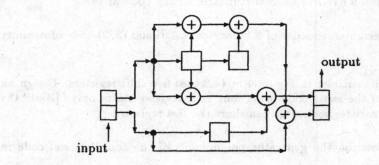

**Figure 12:** An encoder of a $(2,2)$-code

**14I**    Draw the trellis of the $(2,1)$-code with $g_0(x) = 1 + x^2 + x^3 + x^5$.
Use the Viterbi algorithm to decode $\mathbf{w} = 1000001000001000\ldots$.

**14J**    Generalize the concept of a trellis diagram to $(n,k)$-codes.  Draw
the trellis of the $(2,2)$-code in Figure 12.

## Notes

Convolutional codes were introduced by Elias (1954); see also Wozencraft
(1957).  The polynomial treament is due to Masey and Sain (1968) and
Forney (1970), who also presented the description by a trellis.  The decoding
algorithm is due to Viterbi (1967).

# Part III

# Cryptography

# Chapter 15

# Cryptography

In this last chapter, we provide a brief introduction to cryptography, stressing the role error-correcting codes play in this field. In *cryptography*, we assume that a sender wants to send a message to a user in such a way that an enemy with a wiretap on the channel will not be able to understand the message. For that reason, the sender applies a special code (we speak about *encryption* instead of encoding here) and the user *decrypts* (i.e., decodes) to get the original message. See Figure 1.

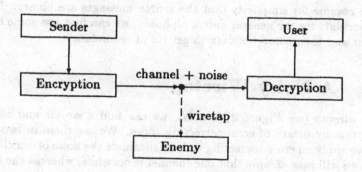

**Figure 1:** A scheme of decoding for secrecy

We present several modern cryptosystems, some of which directly use error-correcting codes. The main connection between the two theories is that cryptography is typically very sensitive to noise. A small change in the encrypted message will usually cause a big damage after decryption. For this reason, it is advisable to combine encryption and error correction,

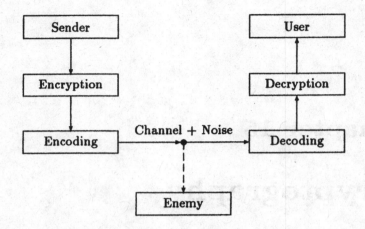

**Figure 2:** A scheme of cryptography with error-correcting coding

as indicated in Figure 2.

It should also be noted that since encryption and decryption are usually quite demanding (a simple encryption would be simple to break), it is always worthwhile to apply data compression before encrypting, see Chapter 3.

We assume for simplicity that the source messages are binary. This is unimportant: for the general source alphabet, we can first use some binary encoder and then compress data to get rid of redundancy.

## 15.1   A Noisy Wiretap

If the wiretap (see Figure 2) is noisy, we can find a simple and effective encryption by means of error-correcting codes. We use them in two ways: first, we apply an error-correcting code to eliminate the noise of our channel. Thus, we will now assume that our channel is noiseless, whereas the enemy has a noisy wiretap. The next application of an error-correcting code will first be illustrated by the simple example of the even-parity code:

**Example.** Suppose that the wiretap is a binary symmetric channel of error-probability $p$. We encrypt as follows: we choose a number $n$, and instead of 0, we send a random binary word of length $n$ and even parity; instead of 1, a random word of odd parity. In other words, if $K_n$ denotes the even-parity code of length $n$, then 0 is encrypted as a random code word and 1 as a random noncode word.

The decryption (in the absence of noise) is easy: decrypt the first $n$ symbols as 0 or 1, according to the parity. On the other hand, the enemy receives an $n$-tuple which either has the original parity or the wrong parity. The latter happens whenever one bit has been corrupted [probability $np(1-p)^{n-1}$] or three bits [probability $\binom{n}{3}p^3(1-p)^{n-3}$], etc. Thus, the enemy decrypts incorrectly with probability

$$P_n = \sum_{i=1}^{n} \binom{n}{i} p^i (1-p)^{n-i}.$$

It is easy to verify that $P_n$ converges to $\frac{1}{2}$ with inreasing $n$. If we choose $n$ with $P_n \approx \frac{1}{2}$, then the enemy is completely baffled: half of his 0's are actually 1's, and vice versa.

## Remarks

(1) More in general, every binary linear $(n, k)$-code $K$ can be used for encryption as follows. Let $H$ be a parity check matrix. For each word $\mathbf{w}$ of length $n$, we can compute its syndrome $\mathbf{s}$ (of length $n - k$) by

$$\mathbf{H}\mathbf{w}^{\mathrm{tr}} = \mathbf{s}^{\mathrm{tr}}.$$

Conversely, all the words $\mathbf{w}$ with a given syndrome $\mathbf{s}$ form a coset, and the number of such words is equal to $2^k$ (= the number of all code words), see 6.2. We divide the source message into blocks of length $n - k$. Given a block $\mathbf{s}$, we choose a random word $\mathbf{w}$ with the syndrome $\mathbf{s}$, and we encrypt $\mathbf{s}$ as $\mathbf{w}$. The information rate $R$ of this encryption is

$$R = \frac{n-k}{n}$$

because the source message $\mathbf{s}$ of length $n - k$ is encrypted by a word of length $n$.

The decryption (in the absence of noise) is easy: given $\mathbf{w}$, decrypt by finding the syndrome $\mathbf{s}$ of $\mathbf{w}$.

(2) The enemy who uses a noisy wiretap will lose a certain amount of information. In fact, Wyner (1975) proved that it is possible to find codes which (like in the above example) lead to a complete loss of information by the enemy, but (unlike the above example) keep a certain information rate. More precisely, suppose that the enemy uses a binary symmetric channel of error probability $p > 0$. We know that the

maximum amount of information per symbol which can pass through the channel is the capacity $C = 1 - H(p, 1 - p)$, see 4.7, and the summand $H(p, 1 - p)$ represents the loss of information per symbol. Wyner proved that there exist codes $K_n$ such that the information rates of the above encryption method tends to $H(p, 1 - p)$, and the information the enemy receives about the source symbol tends to 0 with increasing $n$.

## 15.2   Secret-Key Encryption

The simplest method of encryption which, moreover, is absolutely secure consists in choosing a *random key*, i.e., a long random binary word known only to the sender and the user. The sender adds the key to the message (the length of which must be smaller or equal to the length of the key) and sends

$$\mathbf{v} = \mathbf{u} + \mathbf{k} \qquad (\mathbf{u} = \text{message}, \mathbf{k} = \text{key}).$$

The user also adds the (same) key to the received word $\mathbf{v}$. Thus, the user gets

$$\mathbf{v} + \mathbf{k} = \mathbf{u} + \mathbf{k} + \mathbf{k} = \mathbf{u},$$

the message sent (see Figure 3). The wiretap brings no information: since $\mathbf{k}$ is a random word (obtained, say, by tossing a coin a number of times), the word $\mathbf{v}$ is also random.

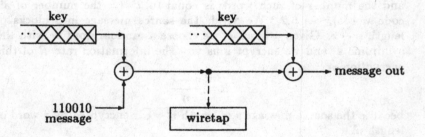

Figure 3: The one-time key

The serious disadvantage of this scheme is the necessity to find a secure manner of delivering the (usually extremely long) key to the sender and the user. One way out of this difficulty is to use a small random key $\mathbf{k}_0$ as a germ for a large "pseudo-random" key $\mathbf{k}$, i.e., a word whose properties resemble the properties of random words. We are going to describe such a procedure which constructs from a random binary word $k_0$ of length $m$ a word of length $2^m - 1$ having the basic features of "randomness". Thus, a key germ of length 100 yields a "pseudo-random" key of length $2^{100} - 1 \approx 1.3 \times 10^{30}$.

The trick is to use the $(2^m - 1, m)$-simplex code $S_m$ [see Example (4) of 8.2]: each key germ of length $m$, considered as an $m$-tuple of information symbols, is encoded into a code word of length $2^m - 1$. We will explain why the code words of the simplex code can be considered to be "pseudo-random". Let $h(x)$ be the minimal polynomial of a primitive element of $GF(2^m)$. Then $h(x)$ is the generator polynomial of a Hamming code of length $2^m - 1$ (see 12.1), which is the dual code to $S_m$. Consequently, $h(x)$ is a parity check polynomial of $S_m$.

**Example.** (1) The minimal polynomial

$$h(x) = x^3 + x + 1$$

of the primitive element of $GF(8)$ found in 11.6 is a parity check polynomial of the simplex code $S_3$. The corresponding parity check matrix is

$$\mathbf{H} = \begin{bmatrix} 0 & 0 & 0 & 1 & 1 & 0 & 1 \\ 0 & 0 & 1 & 1 & 0 & 1 & 0 \\ 0 & 1 & 1 & 0 & 1 & 0 & 0 \\ 1 & 1 & 0 & 1 & 0 & 0 & 0 \end{bmatrix}.$$

It follows that code words are those words $v_0 v_1 v_2 v_3 v_4 v_5 v_6$ which satisfy $\mathbf{Hv}^{tr} = \mathbf{0}^{tr}$, or, equivalently,

$$v_i + v_{i+1} + v_{i+3} = 0 \qquad \text{for } i = 0, 1, 2, 3.$$

In other words, the following recursion formula

$$v_{i+3} = v_i + v_{i+1}$$

determines the code $S_3$. This formula can be "implemented" by the following shift-register sequence:

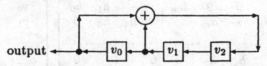

That is, given any initial state (or key germ) $v_0 v_1 v_2$ of the registers, the output word after 8 stages is a code word of $S_3$ (and, conversely, each code word of $S_3$ can be obtained in this manner, since $S_3$ has precisely $2^3$ code words). As a concrete example, let us choose the key germ 101. We obtain the code word

$$1011000.$$

**Remark.** More in general, let $h(x) = h_0 + h_1 x + \cdots + h_m x^m$ ($h_0 = h_m = 1$) be the minimal polynomial of a primitive element of $GF(2^m)$. Then $h(x)$ is the parity check polynomial of the simplex $(2^m - 1, m)$-code $\mathbf{S}_m$. The nonzero code words can be obtained from the shift-register sequence in Figure 4 as follows: insert any nonzero initial word (key germ) $v_0 v_1 \ldots v_{m-1}$ into the shift register, then the output after $n = 2^m - 1$ stages is a code word of $\mathbf{S}_m$. In fact, the output clearly satisfies the recursion formula

$$v_{i+m} = \sum_{k=0}^{m-1} h_k v_{i+k} \qquad (i = 0, 1, 2, \ldots) \qquad (15.5.1)$$

or, equivalently,

$$\sum_{k=0}^{m} h_k v_{i+k} = 0 \qquad (i = 0, 1, 2, \ldots) \qquad (15.5.2)$$

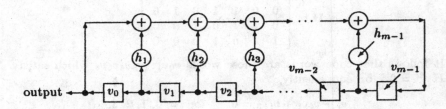

Figure 4: An encoder of the simplex code

It follows that

$$
\begin{bmatrix}
0 & 0 & \cdots & 0 & 0 & h_m & \cdots & h_1 & h_0 \\
0 & 0 & 0 & \cdots & h_m & \cdots & h_1 & h_0 & 0 \\
\multicolumn{9}{c}{\cdots\cdots\cdots\cdots\cdots\cdots\cdots\cdots\cdots\cdots\cdots\cdots} \\
h_m & \cdots & h_1 & h_0 & 0 & 0 & \cdots & & 0
\end{bmatrix}
\begin{bmatrix}
v_0 \\
v_1 \\
\vdots \\
v_{n-1}
\end{bmatrix}
=
\begin{bmatrix}
0 \\
0 \\
\vdots \\
0
\end{bmatrix}.
$$

Thus, $v_0 v_1 \ldots v_{n-1}$ is a code word of $\mathbf{S}_m$.

**Proposition.** *The shift-register sequence in Figure 4 has $n = 2^m - 1$ nonzero states. Given an arbitrary nonzero initial state, each of the $n$ states is taken precisely once during the first $n$ shifts.*

PROOF. Since we have $m$ two-state shift registers, the number of all non-zero states is $2^m - 1$.

Denote by $v_0 v_1 v_2 \ldots$ the infinite output of the shift-register sequence, and assume that the initial state (which is $v_0 v_1 \ldots v_{m-1}$) is nonzero. Then we are going to prove that the sequence $v_0 v_1 v_2 \ldots$ is periodic with period $n$, i.e., $n$ is the smallest number such that $v_{i+n} = v_i$ for all $i$. It then follows that the shift-register sequence does not return to any of the previous states during the first $n$ shifts, and since $n = 2^m - 1$ is the number of *all* possible nonzero states, each state is taken precisely once. To prove that $v_0 v_1 v_2 \ldots$ has period $n$, we form the power series (11G)

$$V(x) = \sum_{i=0}^{\infty} v_i x^i,$$

and we prove that $n$ is the smallest number such that $V(x)$ can be expressed as

$$V(x) = a(x)(1 + x^n + x^{2n} + \cdots), \qquad \text{degree } a(x) < n.$$

For each polynomial $a(x) = a_0 + a_1 x + \cdots + a_r x^r$, denote by $a^*(x) = a_r + a_{r-1} x + \cdots + a_0 x^r$ the reciprocal polynomial and observe that this operation respects multiplication, i.e., $\left[a(x)b(x)\right]^* = a(x)^* b(x)^*$.

We first observe that the product

$$f(x) = V(x)h^*(x)$$

is a polynomial of a degree lower than $m$. In fact, since

$$f(x) = \left(h_m + h_{m-1} x + \cdots + h_0 x^m\right) \sum_{i=0}^{\infty} v_i x^i,$$

$f(x)$ has the following coefficient at $x^j$, $j \geq m$:

$$h_m v_j + h_{m-1} v_{j-1} + \cdots + h_0 v_{j-m} = \sum_{k=0}^{m} h_k v_{(j-m)+k}.$$

The output sequence $v_0 v_1 v_2 \ldots$ satisfies the recursion formula (15.5.2); thus, the last expression is 0.

Next, from the equation

$$g(x)h(x) = x^n - 1,$$

where $g(x)$ is the generator polynomial of the code $S_m$, we get

$$g^*(x)h^*(x) = (x^n - 1)^* = 1 - x^n.$$

Consequently,

$$V(x) = \frac{f(x)}{h^*(x)} = \frac{f(x)g^*(x)}{1 - x^n}.$$

The formula for geometric series (11G) implies that

$$V(x) = f(x)g^*(x)(1 + x^n + x^{2n} + \cdots).$$

The degree of $f(x)$ is smaller then $m$, thus, $f(x)g^*(x)$ has degree smaller than $m + n - m = n$. Consequently, the polynomial $f(x)g^*(x)$ represents a word of length $n$, and the last equation tells us that $V(x)$ is a (cyclic) repetition of that word: $V(x) = f(x)g^*(x) + x^n f(x)g^*(x) + \cdots$. Thus, $V(x)$ is a periodic sequence.

Let $k$ be the period of $V(x)$, i.e., the smallest number such that $V(x) = a(x) + x^k a(x) + \cdots$ for some polynomial $a(x)$ of degree lower than $k$. We clearly have $k \leq n$, and we will prove that $k \geq n$. In fact, since

$$\frac{f(x)}{h^*(x)} = V(x) = a(x)(1 + x^k + x^{2k} + \cdots) = \frac{a(x)}{1 - x^k},$$

we conclude that

$$f(x)(1 - x^k) = h^*(x)a(x).$$

The reciprocal of that equation is

$$f^*(x)(x^k - 1) = h(x)a^*(x).$$

By the unique factorization theorem (11.1), the irreducible polynomial $h(x)$ divides either $f^*(x)$ or $x^k - 1$. The first is impossible since $f^*(x)$ has degree smaller than $m$. The latter implies $k \geq n$: in fact, $h(x)$ is the minimal polynomial of a primitive element $\beta$ of $GF(2^m)$. Since $h(x)$ divides $x^k - 1$, it follows that $\beta^k - 1 = 0$. Because the order of $\beta$ is $2^m - 1 = n$, we conclude that $k \geq n$.                                                             □

*Pseudo-random sequences.* In the following theorem, we list some properties of the nonzero code words of the simplex code, due to which we can consider each of these words as a pseudo-random sequence. We leave it to the reader's intuition to conclude why these properties are sufficient—a detailed explanation can be found in the monograph of Golomb (1967).

Some concepts first. By a *run* of length $k$ in a word $v_0 v_1 \ldots v_{n-1}$ is meant a word $v_i \ldots v_{i+k+1}$ with

$$v_i \neq v_{i+1} = v_{i+2} = \cdots = v_{i+k} \neq v_{i+k+1}$$

($i = 0, 1, \ldots, n - k - 2$). Thus, runs are of two types:

$$\text{a run of 1's: } 0\underbrace{111\ldots11}_{k}0, \qquad \text{a run of 0's: } 1\underbrace{000\ldots00}_{k}1.$$

By the *autocorrelation* of the word **v** is meant the function

$$\rho(k) = \frac{1}{n} \sum_{k=0}^{m-1} (-1)^{v_i}(-1)^{v_{i+k}} \qquad (k = 1, 2, \ldots, n-1)$$

with addition in indices modulo $n$.

**Example.** The code $S_4$ can be generated by the following shift-register sequence [corresponding to $h(x) = 1 + x + x^4$]:

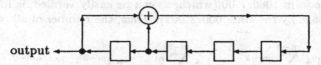

From the key germ, say, 1000, we get the key word

$$100010011010111.$$

It has

(1) eight 1's and seven 0's,

(2) eight runs: four of length 1, two of length 2 and 3 each,

(3) the autocorrelation function $\rho(k) = -\frac{1}{15}$ for all $k$.

**Theorem.** *Each nonzero code word of the simplex code of length $n$ has the following properties:*

(1) *The number of 1's is essentially equal to the number of 0's: they are $\frac{n+1}{2}$ and $\frac{n-1}{2}$, respectively.*

(2) *Of all the runs, one-half have length 1, one-quarter have length 2, one-eighth have length 3, etc. (as long as the fractures are integers). Except for the two longest runs, the number of runs of 1's of a given length is equal to the number of runs of 0's of that length.*

(3) *The autocorrelation has a (very small) constant value:*

$$\rho(k) = -\frac{1}{n} \qquad \text{for } k = 1, 2, \ldots, n-1.$$

PROOF. By the above proposition, the shift-register sequence generating an (arbitrary) nonzero code word $v_0 v_1 \ldots v_{n-1}$ takes each nonzero state precisely once. The $i$th output $v_i$ is the leftmost bit of the $i$th state. This implies the properties (1)–(3) as follows.

(1) Half of all states have the leftmost bit 1, thus, $v_i = 1$ for $\frac{1}{2} 2^m$ indices $i$. Clearly, $\frac{1}{2} 2^m = \frac{n+1}{2}$. Since the all-zero state is not taken, the number of all states with the leftmost bit 0 is $\frac{1}{2} 2^m - 1 = \frac{n-1}{2}$.

(2) Consider first all runs of 0's. A run of 0's of length $k \leq m - 2$ results from a state whose $k + 2$ leftmost bits form the word $1000\ldots001$. The remaining $m - k - 2$ bits are arbitrary, thus, the number of such states is $2^{m-k-2}$. It follows that the word has $2^{m-k-2}$ runs of 0's of length $k = 1, 2, \ldots, m - 2$. One run of 0's has length $m - 1$: it results from the unique state of the form $1000\ldots00$ (which, as can be easily verified, is followed in the next stage by the state $000\ldots001$). Thus, the number of all runs of 0's is

$$1 + \sum_{k=1}^{m-2} 2^{m-k-2} = 1 + \sum_{i=0}^{m-3} 2^i = 1 + 2^{m-2} - 1 = 2^{m-2}.$$

It is clear that no run of 0's has a length larger than $m - 1$ since the all-zero state is never taken.

Analogously, the number of runs of 1's of length $k = 1, 2, \ldots, m - 2$ is $2^{m-k-2}$. However, no run of 1's has a length $m - 1$: The unique state of the form $0111\ldots11$ is followed by the all-one state [which easily follows from the fact that, since $h(0) \neq 0$, the number of summands of $h(x)$ is odd]. The all-one state is followed by $111\ldots110$ [for the same reason]. This leads to a run of 1's of length $m$. The number of all runs of 1' is again $2^{m-2}$.

Consequently, we have $2^{m-1} = 2 \times 2^{m-2}$ runs. Of these, one-half have length 1:

$$\tfrac{1}{2} 2^{m-1} = 2 \times 2^{m-k-2} \qquad \text{for } k = 1.$$

One-quarter, $2^{m-3}$, have length $k = 2$, etc.

(3) Put $w_i = v_i + v_{i+k}$ in $\mathbf{Z}_2$ (addition in the index modulo $n$). Then

$$(-1)^{v_i}(-1)^{v_{i+k}} = \begin{cases} 1 & \text{if } w_i = 0, \\ -1 & \text{if } w_i = 1. \end{cases}$$

Now observe that $\mathbf{w} = w_0 w_1 \ldots w_{n-1}$ is a code word of $\mathbf{S}_m$: it is the sum of the code word $\mathbf{v}$ and the same word shifted cyclically $k$ times. Obviously, $\mathbf{w} \neq \mathbf{0}$ (since the output $\mathbf{v}$ of the shift-register sequence would otherwise have period $k$, in contradiction to the proposition above). Thus, by (1),

$w_i = 0$ for $\frac{n-1}{2}$ indices $i$ and $w_i = 1$ for $\frac{n+1}{2}$ indices $i$. Therefore,

$$\rho(k) = \frac{1}{n} \sum_{i=0}^{n-1} (-1)^{v_i} (-1)^{v_{i+k}} = -\frac{1}{n} \left( \frac{n+1}{2} - \frac{n-1}{2} \right) = -\frac{1}{n}. \qquad \square$$

**Concluding Remark.** One possibility of encryption is to use a secret key **k** whose length is larger or equal to the length of the encrypted mesage.

If **k** is a random word, the encryption method is completely secure (provided that the key can be sent through a completely secure channel).

More realistic, but less secure, is the method of using a random key germ $\mathbf{k}_0$ of length $m$ from which a pseudo-random key **k** of length $2^m - 1$ is created by means of a linear shift-register sequence. The weak point of this method is that the enemy, once deciding that this encryption was applied, can break the code whenever he learns a source message of the (small!) length $2m$ together with its encryption, see Exercise 15A. In this sense, linear shift-register sequences are insecure, and an application of nonlinear elements is advisable. An example of such a method is the DES encryption described in 15.5.

# 15.3 Public-Key Encryption

Modern cryptosystems are often such that the method of encryption is not kept secret. Thus, anyone can send the user an encrypted message. On the other hand, decryption is extremely complicated for everyone except the user—so complicated that it can be considered impossible. Here we describe one public-key cryptosystem based on Goppa codes, and in the next two sections, we will show two other public-key cryptosystems. The following cryptosystem was discovered by McEliece (1978).

Recall from 12.5 that each irreducible polynomial $r(x)$ of degree $t$ over $GF(2^m)$ defines a Goppa $(n, k)$-code with

$$n = 2^m \qquad \text{and} \qquad k \geq n - mt.$$

This code corrects $t$ errors (and a fast decoder is known). Let us choose at random

(1) an irreducible polynomial $r(x)$,

(2) an invertible binary $k \times k$ matrix **S**, and

(3) a permutation $n \times n$ matrix **P** (i.e., each row and each column of **P** has Hamming weight 1).

The encryption is performed by means of the following matrix:

$$G^* = SGP,$$

where $G$ is a $k \times n$ generator matrix of the Goppa code. To encrypt, divide the message into words $v$ of length $k$, compute $vG^*$, and change $t$ randomly chosen bits. Thus, the encrypted message is

$$w = vG^* + e,$$

where $e$ is a random word of Hamming weight $t$. The matrix $G^*$ is public, whereas the matrices $S$, $G$, and $P$ are kept secret.

At the receiving end, we decrypt $w$ as follows. First, compute $wP^{-1}$. Observe that

$$wP^{-1} = (vS)G + eP^{-1}.$$

Now, $(vS)G$ is a code word of the Goppa code (given by the information bits $vS$), and since $P^{-1}$ is a permutation matrix, the Hamming weight of $eP^{-1}$ is $t$. Thus, the word $wP^{-1}$ has Hamming distance $t$ from a code word. Since the Goppa code corrects $t$ errors, we can recover the word $(vS)G$ by applying the decoding technique to $wP^{-1}$. This establishes the information bits $vS$, and the final step is a multiplication by $S^{-1}$: $v = (vS)S^{-1}$.

**Example.** Choose a random irreducible polynomial of degree $t = 50$ over $GF(2^{10})$. It can be proved that there exist more than $10^{149}$ such polynomials. We have

$$n = 1024, \quad t = 50, \quad k \geq 1024 - 50 \times 10 = 524.$$

Next choose a permutation $n \times n$ matrix $P$ (we have 1024! possibilities) and an invertible $k \times k$ matrix $S$ (from among an astronomical number of possibilities). Keep $S$, $P$, and the generator matrix $G$ secret while publishing $G^* = SGP$.

The encryption is performed by blocks of length $k$. From each such block $v$, compute the code word $vSG$, change it in 50 random bits, and send the resulting word $w$.

The decryption of the word $w$ received consists in correcting the 50 errors of the word $wP^{-1}$, thus, retrieving the code word $(vS)G$. The information bits $vS$ are then multiplied by $S^{-1}$.

The enemy, who knows $w$ and $G^*$ and knows the encryption method, will not be able to decrypt $w$ unless he discovers the secret matrices (which were chosen randomly from an extremely large number of possibilities). Moreover, the random change of 50 out of 1024 bits makes the decryption even more difficult.

## 15.4 Encryption Based on Large Prime Numbers

Rivest, Shamir, and Adelman (1978) found a simple public-key cryptosystem based on the following two facts:

(1) A fast algorithm for finding a random prime number of a prescribed size is known.

(2) No fast algorithm for a factorization of a large number into a product of primes is known.

Recall from 11.7 that for two relatively prime numbers $q$ and $n$, we have

$$q^{\varphi(n)} = 1 \pmod{n},$$

where $\varphi$ is the Euler function. Further, if $n = pq$ is a product of primes $p$ and $q$, then

$$\varphi(n) = (p - 1)(q - 1).$$

*Encryption.* Choose two large random prime numbers $p$ and $q$. Put

$$n = pq$$

and use the numbers $0, 1, \ldots, n - 1$ as the source alphabet. (One can, of course, use the binary expansion of those numbers to remain in the binary.) Further, choose a random number $i = 0, 1, \ldots, n - 1$ relatively prime with $\varphi(n)$. Then, by 13C, we can find a number $j = 0, 1, \ldots, n - 1$ such that

$$ij \equiv 1 \pmod{\varphi(n)}.$$

Publish $n$ and $i$, keeping $p$, $q$, and $j$ secret.

A source symbol $v = 0, 1, \ldots, n - 1$ is encrypted as follows: compute the $i$th power $v^i$ and find the remainder $w$ of its division through $n$. That is, the symbol sent is the number $w = 0, 1, \ldots, n - 1$ such that

$$w \equiv v^i \pmod{n}.$$

*Decryption.* The received symbol $w$ is raised to the $j$th power and the remainder of $w^j$ divided through $n$ is computed:

$$v \equiv w^j \pmod{n}.$$

**Proposition.** *The above decryption is correct, i.e., for each number* $v = 0, 1, \ldots, n-1$,

$$w \equiv v^i \pmod{n} \quad \textit{implies} \quad v \equiv w^j \pmod{n}.$$

**PROOF.** The statement is clear if $v = 0$; thus, we can assume $v \neq 0$. Since $ij \equiv 1 \pmod{\varphi(n)}$, there exists an integer $r$ such that $ij = 1 + r\varphi(n)$. Then $w \equiv v^i \pmod{n}$ implies

$$w^j \equiv vv^{r\varphi(n)} \pmod{n}.$$

It remains to prove that

$$v^{\varphi(n)} \equiv 1 \pmod{n},$$

from which it follows that $v^{r\varphi(n)} \equiv 1^r \pmod{n}$. Then we conclude that $w^j \equiv v \times 1 \pmod{n}$.

Suppose $v$ and $n$ are relatively prime. Then $v^{\varphi(n)} \equiv 1 \pmod{n}$ by the Euler-Fermat Theorem (11.7). If $v$ and $n$ are not relatively prime, then $v$ is divisible either by $p$ or $q$; say, by $p$. Then $v^{\varphi(n)}$ is also divisible by $p$; thus, the remainder of the division of $v^{\varphi(n)}$ through $n = pq$ is the same as the remainder of the division through $q$. Therefore, it remains to prove that $v^{\varphi(n)} \equiv 1 \pmod{q}$. This follows from the Euler-Fermat Theorem again: $v$ is relatively prime with $q$ (since else it would be divisible by $n = pq$, but $0 < v < n$); therefore,

$$v^{\varphi(q)} \equiv 1 \pmod{q}.$$

Raising both sides of the last equation to $\varphi(p)$, we conclude [since $\varphi(n) = (p-1)(q-1) = \varphi(p)\varphi(q)$] that

$$v^{\varphi(n)} = \left[v^{\varphi(q)}\right]^{\varphi(p)} \equiv 1 \pmod{q}.$$

□

**Example.** Choose two random 50-digit prime numbers $p$ and $q$. Do not be worried whether there is enough to choose from: for the number $\pi(k)$ of all prime numbers smaller than $k$, it it well known that

$$\lim_{k \to \infty} \frac{\pi(k) \log k}{k} = 1.$$

If we estimate $\pi(10^{50})$ by $\frac{10^{50}}{\log 10^{50}} = 5 \times 10^{47}$, we conclude that the choice is rich enough. The basic fact is that there are fast algorithms for testing primality; thus, the random choice can be practically performed: choose a random fifty-digit number and test it for primality. See Solovay and Strassen (1977) for details.

Once $p$ and $q$ have been chosen, we have a 100-digit number $n = pq$ which we publish. We further publish a number $i$ for which we have found a (secret) number $j$ such that $ij \equiv 1 \pmod{n}$. We encrypt by the public key $v \mapsto v^i \pmod{n}$ and decrypt by the secret key $w \mapsto w^j \pmod{n}$. In order to guess the secret number $j$, it would be sufficient to know the secret number $\varphi(n)$: then $j$ is determined from the equation $ij \equiv 1 \pmod{\varphi(n)}$. However, guessing $\varphi(n)$ is as difficult as factoring $n$, see Exercise 15B.

No algorithm capable of factoring a random 100-digit number sooner than in hundreds of years is known today, and there are good reasons to believe that such an algorithm will not be found in the future.

## 15.5 Encryption Based on Knapsack Problems

Another public-key cryptosystem was found by Merkle and Hellman (1978). It is based on the following *knapsack problem*: given a pile of objects, can your knapsack be filled exactly by some of those objects? More precisely: given a pile of natural numbers $a_1, a_2, \ldots, a_n$, can a fixed number $s$ be expressed as a sum $s = a_{i_1} + a_{i_2} + \cdots + a_{i_k}$ of some of them? This can be reformulated by asking whether $s$ is equal to the scalar product of the vector $\mathbf{a} = (a_1, a_2, \ldots, a_n)$ and some binary word $\mathbf{v}$ of length $n$. In fact, the expression

$$s = \mathbf{v} \cdot \mathbf{a} = v_1 a_1 + v_2 a_2 + \cdots + v_n a_n$$

is exactly the sum we were searching for.

The knapsack problem can be used for encryption as follows: encrypt binary words $\mathbf{v}$ of length $n$ by the formula $\mathbf{v} \mapsto s = \mathbf{v} \cdot \mathbf{a}$. To decrypt, solve the knapsack problem of the number $s$, i.e., find $\mathbf{v}$ such that $s = \mathbf{v} \cdot \mathbf{a}$. Unfortunately, if the knapsack problem is simple, i.e., if the numbers $a_1, a_2, \ldots, a_n$ are such that one can simply find the word $\mathbf{v}$ for the given number $s$, then this method is useless because the enemy can simply decrypt our message. If the knapsack problem is difficult, then this method is also useless because we will not be able to encrypt. What we need is a method of turning an easy knapsack problem into a problem which is difficult for the enemy. We first describe some simple knapsack problems.

**Definition.** *A sequence $a_1, a_2, \ldots, a_n$ of natural numbers is called* superincreasing *provided that for each $i = 1, 2, \ldots, n - 1$,*

$$a_{i+1} > a_1 + a_2 + \cdots + a_i.$$

**Remarks**

(1) The knapsack problem of every superincreasing sequence $a_1, a_2, \ldots, a_n$ is easy: given a number $s$, define a binary vector $\mathbf{v}$ as follows:

$$v_n = 1 \quad \Longleftrightarrow \quad a_n \leq s,$$
$$v_{n-1} = 1 \quad \Longleftrightarrow \quad a_{n-1} + v_n a_n \leq s,$$
$$v_{n-2} = 1 \quad \Longleftrightarrow \quad a_{n-2} + v_{n-1} a_{n-1} + v_n a_n \leq s,$$

etc. Then either $s = \mathbf{v} \cdot \mathbf{a}$ or the knapsack problem has no solution for $s$.

(2) A simple knapsack problem $(a_1, a_2, \ldots, a_n)$ can be turned into a difficult one as follows. Choose relatively prime numbers $i$ and $m$ with $m > \sum_{i=1}^{n} a_i$ and $m > i \geq 1$. Then find $j = 1, 2, \ldots, m$ such that $ij \equiv 1 \pmod{m}$, see 13C. For each of the given numbers $a_k$, find the remainder $b_k$ of the integer division of $ia_k$ through $m$:

$$b_k \equiv ia_k \pmod{m}.$$

The numbers $(b_1, b_2, \ldots, b_n)$ constitute a knapsack problem looking difficult to the enemy. But it is a simple one for us: given a number $s$, find the remainder $s'$ of the integer division of $js$ through $m$:

$$s' \equiv js \pmod{m}.$$

Solve the easy knapsack problem for $s'$: $s' = \mathbf{v} \cdot \mathbf{a}$. The same vector $\mathbf{v}$ then solves the "difficult" knapsack problem, as we prove presently.

**Proposition.** *For each number* $s = v_1 b_1 + v_2 b_2 + \cdots + v_n b_n$, *the number* $s' = 0, 1, \ldots, m-1$ *with* $s' \equiv js \pmod{m}$ *satisfies* $s' = v_1 a_1 + v_2 a_2 + \cdots + v_n a_n$.

**PROOF.** Since $ij \equiv 1 \pmod{m}$ and $b_k \equiv ia_k \pmod{m}$, we have $jb_k \equiv a_k \pmod{m}$. Therefore,

$$s' \equiv j(v_1 b_1 + v_2 b_2 + \cdots + v_n b_n) \pmod{m}$$
$$\equiv v_1 a_1 + v_2 a_2 + \cdots + v_n a_n \pmod{m}.$$

Our choice of $m$ was such that $m > \sum_{k=1}^{n} a_k \geq v_1 a_1 + v_2 a_2 + \cdots + v_n a_n$. Also, $m > s'$. Thus, from the equation $s' \equiv \sum_{k=1}^{n} v_k a_k \pmod{m}$, it follows that $s' = \sum_{k=1}^{n} v_k a_k$. $\qquad\square$

*Encryption.* Choose

(1) an easy knapsack problem $a_1, a_2, \ldots, a_n$,

(2) a number $m > \sum_{k=1}^{n} a_k$,

(3) numbers $i, j = 1, 2, \ldots, m - 1$ with $ij \equiv 1 \pmod{m}$.

Compute numbers $b_k = 0, 1, \ldots, m - 1$ satisfying $b_k \equiv ia_k \pmod{m}$. Publish $b_1, b_2, \ldots, b_n$, keeping $i, j, a_k$, and $m$ secret.

Binary messages are divided into words $\mathbf{v}$ of length $n$. Each word is encoded as the number

$$s = v_1 b_1 + v_2 b_2 + \cdots + v_n b_n.$$

*Decryption.* Find the number $s' = 0, 1, \ldots, m - 1$ with $s' \equiv js$ $\pmod{m}$. The solution of the easy knapsack problem for $s'$ is the encrypted message.

**Concluding Remark.** The security of the knapsack encryption depends on the difficulty of solving the new knapsack problem $b_1, b_2, \ldots, b_n$. Although it is known that solving a *random* knapsack problem is really difficult (as difficult as factoring large numbers), the trouble is that our knapsack problem is not random.

To increase the security, the method can be iterated: from a superincreasing sequence $a_1, a_2, \ldots, a_n$, we create a difficult knapsack problem $b_1, b_2, \ldots, b_n$, which, however, is simple for us. Starting from the latter problem, we create, in the same manner, a new knapsack problem $c_1, c_2, \ldots, c_n$, which we publish (keeping $b_1, b_2, \ldots, b_n$ secret), etc. The advantage of the knapsack encryption over, say, the prime-number method is the simplicity of its implementation.

# 15.6 Data Encryption Standard

We now describe the cryptosystem which has become the Data Encryption Standard (DES) of the National Bureau of Standards in 1977, and which is available on chips suitable for a number of applications. Although theoretical attacks against the security of DES have been launched, no effective way of breaking it has been published yet.

The encryption of DES is based on a key chosen by the user. The key is a binary word of length 64, with 56 arbitrarily chosen bits and 8 parity check bits. We now describe the scheme in detail (see Figure 5).

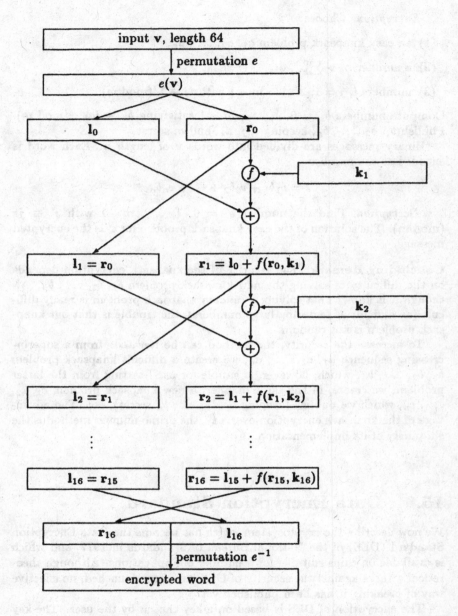

**Figure 5:** DES encryption of a source word **v**

The scheme uses various nonlinear elements, e.g., those of the following type, $\widehat{S}$: let $S$ be a $4 \times 16$ matrix, the rows $s_0$, $s_1$, $s_2$, $s_3$ of which are permutations of the numbers 0, 1, ... , 15 (see Figure 6). The nonlinear function $\widehat{S}$ maps words of length 6 to words of length 4 as follows: the response to $v_1 v_2 v_3 v_4 v_5 v_6$ is the matrix entry $S_{ij} = 0, 1, \ldots, 15$ expressed in the (4-bit) binary expansion, where

$i$ is the number whose binary expansion is $v_1 v_6$,
$j$ is the number whose binary expansion is $v_2 v_3 v_4 v_5$.

For example, if $S = S_1$ in Figure 6, then $\widehat{S}_1$ gives the following responses:

$$
\begin{array}{rcccl}
000000 & \longmapsto & 14 & = & 1100, \\
000001 & \longmapsto & 0 & = & 0000, \\
100000 & \longmapsto & 4 & = & 0100, \\
100001 & \longmapsto & 15 & = & 1101,
\end{array}
$$

etc.

## DES Encryption

Divide the source message into binary words $\mathbf{v}$ of length 64. They are encrypted by means of a key of length 64. The key, chosen by the user, produces 16 keys, $\mathbf{k}_1, \mathbf{k}_2, \ldots, \mathbf{k}_{16}$, of length 48 by means of the key schedule described below (see Figure 7). The encryption is performed in the following three steps (see Figure 5).

**Step 1:** Permute the letters of $\mathbf{v}$ by means of the permutation $e$ in Figure 8. That is, the 58th bit goes to the first position, the 50th one to the second position, etc. Denote by $\mathbf{l}_0$ and $\mathbf{v}_0$ the two halves of the resulting word $e(\mathbf{v})$, i.e., $\mathbf{l}_0$ and $\mathbf{r}_0$ are words of length 32 such that $e(\mathbf{v}) = \mathbf{l}_0 \mathbf{r}_0$.

**Step 2:** Compute words $\mathbf{l}_1 \mathbf{r}_1$, $\mathbf{l}_2 \mathbf{r}_2$, ... , $\mathbf{l}_{16} \mathbf{r}_{16}$ as follows: the left half of each word is just the right half of the preceding one:

$$\mathbf{l}_i = \mathbf{r}_{i-1} \qquad (i = 1, 2, \ldots, 16),$$

whereas the right half is computed using the key $\mathbf{k}_i$ as follows:

$$\mathbf{r}_i = \mathbf{l}_{i-1} + f(\mathbf{r}_{i-1}, \mathbf{k}_i) \qquad (\text{addition in } \mathbf{Z}_2^{32}),$$

where $f$ is the function described below.

| | | | | | | | | | | | | | | | | | |
|---|---|---|---|---|---|---|---|---|---|---|---|---|---|---|---|---|---|
| $S_1$ | $s_0$ | 14 | 4 | 13 | 1 | 2 | 15 | 11 | 8 | 3 | 10 | 6 | 12 | 5 | 9 | 0 | 7 |
| | $s_1$ | 0 | 15 | 7 | 4 | 14 | 2 | 13 | 1 | 10 | 6 | 12 | 11 | 9 | 5 | 3 | 8 |
| | $s_2$ | 4 | 1 | 14 | 8 | 13 | 6 | 2 | 11 | 15 | 12 | 9 | 7 | 3 | 10 | 5 | 0 |
| | $s_3$ | 15 | 12 | 8 | 2 | 4 | 9 | 1 | 7 | 5 | 11 | 3 | 14 | 10 | 0 | 6 | 13 |
| $S_2$ | $s_0$ | 15 | 1 | 8 | 14 | 6 | 11 | 3 | 4 | 9 | 7 | 2 | 13 | 12 | 0 | 5 | 10 |
| | $s_1$ | 3 | 13 | 4 | 7 | 15 | 2 | 8 | 14 | 12 | 0 | 1 | 10 | 6 | 9 | 11 | 5 |
| | $s_2$ | 0 | 14 | 7 | 11 | 10 | 4 | 13 | 1 | 5 | 8 | 12 | 6 | 9 | 3 | 2 | 15 |
| | $s_3$ | 13 | 8 | 10 | 1 | 3 | 15 | 4 | 2 | 11 | 6 | 7 | 12 | 0 | 5 | 14 | 9 |
| $S_3$ | $s_0$ | 10 | 0 | 9 | 14 | 6 | 3 | 15 | 5 | 1 | 13 | 12 | 7 | 11 | 4 | 2 | 8 |
| | $s_1$ | 13 | 7 | 0 | 9 | 3 | 4 | 6 | 10 | 2 | 8 | 5 | 14 | 12 | 11 | 15 | 1 |
| | $s_2$ | 13 | 6 | 4 | 9 | 8 | 15 | 3 | 0 | 11 | 1 | 2 | 12 | 5 | 10 | 14 | 7 |
| | $s_3$ | 1 | 10 | 13 | 0 | 6 | 9 | 8 | 7 | 4 | 15 | 14 | 3 | 11 | 5 | 2 | 12 |
| $S_4$ | $s_0$ | 7 | 13 | 14 | 3 | 0 | 6 | 9 | 10 | 1 | 2 | 8 | 5 | 11 | 12 | 4 | 15 |
| | $s_1$ | 13 | 8 | 11 | 5 | 6 | 15 | 0 | 3 | 4 | 7 | 2 | 12 | 1 | 10 | 14 | 9 |
| | $s_2$ | 10 | 6 | 9 | 0 | 12 | 11 | 7 | 13 | 15 | 1 | 3 | 14 | 5 | 2 | 8 | 4 |
| | $s_3$ | 3 | 15 | 0 | 6 | 10 | 1 | 13 | 8 | 9 | 4 | 5 | 11 | 12 | 7 | 2 | 14 |
| $S_5$ | $s_0$ | 2 | 12 | 4 | 1 | 7 | 10 | 11 | 6 | 8 | 5 | 3 | 15 | 13 | 0 | 14 | 9 |
| | $s_1$ | 14 | 11 | 2 | 12 | 4 | 7 | 13 | 1 | 5 | 0 | 15 | 10 | 3 | 9 | 8 | 6 |
| | $s_2$ | 4 | 2 | 1 | 11 | 10 | 13 | 7 | 8 | 15 | 9 | 12 | 5 | 6 | 3 | 0 | 14 |
| | $s_3$ | 11 | 8 | 12 | 7 | 1 | 14 | 2 | 13 | 6 | 15 | 0 | 9 | 10 | 4 | 5 | 3 |
| $S_6$ | $s_0$ | 12 | 1 | 10 | 15 | 9 | 2 | 6 | 8 | 0 | 13 | 3 | 4 | 14 | 7 | 5 | 11 |
| | $s_1$ | 10 | 15 | 4 | 2 | 7 | 12 | 9 | 5 | 6 | 1 | 13 | 14 | 0 | 11 | 3 | 8 |
| | $s_2$ | 9 | 14 | 15 | 5 | 2 | 8 | 12 | 3 | 7 | 0 | 4 | 10 | 1 | 13 | 11 | 6 |
| | $s_3$ | 4 | 3 | 2 | 12 | 9 | 5 | 15 | 10 | 11 | 14 | 1 | 7 | 6 | 0 | 8 | 13 |
| $S_7$ | $s_0$ | 4 | 11 | 2 | 14 | 15 | 0 | 8 | 13 | 3 | 12 | 9 | 7 | 5 | 10 | 6 | 1 |
| | $s_1$ | 13 | 0 | 11 | 7 | 4 | 9 | 1 | 10 | 14 | 3 | 5 | 12 | 2 | 15 | 8 | 6 |
| | $s_2$ | 1 | 4 | 11 | 13 | 12 | 3 | 7 | 14 | 10 | 15 | 6 | 8 | 0 | 5 | 9 | 2 |
| | $s_3$ | 6 | 11 | 13 | 8 | 1 | 4 | 10 | 7 | 9 | 5 | 0 | 15 | 14 | 2 | 3 | 12 |
| $S_8$ | $s_0$ | 13 | 2 | 8 | 4 | 6 | 15 | 11 | 1 | 10 | 9 | 3 | 14 | 5 | 0 | 12 | 7 |
| | $s_1$ | 1 | 15 | 13 | 8 | 10 | 3 | 7 | 4 | 12 | 5 | 6 | 11 | 0 | 14 | 9 | 2 |
| | $s_2$ | 7 | 11 | 4 | 1 | 9 | 12 | 14 | 2 | 0 | 6 | 10 | 13 | 15 | 3 | 5 | 8 |
| | $s_3$ | 2 | 1 | 14 | 7 | 4 | 10 | 8 | 13 | 15 | 12 | 9 | 0 | 3 | 5 | 6 | 11 |

**Figure 6:** Matrices $S_1, S_2, \ldots, S_8$ of permutations

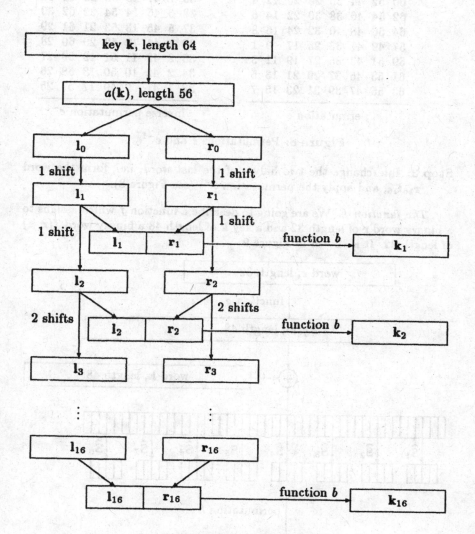

**Figure 7:** Key schedule

| 58 | 50 | 42 | 34 | 26 | 18 | 10 | 2 |
| 60 | 52 | 44 | 36 | 28 | 20 | 12 | 4 |
| 62 | 54 | 46 | 38 | 30 | 22 | 14 | 6 |
| 64 | 56 | 48 | 40 | 32 | 24 | 16 | 8 |
| 57 | 49 | 41 | 33 | 25 | 17 | 9 | 1 |
| 59 | 51 | 43 | 35 | 27 | 19 | 11 | 3 |
| 61 | 53 | 45 | 37 | 29 | 21 | 13 | 5 |
| 63 | 55 | 47 | 39 | 31 | 23 | 15 | 7 |

permutation $e$

| 40 | 8 | 48 | 16 | 56 | 24 | 64 | 32 |
| 39 | 7 | 47 | 15 | 55 | 23 | 63 | 31 |
| 38 | 6 | 46 | 14 | 54 | 22 | 62 | 30 |
| 37 | 5 | 45 | 13 | 53 | 21 | 61 | 29 |
| 36 | 4 | 44 | 12 | 52 | 20 | 60 | 28 |
| 35 | 3 | 43 | 11 | 51 | 19 | 59 | 27 |
| 34 | 2 | 42 | 10 | 50 | 18 | 58 | 26 |
| 33 | 1 | 41 | 9 | 49 | 17 | 57 | 25 |

inverse permutation $e^{-1}$

**Figure 8:** Permutations $e$ and $e^{-1}$

**Step 3:** Interchange the two halves of the last word, i.e., form the word $r_{16}l_{16}$, and apply the permutation $e^{-1}$ (see Figure 8).

*The function $f$.* We are going to describe a function $f$ which assigns to a binary word $r$ of length 32 and a key $k$ of length 48 a binary word $f(r, k)$ of length 32. It is shown in Figure 9.

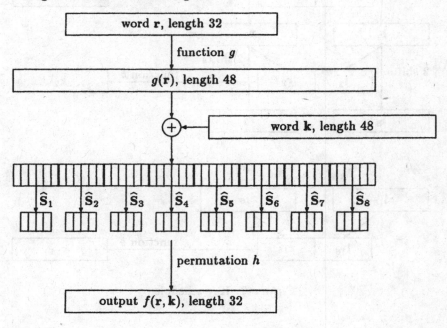

**Figure 9:** Function $f$

| 32 | 1 | 2 | 3 | 4 | 5 |
|----|----|----|----|----|----|
| 4 | 5 | 6 | 7 | 8 | 9 |
| 8 | 9 | 10 | 11 | 12 | 13 |
| 12 | 13 | 14 | 15 | 16 | 17 |
| 16 | 17 | 18 | 19 | 20 | 21 |
| 20 | 21 | 22 | 23 | 24 | 25 |
| 24 | 25 | 26 | 27 | 28 | 29 |
| 28 | 29 | 30 | 31 | 32 | 1 |

**Figure 10:** Function $g$

**Step 1:** Turn the word $r$ into a word $g(r)$ of length 48 by the function $g$ in Figure 10. That is, the 32nd bit of $r$ goes to the first position, the first bit to the second position, etc.

**Step 2:** Add $g(r)$ and $k$ in $Z_2^{48}$. Divide the resulting word into eight words of length 6.

**Step 3:** Apply to the eight words of Step 2 the following eight functions $\widehat{S}_1, \widehat{S}_2, \ldots, \widehat{S}_8$, respectively, in order to compute a word of length $8 \times 4 = 32$. The functions $\widehat{S}_i$ are defined by means of the matrices $S_i$ in Figure 6 (whose rows are permutations of the numbers $0, 1, \ldots, 15$) in the manner described in the introduction of the present section.

**Step 4:** Perform the permutation $h$ of Figure 11. That is, the 16th bit goes to the first position, the 7th one to the second position, etc.

| 17 | 7 | 20 | 21 | 29 | 12 | 28 | 17 |
|----|----|----|----|----|----|----|----|
| 1 | 15 | 23 | 26 | 5 | 18 | 31 | 10 |
| 2 | 8 | 24 | 14 | 32 | 27 | 3 | 9 |
| 19 | 13 | 30 | 6 | 22 | 11 | 4 | 25 |

**Figure 11:** Permutation $h$

*Key schedule.* The user chooses a key $k$ of 64 bits: 56 bits are chosen at random and 8 bits are parity check bits, serving to detect an error per 8 bits. This is performed by setting every eighth bit in such a way that, together with the seven preceding bits, it forms a word of odd parity. The key $k$ is used to compute words $k_1, k_2, \ldots, k_{16}$ as follows (see Figure 10).

**Step 1:** Apply the function $a$ in Figure 12 (which is a permutation of the 56 information bits of the key **k**): the 57th bit of **k** goes to the first position, the 49th bit to the second one, etc. Split the result $a(\mathbf{k})$ in two halves, $a(\mathbf{k}) = \mathbf{l}_0\mathbf{r}_0$.

**Step 2:** Form $\mathbf{k}_i = b(\mathbf{l}_i\mathbf{r}_i)$, $i = 1, 2, \ldots, 16$, where $b$ is the function of Figure 13 assigning to each word of length 56 a word of length 48, and $\mathbf{l}_1\mathbf{r}_1, \mathbf{l}_2\mathbf{r}_2, \ldots, \mathbf{l}_{16}\mathbf{r}_{16}$ are defined as follows: $\mathbf{l}_i$ is obtained from $\mathbf{l}_{i-1}$ by $n_i$ cyclic shifts to the left, and $\mathbf{r}_i$ is obtained from $\mathbf{r}_{i-1}$ by $n_i$ cyclic shifts to the left, where

$$n_i = \begin{cases} 1 & \text{if } i = 1, 2, 9, 16, \\ 2 & \text{else.} \end{cases}$$

The key schedule is indicated in Figure 7.

| 57 | 49 | 41 | 33 | 25 | 17 | 9 |
|----|----|----|----|----|----|----|
| 1  | 58 | 50 | 42 | 34 | 26 | 18 |
| 10 | 2  | 59 | 51 | 43 | 35 | 27 |
| 19 | 11 | 3  | 60 | 52 | 44 | 36 |
| 63 | 55 | 47 | 39 | 31 | 23 | 15 |
| 7  | 62 | 54 | 46 | 38 | 30 | 22 |
| 14 | 6  | 61 | 53 | 45 | 37 | 29 |
| 21 | 13 | 5  | 28 | 20 | 12 | 4 |

| 14 | 17 | 11 | 24 | 1  | 5 |
|----|----|----|----|----|----|
| 3  | 28 | 15 | 6  | 21 | 10 |
| 23 | 19 | 12 | 4  | 26 | 8 |
| 16 | 7  | 27 | 20 | 13 | 2 |
| 41 | 52 | 31 | 37 | 47 | 55 |
| 30 | 40 | 51 | 45 | 33 | 48 |
| 44 | 49 | 39 | 56 | 34 | 53 |
| 46 | 42 | 50 | 36 | 29 | 32 |

**Figure 12:** Function $a$        **Figure 13:** Function $b$

# Exercises

**15A**  In the encryption method using linear shift sequences (15.2), prove that the following system of equations

$$\begin{bmatrix} v_k & v_{k+1} & \cdots & v_{k+m-1} \\ v_{k+1} & v_{k+2} & \cdots & v_{k+m} \\ \cdots\cdots\cdots\cdots\cdots\cdots\cdots\cdots\cdots\cdots & & & \\ v_{k+m+1} & v_{k+m+2} & \cdots & v_{k+2m-2} \end{bmatrix} \begin{bmatrix} h_0 \\ h_1 \\ \vdots \\ h_m \end{bmatrix} = \begin{bmatrix} v_{k_m} \\ v_{k+m+1} \\ \vdots \\ v_{k+2m-1} \end{bmatrix}$$

holds and makes it possible to find $h(x)$ whenever we know $v_k \ldots v_{k+2m-1}$.

**15B**    Prove that the prime-number method in 15.4 has the property that anyone who determines the secret number $\varphi(n)$ knows the factorization of $n$: since $pq = n$ is known, and $p + q = n - \varphi(n) + 1$, it is easy to find $p$ and $q$.

## Notes

Using a secret key for cryptography is an obvious and old method. The trick of using error-correcting codes in the case of a noisy wiretap is due to Wyner (1975). Pseudo-random keys are discussed by MacWilliams and Sloane (1976).

A pioneering paper in cryptography, which introduced the idea of a public key, is Diffie and Hellman (1976). The first satisfactory public-key cryptosystem, based on large primes, was presented by Rivest, Shamir, and Adelman (1978). Soon later the knapsack-problem cryptosystem was proposed by Merkle and Hellman (1978). The cryptosystem based on Goppa codes is due to McEliece (1978). The Data Encryption Standard was created in 1977 by IBM, and then adopted by the National Bureau of Standards.

For more information about the topics of this chapter, the reader is referred to the excellent textbook of van Tilborg (1988).

# Appendixes

Appendixes

# Appendix A

# Galois Fields

We present fields $GF(p^m) = \mathbf{Z}_p[x]/\mathrm{mod}\ r(x)$ (see 11.3), where $r(x)$ is an irreducible polynomial of degree $n > 1$. Every nonzero element is expressed (a) as a polynomial in indeterminate $\alpha$ (of degree lower than $n$) and (b) as a power of $\alpha$. All finite fields of at most 32 elements are represented here (except the trivial case of $\mathbf{Z}_p$, $p$ a prime).

$$GF(4) = \mathbf{Z}_2[x]/\mathrm{mod}\ x^2 + x + 1$$

| 0 | 1 | | $\alpha$ | $1 + \alpha$ |
|---|---|---|---|---|
| – | $\alpha^0 = \alpha^3$ | | $\alpha^1$ | $\alpha^2$ |

$$GF(8) = \mathbf{Z}_2[x]/\mathrm{mod}\ x^3 + x + 1$$

| 0 | 1 | | $\alpha$ | $\alpha^2$ | $1 + \alpha$ | $\alpha + \alpha^2$ | $1 + \alpha + \alpha^2$ | $1 + \alpha^2$ |
|---|---|---|---|---|---|---|---|---|
| – | $\alpha^0 = \alpha^7$ | | $\alpha^1$ | $\alpha^2$ | $\alpha^3$ | $\alpha^4$ | $\alpha^5$ | $\alpha^6$ |

321

$GF(9) = \mathbf{Z}_3[x]/\bmod x^2 + x + 2$

| 0 | 1 | | $\alpha$ | $1 + 2\alpha$ | $2 + 2\alpha$ | 2 | $2\alpha$ | $2 + \alpha$ | $1 + \alpha$ |
|---|---|---|---|---|---|---|---|---|---|
| – | $\alpha^0 = \alpha^8$ | | $\alpha^1$ | $\alpha^2$ | $\alpha^3$ | $\alpha^4$ | $\alpha^5$ | $\alpha^6$ | $\alpha^7$ |

$GF(16) = \mathbf{Z}_2[x]/\bmod x^4 + x + 1$

| 0 | 1 | $\alpha$ | $\alpha^2$ |
|---|---|---|---|
| – | $\alpha^0 = \alpha^{15}$ | $\alpha^1$ | $\alpha^2$ |
| $\alpha^3$ | $1 + \alpha$ | $\alpha + \alpha^2$ | $\alpha^2 + \alpha^3$ |
| $\alpha^3$ | $\alpha^4$ | $\alpha^5$ | $\alpha^6$ |
| $1 + \alpha + \alpha^3$ | $1 + \alpha^2$ | $\alpha + \alpha^3$ | $1 + \alpha + \alpha^2$ |
| $\alpha^7$ | $\alpha^8$ | $\alpha^9$ | $\alpha^{10}$ |
| $\alpha + \alpha^2 + \alpha^3$ | $1 + \alpha + \alpha^2 + \alpha^3$ | $1 + \alpha^2 + \alpha^3$ | $1 + \alpha^3$ |
| $\alpha^{11}$ | $\alpha^{12}$ | $\alpha^{13}$ | $\alpha^{14}$ |

$GF(25) = \mathbf{Z}_5[x]/\bmod x^2 + x + 2$

| 0 | 1 | $\alpha$ | $4\alpha + 3$ | $4\alpha + 2$ | $3\alpha + 2$ | $4\alpha + 4$ |
|---|---|---|---|---|---|---|
| – | $\alpha^0 = \alpha^{24}$ | $\alpha^1$ | $\alpha^2$ | $\alpha^3$ | $\alpha^4$ | $\alpha^5$ |
| 2 | $2\alpha$ | $3\alpha + 1$ | $3\alpha + 4$ | $\alpha + 4$ | $3\alpha + 3$ | 4 |
| $\alpha^6$ | $\alpha^7$ | $\alpha^8$ | $\alpha^9$ | $\alpha^{10}$ | $\alpha^{11}$ | $\alpha^{12}$ |
| $4\alpha$ | $\alpha + 2$ | $\alpha + 3$ | $2\alpha + 3$ | $\alpha + 1$ | 3 | $3\alpha$ |
| $\alpha^{13}$ | $\alpha^{14}$ | $\alpha^{15}$ | $\alpha^{16}$ | $\alpha^{17}$ | $\alpha^{18}$ | $\alpha^{19}$ |
| $2\alpha + 4$ | $2\alpha + 1$ | $4\alpha + 1$ | $2\alpha + 2$ | | | |
| $\alpha^{20}$ | $\alpha^{21}$ | $\alpha^{22}$ | $\alpha^{23}$ | | | |

$GF(27) = \mathbf{Z}_3[x]/\operatorname{mod} x^3 + 2x + 1$

| 0 | 1 | $\alpha$ | $\alpha^2$ | $\alpha + 2$ |
|---|---|---|---|---|
| – | $\alpha^0 = \alpha^{26}$ | $\alpha^1$ | $\alpha^2$ | $\alpha^3$ |
| $\alpha^2 + 2\alpha$ | $2\alpha^2 + \alpha + 2$ | $\alpha^2 + \alpha + 1$ | $\alpha^2 + 2\alpha + 2$ | $2\alpha^2 + 2$ |
| $\alpha^4$ | $\alpha^5$ | $\alpha^6$ | $\alpha^7$ | $\alpha^8$ |
| $\alpha + 1$ | $\alpha^2 + \alpha$ | $\alpha^2 + \alpha + 2$ | $\alpha + \alpha^2$ | 2 |
| $\alpha^9$ | $\alpha^{10}$ | $\alpha^{11}$ | $\alpha^{12}$ | $\alpha^{13}$ |
| $2\alpha$ | $2\alpha^2$ | $a\alpha + 1$ | $2\alpha^2 + \alpha$ | $\alpha^2 + 2\alpha + 1$ |
| $\alpha^{14}$ | $\alpha^{15}$ | $\alpha^{16}$ | $\alpha^{17}$ | $\alpha^{18}$ |
| $2\alpha^2 + 2\alpha + 2$ | $2\alpha^2 + \alpha + 1$ | $\alpha^2 + 1$ | $2\alpha + 2$ | $2\alpha^2 + 2\alpha$ |
| $\alpha^{19}$ | $\alpha^{20}$ | $\alpha^{21}$ | $\alpha^{22}$ | $\alpha^{23}$ |
| $2\alpha^2 + 2\alpha + 1$ | $2\alpha^2 + 1$ | | | |
| $\alpha^{24}$ | $\alpha^{25}$ | | | |

$GF(32) = \mathbf{Z}_2[x]/\mod x^5 + x^2 + 1$

| 0 | 1 | $\alpha$ | $\alpha^2$ |
|---|---|---|---|
| – | $\alpha^0 = \alpha^{31}$ | $\alpha$ | $\alpha^2$ |
| $\alpha^3$ | $\alpha^4$ | $\alpha^2 + 1$ | $\alpha^3 + \alpha$ |
| $\alpha^3$ | $\alpha^4$ | $\alpha^5$ | $\alpha^6$ |
| $\alpha^4 + \alpha^2$ | $1 + \alpha^2 + \alpha^3$ | $\alpha + \alpha^3 + \alpha^4$ | $1 + \alpha^4$ |
| $\alpha^7$ | $\alpha^8$ | $\alpha^9$ | $\alpha^{10}$ |
| $1 + \alpha + \alpha^2$ | $\alpha + \alpha^2 + \alpha^3$ | $\alpha^2 + \alpha^3 + \alpha^4$ | $1 + \alpha^2 + \alpha^3 + \alpha^4$ |
| $\alpha^{11}$ | $\alpha^{12}$ | $\alpha^{13}$ | $\alpha^{14}$ |
| $1 + \alpha + \alpha^2 + \alpha^3 + \alpha^4$ | $1 + \alpha + \alpha^3 + \alpha^4$ | $1 + \alpha + \alpha^4$ | $1 + \alpha$ |
| $\alpha^{15}$ | $\alpha^{16}$ | $\alpha^{17}$ | $\alpha^{18}$ |
| $\alpha + \alpha^2$ | $\alpha^2 + \alpha^3$ | $\alpha^2 + \alpha^4$ | $1 + \alpha^2 + \alpha^4$ |
| $\alpha^{19}$ | $\alpha^{20}$ | $\alpha^{21}$ | $\alpha^{22}$ |
| $1 + \alpha + \alpha^2 + \alpha^3$ | $\alpha + \alpha^2 + \alpha^3 + \alpha^4$ | $1 + \alpha^3 + \alpha^4$ | $1 + \alpha + \alpha^2 + \alpha^4$ |
| $\alpha^{23}$ | $\alpha^{24}$ | $\alpha^{25}$ | $\alpha^{26}$ |
| $1 + \alpha + \alpha^3$ | $\alpha + \alpha^2 + \alpha^4$ | $1 + \alpha^3$ | $\alpha + \alpha^4$ |
| $\alpha^{27}$ | $\alpha^{28}$ | $\alpha^{29}$ | $\alpha^{30}$ |

# Appendix B

# BCH Codes and Reed-Muller Codes

We list parameters of all BCH codes (Chapter 12) and all punctured Reed-Muller codes $\overline{\mathcal{R}}(r, m)$ (see 9.3) of lengths $n = 7, 15, 31, 63, 127$. The number of information symbols is denoted by $k$.

| Length | Minimum distance | BCH codes $k$ | $\overline{\mathcal{R}}(r, m)$ $k$ | $r$ |
|--------|------------------|---------------|------------------------------------|-----|
| 7      | 3                | 4             | 4                                  | 1   |
|        | 7                | 1             | 1                                  | 0   |
| 15     | 3                | 11            | 11                                 | 2   |
|        | 5                | 7             | –                                  | –   |
|        | 7                | 5             | 5                                  | 1   |
|        | 15               | 1             | 1                                  | 0   |
| 31     | 3                | 26            | 26                                 | 3   |
|        | 5                | 21            | –                                  | –   |
|        | 7                | 16            | 16                                 | 2   |
|        | 11               | 11            | –                                  | –   |
|        | 15               | 6             | 6                                  | 1   |
|        | 31               | 1             | 1                                  | 0   |

| Length | Minimum distance | BCH codes $k$ | $\overline{\mathcal{R}}(r, m)$ $k$ | $r$ |
|---|---|---|---|---|
| 63 | 3 | 57 | 57 | 4 |
| | 5 | 51 | – | – |
| | 7 | 45 | 42 | 3 |
| | 7 | 39 | – | – |
| | 11 | 36 | – | – |
| | 13 | 30 | – | – |
| | 15 | 24 | 22 | 2 |
| | 21 | 18 | – | – |
| | 23 | 16 | – | – |
| | 27 | 10 | – | – |
| | 31 | 7 | 7 | 1 |
| | 63 | 1 | 1 | 0 |
| 127 | 3 | 120 | 120 | 5 |
| | 5 | 113 | – | – |
| | 7 | 106 | 99 | 4 |
| | 9 | 99 | – | – |
| | 11 | 92 | – | – |
| | 13 | 85 | – | – |
| | 15 | 78 | 64 | 3 |
| | 19 | 71 | – | – |
| | 21 | 64 | – | – |
| | 23 | 57 | – | – |
| | 27 | 27 | – | – |
| | 31 | 43 | – | – |
| | 31 | 36 | 29 | 2 |
| | 43 | 29 | – | – |
| | 47 | 22 | – | – |
| | 55 | 15 | – | – |
| | 63 | 8 | 8 | 1 |
| | 127 | 1 | 1 | 0 |

# Bibliography*

Abramson, N. (1963) *Information Theory and Coding.* McGraw-Hill, New York [Ch. 1–4].

Berlekamp, E. R. (1968) *Algebraic Coding Theory.* McGraw-Hill, New York [Ch. 5–14].

Berlekamp, E. R., editor. (1974) *Key Papers in the Development of Coding Theory.* IEEE Press, New York [Ch. 5–14].

Birkhoff, G., and MacLane, S. (1953) *A Survey of Modern Algebra.* Macmillan, New York [Ch. 6, 7, 11].

Blahut, R. E. (1983) *Theory and Practise of Error Control Codes.* Addison-Wesley, Reading, Mass. [Ch. 5–14].

Bose, R. C., and Ray-Chaudhuri, D. K. (1960) On a Class of Error Correcting Binary Group Codes. *Inform. Control* 3, pp. 68–79 [Ch. 12].

Diffie, W., and Hellman, M. E. (1976) New Directions in Cryptography. *IEEE Trans. Inf. Theory* IT–22, pp. 644–654 [Ch. 15].

Elias, P. (1954) Error-Free Coding. *IEEE Trans. Inf. Theory* IT–4, pp. 29–37 [Ch. 14].

Fadeiev, D. K. (1956) To the Concept of Entropy of a Finite Probability Distribution (Russian), *Uspechy Matem. Nauk* 11, pp. 1–10.

Forney, G. D., Jr. (1970) Convolutional Codes I: Algebraic Structure. *IEEE Trans. Inf. Theory* IT–16, pp. 720–738 [Ch. 14].

Golay, M. J. E. (1949) Notes on Digital Coding. *Proc. IEEE* 37, p. 657 [Ch. 5].

Golomb, S. W. (1967) *Shift Register Sequences.* Holden-Day, San Francisco [Ch. 15].

Goppa, V. C. (1970) A New Class of Linear Error-Correcting Codes. *Probl. Peredach. Inf.* 6, pp. 24–30 [Ch. 12].

Gorenstein, D. C., and Ziegler, N. (1961) A Class of Error-Correcting Codes in $p^m$ Symbols. *J. Soc. Indus. Applied Math.* 9, pp. 207–214 [Ch. 12].

---

*At the end of each reference, we put in brackets the chapter(s) to which it is related.

Hamming, R. W. (1950) Error Correcting and Error Detecting Codes. *Bell Syst. Tech. J.* 29, pp. 147–160 [Ch. 5].

Hamming, R. W. (1980) *Coding and Information Theory.* Prentice-Hall, Englewood Cliffs, New Jersey [Ch. 1–4].

Hocquenghem, A. (1959) Codes corecteurs d'erreurs.  *Chiffres* 2, pp. 147–156 [Ch. 12].

Karush, J. (1961) A Simple Proof of an Inequality of McMillan. *IEEE Trans. Inform. Theory* IT–7, p. 118 [Ch. 1].

Kasami, T. (1964) A Decoding Procedure for Multiple-Error-Correcting Cyclic Codes. *IEEE Trans. Inf. Theory* IT–10, pp. 134–138 [Ch. 10].

Kraft, L. G. (1949) *A Device for Quantizing, Grouping, and Coding Amplitude Modulated Pulses.* M.S. thesis, Electrical Engineering Department, Massachusetts Institute of Technology, March [Ch. 1].

Lin, S., and Costello, D. J. (1983) *Error-Control Coding.* Prentice-Hall, Englewood Cliffs, New Jersey [Ch. 5–14].

MacWilliams, F. J. (1963) A Theorem on the Distribution of Weights in a Systematic Code. *Bell Syst. Tech. J.* 42, pp. 79–94 [Ch. 8].

MacWilliams, F. J., and Sloane, N. J. A. (1976) Pseudo-Random Sequences and Arrays. *Proc. IEEE* 64, pp. 1715–1729 [Ch. 15].

MacWilliams, F. J., and Sloane, N. J. A. (1981) *The Theory of Error-Correcting Codes* (3$^{rd}$ printing). North-Holland, Amsterdam [Ch. 5–14].

Massey, J. L., and Sain, M. K. (1968)  Inverses of Linear Sequential Circuits. *IEEE Trans. Comp.* C–17, pp. 330–337 [Ch. 14].

McEliece, R. J. (1978) A Public-Key Cryptosystem Based on Algebraic Coding Theory. Deep Space Network Progress Report 42–44, Jet Propulsion Laboratories, Pasadena, California, pp. 114–116 [Ch. 15].

McMillan, B. (1956) Two Inequalities Implied by Unique Decipherability. *IRE Trans. Inform. Theory* IT–2, pp. 115–116 [Ch. 1].

Meggit, J. E. (1960) Error-Correcting Codes for Correcting Bursts of Errors, *IBM J. Res. Develop.* 4, pp. 329–334 [Ch. 10].

Merkle, R. C., and Hellman, M. E. (1978) Hiding Information and Signatures in Trapdoor Knapsacks. *IEEE Trans. Inf. Theory* IT–24, pp. 525–530 [Ch. 15].

Muller, D. E. (1954) Application of Boolean Algebra to Switching Circuit Design and to Error Detection. *IEEE Trans. Comp.* 3, pp. 6–12 [Ch. 9].

Patterson, N. J. (1975) The Algebraic Decoding of Goppa Codes. *IEEE Trans. Inf. Theory* 21, pp. 203–207 [Ch. 12].

Peterson, W. W. (1960) Encoding and Error-Correcting Procedures for the Bose-Chaudhuri Codes. *IEEE Trans. Inf. Theory* IT–16, pp. 459–470 [Ch. 12].

Prange, E. (1957) *Cyclic Error-Correcting Codes in Two Symbols.* AFCRC–TN–57–103, Air Force Cambridge Research Center, Cambridge, Massachusetts [Ch. 10].

Reed, I. S. (1954) A Class of Multiple-Error Correcting Codes and the Decoding Scheme. *IEEE Trans. Inf. Theory* 4, pp. 38–49 [Ch. 9].

Reed, I. S., and Solomon, G. (1960) Polynomial Codes over Certain Finite Fields. *J. Soc. Indus. Applied Math.* 8, pp. 300–304 [Ch. 12].

Rivest, R. L., Shamir, A., and Adelman, L. M. (1978) A Method for Obtaining Digital Signatures and Public-Key Cryptosystems. *Comm. ACM* 21, pp. 120–126 [Ch. 15].

Shannon, C. E. (1948) A Mathematical Theory of Communication. *Bell Syst. Tech. J.* 27, pp. 379–423 and 623–656 [Ch. 1–4].

Slepian, D. (1956) A Class of Binary Signalling Alphabets. *Bell Syst. Tech. J.* 35, pp. 203–234 [Ch. 5].

Slepian, D. (1960) Some Further Theory of Group Codes. *Bell Syst. Tech. J.* 39, pp. 1219–1252 [Ch. 5].

Slepian, D., editor. (1974) *Key Papers in the Development of Information Theory.* IEEE Press, New York [Ch. 1–4].

Solovay, R., and Strassen, V. (1977) A Fast Monte-Carlo Test for Primality. *SIAM J. Comp.* 6, pp. 84–85 [Ch. 15].

Sugiyama, Y., Kasahara, M., Hirasawa, S., and Namekawa, T. (1975) A Method for Solving Key Equation for Decoding Goppa Codes. *Inf. and Control* 27, pp. 87–99 [Ch. 13].

Sugiyama, Y., Kasahara, M., Hirasawa, S., and Namekawa, T. (1976) An Erasures-and-Errors Decoding Algorithm for Goppa Codes, *IEEE Trans. Inf. Theory* IT–22, pp. 238–241.

Tietäväinen, A. (1974) A Short Proof for the Nonexistence of Unknown Perfect Codes ofer $GF(q)$, $q > 2$, *Annales Acad. Scient. Fenniciae*, ser. A, 580, pp. 1–6 [Ch. 10].

van Lint, J. H. (1982) *Introduction to Coding Theory.* Springer, New York–Heidelberg–Berlin [Ch. 5–14].

van Tilborg, H. C. A. (1988) *An Introduction to Cryptology.* Kluwer, Boston–Dordrecht–Lancaster [Ch. 15].

Viterbi, A. J. (1967) Error Bounds for Convolutional Codes and an Asymptotically Optimum Decoding Algorithm. *IEEE Trans. Inf. Theory* IT–13, pp. 260–269 [Ch. 14].

Wolfowitz, J. (1959) Strong Converse of the Coding Theorem for Semi-continuous Channels, *Illinois J. Math.* 3, pp. 477–489.

Wozencraft, J. M. (1957) Sequential Decoding for Reliable Communication. *Nat. IRE Conv. Rec.* 5, pp. 11–25 [Ch. 14].

Wyner, A. D. (1975) The Wire-Tap Channel. *Bell Syst. Tech. J.* 54, pp. 1355–1387 [Ch. 15].

# List of Symbols

# Index